MARKETING RESEARCH IN IRELAND:

Theory and Practice

*Christine Domegan
and Declan Fleming*

GILL & MACMILLAN

Gill & Macmillan Ltd
Goldenbridge
Dublin 8
with associated companies throughout the world
www.gillmacmillan.ie

© Christine Domegan and Declan Fleming 1999
0 7171 2667 6

Index compiled by Warren Yeates
Print origination by Andy Gilsenan
Printed by ColourBooks Ltd, Dublin

The paper used in this book is made from the wood pulp of managed forests. For every tree felled, at least one tree is planted, thereby renewing natural resources.

All rights reserved.
No part of this publication may be reproduced, copied or transmitted in any form or by any means without written permission of the publishers or else under the terms of any licence permitting limited copying issued by the Irish Copyright Licensing Agency, The Writers' Centre, Parnell Square, Dublin 1.

A catalogue record is available for this book from the British Library.

To Peter, Nina and my parents.
CD

To Monique, Leah and in memory of my parents.
DF

CONTENTS

Acknowledgments — vii

PART 1 — Introduction to Marketing Research

- Chapter 1 Marketing Research Introduced — 2
- Chapter 2 The Marketing Research Process — 16
- Chapter 3 Problem Definition and Research Design — 43

PART 2 — Data Collection Methods

- Chapter 4 Secondary Sources of Data — 70
- Chapter 5 Focus Groups, In-depth Interviews and Projective Techniques — 127
- Chapter 6 Surveys, Observation and Panels — 157
- Chapter 7 Experimentation — 194

PART 3 — Data Collection and Acquisition

- Chapter 8 Questionnaire Design and Field Work — 232
- Chapter 9 Measurement Concepts and Attitude Scales — 265
- Chapter 10 The Sampling Process — 302
- Chapter 11 Sample Size Determination — 335

PART 4 — Data Analysis and Presentation

- Chapter 12 Data Preparation and Processing — 354
- Chapter 13 Fundamental Data Analysis — 380
- Chapter 14 Multivariate Data Analysis — 405
- Chapter 15 Communication of Research Findings, Report Writing and Presentation — 427

Appendices — 444
References — 449
Index — 463

ACKNOWLEDGMENTS

To all our marketing colleagues who contributed much needed and valuable Irish case study material, worked examples, illustrations and advice: Professor Jim Ward, NUI, Galway; Dr Aidan Daly, NUI, Galway; Ann Torres, NUI, Galway; Declan Doyle, NUI, Galway; Monica Nielsen, GMIT; Gerry Mortimer, DIT; Dr Tom O'Toole, WIT; Dr Brenda Cullen, UCD; Dr Sean Connolly, IT, Tralee; Ray Collis, MD, Envision Consulting; Roger Jupp, MD, Lansdowne Market Research Ltd; John Casey, Chief Executive, Marketing Institute of Ireland; and Catherine Kilbride, Director-Education, Marketing Institute of Ireland.

To our research assistants, for the many hours of desk research and miscellaneous activities: Una Carey, Mairead D'Arcy, Justin Jennings and Andrea Moloney.

To our marketing department secretary, Mary Greaney, and the librarian staff, NUI, Galway, especially Trish Finan, for their continual assistant and support.

To all those B.Comm and DBS students who asked for the book.

To Ailbhe O'Reilly, Gabrielle Noble and the Gill & Macmillan team for facilitating the production of this book.

To the anonymous reviewers for their kind comments and suggestions.

Finally, to our loved ones and families.

Part 1

INTRODUCTION TO MARKETING RESEARCH

Chapter 1

MARKETING RESEARCH INTRODUCED

> - **Chapter Overview**
> - Introduction • What is Marketing Research? • Why is Marketing Research Essential? • Marketing Research in Ireland • Summary

• Introduction

We have in Ireland, the world's leading cream liqueur manufacturer, the world's leading manufacturer of high quality glassware and china, the European market leader in stout, and a manufacturer of small domestic appliances which leads its chosen markets in many European countries.[1] These firms know that to be successful, a business must gear all its efforts to giving customers what they want, while still earning a profit. To be truly marketing orientated, companies have to be information orientated. As Feargal Quinn of Superquinn reminds us, 'the single most important skill you need to become truly customer-driven is the ability to listen (to the customer)'.[2] So, one of the first steps in marketing is to listen to the customer and gather marketing information, also known as *marketing research*.

This chapter introduces you to the concept of marketing research. Its purpose is to act as a precursor and prelude to an understanding and appreciation of the marketing research process, research tools and techniques. By the end of this chapter, you will be able to:

1. discuss the role of information and data in marketing;
2. define marketing research;
3. detail the role and functions of marketing research;
4. explain the hallmarks of good marketing research;
5. discuss marketing research in Ireland.

• What is Marketing Research?

Marketing research is about generating and interpreting information to assist management with decision-making. It is the principal method for answering questions, such as: Who are my customers? Where do they shop? What do they want? What price will they pay? Who are my competitors? What do my competitors offer?

So, marketing research is an activity that links the customers and competition to the company through timely, valid and reliable data. In this manner, marketing research is a function which supports and implements the marketing concept of customer satisfaction. It is 'the process of listening to the voice of the market and conveying it to management'.[3]

The idea of marketing research being an information-gathering process to assist with decision-making is encapsulated in the many formal definitions of marketing research that exist. Some are displayed in Box 1.1.

Box 1.1
Definitions of marketing research

'The formalised means of obtaining information to be used in making marketing decisions.'
The Marketing Institute of Ireland[4]

'The collection, analysis, interpretation and presentation of information obtained from individuals or groups of people in order to guide decisions on a wide range of matters, affecting consumers, either as buyers or as citizens.'
The Market Research Society (UK)[5]

'The function which links the consumer, customer and public to the marketer through information — information used to identify and define marketing opportunities and problems; generate, refine and evaluate marketing actions; monitor marketing performances; and improve understanding of marketing as a process.'
The American Marketing Association[6]

Whatever definition of marketing research one chooses, there are several important characteristics inherent in the concept. Good marketing research must be *methodology-led, decision-driven* and *information-orientated*.

Firstly, marketing research is a methodology-led process that systematically and objectively investigates a problem or opportunity confronting marketing management. While no two research projects are ever identical, there is a single procedure for all researchers to follow. So, marketing research denotes a process or sequence of steps to gather facts and figures in an objective and accurate manner.

In other words, marketing research stresses *how* to gather accurate, timely, valid and reliable information. It details the accepted method to generate useful data and results. Obtaining information appears deceptively simple — it is easy to walk down Grafton Street on a Monday afternoon and talk with the first twenty shoppers one meets, enquiring after their shopping patterns. This, however, excludes those working, travelling or eating in restaurants, attending college or collecting children from school, for example. The generated data could be misleading — it may not represent the shopping habits of all Dubliners.

So, one critical methodology-led aspect of marketing research is about how to generate objective and accurate data. The process of gathering information and the actual information collected has to be unbiased and untainted. This means that marketing research is scientific in nature. Special techniques are needed to ensure accurate, valid and reliable results. Great care is taken to ensure the research is free from error and that the research bears all the hallmarks of *validity* and *reliability*. These two terms, *validity* (measuring what we actually wanted to measure) and *reliability* (consistency in measurement) are the hallmarks of good research.[7] When present, marketing research is free from error, objective in nature and scientific in character. This scientific nature is referred by Baker[8] as the 'look before you leap' phenomenon. The word 'research' means to search again, re-search what we think we already know. The term 'research' is used by all sciences and is not confined to marketing.

The second trait of marketing research is that it is *decision-driven*. The purpose of conducting research is to aid management decisions. Research is always undertaken with a specific decision in mind. The collected information should decrease the risk and uncertainty associated with a decision and in this manner, improve management decision-making.

Specifically, marketing research is concerned with a particular decision — an opportunity or problem — facing a company at a point in time. Normally, a company has to make a strategic or tactical decision to rectify a problem. Some examples: sales are decreasing in the Cork region and the company does not know why; the firm is ready to launch a new advertising campaign, and wants to know how existing customers will perceive the potential new copy and message; the firm is already selling to multiples through a wholesaler in Britain and needs to make a decision about price points and margins to make more sales; or the company needs to decide whether to enter the Dutch market with its new range of slimming products.[9] In all of these cases, the decision is time-bound. As a result, marketing research has a definite beginning and a definite end.

Thirdly, marketing research is about information. With the myriad of occasions that customers come into contact with the company and with the numerous activities that have to be undertaken to achieve customer satisfaction, it comes as no surprise to find that the marketing research process can be applied to a huge variety of marketing problems that can arise for a firm. Different types of marketing research project span all aspects of the macro and micro environment, and so marketing research studies are to be found in every context that links the company with its environment. In reality, marketing research can be applied to any industry sector, any product or service, any country or used by any firm, large or small. So, while the decision is action-orientated for the manager in question, marketing research is information-orientated for the investigator.

Box 1.2
Types of marketing research studies

Market research
What is the market size by value and volume? What are the trends? What is the market structure — breakdown by customer type, geography, distribution methods? Who are the competitors, what are their market shares and volumes? What are their strengths and weaknesses? What are their competitive edges or advantages?

Consumer research
Who are the customers and consumers? What is their profile? Why do they buy the product, what needs does the product meet, what product features are they interested in? Where do customers get information about the product? What are their attitudes to the product/service?

For example, consumer research informed Baileys,[10] producers of Sheridans liqueur, of the difficulties consumers had with the innovative packaging of the liqueur. The bottle is divided into two sections and early growth was hampered by concerns about how to pour the product (initially, Sheridans had two corks). This was upgraded to the 'perfect pour' cap, which delivers the dark liqueur and creamy top in the right combinations. However, further consumer research revealed that some people who liked the product were still a 'little apprehensive' about how to pour it, leading to the possible introduction of some form of twist cap.

Distribution research
What are all the potential distribution outlets for the product? What incentives work best for the different outlets? What is the best distribution system? What options are available if exporting? Which agent? What about shop assistants, what role do they play? How can they be assisted?

On this last point about the role of staff, one report[11] states that 'the majority of very satisfactory service incidents resulted from employees breaking the rules of their own organisations'.

Product/services research
How important is service, fast delivery, back-up facilities and warranties as part of the product? Is the quality right for the market segment? What could/should be added to the existing product to augment it? Is the packaging attractive?

Golden Vale[12] for example, engaged in eighteen months of research prior to their launch of Cheestrings — cheese sticks that can be peeled into strings. The company's product research uncovered that fun and not flavour was the source of real appeal to young children when eating cheese.

Brand manager for Goodfella's pizzas at Green Isle Foods, Kristi O'Sullivan, maintains that superior product quality, value for money, pricing appeal and relevant brand imagery are the three contributions to the success of Goodfella's pizzas, all unearthed by product, pricing and promotional research.[13]

Pricing research

How should prices be set? What will the market bear? What are competitors charging? Should different customers be charged different prices?

Promotion research

What is the best way to promote the firm and its products? How much should be spent on promotions? Should you advertise on national radio, local radio, in print media or on the internet? How do you reach the target audience? How often should you talk with the target market? Should there be point-of-sale material?

HB launched a new corporate identity in 1998 as it was discovered, through promotional and consumer research, that their logo was becoming outdated. The new logo, a heart-shaped symbol in yellow and red with the HB letters underneath in blue, is intended to reflect consumer perceptions of ice cream — warmth and affection. The new logo was deemed necessary as the previous one reflected the fact that ice cream was traditionally regarded as a summer refreshment product, but now is becoming a year-round product. Promotional research, therefore, informed the company of the need to change their identity in line with the market.[14]

In cod's name, what became of Captain Birdseye? Recent promotional research showed that pre-teens thought the old Captain Birdseye was just that — old. 'These are kids that are very familiar with computer games and fast-moving action' says Terry Byrne, marketing manager for Birdseye. Hence the transformation from a Gilbert and Sullivan-type scenario to an Indiana Jones-inspired action hero, who roams the seabed in his space-age sea mobile accompanied by a Star Trek-type crew protecting the recipe for fish fingers from the piranha gang.[15]

• Why is Marketing Research Essential?

One reason why marketing research is essential to firms is because marketing research provides answers to key questions, e.g. Who are my customers? What do they want? What price will they pay? What do they read? Where do they shop?

For example, the major banks in Ireland often conduct customer satisfaction surveys to investigate how satisfied customers are with their services. In a recent study,

Bank of Ireland asked customers about their telephone services, staff friendliness, credit card facilities, opening hours, statements, and loan facilites.[16] This has resulted in initiatives such as 'Banking 365' and '100Y2000'. Another firm, Goodfella Pizzas, before entering the Irish market, investigated when and why people eat pizzas — to find that Irish consumers associate pizzas with fun.[17]

Firms also engage in marketing research to reduce risk and uncertainty and so aid decision-making. Information helps management make better and more informed decisions about customer needs, the market, competitors and potential changes in the firm's offerings. Better information leads to better decisions, customer satisfaction and profitability. Good decision-making relies upon a sound information base. The value of information lies in its assistance in decision-making. In the face of intense competition, increasing service requirements of customers, shorter product life cycles and greater segmentation, an efficient and effective marketing information system enables marketing managers to make better-informed decisions. Managers can respond to changing environment and customer stimuli with greater speed. New opportunities can be capitalised upon, increasing profitability and market share. As put by Roger Jupp, Lansdowne Marketing Research,[18] 'Good research is equivalent to the lights on a car — you can see where you are going.' Managers can thus use information at:

- An operational level, e.g. a customer complaint has been received about late deliveries and management need information to diagnose the problem — was it a transport difficulty; traffic delays; or an incorrect delivery docket?
- A tactical level, e.g. sales-force management and measurement of sales levels, market share, brand awareness, preferred brands and brand loyalty are used to describe how effective the firm was in pursuing their marketing strategy. Michael Brophy, MD of the *Sunday World*, maintains that marketing research informs the company of the variety of reasons why people buy and read newspapers. By fulfilling one of these requirements to the satisfaction of a reader, brand loyalty is established.[19]
- A strategic level, e.g. new target market identification within the company to enhance performance or development of a sales forecast to help strategy-setting issues. To illustrate, Helen Harrington, brand manager at Dairygold[20] food products, maintains that the first step in the creation of a national brand, such as Sno Yogurt, was the comprehensive research looking into the potential of the market, the strengths and weaknesses of other brands, whether or not there was room for a new brand, and how best to penetrate the market. In a similar manner, Biosite Diagnostics Inc.[21] prior to the introduction of a new product, Triage, engaged in market research to ascertain whether or not a market existed for the 'novel technology' they had produced. As a result, the company was able to identify one market out of five or six potential end-user segments. Thanks to this early marketing research, the firm chose the best market niche and selling strategy

for its drug-testing device, and so used strategic marketing research as an antidote to the seduction of science!

Box 1.3
Examples of companies using research to aid decision-making

A small entertainment company needs information about the multimedia industry. They have to decide what segment to enter to ensure future survival. Accordingly, they want to know:

(a) about the type of products being sold — CD-roms for games, for entertainment, and/or for education;
(b) where the products are selling: USA, Europe and/or Japan;
(c) market segments, such as Internet, interactive television, and/or CD-roms;
(d) which are growing, at what rate, where and why.

A fast-food chain wants to expand. They have to decide between four different towns as to where the next shop will be located. Information is required about: population trends — age, income, social class, occupation; consumption patterns of fast food and convenience food; and existing competitors in the areas. Traffic flow, parking facilities and many more issues need to be investigated before reaching a conclusion as to the most suitable location.

A well-recognised group of hotels in Ireland have been up-grading their leisure facilities in their hotels to include gyms, swimming pools, sauna and outdoor sports such as tennis. One particular hotel in the chain is different to the rest — it has traditionally catered for the American tourist market, a market not demanding extensive leisure facilities. The question now arises — does the group invest in extensive leisure facilities in this particular hotel? As well as needing information about the changing needs of the American market, the decision-makers also need to know about other segments that they have not catered for in the past, but may wish to serve now. For example, many local residents are now joining health clubs in the area for relaxation, exercise and social reasons. What are their needs? Who are they? When do they use leisure facilities — Why? Where? What do they like and dislike in a leisure centre?

In summary, marketing research is essential because it can:

- identify problems in current marketing strategies;
- aid and improve management decision-making;
- reduce the business risk associated with a management decision;

- identify new opportunities;
- improve the firm's ultimate objective of profitability through customer satisfaction;
- act as the linkage between the firm, its environments and customers.

A word of caution: managers can suffer from three potential inertia difficulties where information is concerned. Firstly, too much information can result in information overload — managers experience 'paralysis by analysis'. Secondly, there is information deprivation — managers can 'drown in data, but lack information to make an informed decision'.[22] Thirdly, while marketing information can greatly enhance a manager's judgment about the marketing strategies, it never eliminates risk or uncertainty surrounding a decision. Information is not a substitute for management judgment.

• Marketing Research in Ireland[23]

Marketing research in Ireland has developed enormously since the early 1960s, which was the period of founding of two of the first indigenous market research agencies — Irish Marketing Surveys and Market Research Bureau of Ireland. Since that time, the number of companies has grown slowly but steadily, and now includes a range of companies operating as all-purpose generalist market research agencies and many small organisations who specialise in particular market niches, for example, qualitative research. Thus, marketing research in Ireland is a well-developed industry, relative to the size of the economy. The current field of research companies includes multinationals such as AC Nielsen, who undertake a wide range of retail audits and are now responsible for measurement of the television audience in Ireland via the Nielsen TV ratings surveys. The industry also includes other companies owned by non-Irish interests such as TNAGB MRBI-SOFRES. It is generally recognised that Nielsen represents the largest market research agency in Ireland. Lansdowne Market Research is the largest *ad hoc* research company, followed by Irish Marketing Surveys, TNAGB MRBI-SOFRES and Behaviour and Attitudes (these companies are frequently quoted in national newspapers). Most of the leading companies now have links with international partners in order to satisfy demand for co-ordinating research outside Ireland and to remain in continuous contact with developments in Europe and America.

The overall size of the Irish industry was estimated at over IR£24.4 million in 1998 by AIMRO (the Association of Irish Market Research Organisations, which includes the six largest market research firms in the Republic of Ireland). Europe has the largest research market in the world, 46% of the world-wide total of US$11 billion — a significant market by any standards.[24]

The profile of the Irish market research industry is broadly similar to the rest of Europe. Fast-moving consumer goods, the original life-blood of market research, represents a continuing important flow of business to market research agencies. It is estimated that 80% of market research expenditure is upon consumer products,[25] the majority of which comes from manufacturers, followed by the service industry. Yet while consumer research represents the backbone of the marketplace, business-to-business research is rising in terms of its importance. Coupled with this, the growth of the service economy and proliferation of marketing practices in such industries as financial service provision, telecommunications, the retail industry and media has led to the increasing importance of research for companies involved in these industries in recent years.

Market research is not undertaken only by the largest companies in Ireland, but certainly, as in many other spheres, they constitute the largest buyers. This is, in part, a reflection of their substantially larger marketing budgets *vis-à-vis* small to medium enterprises. For the vast majority of smaller firms, market research is about assessing the firm's ability to match their resources with the customers' needs, in light of the environment within which they operate. So, essentially, marketing research in Ireland for small firms is about:

- the market;
- the 'W' issues — What?, When?, Where, Why?;
- the effectiveness of the firm (versus competitors).

Box 1.4
Examples of marketing research studies undertaken by Irish firms

Thermo King
Customer perception feedback
Competitive profiling
Price positioning
Environmental changes and forces
Bank of Ireland and AIB
Customer service analysis
Customer satisfaction
Communication research
Customer image
Irish Life
Image studies
Segmentation research
Distribution research

Goodfella's
Pizza buying behaviour
Market size
Brown Thomas
Corporate identity and positioning
Dubarry
Brand recognition
Attitude study
Guinness
Test marketing — beer
Chanelle Veterinary
Awareness and image studies
Usage patterns
Effective promotional methods

Bord na Mona	**Dairygold Food**
Consumer buyer behaviour	Competitive analysis
Usage patterns	Market studies, e.g. yoghurt
Jury's	**National Dairy Council**
Tourism trends and changes	New product development
Customer satisfaction surveys	**Haagen-Dazs**
United Beverages	Market segmentation
New product development	**Mars Ireland**
Brand name — Finches	Test market — celebrations

According to a study about marketing practices in Ireland,[26] there is an overall trend among small Irish firms towards informal information usage, with two-thirds of respondents reporting 'word-of-mouth' information as the dominant information source. This strong reliance on informal sources of information is also documented,[27] with 81% of respondents expressing the view that informal chats with colleagues about the market were more insightful than formal reports. This use of 'gut feelings' by Irish managers does not exclude marketing research. Rather, Irish managers appreciate the use of 'instinct' and combine it with the formal scientific approach of marketing research to give a holistic and complete picture. As a result, talking with people is the most profitable avenue of investigation for marketing researchers in Ireland. This is reinforced by the tendency to find 'information in people's heads as opposed to in a report'.[28]

The particular types of projects undertaken are extremely diverse, as they now are throughout the world. The range of project types is just as diverse as the needs of the companies themselves. Usage and attitude surveys, providing market overviews and market share data, remain relevant, especially in the light of greater emphasis on truly understanding the image positioning occupied by specific brands *vis-à-vis* their competitors. Changes in customer profiles and penetration of brands remain a constant source of customer research, but these are often allied to more complex studies which look at issues such as customer segmentation into particular typologies or customer satisfaction. The Pareto principle (80/20 rule) has ensured a strong focus on identifying the most relevant and important customers, for the main buyers of market research. It has led to an emphasis on understanding the customer, in keeping with the need to provide appropriate communications strategies to enhance customer retention, loyalty and satisfaction.

In the business-to-business arena, similar marketing philosophies have been applied in recent years; but it is fair to say that business-to-business research is probably of a lesser scale in Ireland than elsewhere, by virtue of the relative smallness of the economy. A greater need exists in larger markets such as the USA, Britain, Germany etc. to understand business-to-business habits than appears to be the case in the Republic of Ireland.

The proximity of the United Kingdom, in part, has an impact on the types of research undertaken in Ireland and also on the current topicality of specific research areas or research techniques. The arrival of computer aided telephone interviewing (CATI) in Ireland in the mid-1990s came at a time when telephone penetration was still below the European average. This has not prevented CATI interviewing from becoming a major aspect of the existing market research scene, covering projects in both the general public and business-to-business sectors. The importance of technology is becoming ever more widespread within the industry, in respect of both data collection and data analysis, again reflecting trends in business as a whole. (These trends are discussed in more detail in chapters to follow.)

Overall, the marketing research industry in Ireland is growing and varied. It has learned to apply technology-based techniques, while maintaining a broad focus across industries. In so doing, the marketing research industry in Ireland continues to advise leading companies about their marketing decision-making processes.

• Summary

Good marketing practice requires a firm to be both customer-orientated and information-driven. Marketing research complements the marketing concept of customer satisfaction. Marketing research is an all-pervasive information activity that is necessary in implementing the marketing concept.

The purpose of this chapter has been to reflect upon what marketing research is — a valuable tool in the evaluation of different courses of action. Marketing research cannot make the decisions for managers, it is not a substitute for management decision-making. However, marketing research can help decrease the risk and uncertainty connected with many marketing decisions by delivering accurate and relevant information.

Marketing research is defined as the systematic planning, gathering, analysis and reporting of information to management to assist with a specific decision. A firm engages in marketing research because research improves decision-making. Marketing research also reduces risk and uncertainty. Marketing research is the strategic link between the firm, its customer and environment. We can conclude that marketing research is:

- a building block of marketing;
- a function in its own right;
- a management responsibility;
- an asset to be invested in;
- a source of competitive advantage or differentiation.

The marketing research industry is well developed in Ireland. First established in the 1960s, it embraces consumer and business-to-business research across a wide variety of sectors, with links to international partners. Valued at IR£21 million, it is set to continue to grow and advise leading companies about their marketing decision-making processes, through the provision of accurate, timely and relevant information.

Key Terms

Marketing concept
Marketing research
Methodology led
Uncertainty
Decision-making
Valid
Decision driven

Customer satisfaction
Scientific approach
Information intense
Risk
Management function
Reliable
Systematic

Questions

1. What is marketing?
2. Describe the role information plays in marketing research. How important is it?
3. What are the three levels at which managers utilise information?
4. Why is the management of information so important to decision-making?
5. What are the implications for information management over the next few years?
6. What is marketing research?
7. What are the main characteristics of marketing research?
8. How would you argue that some form of marketing research is needed in all organisations?
9. Does the type of marketing research a company needs depend on the nature of its customers? Why?
10. How would you describe the marketing research industry in Ireland?

Problems and Assignments

1. How might the following use marketing research? Be specific:
    (a) A small sports shop.
    (b) A fast-food chain.
    (c) A major television network (RTE or UTV for example).
    (d) A computer firm.
    (e) A university.
    (f) Manchester United football club.
2. One of the key marketing trends of the 1990s is that organisations are trying to be more market-driven. What role should marketing research play in the process?
3. A marketing manager responsible for CD-rom-based video games (CD-rom stands for compact disc read-only memory) for personal computers (PCs) has

received a copy of ten new books on this industry and five new industry reports prepared by industry consultants. These items total over 3,000 pages. 'All this data will be great help with the new games we are playing', noted the analyst who delivered the documents. Comment on this quote, and describe how the manager should proceed.

4. The new president of an old, established company, selling a wide variety of equipment and supplies to the dairy industry, is facing a problem. The company is currently unprofitable and is, in the president's opinion, operating inefficiently. Some items it manufactures, and many it wholesales to dairies, creameries, and similar plants. Because the industry is changing in several ways, survival will be more difficult in the future. In particular, many equipment companies are bypassing the wholesalers and are selling directly to dairies. In addition, many of the independent smaller dairies are being taken over by larger dairies. How might research help the new president make the right decisions?

5. You have received a report from a consultant hired by your firm — a life insurance company. The study is a survey of morale in the head office and covers the opinions of about 30 secretaries about 100 executives and actuaries. You are asked to comment on its quality. What would you look for?

6. Use a web browser to visit Ireland On Line at: http://www.iol.ie. What type of information can be accessed?

7. The owner of 22 fast-food restaurants was asked how he does marketing research. He answered that he did it by driving around. 'I stay up late. If it's midnight and I don't have anything else to do, I drive around town and look at the lines in front of places. I'll look at the rubbish and see if the guy's doing business. If he's got real clean rubbish bins and an empty car park, he's not doing any business. I also find out a lot by talking to my suppliers. I ask the bread guy how many boxes of buns the drive-in down the street is buying. Very few managers do that.' Is this manager conducting marketing research? Justify your answer.

8. Look through recent issues of newspapers and magazines to identify five examples of marketing research.

9. List one kind of marketing research that would be useful to each of the following organisations:
   (a) Your campus bookshop.
   (b) A major department store in your area.
   (c) A restaurant located near your campus.
   (d) A museum or heritage centre near you.
   (e) A nearby hospital.

10. Use the Internet to locate and examine:
    (a) ESOMAR's Code of Conduct.
    (b) The Market Research Society (UK) and its code of conduct.
    (c) Marketing associations in Ireland (name, address, phone, fax etc.).
    (d) Marketing research firms in Ireland and other European countries, together with the facilities they offer to clients (via ESOMAR).

Case Study
The Norwegians Invade Ireland*

An Irish plant manufacturing solid fuel is for sale. A Norwegian company is investigating the option of purchasing the Irish plant. The Norwegian firm have considerable expertise in this area in their home market. They are examining the Irish plant with a view to developing a new fuel for the Irish market. The fuel would be a cross between peat and coal. It would be targeted at households all over Ireland.

Assignment

1. Make a detailed list of all of the marketing questions you will ask as marketing manager of the Norwegian company faced with the decision to purchase or not to purchase the plant.
2. What types of marketing information will help you in decreasing the risk related to the purchase decision? Be specific.
3. Where will you find this information?

*This case was written by Ray Collis, Managing Director, Envision Marketing. It is intended to be used as a basis for class discussion rather than to illustrate either effective or ineffective handling of an administrative situation. The case is based on a real situation, though certain information has been disguised.

Chapter 2

THE MARKETING RESEARCH PROCESS

> - **Chapter Overview**
> - Introduction • The Marketing Research Process • Some Additional Comments on the Marketing Research Process • The Characteristics of Good Research • Marketing Research Errors • General Trends in Marketing Research • Ethics in Marketing Research • Summary

• Introduction

The challenge for marketing managers is to obtain and use accurate information upon which to base good decisions, as we saw in Chapter 1. This may appear to be making an essentially simple process of gathering information into a very complicated and complex procedure. This is not so, as gathering information is not simple — not if you want that information to be accurate, objective, valid and reliable. Any manager can talk informally with several customers who just happen to be in the shop. But what about the customers who are not in the shop? What about their likes and dislikes, their complaints, their changing requirements? What about those people who are buying from competitors — Why? What are they buying? How could they buy from you? These types of questions and many others offer some insight into why gathering information must first be planned, and then collected. If the information is to assist with a decision about a problem or new opportunity, the manager must have complete confidence that the correct information was gathered in a reliable and accurate manner.

Enter marketing research. Marketing research is merely a label we give to a sequence of stages for gathering decision-making information using scientific techniques. This chapter is devoted to an overview of the stages involved in research, i.e. the marketing research process. That done, we turn our attention to the methodological and conceptual foundation underlying the process of good marketing research. To this end, we introduce the terms *validity* and *reliability*, and examine the concept of error management. Lastly, the chapter describes marketing research and the general trends that are affecting it. Having completed this chapter, you will be able to detail and describe:

1. the stages necessary to undertake a marketing research study;
2. the role of validity and reliability in marketing research;
3. how error can detract from the usefulness of marketing research;
4. error management;
5. general trends in marketing research.

The stages outlined in this chapter are used as a structure for the remainder of the book. Many of the concepts and terms raised here may be unfamiliar to you at this point. They are the tools and techniques of the marketing researcher and are repeated and detailed in more depth as we move through the book to facilitate your learning.

• The Marketing Research Process

The marketing research process refers to a set of stages that detail a number or sequence of tasks a researcher undertakes to gather and report valid and reliable information to assist with decision-making. Different authors categorise the various stages in marketing research differently. This arises due to the inter-related nature of marketing research activities. For the purposes of this book, we present the marketing research process as a set of seven stages that encapsulate the major concerns of the researcher in conducting a marketing research study. Each stage has both a conceptual dimension and activities facet for the investigator to consider. The following stages are overlapping and complementary to each other; they serve the purpose of providing a general structure for planning a research project. They are depicted in Figure 2.1.

Figure 2.1 The marketing research process

We now present a general discussion of the stages involved in any marketing research project, according to Figure 2.1. The above presentation of marketing research is adopted to capture the complexity and structure needed to understand the concept. Remember, many of the terms introduced here are explained in further detail in the relevant following chapters.

Stage 1 — Problem Definition

A research project is first concerned with correct and proper *problem definition*. This stage is essentially about the researcher deciding what information is needed to solve the problem on hand. The researcher has to determine the purpose of the study and why it is being undertaken. For example, the British Newspaper Society[1] initiated a study into the relative strengths of colour in advertising, and to this end, defined the objectives of the project as follows:

- to measure the difference in effectiveness between colour and mono advertising;
- to ascertain why some advertisements work more effectively than others;
- to develop an understanding of what elements within an advertisement will (a) make it more effective and (b) make the colour work harder.

Thus, the management decision has to be stated by the researcher as a question- and/or an information-oriented statement. This consists of a number of activities and involves the manager and researcher working closely to identify the problem.

In this manner, the tasks involved in problem definition: problem identification, clarification, formulation and objectives, are highly inter-related and dependent upon each other, as Figure 2.2 depicts. The marketing research problem or opportunity cannot be formulated without a tentative list of the information needs. To this end, a marketing information system (discussed in Chapter 3) is an important mechanism for accessing numerous sources and persons who can potentially help in defining the information needs of the project on hand.

Figure 2.2 Problem definition stages

Problem definition ends with, and results in either (a) a list of objectives or (b) a hypothesis. Objectives are broad statements of intent, while a hypothesis is a tentative answer to the question being considered. These are discussed in more detail in Chapter 3, as are all the individual aspects to this first stage in marketing research.

A decision at Stage 1, problem definition, automatically, directly and explicitly affects the remaining stages of research. While the stages of a marketing research study appear at face value to be mutually exclusive, they are highly dependent upon each other.

At some point early on in the research process, budget and costing have to be considered in light of required information and proposed methods for collecting the data. A research proposal may also be necessary, especially if the research is being undertaken by a research agency on behalf of the firm.

Box 2.1 Main components of a research proposal

A good research proposal will incorporate the following headings:

1. Background
A broad overview and introduction to the present situation, covering the firm, person requesting the research, an outline of the product/service, market segment etc. to be researched.

2. Research objectives
A clear statement of the research objectives and aims. The research question behind the objectives is discussed. The research can be expressed as a hypothesis.

3. Required information
A discussion of the needed information and data, along with the decision facing management and potential outcomes. The decision implications of potential findings are examined. The research parameters agreed with management are presented, e.g. products, markets, topics and key issues.

4. Research methods
Based upon the (a) nature of the problem in hand; (b) time and resources and (c) nature of the decision, the researcher chooses the research techniques, in light of the accuracy and objectivity sought by management. The planned secondary and primary research is documented.

5. Terms of reference
The researcher sets out clearly what is to be undertaken, the time frame, when, where and how he/she will report to management. The key assumptions with respect to the research are also given.

6. Costs
All direct and indirect costs for the entire project are given, with breakdown for each of the individual stages. Financial constraints are clearly outlined.

7. Presentation
The presentation has to be prepared with the client's needs clearly in mind. It will include a written report and one or more oral presentations.

In summary, finding the starting point for any marketing research project can be the most difficult part. Once the problem has been correctly identified and the information needs and objectives have been established, the research task gains momentum and starts to unfold.[2]

Stage 2 — Choose a Research Design

Choosing a research design is the second stage in marketing research. A research design is an overall blueprint, guideline, plan of action or framework for the rest of the research process to facilitate later decisions that need to be made. One way to classify the nature of the required information, and hence research designs in marketing research, is according to the three terms: *exploratory*, *descriptive* or *causal*, as shown in Figure 2.3.

Figure 2.3 Research designs

Exploratory research is research that aims to explore and to discover issues about the problem on hand, because very little is known about the situation by anyone inside or outside the firm. A research project is exploratory when there is uncertainty about the dimensions or characteristics of a problem or opportunity. Golden Vale[3] conducted a pan-European food research project, with the aim of the research being to find out more about the health benefits of Omega 3, the fish oil used by Golden Vale in its spread, Live. In this manner, you are 'putting your toe in the water'. This need by exploratory research to explore and discover, leaves it as response driven, i.e. it's the respondents' responses that matter to the investigator and not the questions posed by the researcher.

In contrast to this, you may already know a lot about the market and its behaviour, and you may want to describe this market or facets of it in more detail. You may want to categorise existing distribution outlets according to size, turnover, customer type and geographical spread. This kind of research is about quantifying some aspects of a market and so is referred to as *descriptive research*. Descriptive research is concerned with describing the associations between two or more variables, e.g. how advertising affects sales, how price and quality are related, the degree to which product usage varies with income. Alternatively, descriptive research could describe one phenomenon or variable in detail, such as brand loyalty. Thus, this type of research seeks to document the number of people who behave in a certain way or the number of units who have a certain characteristic. It is question driven. Descriptive research is highly structured, formal, and mathematically-based. For this reason, you will often hear that exploratory research generates data that is dubbed as 'soft' and descriptive research data is labelled as 'hard' data.

Causal research aims to establish a cause and effect relationship between two or more variables, for example, x causes y. Cadbury[4] test marketed three new chocolate assortments for the Christmas gift market: a high-class prestigious gift, a woman-to-woman gift, and a box of chocolates for men, in order to predict potential sales and the most likely new product to succeed. So, causal research describes a specific type of relationship between two or more variables. Therefore, the distinction between descriptive and causal research is one of degree, as both are dealing with quantifiable data.

Stage 3 — Planning the Data Collection Method(s) and Instrument(s)

With problem definition and research design already decided upon, the researcher is now in a position to decide how, when and where the required information is to be gathered. This stage of the marketing research process incorporates choosing a data collection method and relevant data collection instrument, in light of the problem, and the research design.

Data can be collected from *secondary* sources or from *primary* sources. Secondary data is information that has already been collected by someone else for another reason, other than the one on hand. It can be either internal or external to the firm. For example, internal source is a set of accounts or an invoice, whereas government-published figures are an example of external secondary data. Primary data is defined as data or information collected first hand by the researcher to solve the specific problem/opportunity on hand.

Here, one comes across an important rule of marketing research. You always exhaust your secondary sources of data before planning to collect any primary data. In practice, this means that as a researcher, you first plan what information you need, and then check that the required information is not already in a written report that you could access in a library. If not, you again plan what primary research to conduct before actually gathering data from respondents. For example, as a furniture manufacturer wishing to export to the Swedish market, before going to Sweden to talk with potential customers (primary research), you would visit the Enterprise

Ireland library in Sandymount Dublin (or other sources) and consult a marketing report that they commissioned about the furniture market in Europe (secondary research).

However, in many cases, secondary sources of data are not sufficient to solve the problem. The marketing researcher then turns her/his attention to primary data collection methods.

The choice of primary data collection method is closely tied to the type of research design that is being pursued. Generally speaking, *focus groups*, *in-depth interviews* and *projective techniques* are generally, though not exclusively, associated with *exploratory research*. Food manufacturers often talk with small groups of seven to ten housewives to find out about their food concerns, changing opinions on nutrition and brand preferences. Medical companies conduct in-depth interviews with doctors to uncover their attitudes and opinions about new medical devices. Extensive exploratory research in Ireland convinced Murphy Brewery in Cork that the brand's traditional burgundy-coloured livery and counter mounts were too conservative and did not appeal to drinkers in the important 18–25 age category, now being targeted.[5] Likewise, Gilbeys, in a bid to increase their share of the Irish wine market by targeting 'middle of the road' wine consumers, conducted focus-group research which showed that independently minded wine consumers and connoisseurs make up about 20% of the Irish market. They discovered that these consumers don't want the 'hard sell' approach but want quality information and will pay up to £15 a bottle.[6] Focus groups were also used to identify the name and product positioning for a male contraceptive pill.[7] To utilise these data collection methods, data collection instruments or tools, such as a moderator's script, interviewer guidelines and tape recorders are necessary.

Surveys, either personal, telephone or postal, are the data collection methods available to the researcher when conducting descriptive research. For example, Bank of Ireland and AIB regularly conduct personal interviews with customers to monitor the level of satisfaction with services and product offerings. These utilise the questionnaire as the main data collection instrument. The survey approach was also used to identify the value of the Internet as a marketing tool among Ireland's Top 500 companies.[8]

With the advent of computers and telecommunications, the traditional data collection methods, e.g. surveys, are being modified. That is, data can now be collected by electronic means. For example, the Internet provides a variation on the generic idea of a postal questionnaire, as does the fax. Computers can also be used to conduct CATI, computer-aided telephone interviews or CAPI, computer-aided personal interviews. In these circumstances, the questionnaire is displayed on a screen, the responses are captured on the keyboard, the computer inserts the correct skip patterns and prepares the data for analysis.

Panels are made up of people, business firms or households who record their purchasing activities over a long period. The ever-changing children's market was monitored by use of school panels,⁹ and Superquinn use consumer panels to identify ways of improving customer service and augmenting product ranges.¹⁰ In Ireland, the two major types of panels are household and retail. Nielsen (formerly TAM), a television audience measurement, is the most sophisticated measurement of household panels in Ireland.¹¹

Observation is another data collection method suitable for descriptive research. Here, the researcher observes behaviour instead of asking a respondent about their behaviour. Retailers such as SuperValu and Roches Stores utilise Electronic Point of Sale (EPoS) to observe sales of products and trends, and infer from this the purchasing behaviour of consumers.

Finally, the recognised data collection method for causal research is the *experiment*. As a method of gathering data, the experiment is characterised by manipulation of variables to establish the cause and effect relationship between variables. For example, to measure the effectiveness of a new educational intervention, a distant learning marketing course, the owner/managers of small Irish companies are examined before and after the course.¹²

Figure 2.4 Data collection methods

The data collection instrument normally associated with surveys, observation, panels and experimentation is the *questionnaire*. By definition, a questionnaire is a structured list of questions asked of the respondent. Other instruments, such as interviewer checklist, can also be used.

This stage of the research process, primary data collection, is essentially concerned with *measurement*, measuring the amount of characteristic present or not present. To help us in measuring whether a person has a positive attitude, their consumption or usage rates or any of the other numerous variables that marketers are interested in, we have access to four mathematical measurement scales — the nominal, ordinal, interval and ratio scales. These measurement scales underlie all data collection instruments.

Stage 4 — Sampling

The fourth stage of a marketing research project centres around deciding who to talk to or observe, i.e. identifying who or what has the required information. The technical name given to this stage is *sampling* — choosing a small number of people or objects to represent the larger population or universe from which they are drawn. As is seen in Figure 2.1, many researchers like to consider this question before selecting a data collection method, as the form of the primary research can be influenced by who you are talking with. For example, if you are a toy manufacturer and wish to evaluate the best colour for your new product, you might give the toy in different colours to a group of children, similar to your expected target market, to play with, and observe which colour they favour. If the top five retail grocery buyers are the persons you identify as having the needed information, you may decide to e-mail or fax them a list of your questions, in light of the heavy demands placed upon their time.

The first stage in sampling is to decide upon whether a *sample* or *census* will be undertaken. The *population* of interest needs to be defined and a *sampling list* or frame of all the relevant parties has to be generated.

At this point, the researcher has to choose a sampling method. **Probability** sampling uses a procedure that is based upon statistics, and so every unit within the population has a known chance of being selected as part of the sample. This use of statistics allows the researcher to be objective in selecting who to talk to, and so increases the validity of a study. Types of probability sampling include simple random sampling, systematic random sampling, stratified random sampling, cluster and area random sampling. For example, a paint manufacturer could use the electoral register (list of every single person over the age of 18 registered to vote) for simple random sampling, whereby x number of names are randomly chosen from the said list.

Non-probability sampling, an alternative form of sampling, is not based upon probability. It is therefore more subjective in character. It depends upon criteria such as the researcher's judgment, access to the population, cost and time constraints. It includes quota, convenience, purposeful and judgment, which are different types of non-probability sampling. For example, due to time and cost constraints, a local Dublin firm may conduct personal interviews with the first 100 people walking down Grafton Street on any given Saturday afternoon about a new coffee shop in the area — a convenience, non-probability sample.

As part of sampling, the *sample size* has to be decided upon too, i.e. how many people do you talk to or observe? Sample sizes can vary from one to many thousands and really depend on how confident the manager wants to be about the information collected. The confidence level is one way of expressing the desired accuracy of the sample — how closely the sample mirrors and reflects the population. Accuracy and confidence are measured under the concept of sampling error — the degree to which sample values vary from the population values. The general rule of thumb is that the more accuracy or confidence required in the collected data, the larger the sample size. The available budget will also influence the necessary sample size.

Having got to this point in the research process, the investigator has now planned out in advance all expected actions to acquire the needed information. The marketing research process now moves into the fifth stage.

Stage 5 — Fieldwork, Gathering the Required Information

Knowing who, what, where, how, and why, about the required information, the researcher commences the plan of action and physically collects the primary data. This is often referred to as *fieldwork*. This stage may incorporate the selection, training, controlling and evaluating of a field force, a team of researchers.

Stage 6 — Analysis of the Data

Once all fieldwork is completed, the data has to be translated into information to satisfy the objectives of the study. So the *analysis* stage of marketing research is about the processing or translation of data into information.

Prior to any detailed analysis, the data collection instruments and procedures will have to be checked for completeness and accuracy. This is data preparation and includes the functions of *editing* and *coding* the data. The data can then be entered into a computer for analysis. A computer package is used at this point, such as Minitab, SPSSX or SAS. This is often referred to as *data reduction*.

To further describe or detail various aspects of the market, the consumer, behavioural patterns or attitudes, the data has to be examined for associations, trends and patterns. Simple and cross tabulations, and frequency distributions are the basic form of *data analysis* in marketing research. Measures of central tendency or location, e.g. mean, mode median and measures of dispersion, e.g. range and standard deviation, are also used to summarise the data in basic data analysis. Other data analysis techniques, such as significance testing, correlation, regression, factor analysis, cluster analysis and multidimensional scaling lend richness and depth to the analysis phase.

We often refer to the type of analysis as *univariate, bivariate* or *multivariate analysis*. This refers to the number of variables concerned in the analysis. Univariate analysis denotes one variable, such as the average amount spent on beer by tourists visiting Ireland. Bivariate analysis examines two variables — for example, the relationship between price and quality; while multivariate analysis investigates a variety of variables, e.g. the market share for a particular brand of coffee is influenced by the price of the coffee, the competitors' price, the size of the jar, the competitors' jar size, special promotions, advertising and competitor advertising, shelf spacing and competitor shelf spacing, to name but a few. The National Dairy Council used factor analysis, a multivariate analysis technique, to establish an opening for a hard, white, low-fat cheddar cheese in the Irish market.[13] The actual choice of analytical technique will be dependent upon a number of issues — the problem; the required information; the nature of the collected information; whether the analysis is bivariate or multivariate in nature and whether the variables are dependent or independent. These and other analysis techniques used today are available on computer-based statistical packages used by other social sciences as well as marketing. SPSSX, SAS, MICROSTAT, and SYSTAT are a few of the computer-based statistical packages widely available and used by marketing researchers worldwide. Computer-based statistical analysis methods such as factor analysis are examined and described in depth in Part 4.

Stage 7 — Presentation of the Results and Findings

[margin note: should have solved prob or identified opportunity]
[margin note: written report / oral presentation]

The final and remaining stage in any marketing research process is to communicate the findings and information to solve the problem/opportunity. This involves the researcher preparing and presenting a written report for the client.

To write such a report, the researcher must first understand the audience for the report. For example, most managers, of either small or large firms, do not want to hear about the pro's and con's of the chosen data collection method. Such information is too technical for many managers. So, while this technical dimension to the study would be included in a report, it would not be the focal point. If the *raison d'être* of research is to assist with decision-making through the provision of information, then the marketing research report reflects this, by primarily discussing and explaining the findings and results, and not the methodology followed. The limitations of the study would also be acknowledged at this point — limitations are actual errors or shortcomings which occurred in reality. The validity and reliability implications for the study as a whole are thus documented.

Secondly, the written marketing research report follows the standardised reporting format used among the business and marketing community, unless otherwise specified by the manager in question. For example, all research reports have an executive summary — one or two pages of statements summarising the key/core findings of the research.

The presentation of results normally incorporates an oral presentation to the manager and other relevant decision-makers within the company. Again, the crux of the presentation is the findings and results of the research process and not the actual research process itself. This follows a generally accepted number of guidelines, as outlined in Chapter 15, and affords the manager a question and answer period.

• Some Additional Comments on the Marketing Research Process

There are some hidden issues surrounding any basic marketing research model, such as the one above, which a researcher needs to be aware of.

1. In practice, the stages in any marketing research process are more interactive than the stage-by-stage model, presented in this chapter, tends to suggest. For

example, it is common for a researcher, while considering the data collection method best suited to the project on hand, to also think about sampling and fieldwork, as all three issues impact upon each other. The marketing research stages are very interdependent upon each other, and overlap.   *not mutually exclusive*

2. Each stage in the marketing research process is, in reality, very complex. Each stage of the research process is fraught with difficulties and potential pitfalls. To illustrate, when doing survey work, it is possible that the respondent will not remember the required information (do you know how many pints you have consumed in the past year?), will reveal the true answer (how much did you earn this year?), or will answer yes or no to make the researcher happy. These are merely examples of respondent error.

3. As presented, the marketing research stages appear very rigid; in practice they are much more fluid than first appears. Marketing research is not as linear as depicted by any model. To illustrate this point — firms can undertake an exploratory research and then turn around and use this to feed into a second descriptive research study. Given this, we can now introduce a feedback loop into our basic marketing research model, as shown in Figure 2.5.

Good Mkting Research is:-
- *Systematic* (@ stage 7 should have solved prob or id'd opportunity)
- *well organised*
- *well planned*
- *Objective*
  - *unbiased*
  - *untainted*
  - *free from error*
- *Reliability*
  - *measuring instruments used deliver consistent findings over time*
- *Validity*
  - *measuring what one truly wants to measure*

Figure 2.5 The marketing research process

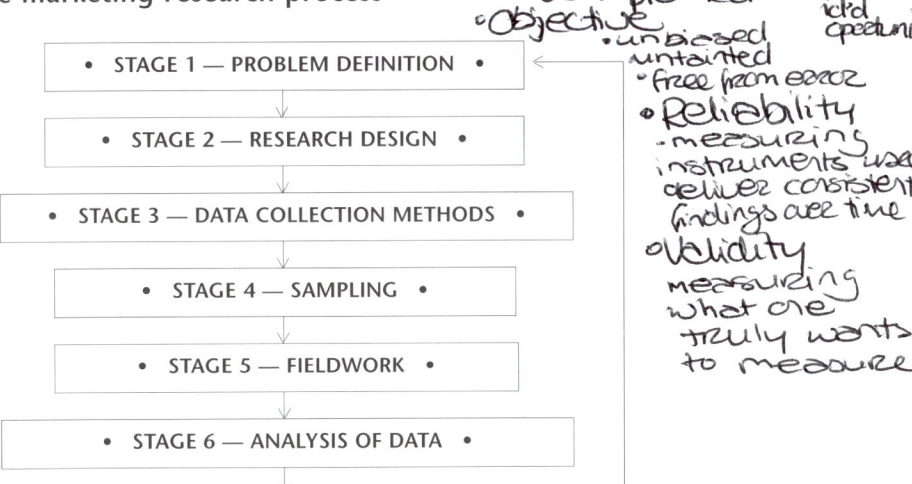

4. Sometimes, secondary sources of data can supply enough information to solve the problem and thus allow the manager to make a decision. In this situation, you would then move to the analysis stage of the marketing research process and continue on from that point. A firm, having defined the information needs, may locate and access a secondary source of data, a report or study, that provides answers to the problem on hand. By analysing the report and documented

information within, the researcher may be in a position to write up the results and present them to the manager. This type of research is still a marketing research study, except that in these circumstances, no primary research was needed. So, our marketing research model looks like that presented in Figure 2.6.

Figure 2.6 The marketing research process

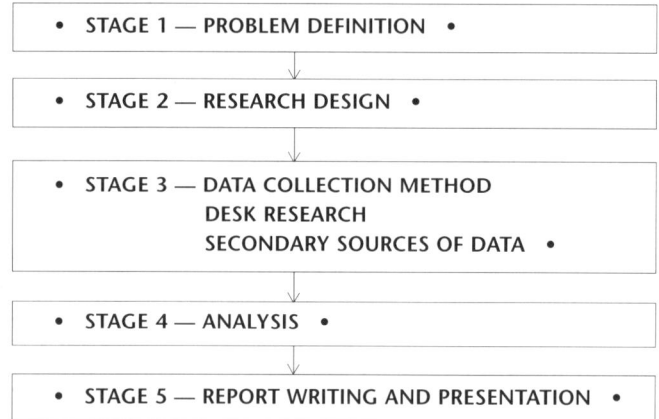

• The Characteristics of Good Research

An important question for an investigator to consider is 'What makes for good marketing research?' To answer such a question, we must consider a web of factors. Firstly, management must be confident in the information gathered. Secondly, the collected information has to be in accordance with scientific principles. If the provided information is to be accurate and relevant, it has be valid and reliable. Thirdly, planning every stage is essential to good research. The nature of marketing research involves much planning, attention to detail and a scientific approach to information gathering. These factors translate into four key characteristics of good marketing research: systematic, objective, valid, and reliable.

Systematic

Marketing research has to be well organised, well thought out and planned in advance. As an approach to collecting relevant information, marketing research is a logical and defined method. Thus marketing research is, by definition, systematic.

Objective

The process of gathering information and the actual information collected has to be unbiased and untainted. There is great care taken to ensure the research is free from error (random and systematic error), and that the research bears all the hallmarks of validity and reliability. These two terms, validity (measuring what we actually wanted to measure) and reliability (consistency in measurement) are required of good research. When present, marketing research is free from systematic and random error and is therefore 'objective' in nature.

Valid

Results are valid when we measured what we truly wanted to measure. This concept of validity underlies each and every stage of any marketing research process, and is considered necessary for the soundness of the research.

Reliable

Results are reliable when the measuring instruments used deliver consistent findings over time. It assists us in generalising the results from our study to other persons, objects, stores or entities.

Throughout the remainder of this book, the concepts of validity and reliability are given due consideration as they conceptually underlie every stage of the marketing research process. To manage for and ensure they are both present, we consider the likelihood of error detracting from our findings and results.

• Marketing Research Errors

Precautions must be taken at all times to guard against error, bias or shortcomings in the findings, as these detract from the research being valid and reliable. So, it is equally important for a researcher to consider what makes for poor research.

To understand error, we introduce the concept of measurement. Error is said to have occurred when our obtained measurement deviates from the real or true measurement. By virtue of the fact that the researcher is taking a measurement (M) of a characteristic (C), there is a distortion in the measurement of the true characteristic. So, instead of M = C, in reality M = C + E, where E is the amount of total error present. This error can come from random events (and so affect the reliability of the study) or it can surface from systematic error (thus bringing into question the validity of the research). However, on a more practical level, we can say that overall, there are two general or broad types of error that can affect any marketing research. These are *systematic error* and *random error*. Systematic error is bias or shortcomings that detract from accuracy and usefulness of the measurements. It occurs because of faults in the measurement procedure. Random error is *ad hoc* bias that results in an inconsistent measurement. Both can occur at any time during the research process. Systematic error is within the control of the researcher, while random error is not. To simplify a discussion of error and its effect on any research process, we will coincide our discussion of error with each of the marketing research stages and possible errors, as outlined in Table 2.1.

Table 2.1 Sources of error in marketing research

Marketing research stage	Source of errors	
	Systematic errors	Random errors
Problem definition	Informational error	Random error
Research design	Informational error	Random error
Data collection	Non-sampling error (Response error) (Non-response error) (Interviewer error) (Measurement error)	Random error
Sampling	Sampling error (Population error) (Frame error)	Random error
Analysis of data	Analysis error	Random error
Presentation of the results	Communication errors	Random error

Regardless of the classification system used to understand the impact of error in any given project, the tasks and activities undertaken in *each* stage of marketing research are aimed at reducing or eliminating total error, so as to increase the overall objectivity, validity and reliability of the project.

The remainder of this book presents a more in-depth understanding and examination of error in each of the stages in the marketing research process, along with the different management strategies used to eliminate or minimise error.

• General Trends in Marketing Research

To complete our overview of the stages of marketing research, it is necessary to appreciate the broad trends impacting upon the topic. Just as marketing exists in an ever-changing world, so too does marketing research. More so than ever before, research is experiencing tremendous changes.[14, 15] Problem definition becomes more complex and complicated in the 'global village' and in the face of intense competition. As the abundance of internal and external secondary sources of data continues to grow, the issue confronting managers is not lack of information *per se*, but lack of relevant information and information overload. A number of trends are affecting marketing research worldwide. These trends are discussed at the end of each chapter, as they specifically impinge on the topic under discussion. To keep up-to-date with such developments, you are recommended to join a professional research or marketing association, such as the Marketing Institute of Ireland, the MII, the Market Society (UK) and ESOMAR. For the present, an overview of the major trends will provide the necessary background against which the more detailed trends are set.

> ### Box 2.2 Summary of overall trends in marketing research
>
> 1. Traditional marketing research to broaden into relationship and extended marketing research, as the business world becomes more complex and dynamic.[16]
> 2. Continued growth and augmentation of exploratory research.[17]
> 3. More use of research methods to 'get into customer shoes'.[18]
> 4. Increased penetration of Information Technologies into all marketing functions, especially marketing information and information management.[19, 20]
> 5. Concentrated efforts and focus upon ethics and code of conduct within the industry.[21]

We will now outline each of these trends, with further discussion to follow in the relevant chapters to come.

Types of Research

With the advent of customer service and 'relationship marketing', more and more research studies look to the criteria necessary for building long-term relationships with some market segments. This results in detailed 'psychographic' information about customer preferences, lifestyles, personalities, to augment the existing demographic data which many companies tend to have. Dubbed as 'relationship marketing research', Pat Cody,[22] Director of Kompass, Ireland, predicts that this trend will continue, as 'detailed information gathering will soon become as routine as book-keeping; marketing will move away from average customers and towards individual customer analysis to facilitate one-to-one marketing'. Guinness discovered, through research, that because of the specialised nature of their new brand of beers — St James' Gate Beers — drinkers want to be engaged in a dialogue with the brand in order to feel more involved with it. Hence Guinness plans to establish a one-to-one relationship with St James' Gate beer drinkers through an innovative relationship marketing campaign.[23]

Coupled with this, in an accelerating competitive environment, companies have to keep in touch with other external agents in their environment. For example, Digital, in researching the environmental technology in Europe, included the suppliers as well as the users of such technology to ensure a profitable market existed.[24] This is referred to as 'extended research' and can be expected to continue to grow as markets become less clear and as macro environmental factors impact on marketing strategy more and more.

Data Collection Methods

Traditionally, marketing research has been dominated by descriptive research. Describing a customer's age, income level, social class and occupation has enabled firms to better segment markets and fine-tune their offer to these segments. However, shorter product life-cycles, intense competition, outsourcing of raw material and deregulation has led to the need for more detailed, exploratory or 'soft' data about customer needs, preferences, expectations and motivations. This has led to a rise in the use of data collection methods such as focus groups and depth interviews. This trend towards greater utilisation of exploratory research designs and related data collection methods will continue to evolve. Such humanistic data,[25] once generated and gathered, can then be used to feed into more sophisticated marketing computer models, to generate satisfaction models and scenarios of different strategies for companies.[26]

The new interest in exploratory research does not imply a neglect of descriptive or causal research. On the contrary, exploratory research can be undertaken and complemented with a follow-up descriptive study.

Although focus groups and in-depth interviews are generally associated with exploratory research, there has been a strong trend in the 1990s to use focus groups to generate descriptive data.

Technology and Research

Marketing and marketing research is being transformed like never before with the advent of new technologies. MRNet or marketing research in Cyberspace is a new departure for many practitioners.[27] 'Inforsuring' (secondary research medium) and 'Cyberesearch' (through the on-line world at household and individual level) offer new ways of accessing, storing, collecting, generating, processing and reporting data and information. Thus, it comes as no surprise that every phase of marketing research is being impacted by information technologies.[28] Nowhere is the technology effect more evident than in secondary sources of data. The advent of the Internet, web sites and on-line databases is transforming desk research, as discussed in Chapter 4, giving rise to what many call the 'digital age' of information.

In this vein, researchers have better storage and analysis tools to apply to qualitative and quantitative data, e.g. the recent introduction of a new statistical package in Ireland specifically aimed at researchers who conduct exploratory research.[29] Other packages, such as Quantum and SAS, can be used for developing and processing questionnaires.[30]

With sophisticated computer hardware and software readily available, and becoming more affordable every week, marketing models will become more popular, as market behaviour is mathematically modelled.[31] Many computer packages are readily available for assisting with the interviewing process (referred to as CATI, computer-aided telephone interviewing). Such advances are discussed under the relevant topic in forthcoming chapters.

• Ethics in Marketing Research

The ethical concerns in marketing research have been the subject of an ongoing debate in the industry for a long time. The trends discussed above continue to fuel this debate. Professional marketing researchers and practitioners adhere to a strict 'code of conduct' to support those engaged in maintaining professional standards throughout the industry. Ethical issues cluster around the researcher's integrity, fair and just treatment of respondents and clients, and anonymity and confidentiality to respondents and clients alike.[32] For these reasons, reputable research companies require their interviewers to show a photo-identity card to respondents if asked, and provide a contact name and number for respondent access to a field controller or manager.[33] Such 'codes of conduct' are readily available from professional organisations such as the Marketing Society of Ireland, ICC/ESOMAR (International Code of Marketing and Social Research Practice; ESOMAR published their first code in 1948), the Market Research Society (UK) (Code of Conduct) and are in keeping with data protection and other relevant legislation (national and international).

The key principles of a 'code of conduct' for the industry are based upon the willing co-operation of the public and of business organisations — hence the over-riding need for research to be conducted with honesty, objectivity, with co-operation and respect for respondents. The general public is entitled to complete assurance that every research project is conducted with strict adherence to this code, and that their rights of privacy are respected. The information supplied by respondents cannot, without their express agreement, be supplied to other organisations. Wherever possible, respondents should be informed of the purpose of the research and the length of time needed to collect the information.[34] Thus, practices such as slugging (selling under the guise of market research) is unacceptable in the industry. For example, to protect the general public and uphold performance standards in marketing research, the ICC/ESOMAR International Code for Internet Research has been adopted by over 60 research and marketing associations worldwide. It states that:

1. respondent's co-operation is voluntary;
2. the researcher's identity must be disclosed to respondents;
3. the respondent's rights to anonymity must be safeguarded;
4. adequate security of data must be provided;
5. survey reports should describe the methods used and possible limitations on the reliability and validity of the findings;
6. special care must be taken when interviewing minors;
7. unsolicited e-mail must be kept to a minimum.[35]

With respect to EU directives and legislation, data protection legislation is stringently followed in respect of all market research data, which continually reflects the need to avoid any possibility of identifying any individual with any information they may provide to a market researcher. A ban on unsolicited telephone calls, such as those typically used in direct marketing of telephone market research, was debated by the European Union some years ago, but was indefinitely deferred as a result of objections to its potential effect on customer freedom.[36]

• Summary

There is a myriad of occasions when customers come into contact with a company. There are numerous activities undertaken by a firm in dealing with the customer. So it comes as no surprise to find that the marketing research can be applied to a huge variety of marketing problems facing a firm.

While no two marketing research projects are the same, there are common stages that always emerge to enable us to talk about a marketing research process.[37] This process consists of a number of generic stages, seven in total, which provide a general framework to follow when engaging in research. The seven stages in the marketing research process are overlapping and complementary as shown in Box 2.9.

Box 2.3 Summary of the marketing research process

Marketing research stage	Typical concerns
Problem definition	What decision has to be made? What are the problems facing management? What information is required?
Research design	What type of information is needed? How much is already known? Are we looking for insights or facts and figures? What is the aim of the study?
Data collection	What information exists within the firm? What information exists outside the firm? Do we need to gather the data ourselves? How? Where/when?
Sampling	Who has the necessary information? Where can we talk with them? How many people do we talk with?
Fieldwork	What time do we visit people? How many researchers are needed? How much are they paid? Who will supervise them?
Analysis of data	How do we translate the raw data into a meaningful picture? What computer package will we use?

| Presentation of findings | Who is the report for? What are their needs and interests? What do they expect in the report? How many copies of the report do they want? Is an oral presentation required? |

The aim of these stages is to rid the research process of errors or mistakes that detract from the accuracy, relevance and confidence of the results. Thus, error management is an important dimension to any research investigation.

The major trends presently evident in marketing research revolve around the use of IT (Internet, web sites, on-line databases, systems and software packages); the growth of exploratory research and qualitative data collection methods; extended research into relationships; and the central role of ethics in marketing research and the industry.

With this overview of the marketing research process completed, we are now ready to examine in detail each stage in its own right, starting with problem definition and choosing a research design in Chapter 3.

Key Terms

Objective	Exploratory research
Systematic	Planned
Marketing research	Measurement
Secondary data	Sampling error
Internal data source	Error
Validity	Reliability
Causal research	Descriptive research
Problem definition	Research design
Data collection	Analysis
Primary data	Sampling
Probability sampling	Non-probability sampling
Systematic error	Random error

Questions

1. Specify and briefly detail the seven stages involved in the marketing research process.
2. Why is accurately identifying the problem definition/opportunity so important to the subsequent six stages of the research process?
3. What are the three basic types of research design? In what circumstances would each be used? When might the three types be used?

4. What is the most popular type of data collection method and why? Why is there a growing trend towards qualitative research?
5. Which should be collected first: primary data or secondary data — and why?
6. What are the various data collection methods available to the researcher?
7. What role does sampling play in the whole research process?
8. What are the stages involved in sampling?
9. A major marketing research firm once declared one of its survey-based services to be 'free from all error, except sampling error'. Do you think this could be a true statement?
10. What is a non-sampling error?
11. What is meant by the term 'fieldwork'?
12. How might the choice of analytical technique depend on the previous stages of the research process?
13. Why is it important for the researcher to understand the audience for the report prior to writing and presenting it?
14. How might the various stages in the research process loop back to each other?
15. Name the types of error found in the research process and where they might occur within the process.
16. What are some of the trends in marketing research?
17. Detail the forces that are significantly affecting the Irish marketing research industry.

Problems and Assignments

1. In Ireland, cars are polished more frequently when the owners do not have garages. Is the lack of a garage a good variable for predicting sales of car polish? Are there other hypotheses that might explain this finding?
2. You have been retained by a manufacturer of major appliances to investigate the probable colour preferences for ovens and refrigerators in 1999. What is the purpose of the research? Are there different purposes that might require different research approaches?
3. Give some hypothetical examples of situations when you would undertake (a) exploratory research; (b) descriptive research; and (c) causal research.
4. What are some management and accompanying research questions that might be useful to the following executives:
    (a) The president of a college sports club.
    (b) The production manager of a jeans factory.
    (c) The vice president of a software manufacturing firm.
5. Which research design seems appropriate for the following studies?
    (a) The manufacturer and marketer of flight simulators and other pilot training equipment wishes to forecast sales volume for the next five years.

(b) A major food company researcher wishes to know what types of food are purchased in small corner shops or petrol court outlets to learn if the company can capitalise on this phenomenon.
(c) A petroleum company is concerned with the increased costs of marketing regular leaded petrol and is considering dropping this product.
6. Examine a recent marketing research report in a local library (such as those reported in the business news). Identify the stages undertaken. Identify the sources of error that affected the study.
7. Read the business section of any national daily or Sunday paper for the past month to identify Irish companies that undertook or commissioned marketing research.
8. Select a well-known Irish consumer branded product. Conduct a database search in a local library to determine what has been published about the brand in Ireland.

Case Study
Electronic Engineering Systems*

Karin Grieves has built up her small electronic engineering business over the past seven years. A successful operation, manufacturing electrical control devices for government departments, Grieves has hitherto relied upon her own extensive knowledge of government and tender procedures to outbid rival competitors.

Now, she is faced with some equipment adapted by one of her senior engineers while on a trip to the USA. The device basically is an automatic garage door-opening mechanism. A switch is activated on the garage door when a beam located on the garage forecourt passes through a small electronic package and the door opens. Grieves and the engineer have been using the device on their own garages and are quite happy that the device works well.

Grieves is keen to embrace the idea and is willing to spend a small amount of money to enter the market. She finds herself wondering who would be interested in buying the product and why. She is well aware that the device is unlikely to have extensive appeal to the mass market.

Questions
1. Discuss all the facts, figures and statistics etc. you can think of that would be of value to Karin Grieves.
2. Discuss as many sources of information as possible that will provide this data.
3. Propose a marketing research study, detailing all the relevant stages, that you will undertake on behalf of Grieves to solve her dilemma.
4. Identify likely errors that would be of concern to you.

*This case was written by Christine Domegan. It is intended to be used as a basis for class discussion rather than to illustrate either effective or ineffective handling of an administrative situation.

Case Study
The Society for the Prevention of Cruelty to Animals*

The SPCA has been increasingly concerned over the past year at the number of stray cats and dogs in Irish cities. As a voluntary organisation established to care for neglected and abandoned animals, they are often the first to receive calls from the general public when an animal is in need of care or rescue. However, the increased number of calls and stray dogs has not been matched with an increase in money from the general public. The society is seriously concerned about their ability to care, feed and re-home the unwanted animals. Coupled with this, the society faces huge veterinary bills — in line with its policy, it holds onto all animals until they can be settled into a new home.

The situation is further compounded, as the county councils are the bodies charged with responsibility for the dog problem. To date, they too have experienced problems in dealing with the increasing numbers of stray dogs in cities and been unable to provide a solution. In the meantime, the SPCA struggles to cope with the stray dog and cat problem.

Questions

1. How can the SPCA use marketing research to find out about residents' knowledge and understanding of the stray dog problem?
2. What data collection method(s) could be used to identify potential sources of funding?
3. Who should the SPCA talk with to gather this needed information?

*This case was written by Christine Domegan. It is intended to be used as a basis for class discussion rather than to illustrate either effective or ineffective handling of an administrative situation. The case is based on a real situation, though certain information has been disguised. The author wishes to thank SPCA for their kind permission to use the material in this case.

Case Study
Dubarry Brands*

In the autumn of 1996 Michael Walsh, the Marketing Manager of Dubarry, was faced with a dilemma in one of the company's important market segments, the young fashion market. Dubarry had developed a line of brands for this segment which included the AV8, Hobos and Trucker brands.

Each of these brands had developed a significant market position and personality. Each was supported by innovative point-of-sale materials and by print and TV advertising. The issue for the company was whether to combine the three lines under one brand or to continue to market them separately with their own unique support and positioning.

Dubarry was a well-known brand on the domestic shoe market which sold in all major retail shoe outlets nationally. Total sales of the company in the previous year were over £8 million. Dubarry prided itself on selling 'shoes for all the family' and tried to cater for all major segments of the shoe market.

Established in Ballinasloe, Co. Galway over 60 years ago, the company was one of the few remaining shoe manufacturers in the country. The shoe industry in Ireland had diminished from a formerly significant one to leave just Dubarry and a few other small players. Imports now accounted for most of the shoes sold in Ireland.

However, Dubarry was still a significant force with over 200 employees, a strong design department and a team of young, but experienced managers. The company had grown rather than vanish like its former domestic competitors because it had focused on developing good quality shoes for specific market segments such as the youth market. Internationally the company was very well known in the sailing shoe market for its Broga line. Dubarry sailing shoes were recognised throughout Europe as the leading brand technically. Their Goretex-lined Shamrock sailing boot was a much-prized item, eagerly sought out by serious yachting teams. Dubarry sailing shoes and boots were worn by a number of crews on the Whitbread round-the-world race. These products had won international awards for design and were lauded by international sailing magazines.

The issue under consideration in the youth market was a critical one for Dubarry. Marketing under one brand would enable considerable savings to be made, particularly on promotion. However, there was a danger attached to such a strategy in that each individual brand had its own identify and target market. For example, the AV8 line was primarily a casual back-to-school line with a moccasin construction. Hobos were young teenage girls' shoes, worn for a wide range of uses and occasions, from sports to school to going out. Truckers were heavy, worker type, aggressive soled casual shoes and boots primarily for men.

If the decision was to drop two names, the question was not only which one to keep. It was possible that it might be better to consider a completely new name for all three. A number of names were under consideration, including Code, Tribe and Federation.

A further issue concerned the use of the name Dubarry. Michael Walsh was unsure how explicit the association should be with the youth line, if at all. Would the name Dubarry be a positive or negative association for the youth segment if it was more identified as an adult comfort brand? Michael was preparing a research proposal to present to his Board to help answer these questions. However, he was not at all sure what form this research should take. Would he need to do field research and, if so, what type? Who should he talk to? What role did parents play in shoe purchasing decisions?

In addition, the marketing considerations involved in the decision needed to be clearly articulated.

Assignment

Design a full marketing research study that will assist Michael Walsh in making all the necessary decisions facing Dubarry.

*This case was written by Professor Jim Ward, NUI, Galway. It is intended to be used as a basis for class discussion rather than to illustrate either effective or ineffective handling of an administrative situation. The case is based on a real situation, though certain information has been disguised. The author wishes to thank Dubarry for their kind permission to use the material in this case. © Jim Ward, NUIG.

Case Study
Trócaire's Double-Sided Jigsaw*

Trócaire is one of the largest charities in Ireland. It is dedicated to relief and development work in third-world countries. Mike Garvey joined Trócaire in 1995 with the objective of accelerating fund-raising activities for the organisation. He believed Trócaire would benefit from the development of a product which would generate revenue and also provide a vehicle to give donors visible evidence of their support for the charity.

The concept of a double-sided jigsaw was novel and potentially attractive commercially. A decision was taken to commission a research team to assess the size of the market for jigsaws, to identify the appropriate jigsaw theme, optimum number of pieces, pricing, distribution, and launch strategy.

The Jigsaw Market

The jigsaw market in Ireland is valued annually at approximately £3 million and is dominated by three large manufacturers: Ravensburger, Milton Bradley and Waddingtons, in addition to a number of smaller players. The market leaders offer a very extensive range of jigsaws which incorporate a wide variety of themes with variation in the number of pieces to cater for the different market segments.

Initial secondary research indicated that the target market for jigsaws was segmented by age and that it would be difficult to identify an appropriate theme and jigsaw size to appeal to a broad target market (Table 2.2). Furthermore, jigsaws were typically purchased as gift items (over 70% of all sales are at Christmas) by adults for children or for adult jigsaw enthusiasts.

Table 2.2

Target market	Price	No. of jigsaw pieces	Purchase location	Attractive themes
Children 4–10 years	£2.50–£3.99	25–100	Toy stores	Licensed movie themes e.g. Disney
15–adult	£4–£12	200–8,000	Department stores, supermarkets and toy stores	Cars, classical themes, art, landscapes

Market Research

The first stage of the research involved running a number of focus groups comprising jigsaw puzzle consumers in order to identify market segments and related themes. The feedback from this research indicated that the puzzle illustration was the most important selling issue for consumers and a wide range of themes was generated through the research. Two key market segments were identified, the 8–10-year-old age group, and the family jigsaw.

Trócaire decided that the 'family' segment would have most potential, and two Irish themes were chosen as no other jigsaw manufacturer had developed this concept. The design incorporated a Celtic print of the Children of Lir by a well-known Irish artist on one side, and a satellite photograph of Ireland on the other. It was decided to brand the jigsaw subtly with the Trócaire logo. Consumers in this market had a preference for a jigsaw of approximately 1,000 pieces with a maximum retail price of £10.

A prototype was produced with 1,000 pieces with an expected retail price of £9.99. A second phase of focus group research was commissioned to test the design. The feedback was positive. The main retail outlets in which consumers were likely to purchase the jigsaw were toy stores, department stores, and supermarkets. Following this stage of research it was also clear that the jigsaw could be targeted at a second market segment — the tourist market. The tourists were most likely to purchase through book stores and tourist craft shops.

Channels of Distribution

The games market is very competitive and a second concern for Trócaire was ensuring access to channels of distribution. Key buyers across a range of retail store types were contacted and invited to comment on the prototype and their willingness to participate in a test market (Table 2.3).

Table 2.3

Type of outlet	Feedback	Suggested RSP
Department store	Positive — agreed to discuss the possibility of test marketing.	£4.99–£5.99
Department store	Positive — agreed to discuss the possibility of test marketing.	£7.99–£9.99
Book store	Positive — agreed to discuss the possibility of test marketing.	£14.99
Toy store	Positive — agreed to discuss the possibility of test marketing.	£6.99–£7.99
Souvenir shop	Positive — will not stock the product this year but possibly in 1997.	£4.99–£5.99
Supermarket chain	Will not stock the product in their stores but possibly in store catalogue.	£6.99–£7.99
Book store	Negative — indicated that the product would not fit in with their portfolio.	Unable to indicate.

Trócaire was happy with the response and planned to test the product further by putting it in a selection of outlets for the Christmas period. The key issue for Trócaire following the test market would be to establish criteria by which they could evaluate the results of the test market and plan a launch strategy.

Questions

1. How would you research and define the target market for a double-sided family jigsaw?
2. Evaluate the different research stages identified in the case.
3. What would you consider the most appropriate composition of the two sets of focus groups?
4. What are the key factors which would ensure the success of this product?
5. Recommend an appropriate market entry strategy for Trócaire's double-sided jigsaw.

*This case was written by Brenda Cullen, UCD, and John McGrath, UCD Marketing Development Programme, Researched by John McGrath. It is intended to be used as a basis for class discussion rather than to illustrate either effective or ineffective handling of an administrative situation. The case is based on a real situation, though certain information has been disguised. The authors wish to thank Trócaire for their kind permission to use the material in this case. © Brenda Cullen and John McGrath UCD.

Chapter 3

PROBLEM DEFINITION AND RESEARCH DESIGN

- **Chapter Overview**
- Introduction   • What is Problem Definition?   • Tasks and Activities to Define Problem Definition   • Problem Definition Error   • Problem Definition and the Marketing Information System   • Research Design Defined   • What Types of Research Designs Exist?   • How to Choose the Best Research Design   • Summary

• Introduction

The basic nature of research, decision-making, information needs and the steps in marketing research have been discussed in the preceding chapters. We've also explained the concept of marketing research and where it fits into the overall information needs of an organisation. This discussion so far has been broad and general in tone, to introduce the reader to the area.

In this chapter, we detail the first two major steps of marketing research — *problem definition* and *research design*. The focus is now on the specific tasks and activities that cluster around defining the aims of the study. Regardless of the market, customers or difficulties facing the marketing manager, the investigator begins a research project by defining the problem. Correctly defined problems allow the investigator to anticipate activities, information requirements, data sources and likely errors. As management action is dependent upon research results, time taken at the problem definition step is time well spent. As the old adage goes: 'a problem well defined is a problem half solved'. By the end of this section, you will be able to:

1. explain what problem definition is;
2. undertake all the tasks and activities needed to complete problem definition;
3. choose a research design;
4. draw up a list of research objectives;
5. translate management decision needs into information requirements;
6. develop hypotheses.

• What is Problem Definition?

Problem definition is the first, initial step in any research project. The researcher questions what the problem is, what decision is necessary and what information is needed for management to make a decision. It is about examining the true problem, related decision and needed information.

Figure 3.1 Relationship between problem, information and decision

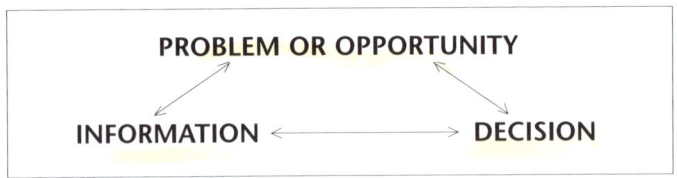

At this stage of the study, the investigator is querying what the purpose of the study is. Generally, a problem confronts the manager and he/she wants information to assist in making a more informed decision. Occasionally, there can be an opportunity presenting itself to the management team and the firm want information to capitalise upon the opportunity. In this sense, the title 'problem definition' is a misnomer, as it incorporates marketing opportunities facing a company. Correct, complete and thorough problem definition focuses the study and lends direction to the investigation and subsequent research steps. Problem definition translates the management decision and problem into research information needs.

So when a problem or opportunity occurs, information is needed to clarify the issue, and then information is sought on which to base a decision. Problem definition can be thought of as a needs assessment — what relevant information is missing at present? The ethos of problem definition is to be creative, investigative, probing and clear minded as to the information needs for decision-making.[1] More formally, problem definition is identification, clarification, formulation and definition of the specific marketing difficulty that necessitates decision-related information.

• Tasks and Activities to Define the Problem

To uncover the true issues and the decision confronting managers, an intricate web of tasks and activities faces the researcher. Since most marketing decisions are complex, and numerous factors affect the outcome, careful investigation of the cause and symptoms is needed. Another old adage 'what comes out very much depends on what goes in' is relevant here — the greater the effort, the better the problem definition step and the better the whole project.

It is helpful to think of problem definition as having four sub-sections for the researcher to work through, to ensure adequate and correct problem definition.

These are identification, clarification, formulation and definition of the presented problem or opportunity facing the firm.

Figure 3.2 Problem definition

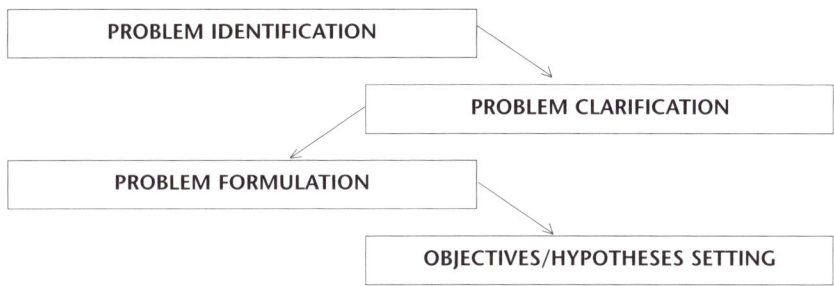

Each of these consists of distinct, yet intertwined activities and duties for the researcher to complete, before moving on to any other research phase.

> **Box 3.1 Step one, problem definition, researcher activities and tasks**
>
> | | |
> |---|---|
> | **Problem identification** | Dialogue with managers |
> | | Dialogue with relevant staff |
> | | Identify problem, decision, information needs |
> | | Identify *content* of decisions |
> | **Problem clarification** | Immerse yourself in the background |
> | | Conduct a literature search |
> | | Conduct a situational audit/ environmental audit |
> | | Talk with knowledgeable people |
> | | Clarify the *context* of the problem |
> | **Problem formulation** | Isolate cause from symptoms |
> | | Differentiate between management decision and research decision |
> | | Undertake a problem audit |
> | | Determine the unit of analysis and relevant factors |
> | | Select appropriate analytical/theoretical model |
> | **Objectives/hypotheses setting** | List outcomes of investigation |
> | | List research objectives |
> | | Phrase research questions to be answered |
> | | Write down the research hypothesis |

Dialogue between management and the researcher marks the starting point for problem/opportunity identification. Management generally talk through their perception of the problem and the decisions they need to make with the researcher. The researcher has to understand how any gathered information will be used in the decision-making process to truly appreciate the kernel of the problem.

Generally speaking, managers have a feel for the problem/opportunity, but may not be able to communicate their exact information needs to the researcher. Managers have to be active participants at this point in the research process. Clearly, the greater the co-operation, discussion and commitment between management and researcher at this preparatory phase, the better the quality of the information supplied and decision made.

Some managers will want assistance with very specific problems. They will want very specific answers to specific questions. Typical examples include:

1. Of the three proposed package designs, which will result in the highest usage?
2. Should we offer a 20p discount or a token free gift to stimulate sales?
3. Which product features, freshness, convenience or nutrition will increase the probability of sales by 5%?

However, some studies will require more information before the problem can be identified. In such cases, specific questions have not been asked. Consider the situation where sales of a product are static — a lack of advertising, changing consumer tastes or competitive actions could all explain static sales.

So, problem identification leads to a management decision problem and a research problem. Such a distinction is necessary, as simply responding to information requests will not result in the needed answers. This aspect of problem definition identifies the content of the decision.

Box 3.2 Management decisions versus research problems

Management decision	Research problem
Develop a new advertisement	Evaluate effectiveness of alternative advertisements
Increase store traffic	Measure current customer satisfaction of store
Introduce new product	Forecast potential sales levels
Increase sales	Assess penetration level of existing outlets
Launch new product	Identify emerging consumer trends and changing tastes
Decrease costs	Determine non-price basis for competition

While managers may have a perspective on the problem, their insights may actually be limited. The *iceberg principle* operates here. The visible aspect of the presented problem is really only a small dimension of the real or true difficulty. Coupled with this, the scientific nature of the research process beholds the researcher to be objective and exhaustive. So, the researcher moves into a clarification phase. To this end, the researcher must establish the *background* to the problem/opportunity. Much background information can be gleaned from reports, letters and documents, trade material and strategic plans. This is labelled as a *literature search*. It is first conducted in-house and then externally, making use of library facilities. Once completed, the researcher turns her/his attention to experts to complete the problem clarification phase. Referred to as an *expert survey*, it usually requires the researcher to have discussions and meetings with knowledgeable persons related to the topic/problem. These can be personnel within the firm, such as production managers, accounts, delivery and telephone receptionists and these can also be experts outside the company, e.g. trade associations, state bodies, government officials — to name but a few. The researcher, to provide a better appreciation of the problem/opportunity, combines the literature and expert survey. This phase of problem definition can be referred to as a *situational analysis*. It covers buyer behaviour and market characteristics that affect demand, coupled with competition and the micro and macro environment — the uncontrollable variables facing managers.

Box 3.3 Problem formulation in the Irish bottled gas market[2]

A company was considering entering the Irish bottled gas market. To decide if entry was feasible and, if so, to design a strategy to do this, the company managers wanted to know about the various market characteristics. In discussions with the researchers, this market entry problem turned into a need for information about end consumers, their current usage patterns, degree of brand loyalty and their perceptions of competitors. To this end, the researcher planned to gather information about:

- gas usage and consumption;
- brands used;
- bottle gas regulators;
- gas bottle physical characteristics;
- contents of gas bottles;
- stocking/storage of gas bottles;
- purchasing procedure;
- awareness of and attitude towards price;
- awareness of and interest in the origin of gas;
- purchasing criteria;
- safety concerns;
- reaction to the idea of a coalman-type delivery service.

At this point, the researcher will have developed a good understanding of the problem facing management, the related decision managers want to make and the necessary information to be supplied for a solution. This leads the researcher into the problem formulation element of problem definition. This is where the investigator is able to differentiate between the symptoms and the true cause of the problem. The researcher stands back from the problem and takes a broad perspective by setting the problem in an appropriate *analytical/theoretical* model to reflect and present all the variables of interest. The relevant model is drawn from the existing body of knowledge. Let's say you are the manager of a new 'paint-your-own-pottery' shop. The first of its kind in Ireland and Europe, the concept of painting your own pottery has taken America by storm. You are now faced with the challenge of promoting the shop. The 'Hierarchy of Effects' model states that you must first create awareness, then interest, followed by desire before a consumer will come to your shop to paint a piece of pottery. So, any research must measure and assess the current level of awareness, then interest, desire and action, in that order, so as to guide an effective promotional strategy.[3]

In this manner, the theory acts as a *problem audit*, as the model must capture all necessary variables impinging on the problem/opportunity and how they are related. The researcher must ensure that all important and necessary issues have been included. Failure to incorporate all issues results in inaccurate data and error. The problem audit requires the researcher to choose a *unit of analysis* — an entity to focus upon, at the micro level, from which to collect the necessary data. The unit of analysis in marketing is commonly the end consumer. For some products, e.g. children's toothpaste and cereals, the unit of analysis may be both the purchaser and the consumer, normally the mother and the child respectively. Other common units of analysis used much in marketing are retail buyers, retail stores, wholesalers, importers, agents, managers, advertisers, shop assistants, etc. (all people who may have valuable information about the consumer). A common mistake in considering the unit of analysis is to overlook the product, shelf spacing, price or an advertisement etc. as entities that may contain the much-needed information. Thus, the researcher has now determined the context of the problem, as well as the content.

Now the researcher is ready to define the problem. Problem definition results in a list of research objectives, and/or a research hypothesis. Research objectives are a statement of specific and limited information needs. There is one overall broad statement — referred to as the *primary objective*. This is divided into sub-components, namely *secondary objectives*. The relationship between the primary and secondary objectives operates upon the umbrella principle. The secondary objectives come together as a whole. The research objectives are specific, action-orientated statements of intent. The researcher, having prepared a list of needed information, evaluates the usefulness of the objectives by anticipating possible findings. This exercise in caution enables the researcher to weed out unrealistic aims and unnecessary goals (these can generate interesting information but irrelevant to the problem on hand and a drain on limited resources).

A research hypothesis is a tentative answer to the problem, or more specifically a research question. It requires empirical research to support or refute the proposition. It is an assertion as to the likely outcome. For example, a manager might question the most advantageous course of action — to run an advertisement during 'Top of the Pops' or 'Friends'? Given this, one research question might be 'Which programme has the highest viewership among 15- to 18-year-old teenagers?', while one hypothesis could read 'More 15- to 18-year-old teenagers watch "Friends" than "Top of the Pops".'

To develop a hypothesis the researcher must identify the independent and dependent variables, coupled with the relationship between the two. Consider a manager who is reducing the price of his product. He will postulate the effect on sales, whether there will be a 2%, 3% or 5% increase in sales, or none as may be the case. Such an assumption or expectation is a hypothesis — a tentative statement about the expected outcome. In this case, the price decrease is the independent variable affecting the level of sales, which is the dependent variable. The independent variable comes before the dependent in time and alters the dependent variable in some manner.

Hypotheses are based upon, and generated by management experience, literature reviews or insights. It is critical that these (like objectives) are in written form and agreed by all before proceeding with the remainder of the research process.

The final list of research objectives and/or hypotheses is presented to management to ensure that their interpretation of the problem is in keeping with the researcher's understanding of the information requirements. In this way, the project results will not surprise or disappoint the manager.

Box 3.4 The Deerhaven Lawn Tennis Club — problem definition

In 1998, the Deerhaven Lawn Tennis Club sought to address both its financial and membership crisis which was evident from internal records in recent years. Income came primarily from annual subscriptions from club members. These had fluctuated considerably over the past few years.

Income from subscriptions (£s)

Year	Amount
1992	69,000
1994	82,000
1996	76,000
1998	70,000

Unfortunately, the club's problem seemed likely to worsen as the Deerhaven Lawn Tennis Club faced serious membership problems.

Year	Combined membership	Squash membership	Badminton membership	Tennis membership	Total membership
1992	130	300	160	260	850
1994	300	263	154	207	924
1998	126	90	70	197	464

The membership crisis raised several questions. Club statistics have already revealed that in recent years, 30% of new members failed to renew their membership. The Deerhaven Lawn Tennis Club was particularly interested in obtaining the views and opinions of non-members in the 18—35 age group category, since it was considered a potential growth area. Management was also especially interested in this category in light of the drastic decline in membership figures among this age group.

Membership figures in the 18–35 age group

1992	127
1994	211
1998	29

These figures also raised several questions concerning the popularity of tennis, squash and badminton. By using the above approach to problem definition, a number of research objectives emerged. These read as follows:

Primary Objective

The primary objective of this study is to ascertain the reasons for the decline in membership of the Deerhaven Lawn Tennis Club in the past six years.

Secondary Objectives

The primary objective was broken down into the following secondary objectives in order to establish which information had to be collected via research:

- Establish the perceptions of the tennis club by non-members.
- Determine why the membership in the two-mile catchment area is particularly low.
- Analyse whether the location of the club (in a traditionally middle-class area) is a deterrent to joining the club.
- Ascertain whether the distance of the club from city centre acts as a deterrent to the 18–30-year-old age group from joining the club.

- Analyse whether racquet sports (i.e. tennis, badminton and squash) have become less popular.
- Establish why people with relatively high disposable incomes in the immediate areas are not becoming members.
- Determine the effect of direct competition and indirect competition, in the area, on the club.
- Ascertain whether the lack of a promotional and advertising campaign had been a major factor in the decline in membership.
- Analyse why this era of health consciousness and sport-orientated leisure activities has not spurred membership numbers to increase in recent years.

• Problem Definition Errors

On the surface, problem definition appears easy — deceptively so as many firms often find out to their peril. The process of problem definition is slow and fraught with difficulties. The research process is only as good as the problem definition stage. Error can occur at any point — one major source of research error seriously affecting the scientific credibility of the project is poorly defined problems.

One of the biggest causes of incorrect or inappropriate problem definition occurs because of improper communication between the manager and researcher. Management tends to have a feeling for what's wrong, but cannot pinpoint exactly what the root cause of the problem is — akin to not being able to see the wood from the trees. Lack of communication results in vague goals at the outset of the study giving rise to vague or ambiguous results at the end. Managers tend to think in terms of decisions and not the information needed to make an informed decision. Managers can and do have serious difficulties articulating the detailed data they need. The translation of the problem and decision into information requirements by the researcher is highly dependent upon good communication between all concerned. Close co-ordination and genuine dialogue between the researcher and managers can minimise such communication pitfalls. Conflict between management and researcher can be minimised. Managers can be too involved and have to guard against the professional knowing best. Managers as active participants are the best defence against improper definition of the problem. The researcher's perspective dictates that problem definition be approached as research-based decision-making.

Researchers should not assume that the presented difficulty is the true or real one. Problems are never taken at face value, often what the researcher sees first are the symptoms and not the cause of the difficulties. For example, the general trend evident across Europe is for problem definition to be more complex than ever before. As companies move into relationship marketing, networking, interactive marketing, and globalisation, distinguishing the marketing symptoms from the cause is increasingly more difficult for managers and researcher alike. The boundaries between the firm and its environs are hazy and unclear. Given this, problem definition can seem limitless. So, it is critical for the investigator to continually probe to uncover the real problem.

Research produces data and information, not decisions. Management sometimes has greater expectations than research can deliver. Presenting the list of research objectives to managers can be a worthwhile exercise as it lays a common foundation as to expectations and potential findings. It ensures that the research process stays focused upon a solution and the necessary information needed to make a decision.

All of these issues — lack of communication, lack of co-operation, incorrect communication, ignorance of the role of research, and inappropriate time given to problem definition — can result in informational error. Worse still, problem definition error (or informational error) is carried throughout the entire project, tainting all subsequent steps. For this reason, we refer to it as systematic error. A mistake now by the researcher, for whatever reason, systematically affects all other phases and seriously threatens the validity of the research findings.

• Problem Definition and the Marketing Information System (MkIS)

Before leaving the discussion of problem definition, it is worthwhile to note the role of the marketing information system in problem definition. Many of the tasks and activities in problem definition dictate that the investigator draw heavily upon the marketing information system within the company in question.

A marketing information system (MkIS) is a framework or structure for marketing information management. It is a system of processes, procedures and people to support marketing management. It generally incorporates the use of computers and software. It is about the collection, organisation, storage, communication and dissemination of information relevant to marketing managers.

An MkIS is an organised flow of information about customers, competitors and the company's performance in support of marketing decision-making. An MkIS is not about information automation, as the computer acronym says: GIGO — garbage in, garbage out. Rather, an MkIS is about information enhancement and management improvement.[4] It is designed to collect, gather, analyse, disseminate, store, retrieve and communicate both internal and external secondary marketing research and marketing intelligence data to marketing managers in order to improve decision-making. Thus, a marketing information system is charged with the responsibility of aiding and assisting marketing decision-making; filtering timely, accurate and relevant information and translating data into meaningful decision-related information. It enables the company to gather facts about the micro and macro environment within which the firm competes. In this manner, the marketing information system can be of immense value to an investigator grappling with problem definition.

Problem Definition and Research Design 53

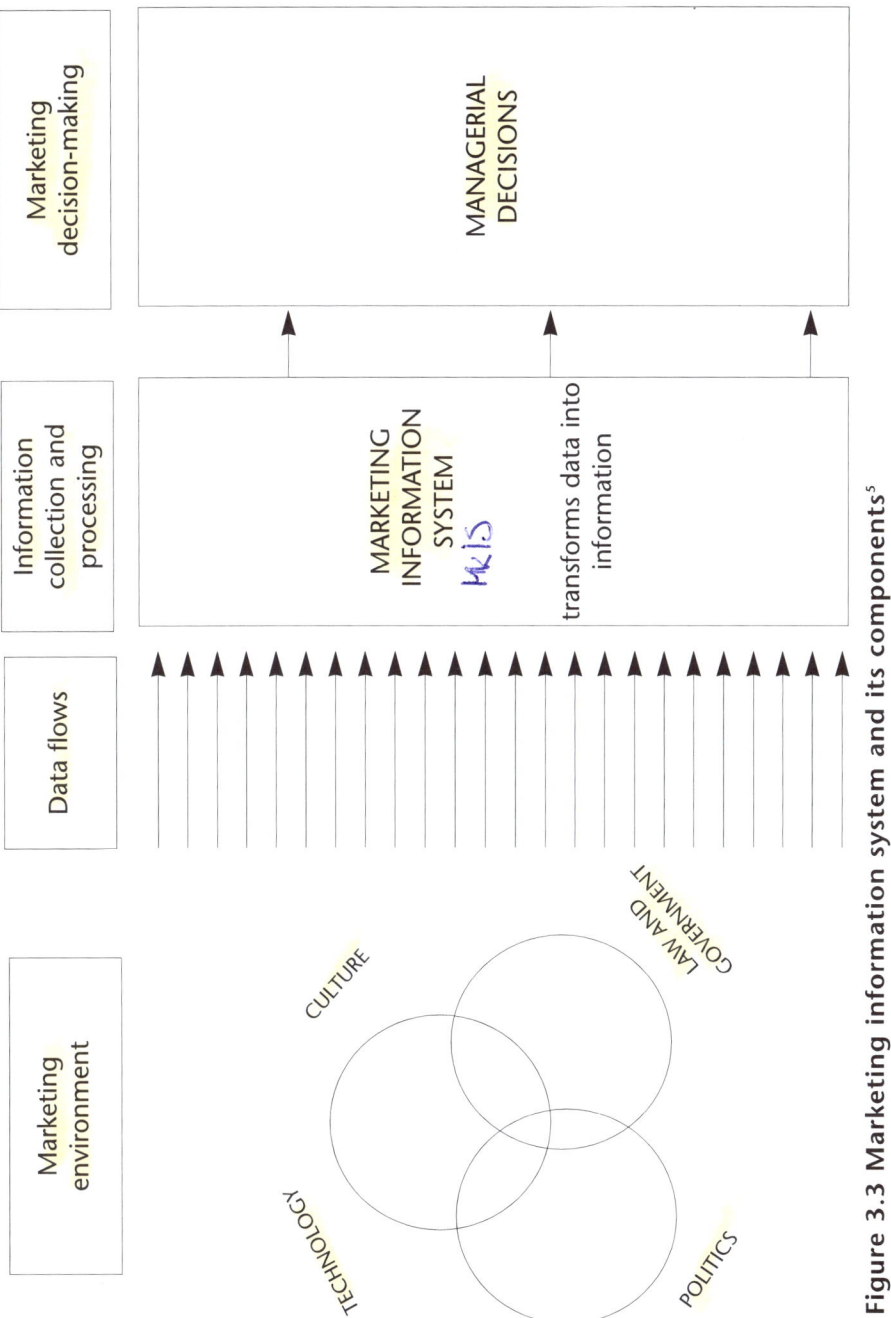

Figure 3.3 Marketing information system and its components[5]

Source: J. Murray & A. O'Driscoll, *Managing Marketing, Concepts and Irish Cases*, Gill & Macmillan, 1993, p.134.

The limitations of an MkIS are hard to imagine, apart from the time and cost necessary to manage it efficiently. However, the main drawback is the lack of information orientation in a firm, as this results in the trappings of an MkIS with no substance. MkISs have to assist management with decisions to be of use.

It can be very simple, such as an index card of customers, or very elaborate such as a network of computer databases. Larger Irish firms, such as Smurfit's, Kerry, Avonmore, Waterford, Superquinn, Bank of Ireland, and AIB, to name but a few, have a complex and elaborate web of computers that constitute their MkIS. However, an MkIS can also be informal with basic or even no technology, as tends to be the case with many smaller Irish firms. When Aer Arran[6] began building an MkIS, customer names, addresses, phone numbers, usage patterns and complaints were initially held on an alphabetically sorted index card system. For smaller firms that are owner managed, once the basic elements or rudiments are present, the information link between the firm, the customer and environment can exist. So, while the degree of structure and formality of an MkIS can and does vary among Irish firms, the existence of an information flow and process is the kernel of the MkIS and the marketing attitude.[7, 8, 9]

• **Research Design Defined**

Closely allied to problem definition is the second step of the marketing research process — research design. Formulating the study goals is highly inter-related to the general information design of the study. Different problems lead to different research designs. Many research models subsume this step into problem definition and present them as one, as both are dependent on the amount of existing information about the problem. For the sake of simplicity, we consider the process of choosing a research design as a step in its own right. First, we discuss what a research design is.

A research design is a blueprint or overall action plan for the remaining marketing research study. It is a grand or master framework to guide the remaining steps of the research process — data collection, measurement, analysis and reporting. The research design is based upon the nature of the information required by management. It dictates the scope and boundaries of the study.

The research design can only be chosen after the objectives have been finalised. It co-ordinates the methodology issues with the stated objectives and so acts as a guiding light for the researcher in deciding the when, where, how and why of information collection. It gives structure, order and logic to the remaining marketing research steps, in light of the study objectives. A research design is the bridge between the research objectives and the methodology used to fulfil these objectives.

While it is true that marketing problems are limitless and no two problems are the same, similarities do exist as to the type of information needed. The information type allows for the classification of a research project.

• What Types of Research Designs Exist?

As noted in the previous chapter, a research design can be classified as exploratory, descriptive or causal in nature.

Figure 3.4 Research design classification

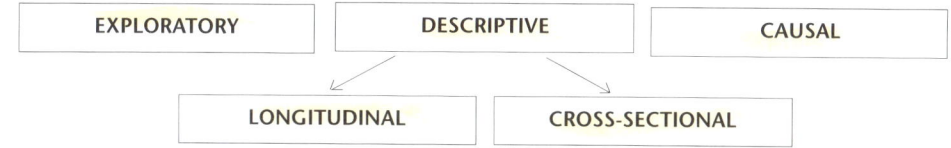

Exploratory research is about establishing trends, patterns and ranges of behaviour that are unknown. Exploratory research uncovers unknown and previously undocumented marketing variables. It aims to identify and establish the very existence of variables. For this reason, hypothesis generation is a feature of such research. An exploratory study is, by definition, a study exploring an area to understand it better. Flexibility, ingenuity and imagination are the traits of such research. This work is relatively non-mathematical and non-statistical in form. For this reason, exploratory research can be likened to Christopher Columbus charting new lands, or Star Trek, 'going where no man has gone before'. The researcher has the freedom to explore different avenues of interest and change the direction of enquiry. Such work is often referred to as *qualitative data.* This denotes the types of data collection methods likely to be used, e.g. literature review, expert survey, focus groups, in-depth interviews or projective techniques.

Exploratory research is especially useful in new product development, creative aspects of advertising, media selection and promotion in general: unearthing new segments, shifts in cultural values and changing attitudes.[10]

Box 3.5 Homeopathic remedies for pets and exploratory research

As a homeopathic manufacturer of medicines, the firm has recently had a number of enquiries about remedies for pets. Management decide to explore the idea of homeopathic remedies for pets as a possible new and emerging market.

To gain some insights and a basic understanding about an area that management know little about, they engage in exploratory research. This involves talking with leading vets in the area about their perceptions, experience and knowledge of homeopathic remedies for pets. Animal clubs and associations are contacted to learn of their experiences and needs. Finally, a number of groups of consumers are brought into the firm to hear first hand from them about their use of alternative medicines for their pets.

In contrast, descriptive research quantifies known consumers, markets and known marketing issues. It measures the number and amount of a variable present. Quantitative research details the percentage or proportion of a characteristic present. It is heavily reliant on mathematics, statistics and probability theory. Quantitative research assumes prior knowledge exists, and background information is readily available. To this end, hypothesis testing is indicative of quantitative research.

Quantitative research is used to describe existing market segments, competitors, current marketing offerings. It lends itself well to evaluating and assessing various aspects of product, price, promotion and place.

> **Box 3.6 Entry into the pre-packed stuffing market and descriptive research**
>
> The family has been in the bakery business for three generations. As one of the largest suppliers to supermarkets all over the country, you are deciding whether to enter the pre-packed stuffing market. You require much information about all facets of the marketing mix. For example, some of the information will be concerned with:
>
> (a) The actual market size — how many packs of pre-packed stuffing are sold each year? How much is the market valued at? By how much is the market increasing or decreasing on an annual basis? What are the market segments?
> (b) The competitors — how many firms are already supplying the market? What is their market size? What are their strengths and weaknesses?
> (c) The customer — what benefits are customers looking for when they buy such a product? What are the three most important features? Who are the customers, age, income, social class, lifestyle, and family life cycle?

Thus, descriptive data, as the name suggests, describes various facets of the problem on hand in mathematical terms. It requires a clear statement about the who, what, where, when, and how of the relevant issues. It is traditionally the most common form of research in marketing. Descriptive data can be further divided into either *longitudinal* or *cross-sectional* data. Longitudinal descriptive data is equivalent to a movie picture — describing the elements, variables and their relationship over a length of time. It incorporates repeated measurement of the relevant characteristics. Panels and EPoS (Electronic Point of Sales) are the data collection tools used. A cross-sectional study is like a snapshot — a description of variables and their association at one point in time. This is a once-off measurement — observation and surveys are utilised here.

Causal data proves a cause and effect relationship between two or more variables. It is the most demanding and rigorous of all research — the investigator must know, first, the exact variables, and also the effect they have on each other. The researcher must also be able to control outside factors and their influence on the variables being manipulated. Causal data can be collected in a field or laboratory setting, by utilising an experimental design. It is frequently associated with test marketing or simulated test marketing. Thus, this type of a research design is very demanding and rigorous.

First impressions tend to suggest that exploratory, descriptive and causal research are at odds with each other. In practice, they are not separate but complementary to each other. The Chinese idea of the yin and yang symbol captures the twinning essence of all three research designs. Exploratory research is often conducted before descriptive or causal work is undertaken.[11]

• How to Choose the Best Research Design

It is the researcher's responsibility to choose an appropriate research design for the study. Regrettably, there is no formula to help choose the best design. Equally, no one design is better than the other — it's really a question of which is best suited to the particular problem in hand. In practice, the information-based decision guides the choice of research design. That is, the aims of the study, to explore or describe or establish a cause and effect relationship, dictate the research design. Costs and timing are also borne in mind, as they influence the choice of design. So the choice of design is a matter of distinction and not absolute.

Table 3.1 Choosing a research design

	Exploratory research	**Descriptive research**	**Causal research**
Data type	Qualitative	Qualitative or quantitative	Quantitative
Aims	To explore, chart, identify	To describe, quantify	To establish cause and effect
Nature of variables	Unknown Undocumented	Known associations and documented	Known exactly, Clearly supported
Degree of formality	Relatively little	Some to extensive	High mathematical content
Data	Literature review Expert survey Focus groups In-depth interviews Projective techniques	Literature review Expert survey Surveys Observation Panels (Focus groups)	Literature review Expert survey Experiments (Surveys) (Observation)

	Exploratory research	Descriptive research	Causal research
Sample size	Small	Small to large	Large
Question types	Probing Response driven	Some probing Interviewer driven	No probing
Hypothesis	Generates, Develops	Tests and/or Generates, Develops	Tests

Some concluding remarks about research designs include the following points:

First, the selection of the wrong or inappropriate design is the biggest mistake made at this stage of the marketing research project. Such a research error arises due to poor problem definition. It results in systematic error throughout the remainder of the project. The validity content of the study is jeopardised if such an error occurs.

Second, information is growing exponentially, that is, all three types of research designs are utilised more than ever before by all industry sectors. Recent evidence[12, 13, 14] certainly suggests that this trend will continue in an effort to present a more holistic picture of consumers and markets.

Third, new exploratory techniques such as games, time travel visualisations, museum and role playing, are all continuing to gain favour with Irish and European research firms alike — these are given detailed consideration in later chapters.

• Summary

In planning for a specific research project, the first step is problem definition. It is about defining the decision, the related problem and relevant information needed. It consists of problem identification, clarification, formulation and objective setting. It involves a multiplicity of interactive activities, for example, management discussions, literature review, situational audit, problem audit, and expert survey. It can draw heavily upon the marketing information system. The aim is to state the information needs of the decision as a list of objectives or hypotheses. It concludes with a list of research objectives and/or hypotheses.

Problem definition or informational error is the mistake most likely to occur. It is where the incorrect or improper definition has been made. To prevent such a threat to the validity of the study, it is vital that managers and researchers work closely to ensure correct definition of all issues.

The second step in marketing research is choosing a research design. A research design is a blueprint or framework for the methodological issues of the study. A research design can be either exploratory or descriptive or causal in character. The chosen research design is a function of the problem, the required information, the decision, the nature of the desired data and research concerns such as sample size, data collection methods and degree of formality.

Key Terms

Problem definition
Problem clarification
Expert survey
Marketing information system
Secondary objectives
Hypothesis
Research design
Quantitative
Exploratory
Independent variable

Problem identification
Problem formulation
Situational analysis
Macro and micro environment
Primary objective
Unit of analysis
Qualitative
Descriptive
Causal
Dependent variable
Information error

Questions

1. What is problem definition and what are the four sub-sections of problem definition that the researcher should work through to ensure that the problem is accurately defined?
2. What is the starting point of problem definition?
3. Why is it important to define the marketing research problem appropriately?
4. What are the differences between research questions and hypothesis?
5. What is a situational analysis? What is involved in a literature search and an expert survey?
6. What is involved in formulating the problem?
7. What is the relationship between the primary objective and secondary objectives?
8. What is meant by the term 'research hypothesis'?
9. What trends are evident with relation to problem definition across Europe?
10. What is the biggest cause of incorrect problem definition?
11. Discuss the nature and role of research design in marketing research.
12. Define research design. What is its role within the overall research process?
13. Differentiate between the three basic types of research design. What are the characteristics of each and under what circumstances would each one be used?
14. If one is using both exploratory and descriptive research, which research design is normally undertaken first, and why?
15. How do the three categories of exploratory, descriptive and causal research design differ from each other?
16. What guides the choice of design that the researcher adopts?
17. What are the potential sources of error that can affect the beginning stages of any marketing research project?

Problems and Assignments

1. How would you go about determining why market share for a particular brand has declined in the past year, i.e. what research design(s) would you use, and why?
2. In a research project for a chain of shoe stores, mothers of young children were asked the importance of various features of children's shoes and shoe outlets. Which type of error do you think would be most critical for the study?
3. Given the following decision problem, identify the research problems:
   (a) What pricing strategy to follow for a new product.
   (b) Whether to change the sales force compensation package.
   (c) Whether to increase in-store promotion of existing products.
4. Food Inc. is a chain of restaurants located in major cities in Ireland. Sales have been growing very slowly for the last two years. Management has decided to add some new items to the menu, but first they want to know more about their customers and their preferences.
   (a) List two hypotheses.
   (b) What kind of research design is appropriate, and why?
5. Propose one or more hypotheses for each of the following variable pairs, specify which is the independent variable and which the dependent variable.
   (a) The Consumer Price Index and the economic climate.
   (b) The level of worker output and the closeness of supervision of the worker.
   (c) The degree of personal friendship between customer and salespeople and the frequency of sales calls on the customer.
6. You have been hired by a group of hotel owners, restaurant owners and other business owners whose business benefits from tourism on one of the Aran Islands, just off the coast of Galway. They wish to learn how they can attract a larger number of college students to the islands during the Easter holidays. Define the marketing research problem.
7. You have been asked to determine how large corporations prepare for contract negotiations with labour unions. Since you know relatively little about this subject, how would you find out? Be as specific as possible.
8. A manufacturer of hand tools uses industrial agents to reach its major European markets. The company is considering a new automatic inventory control procedure. How would you proceed with an exploratory study in advance of a larger study of the dealers' reactions to this new procedure?
9. You have been hired by a local charity organisation to learn how they can increase the number of persons who volunteer to help with annual fund-raising activities. Define your research objectives.
10. You are the administrative assistant of a small hospital in a health board region. You and the hospital chief have just come from the general health board annual meeting of all hospital chiefs, where you were informed that your staff

performance was unsatisfactory. You had sensed the tension among the staff but had not considered it unusual. The chief calls you into the office after the meeting and instructs you to investigate. Suggest at least three types of research that might be appropriate in this situation.

Case Study
Woolly Jumpers for Men*

An Irish knitwear company, based in Dublin, is aware that its sales in the men's market are static and have been for twelve months. At a stormy meeting between the board members, the founding directors voiced their opinions:

Doyle: 'My sales representatives tell me that retailers want cheaper garments, perhaps 25% wool and 75% acrylic.'
O'Shea: 'High production costs associated with a 100% wool jumper are responsible for our lack of sales.'
MacCraith: 'The way I see it, the product is losing its premium image among customers and can be found in bargain bins in many of the outlets which stock our product. We're losing our quality image.'

While management are of differing opinions as to what the problem is, all feel that sales decline is imminent. They react to this situation by deciding that the company needs more advertising.

As a marketing research consultant, the MD has come to you for assistance. The MD isn't sure the company understands what is happening with their customers, the retailers or even with the market. He has asked you to reconcile the different views of the various directors, before making a final decision on the best way forward for the company.

Questions
1. What information is needed by the MD?
2. How would you define the problem — give a list of objectives.
3. What type of research design would you choose to solve the dilemma facing the MD, and why?

*This case has been adapted from material presented at a FAS training course by Ray Collis, Managing Director, Envision Marketing, 1998. It is intended to be used as a basis for class discussion rather than to illustrate either effective or ineffective handling of an administrative situation. The case is based upon a real situation, though certain information has been disguised.

Case Study
Skin Care Lotion*

A new brand of winter skin care lotion was launched on the Irish market in 1994, targeted at the users of cold creams: it was designed and developed to capitalise on the fact that cold-cream users found their product inconvenient to use and a bit old fashioned. Coupled with this, no cream existed on the market which matched the winter care capabilities of cold cream.

However, while the sales of Brand X grew in the first year, so too did the sales of cold cream. 'We need to do some research to check out how Brand X is performing in the market. We also want to know how consumers feel about it' said the manufacturer to the research client.

Would such a 'post-launch evaluation' study truly address the decisions confronting the brand manager?

*Adapted from Bijapurkar, Rama, 1995, 'Does marketing research really contribute to decision making?', in the 48th ESOMAR Marketing Research Congress, 'Making the Decision', The Hague, 17–20 September, pp. 1–14.

Case Study
Green Isle's Goodfella's Pizza*

O'Rourke sits behind his desk gazing at the latest pizza sales figures for the UK and Irish markets. He is well pleased, sales have surpassed all expectations in the past five years.

He can still clearly remember the day it all started, back in 1992. Green Isle Foods markets convenience foodstuffs and had been looking around for an opportunity for a high quality, mass market product. O'Rourke himself had been monitoring the fast-food market and saw pizzas as the food of the 1990s. As he told the then board of directors, 'People are eating pizzas for breakfast, dinner and tea, for snacking and grazing or main meals.' However, the pizza market was not without its difficulties at the time. It was already growing and had several strong key players such as San Marco with its traditional Italian image, and McCains which competes on a price basis. Coupled with this, Green Isle themselves were already a player in the pizza market, but competing in traditional sectors with outdated technology.

Against this background, O'Rourke persisted and convinced top management that the challenge was for Green Isle to 'move the goalposts' in setting a new standard in quality and taste for main meal pizzas. With this in mind, he undertook extensive market research.

The research objectives were to:

1. identify a major development opportunity for a premium quality frozen pizza;
2. identify the positioning for a premium mass market pizza brand;
3. forecast the market growth for frozen pizzas.

The consumer: secondary data indicated that consumption of pizzas and pizza-based products has been on the increase during the past number of years. However, along with this, survey research showed the consumers had become more discerning in their purchases. In relation to pizza, Irish consumers have become familiar with Italian foods and have good discrimination with respect to what offers good quality and value.

Consumers viewed pizza as a convenience food to be eaten at any time. It was reasonably nourishing and healthy and provided a variety of flavours and tastes. Qualitative research showed emotional aspects of fun, freedom, social and a cosmopolitan outlook associated with pizza.

The findings also indicated that the single nine-inch pizza is the driving force behind the market's dynamic growth, while the largest segment, the five-inch pizza, was static as consumers sought better value in the nine-inch range.

The product: In the market, pizzas were cheap convenience foods often bought for children. Product quality was neither high nor consistent and a key point of differentiation was the deep-pan pizza base. A real opportunity existed if total product quality, ingredient appeal and price-pointing could be married together.

A number of 'blind' taste tests were conducted with panels of consumers. Without knowledge of the brand, the Goodfella's pizza scored a satisfaction rating 25% higher than the market leaders. As a result of extensive product testing, the range of deep-pan pizza includes: Bacon and Mushroom, Cheese Supreme, Pepperoni, Ham and Pineapple in nine-inch format and The Big Cheese and Pepperoni Plus twelve-inch pizzas.

Imagery: All research consistently showed that the imagery of the new product was the key to success. The consumer already had a very distinct image of pizza, so just reproducing this imagery ran the danger of replaying the stereotype. However, viewing this problem as an opportunity, the new brand could create a point of difference in its imagery. As a result, Italian and US images of pizza were examined closely and the US images of friends, beer, the dinner culture, and deep-pan provided the basis for the 'difference' which was needed. From this image and brand research the Brand Strategy was defined — the new brand was to be positioned as THE American Pizza, and the brand identity was created to achieve differentiation — appetite appeal and shelf appeal.

Target market: Goodfella's targeted the households with children and young adults. Informal focus groups showed a positive response to advertisements among this segment.

Goodfella's Success

Armed with this information, October 1993 saw the launch of Goodfella's American Style Pizza into the highly competitive frozen food sector, both in the Republic of Ireland and Northern Ireland. Goodfella's appeal has successfully tapped into latent demand for quality frozen pizza and its launch has subsequently led to a massive growth in demand for pizza. Green Isle Foods is currently market leader in pizza, commanding over 70% of the Irish market. To continue the growth of the Goodfella's brand, Goodfella's was successfully launched into the UK market in February 1995 where it has remained a permanent fixture within the top three deep-pan frozen pizza brands there.

Goodfella's continues to be an Irish product, manufactured in a state-of-the-art pizza plant in Naas, one of the largest pizza manufacturing facilities in Europe. The plant produces 11,000 pizzas per hour — enough to satisfy the total UK daily consumption. The success of Goodfella's to date is largely attributed to a textbook marketing campaign. Quality and high value are an unbeatable combination for any new product, as O'Rourke well knows, and Goodfella's has both.

Questions

1. What do you consider to be the key to Goodfella's success story?
2. What types of research designs were mentioned and/or used in the case study and how do you think they contributed to the success of Goodfella's?
3. If you were Marketing Director of Green Isle, how would you approach researching the potential of the frozen pizza market? What research design(s) do you think would obtain the necessary information to enable you to confidently make the decision to enter or withhold from entering the frozen pizza market?
4. What consumer trends were identified by research carried out in the marketplace? How has Michael O'Rourke capitalised on these trends in the marketing strategy guiding the launch of Goodfella's pizzas? How do the product's design, packaging and advertising campaigns reflect the marketing strategy, given that you are aware of these?

*This case study, written by Christine Domegan and Justin Jennings, draws heavily from 'Goodfella's — developing consumer food products' in the Marketing Institute of Ireland Newsletter, March/April 1995, p. 3; 'Goodfella's market share', *Sunday Business Post*, 23 December 1994; 'Commerical profile: Green Isle Foods', *Sunday Business Post*, 5 June 1994; 'Goodfella's pizza proves a supermarket winner', *Sunday Business Post*, 3 April 1994.

Case Study*
The New Logo for Tourism Brand Ireland Initiative

Tourism has been one of Ireland's growth industries over the past decade. Mr Noel Toolan, the then international marketing director of Bord Fáilte, maintained that major changes have to be introduced to continue on that growth path to bring the industry into the twenty-first century.

Startling results of a survey revealed that despite 50 years of promoting Ireland as a holiday destination, tourists are still in the dark about what the country has to offer. Therefore, Noel Toolan planned to revitalise Ireland's image along the same lines as Spain which introduced a whole new brand image for the country with a concept entitled 'Espana, Everything Under the Sun'.

In 1994, Noel Toolan and his new marketing team in Bord Fáilte conducted extensive research on international images of Ireland. The resulting initiative became known as 'Tourism Brand Ireland' (TBI) which is an Overseas Tourism Marketing Initiative (OTMI).

As part of the £30 million initiative adopted to market Ireland as a branded product to tourists abroad, a new tourism logo, which was to complement the new strategy, was unveiled worldwide in November 1996. It was to replace the traditional shamrock motif that Bord Fáilte had used for over 50 years. The reason for the change in logo was triggered when initial research revealed that Ireland did not have a clear identity overseas.

Marketing Research

In developing the new logo, Bord Fáilte engaged in a huge amount of marketing research internationally in order to develop it to fit into the overall message of the campaign.

An initial large-scale consumer research exercise involving focus groups in Britain, France, Germany, the Netherlands, the USA and Ireland was conducted to test the potency of alternative logos. The findings indicated that while Bord Fáilte's logo should continue to use green, the colour associations for Ireland could be widened somewhat and the shamrock on its own was not a powerful or motivating symbol. Representatives from An Bord Trachtala, An Bord Bia, the IDA and the Department of Foreign Affairs were briefed throughout all the research for the new logo.

Bord Fáilte then took the results of the initial research to seventeen different research groups around the world before the final logo was decided on. The chosen logo that reflects Bord Fáilte's repositioning was tentatively expressed as 'Ireland — An Emotional Experience'.

Research found that while the shamrock was a familiar symbol for Ireland in Britain and the US, there was little recognition of it on most of the continent. Apart from confirming a green association, it had little representational meaning.

The New TBI Logo

The new £100,000 logo depicts two people embracing and exchanging a shamrock. It consists of four colours including red, yellow, and two shades of green. It is meant to symbolise the warmth and friendliness of the Irish people.

Designed by Design Works, an Irish company, its aim was to attract higher spending, younger and middle-aged visitors to Ireland. It portrays an image of the country which is younger and more attractive and different to the usual clichés and stereotypes of Ireland. The idea was to create a new experience for the visitor. There is a lack of awareness about all Ireland has to offer. As mentioned earlier, the logo was designed to complement the overall repositioning strategy by representing what an Irish holiday experience should be.

The New TBI Logo Gets Axed

Leading designers have condemned the decision on 28 July 1997 that the Minister for Tourism, Jim McDaid, took to scrap the Bord Fáilte Tourism logo. He called for the big green shamrock to be reintroduced as soon as possible. McDaid said that dropping the shamrock was cutting off all the links with Ireland's rich tradition and heritage and that there was absolutely no reason to replace the traditional logo.

Jim Dunne, Director of Identity Business and who was involved in the initial research that led to the design of the logo, stated: 'This is a very rash decision by the Minister if there is no research to back it up.' Minister McDaid appealed to common sense and felt that a lot of people agreed with his decision. His decision will be welcomed by those who believed the logo designed for the TBI campaign left many people scratching their heads about what it was supposed to convey and finding it difficult to decipher.

Questions

1. What was the problem definition that led to the undertaking of research into the Bord Fáilte tourism logo?
2. How would you have gone about researching whether or not there is a clear connection between Ireland as a tourist destination and Bord Fáilte's traditional shamrock logo if you were marketing director of Bord Fáilte? What research design(s) would you choose, and why?
3. What research design(s) would you use to test the effectiveness of various new alternative logos in order to decide on the final one?
4. Suppose that the design had not been dropped. What research design(s) would you adopt to test whether the new logo was effective, i.e. whether the new logo was a success or failure. When would you undertake this research? Give reasons to support your answer.
5. Objectively analyse the two opposing views adopted by Jim McDaid and Noel Toolan; one based on common sense and one on extensive research, respectively. Do you think research always provides the answer or does common sense sometimes prevail?
6. Outline the steps in the marketing research process that you think were undertaken in researching the new tourism logo.

*This case study, written by Christine Domegan and Justin Jennings, draws heavily from 'Row flares over Bord Failte survey', *Sunday Tribune*, 16 June 1994; '9% revenue growth is forecast', *Link*, May 1997; 'New emotive image for Irish tourism', IMJ, 1995; 'Tourism — the cost of branding Ireland', *Business and Finance*, 1996; 'Tourism Brand Ireland', MII Newsletter, January/February 1997; 'Bord Failte, uncomfortable with new image', *Sunday Tribune*, 18 May 1997; 'Toursim, A Radical Review', Noel Toolan, Guest lecture at NUI, Galway, 26 November 1996.

Part 2

DATA COLLECTION METHODS

Chapter 4

SECONDARY SOURCES OF DATA

> - **Chapter Overview**
> - Introduction • Desk Research and Secondary Data Defined
> - Advantages and Disadvantages of Secondary Data • Conducting Desk Research and Gathering Secondary Data • Classification of Secondary Sources of Data • Internal • External • Government • State-Sponsored Bodies • Directories • Trade Associations and Other Professionals • The Digital Age of Secondary Data; Databases and CD-roms • The Internet and the WWW • EU and European • Syndicated Services • Grey Material • Summary

- **Introduction**

The central issue of the research process so far has been 'What information do we need?' The focus of this chapter is 'What information already exists?'

Very often, much information is close at hand and can be obtained with ease. Desk research is about collecting data already there, from existing published sources. It is the first step in the data collection phase of a research study. It is the next logical step once the problem is clearly defined. Desk research is concerned with secondary sources of data.

This chapter outlines the secondary sources of data in Ireland that can be used for desk research. *Be very mindful, given the tremendous amount of published information from official and other sources, of the dramatic changes that occur on a daily basis with respect to information sources, government bodies, the Internet and web sites etc. Many of these information sources change or become redundant in a short space of time. As a result, the material presented in this chapter is not a fully comprehensive guide to every single source of secondary data. Rather, it provides an important starting point and framework for desk research.* So, by the end of this session, the reader will be able to:

1. distinguish between desk and field research, secondary and primary data;
2. detail the nature of secondary data;
3. describe the advantages and disadvantages of secondary data;
4. identify key Irish sources;

5. describe their use in marketing;
6. conduct an efficient desk search.

• Desk Research and Secondary Data Defined

A researcher conducts desk research to gather secondary data. Desk research is the systematic collection and analysis of secondary sources of data. Secondary data is data collected by another person for reasons other than the problem in hand. For example, when a researcher goes to a library and obtains population statistics, they are conducting desk research by gathering secondary data.

In contrast, a researcher is conducting field research when they talk to people such as consumers, product purchasers, shop managers or housewives. Field research generates primary data. Primary research is data collected first hand by the investigator for the specific problem on hand. Field research is original data and is synonymous with primary data. Primary data is new data — unpublished and undocumented anywhere else, as captured by Figure 4.1.

Figure 4.1 Research and data types

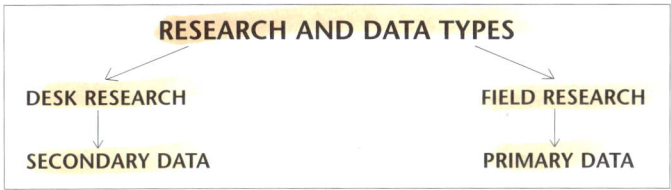

One of the biggest follies in marketing research is to collect primary data before exhausting secondary sources of data. On many occasions secondary data can provide inexpensive answers to posed research questions. The employment of secondary data can even rule out the need for costly primary data. It is assumed that all necessary desk research is completed before considering field research.

• Advantages and Disadvantages of Secondary Data

The reasons behind such generally accepted practice lie in the advantages of secondary data over primary data. Secondary data is relatively cheaper than primary data to gather. It is less time-consuming and so is gathered faster than primary data. Against these advantages of secondary data, possible difficulties in using secondary data relate to the recency and origin of the data itself. A serious time lag can occur between the publication of the secondary data and the project on hand. In effect, such lack of recency renders the data obsolete. Today, this is less of a problem in light of the Internet, the World Wide Web and CD-Rom technology (discussed later in this chapter). Table 4.1 presents the major advantages and disadvantages of secondary and primary data.

Table 4.1 Distinctions between secondary and primary data

	Secondary data	**Primary data**
Purpose	Collected for other reasons by others	Collected for specific problem in hand by researcher
Relevancy	Some to little	Complete
Objectivity	Unknown	High
Process	Easy to gather	Difficult to gather
Cost	Relatively cheap	Relatively expensive
Time required	Relatively little	Relatively much

A researcher should never assume that primary data will provide the absolute answer. In reality, primary data is the last resort to solving the problem. Secondary data is not to be underestimated. In such a situation, the investigator analyses the secondary data and writes up the results.

Figure 4.2 The role of secondary data in the research process

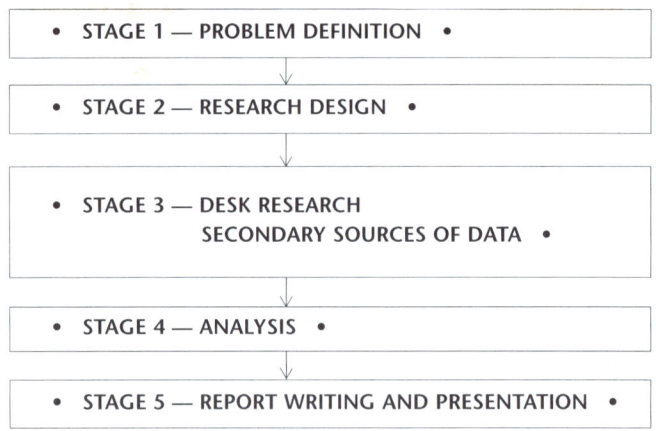

Once the decision has been made to collect secondary data, the data needs to be judged or evaluated before inclusion in the project.

Objectivity is used to evaluate desk research. This term refers to how scientifically the secondary data was originally collected. At some point, the secondary data being considered was primary data. To judge how valid and reliable the original research plan was, the following questions are asked of all secondary data:

- How was it collected?
- Why was it collected?
- When was it collected?
- Why was it published?
- How dependable is the data source?

Essentially, these questions are assessing the quality of the original data. They may highlight some problems or deficiency within the secondary data source. If these arise, the value and the effectiveness of the secondary data is queried. On occasion, it may be deemed inappropriate or even dangerous to utilise the data source.

The second criterion for judging secondary data relates to *comparability* with the current project. Specifically, measurement units and classification schemes being different can be a serious drawback to the use of the secondary source. For example, in Ireland we define a small firm as one employing fewer than 50 people. In many European countries, small firm equates with 200 or fewer employees. As traditional boundaries are becoming blurred in domestic and international marketplaces, measurement units and their definitions are constantly changing. This detracts from the objectivity and comparability of data emanating from different sources and hence its usefulness to a marketing researcher.

The third criterion relates to the *time dimension* of the data. There can be a significant time lag between the data collection and data publication to the extent that the data is too dated for use. Such data is unhelpful or misleading and therefore should not be used. No information is better than poor or wrong information. One exception to this rule is when secondary data, while dated, can be adapted to account for its ageing. The Consumer Price Index is used to this effect in Ireland — it allows a researcher to account for the effects of inflation over time.

In summary, secondary data fulfils a number of important roles in any research process. It:

- is a data source in its own right;
- can provide a solution to the problem;
- acts as background to primary data;
- can be a substitute to primary data;
- aids in problem clarification (literature review).

• Conducting Desk Research and Gathering Secondary Data

Often, it is an overabundance of information and not a lack of it which confronts the researcher at this point. The task is to sift through published sources, selecting those most pertinent to the study. Like all other steps in marketing research, the process of gathering secondary data is ordered and systematic. The researcher, to be exhaustive:

- goes from *internal to external* sources — that is from company documents such as invoices and customer letters to external reports and documents, e.g. government census data;

- goes from *general to specific* sources — the researcher starts with broad general issues and then to specific industry sources. This can be referred to as the *funnel effect*. Key search words and terms are also approached using the general-to-specific guideline. The help of an expert or librarian may be needed at this point, as one investigates more specific sources of data;
- is *methodical and logical* — to ensure effective use of resources and time, an ordered approach to potential sources is needed. A planned and careful approach minimises the likelihood of problems or deficiencies occurring in desk research;
- tries not to rely upon a single source of data — the old saying, 'two heads are better than one' applies to desk research — where possible, *two, three or more sources of data* are used;
- *writes* everything down — at a later stage, you or another researcher may wish to refer to a minor point of information, so it is a time-saving device if there is a paper trail to follow.

Generally speaking, an effective, exhaustive research can be completed of all secondary data using an approach similar to the one described above. In calculating market size estimates or consumption rates, two or three sources will need to be combined. For example, the Census of Population, Household Budget Survey and the Consumer Price Index are necessary to determine the market size of many consumer products here in Ireland (we examine this issue at a later stage in this chapter).

In practice, one exception can arise, where the combination of sources does not give the desired information. In such circumstances, ingenuity and creativity are required in utilising the secondary data. Jane Williams[1] tells of an occasion when a firm wished to estimate the number of fire doors in Ireland. Unable to locate a source or sources of secondary data which quoted a figure, the firm in question used the number of fire signs in existence as an indication of the possible number of fire doors. Such an approach is not uncommon in Ireland. Assumptions, scenarios or lateral thinking are often required to calculate figures etc. It is clearly important that there is a solid foundation for the assumptions and that the assumptions are explicitly documented in all calculations.

• Classification of Secondary Sources of Data

Secondary data can be classified broadly as either internal or external. This internal/external division refers to the origin of the data in the first instance — that is, whether the data was first conceived within the firm or outside.

Internal data is data already in existence within the firm. Accounting documents, sales reports, customer files, invoices and delivery dockets typify internal secondary data. Such secondary data can also be referred to as in-house data and historical data. External data is data in existence outside the organisation. It consists of all published material, information and statistics from official, public and state bodies and other entities.

Secondary Sources of Data

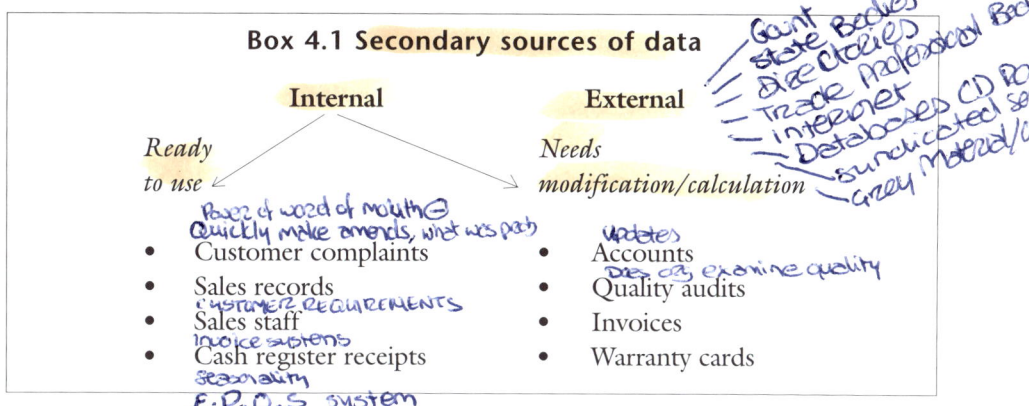

Box 4.1 Secondary sources of data

Internal	External
Ready to use	*Needs modification/calculation*
• Customer complaints	• Accounts
• Sales records	• Quality audits
• Sales staff	• Invoices
• Cash register receipts	• Warranty cards

Handwritten annotations: Govt Bodies, State Bodies, Directories, Trade Professional Bodies, Internet, Databases CD Roms, Syndicated services, Grey material/other. Power of word of mouth, Quickly make amends, what was past, Customer requirements, Invoice systems, Seasonality, E.P.O.S system. Updates, Dig as examine quality.

• Internal Data: Ready to Use

Most of the ready-to-use internal data originates from the marketing function. For example, customer information held on a customer database can be a complementary force for marketing research[2] and can be used to:

- classify customers — gold, silver, bronze according to the amount of business done with the firm;
- assess the probability of closing sale, e.g. 1–9 ranking, where 1 = signing within next day, 2 = within next week . . . ;
- determine the amount of purchase.

In the hotel industry, for example, hotel managers use reservations records and registration information to help in timing their advertising and sales calls. If most tourists book July and August holidays by February, advertising at Easter will be too late. Reservation records also provide information concerning the hotel's top producing travel agents and corporate clients. Hotel sales staff can phone, fax, or visit the travel agents or corporate clients to inform them of future promotional activities and identify new business opportunities. The salesperson can ascertain if the travel agent or corporate client has other needs that the hotel can satisfy, e.g. a conference that is just being planned, as highlighted in Table 4.2.[3]

Table 4.2 Internal records — customer information

Guest information
Personal guest information
Name
Address
Phone numbers: Work
Home

> Mobile
> E-mail
> Number in party
> Reason for trip
> > Business
> > Pleasure
> > Study
> > Other
> Name and address of employer
> Occupation
>
> **Types of tourism products/services purchased**
> Single/double room/suite
> Restaurant
> Room service
> Health club
>
> **Details of trip**
> Length of stay
> Method of arrival — car/bus/train/taxi/other
>
> **Method of payment**
> Credit card/cash/cheque/bill to company
>
> **Membership of frequent guest programme**

Salespeople come in contact with customers in the marketplace every day. They are used as information hounds — the ears and eyes of the firm. They pick up information on a continuous basis about customers, competitors and the marketplace. Sales records can keep the firm abreast of:

- competitor activity;
- market trends;
- customer problems;
- sales activities;
- sales expenses;
- trends in customer business;
- order status;
- potential new needs;
- shifts in customer tastes.

Internal Data, Modification and Calculation

Many researchers and firms don't use the information already available in their own records. They tend to ignore such data. However, simple modification or recalculation enables the researcher to use existing organisational records. More data exists than people know of. In many cases, the researcher must 'dig and delve' to find data that answers the query on hand. This modification to data is needed as many firms have incomplete, inaccurate filing systems.

Accounting data and records are used by marketing managers to:

- keep track of marketing expenses;
- relate performance to targets;
- analyse sales;
- relate profits to sales.

Often, such historical data needs minor rearrangement to assist the marketing function. Here are some examples to demonstrate how a researcher can make company records work for them using profit and loss accounts and invoices.

Keeping Track of Marketing Expenses

Suppose your profit and loss statement for the last six months looks like Table 4.3.

Table 4.3 Profit and loss statement

Sales		50,000
Expenses		
1. Rent	4,000	
2. Supplies	3,000	
3. Selling expenses	5,000	
4. Salaries	9,000	
5. Advertising	1,000	
	22,000	

Your only marketing costs are selling expenses and advertising. So, what information could you obtain from this profit and loss statement? Firstly, information might become more clearly visible if you rearrange the items as shown in Table 4.4.

Table 4.4 Analysis of profit and loss statement

1998 January–June		
Total costs/sales	Selling expenses/sales	Advertising/sales
£22,000/£50,000	£5,000/£50,000	£1,000/£50,000
(44%)	(10%)	(2%)

Having rearranged the data in your profit and loss statement, you can see that, in 1998, costs are 44% of sales, that selling expenses are 10% of sales and that advertising is 2% of sales. These figures can now be used as a basis for controlling future costs. For example, if your present advertising level is satisfactory at 2% of sales, then this figure could be used as a benchmark for your future advertising expenditure. If your selling expenses rise above 10% of sales, then you might try to cut back on costs. Of course, the figures quoted here are merely examples and should not be taken as recommended guidelines.

Relating Performance to Targets

From the accounts one can extract figures which will help to assess sales performance. However, it is essential that two things are done first: quantify benchmarks and set targets. A benchmark is merely a starting point which identifies how many sales you have now. Sales targets are the specific sales goals you anticipate your firm to achieve within a given time period, usually quarterly and/or annually.

Once benchmarks and targets are established, one can accurately measure progress. In this manner, a firm has the means of spotting trends; recognising problems, such as accounts that may have fallen in value; and identifying opportunities, such as fast-growing customers. Additionally, there is the information necessary for planning future action and handling questions.

So, what information do you need if you are to keep track of sales performance?

- Total sales.
- Sales per region.
- Sales for each product or product group.
- Sales for each salesperson.

Once this information is gathered, it is useful to display it on graphs or charts. Then one can see at a glance how a business is doing. Table 4.5 is an example of how one may want to organise sales data to help analyse sales performance.

Table 4.5 Sales analysis

	Target	Actual	Difference
Total sales	900	700	−200
Sales by area			
Area 1	300	200	−100
Area 2	300	275	−25
Area 3	300	225	−75
Sales by product			
Product 1	400	350	−50
Product 2	300	200	−100
Product 3	200	150	−50

Relating Profit to Sales

Finally, a quick calculation of profit-to-sales ratio will help track trends in profitability. If this figure shows that sales are increasing, but that the profit rate is falling, then it is time to look more closely at expenses or prices.

What You Can Learn From Invoices

- Do you know what your average sale is per customer?
- Do you know who are your top five customers? Your top ten? *Rank customers*
- Can you say what is the average credit your customers take? *Why you gave them credit?*
- What time of year do you make the most sales? By volume? By £?
- What is the monthly sales pattern for each product or product group?
- What is the geographic breakdown of your sales?
- How would you break down your overall sales into differing customer groups? (i.e. your firm's sales to different groups, such as builders, new home-buyers and engineering companies.)[4]

• External Sources of Secondary Data

There is also a large quantity of published information which is readily available, easy to consult and relatively inexpensive to gather. Such published information is external to a company. It is available from official sources, the government, trade bodies, the World Wide Web and a myriad of other sources. This type of information is not gathered specifically for marketing purposes. To this end it will need to be adjusted. On many occasions, two or more sources will have to be combined to answer the queries posed by the researcher, as the following example illustrates.

Box 4.2 The Irish alginate market and some secondary sources of data

Alginate is extracted from brown seaweed and is firmly established as one of the most versatile biopolymers available for industrial use. It is used to thicken solutions, to stabilise suspensions and emulsions, to gel a wide range of mixtures, and to form films on various surfaces. To establish an alginate extraction facility and thus spearhead a new initiative aimed at developing the seaweed resources of Ireland, the market size for alginates has to be estimated.

While there was no prior research information available regarding the Irish alginate market, the following secondary sources are useful in tackling the market size issue.

The Irish Trade Statistics is one potentially important source of information on the Irish alginate market. These statistics list the exact amount of alginate imported into this country.

Table 4.6 Alginic acid (Imp./Exp., 1988 to 1992)

	1988	1989	1990	1991	1992
Imports £	108,400	638,900	587,000	428,150	207,250
t	14	80	89	72	24
Exports £	14,000	0	18,000	1,600	246,600
t	12	0	2	1	35

However, the statistics fail to classify alginate into its various grades, and as such the information on average prices is not accurate enough to provide any meaningful picture of the pricing structure.

Much research on the supply and demand for alginate in the US and Western Europe has already been completed by the IMR (International Market Research) agency in San Diego. They provide answers to many of the questions raised above. They identify the main value-added regions of demand, and the main suppliers: USA, France, Italy, Germany and the UK.

A list of all possible areas of usage of alginates can be compiled by referencing promotional literature distributed by the current alginate-producing companies. For example:

1. Food industry: dairy spreads, ice creams, sauces and dressings, pet food and fish food.
2. Industrial sector: textiles, welding electrodes and paper coating.
3. Pharmaceutical/medical applications: gastric ulcer preparations and calcium alginate dressings.

A list of companies within each of these categories of production, and those using alginates in their production, can be compiled using the *Kompass Directory*.[5]

• Classification of External Secondary Sources of Data

From a marketing perspective, this rich array of information sources can be divided into seven main areas, as illustrated in Figure 4.3.

Figure 4.3 Secondary sources of data

Each of these major external data sources is now described. Remember, this discussion is meant as an indication of the wealth of information that is available to the marketing researcher in Ireland, rather than an exhaustive, finite listing of such!

• Government

The Government constitutes one of the most important sources of external secondary data in Ireland. Vast amounts of data, from national to regional, and from urban to rural, are collected and published by the government. The government collects and publishes censuses, statistical information and other data generated in the normal course of operations, e.g. taxes collected and unemployment benefits paid.

Government data is generally of high quality. Such data tends to be readily available to the researcher at little or no cost. Its major value is in assessing the market size, market trends, consumption and expenditure patterns. Its main drawback relates to much of the data being aggregate in nature, i.e. it details product groups rather than brands; regions rather than towns. Coupled with this, the delay from time of collection to time of publication can be substantial, often two or more years. This can require the researcher to supplement the data to account for factors like inflation.

Government data can come from two broad sources, the Central Statistics Office (CSO) and government departments, as Figure 4.4 shows. The description here of the Central Statistics Office, CSO, and associated material draws heavily upon the CSO annual guide to CSO publications and information services.[6]

Figure 4.4 Government sources of secondary data

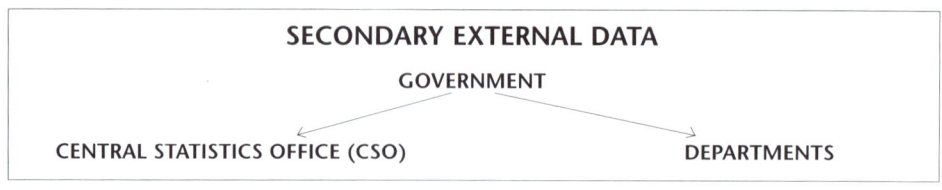

Central Statistics Office (CSO)

The Central Statistics Office (CSO) is the largest gatherer of statistical information in the country. The CSO is the Government agency charged with the responsibility of collecting, compiling and disseminating the results of its statistical enquiries. It publishes official Irish statistics. It is also responsible for the co-ordination of official statistics produced by other public authorities. General publications by the CSO fall under three main headings:

1. Statistical Abstract (annually)

This yearbook is the most comprehensive source of statistical data published in Ireland. It contains not only statistics compiled by the Central Statistics Office, but also a considerable amount of statistical information which is compiled in the course of the administrative work of other government departments and state-sponsored bodies.

The abstract is divided into sections giving detailed information on the following:

- Area and meteorology.
- Population and vital statistics.
- Agriculture, forestry and fisheries.
- Industrial production.
- Building and construction.
- External trade.
- Services and distribution.
- Housing and social statistics.
- Education.
- Justice and defence.
- Tourism, transport and communication.
- Prices.
- Miscellaneous.

Retrospective data is given in all sections. The abstract also includes an appendix which contains published statistics relating to Northern Ireland.

2. Statistical Bulletin (quarterly)
This bulletin is primarily the formal publication medium for the detailed results of all the regular short-term CSO inquiries.

3. Economic Series (monthly)
This publication provides five years retrospective data for a selection of over 150 principal short-term economic series grouped into the following ten categories:

- Prices
- Industry
- Building and construction
- Agriculture
- External trade
- Distribution, transport and tourism
- Services
- Finance
- Labour
- Vital statistics

Census of Population

The Census of Population is the largest statistical enquiry conducted by the Central Statistics Office. First undertaken in 1821, the census was merely a head count. It has now been expanded to the point where there are seven different sections to the census, all of interest to the marketing researcher. The most recent Census was carried out on 28 April 1996.

The Census questionnaire is issued to every household and to every other type of location where persons may be present on Census night. The 1996 Census form contained 24 questions relating to individuals and nine housing questions. In addition to the usual demographic questions on age, sex and marital status, topics such as religion, ability to speak the Irish language, usual residence, means of travel to work, education received, occupation, employment status and involvement in farming, were also covered. Full-time, part-time and duration of unemployment were covered for the first time. The household questions included the nature of occupancy of house or flat, the number of rooms, the year in which the house was built, water supply and sanitary facilities and the principal method of heating the household in winter time. The final Census results include:

- Local population reports — a series of 32 reports for individual counties and county boroughs.
- Small Area Population Statistics (SAPS). This contains detailed classifications of:
  (a) The population by age, sex and marital status.

(b) Households by type, size and by age, sex and marital status of the head of the household.
(c) Family units by size and age of youngest child.
(d) The population aged 15 years and over by principal economic status, age and sex.
(e) Persons at work by sex, employment status and broad industrial sector.
(f) Persons at work and unemployed by sex and occupational group.
(g) The entire population by socio-economic group and social class.

Detailed classifications by means of travel and distance travelled to work, education, ability to speak Irish, religion and housing characteristics, etc. are also provided for urban districts, rural districts, towns and district electoral divisions, under such heading as:

Volume 1 — Population by area.
Volume 2 — Ages and marital status.
Volume 3 — Household composition and family units.
Volume 4 — Usual residence and migration, birthplaces.

The 1991 Census of Population, detailed report covers the above information plus principal economic status and industries; religion; occupations; An Ghaeilge/Irish language; education; housing and travel to work, school and college. Other demographic publications include:

- Population and Labour Force Projections.
- Quarterly Report on Vital Statistics.
- Life Tables.

Marketing Research Uses

Population data is used in marketing to estimate the market size and structure. It indicates whether a socio-economic or geographic market is growing or decreasing. Comparing previous years of census data will reveal if a target market is expanding or contracting. For example, a company in the Munster area manufacturing clothes for girls aged 5 to 9 wants to know the total relevant population. Total population in this category in 1991 was 44,503. In 1996, the total population of 5–9-year-olds was 38,826. This shows a significant drop in the size of this particular market segment and has serious implications for the marketing strategy pursued by the firm. The population census also provides a range of other useful information such as:

- a demographic profile of target markets;
- trend data in the number of births, deaths, marriages, those emigrating, mobility patterns;
- distribution by social class;

- household composition;
- at local, regional or national level;
- employment status by occupational group;
- numbers at each level of education.

The biggest drawback to the use of the Census of Population is the time gap between the collection of data and its publication, with a lead time of three to five years in some cases.

Household Budget Survey

The large-scale national Household Budget Surveys cover 7,000–8,000 urban and rural households. The HBS provides estimates for household composition, accommodation facilities, weekly income, weekly expenditure (over 300 categories of goods and services are distinguished) and other miscellaneous items classified by various household characteristics, e.g. size, composition, gross income level, location, etc. To this end, it shows the actual amount of expenditure and the percentage of the total weekly budget spent on a named household item, such as bread, fish, meat, shoes, petrol and newspapers. It also indicates different patterns of spending in different categories of households, e.g. between urban and rural households and those on different incomes.

A large-scale national survey was conducted in 1994/95. The sampled households give a sufficiently representative picture for all of Ireland's households. Two detailed volumes are readily available — Volume 1 presents detailed results for all households and Volume 2 covers detailed results for urban and rural households. Such HBS results are on a harmonised basis with other EU member states to allow for comparisons — a very useful facility for Irish firms exporting and serving markets abroad. The last Household Budget Survey took place in May 1999. For further details, please contact the CSO.

The Household Budget Survey is a critical source of data on expenditure for a marketer. It enables a manager to estimate the level and trends in expenditure on individual products or services. In this capacity, market potential and market penetration targets can be realistically set. In practice the HBS is used in conjunction with the Census of Population to estimate market sizes, market trends, consumption patterns and demand at local and national level, as shown in the worked example below.

Consumer Price Index

The Consumer Price Index (CPI) is compiled in respect of the second Tuesday of the months of February, May, August and November. Results are released five weeks later. This Index is the official measure of inflation. The Index measures the change in the average level of prices paid for consumer goods and services purchased by Irish households. Separate indices are also provided for the ten main groupings of consumer goods and services.

Categories for which price changes are available include: food; alcoholic drink; tobacco; clothing and footwear; fuel and light; housing; durable household goods; other goods; transport; services and expenditure; all items and energy products.

The Consumer Price Index is used by marketing people to adjust figures on expenditure for inflation. The indices are especially useful when considering monetary trends. For example, sales of a specific product may have increased from £100 in 1995 to £150 in 1999. This appears to be a 50% increase in the value of sales for this item. However, if prices rose by 20% during this period, then the increase in the value of sales in real terms was much less (allowing for inflation).

Estimating the Market Size

For many companies, especially those in the consumer goods field, market estimates can be found by using data published by the Central Statistics Office (CSO). An estimate of the market size can be calculated using three CSO publications:

- Household Budget Survey (HBS).
- Census of Population (COP).
- Consumer Price Index (CPI).

Whether it be a national or a local market, most managers would like to be able to determine the size of the market to which they are selling. It is essential to have an estimate of market size in start-up situations so as to decide whether a venture is worthwhile. Established companies need to know market size to assist in planning. You cannot formulate financial projections or a marketing plan unless you can forecast sales, and in order to forecast sales, you need to know market trends and the overall market size.

For example, according to the Census, the population of Galway city in 1996 was 57,241. How many households does this represent? The HBS tells us that there are 17,168 private households in the city area. Hospitals, army barracks etc. are excluded. The next question asks how much these households spend on a number of items per week. Average weekly expenditure is displayed in Table 4.7.

Table 4.7 Average size, composition, household income and expenditure, 1994–95 classified by urban/rural location

Item description	Urban areas	Rural areas		All rural households	State
		Farm households	Other households		
Average weekly household expenditure:					
	£	£	£	£	£
Food					
Potatoes	1.84	2.69	2.20	2.32	2.02
Drink and tobacco					
Cigarettes	8.55	5.64	7.34	6.91	7.95
Clothing and footwear					
Men's shoes	1.20	1.13	1.01	1.04	1.14
Miscellaneous goods					
Newspapers	3.29	3.57	3.22	3.31	3.30
Household durable goods					
Curtains	0.56	0.52	0.57	0.55	0.56
Transport					
Petrol	8.66	10.85	11.87	11.62	9.75

Multiplying each weekly expenditure by the total number of households in Galway provides the market size. Therefore, for the items listed in Table 4.7, an estimate of the 1996 Galway City market would be as shown in Table 4.8.

Table 4.8 Estimate Galway City Market average weekly expenditure 1996

Potatoes	£31,589 per week	(£1,642,634 per year)
Cigarettes	£146,786 per week	(£7,632,892 per year)
Men's shoes	£20,601 per week	(£1,071,283 per year)
Newspapers	£56,482 per week	(£2,937,101 per year)
Curtains	£9,614 per week	(£499,932 per year)
Petrol	£148,674 per week	(£7,731,093 per year)

Since all these figures were for 1996, they need to be adjusted for inflation. If one assumed that, on average, inflation had been 5.7% per year, then the present market for curtains would be over £10,160. The correct inflation figures for different categories of items can be obtained from the Consumer Price Index (this calculation reflects the figure for inflation from May 1995 to May 1998, as per CSO 16 June 1998).

By knowing the number of households in the country as a whole, you can calculate a national figure and estimate market sales. You can also examine previous Household Budget Surveys to establish trends and new patterns of consumption and expenditure.

Labour Force Survey (Annual)/Quarterly National Household Survey

The Labour Force Survey is the definitive source of data on employment and unemployment. A sample of about 45,000 households is surveyed. The reports provide estimates of the total population classified by age, sex and planning region and of the population aged 15 and over classified by principal economic status (at work, unemployed, etc.), industrial group, occupational group, marital status, etc. Since 1988, the reports have also contained internationally comparable data on the labour force.

September 1997 saw the first Quarterly National Household Survey which replaces the annual tradition Labour Force Survey. It presents quarterly data on employment and unemployment using ILO labour force classifications.

Census of Services (Including Distribution)

This Census covers the distribution sector and all other service sectors excluding the financial sector and the public sector. It provides information on the number of establishments, turnover, purchases, stocks, persons engaged and wages and salaries for various retail and wholesale business descriptions classified by size, legal status, geographic area, etc. Retail results are given for individual towns with 1,000 or more inhabitants.

The census takes place at irregular intervals. A Census of Services was last held in 1988. Volume 1 presents results for the retail and wholesale trade. Volume 2 gives details of the type of business conducted and of the numbers of persons engaged, in respect of the non-distribution services sector. Volume 3 concerns enterprise results. In addition, an Annual Services Inquiry provides some of the data, on an annual basis.

This information is commonly used in marketing to understand the distribution structure in the Irish market. It can also be used to identify:

- broad competitors;
- new distribution outlets;
- distribution patterns and coverage.

Annual Services Inquiry

Estimates of accounting and employment variables are provided by this survey of over 10,000 Irish service enterprises. Findings cover annual turnover, purchases, stocks, capital expenditure/disposal and employment/earnings estimates for the retail and wholesale trade. Real estate, renting, and other selected services are covered, though not to the same level of detail as wholesale or retail.

Retail Sales Index (Monthly)

This series measures changes in both the value and volume levels of retail sales on a seasonally adjusted basis for fourteen types of retail businesses, for all businesses excluding garages and for all businesses combined.

Categories included in the volume index of retail sales:

- Grocery.
- Grocery with public house.
- Public house and off-licence.
- Tobacco, sweets and newspapers.
- Fresh meat.
- Garage and filling station.
- Chemist.
- Hardware.
- Electrical goods.
- Footwear.
- Drapery and apparel.
- Other non-food.
- Total retail sales, i.e. excluding garages and filling stations.
- Department stores: clothing and footwear, furniture, soft furnishings etc., and other goods and services.
- All businesses combined.

Marketing Research Uses

Using this data, it is possible to see, at a glance, the sales progress of particular product groups. This type of information can provide a basis for assessing a company's performance. For example, a shoe company can compare its monthly sales trends with that for the footwear industry overall to judge its performance. The Retail Index can also indicate product groups that are experiencing buoyancy, e.g. frozen pizzas, ice cream cakes and flavoured water drinks. It will also indicate those product groups in decline.

Business of Advertising Agencies

This annual series gives details of the gross amount charged by advertising agencies to clients for advertising space, production work and other work such as research and promotions. Information is also provided on the number of people engaged and the total wages and salaries paid.

Trade Statistics

The most detailed published trade statistics appear in the Monthly Trade Statistics publication. This provides details for over 1,900 items classified according to the

United Nations Standard International Trade Classification. Both quantity and value of imports of each type of product are given for each month, for the year to date and for the same period in the previous year. The December issue gives total figures for the full year. A breakdown of imports by country of origin is also included in each issue.

The monthly releases contain figures for total imports and exports. Cumulative data as well as data for the previous year are provided. Summary commodity and country analyses are also given. Some of the categories may be too broad or too narrow for the research purposes in hand, but it is possible to get a more detailed breakdown by visiting the CSO.

Marketing Research Uses

Such import figures provide information about customer demand and hence market size. In doing so, this data indicates import competition facing Irish companies and suggests opportunities for import substitution.

Import data can also be used in conjunction with production figures and export levels to estimate the market size for a product. Production, plus imports, minus exports, gives a market size estimate.

Industrial Production Index

This index monitors current trends in the volume of production by industrial establishments with three or more people. Seasonally adjusted and unadjusted indices are published for 49 industrial sectors and groupings. For each product group, the annual percentage change and that of the preceding month are given.

This data is used by marketers to benchmark a company's performance against the output of the industry.

Census of Industrial Production

This provides more comprehensive data on industrial production, but there is a greater time lag in the release of figures. The Census of Industrial Production is based on an annual survey of 4,800 industrial establishments known as local units. It details gross and net output overall, per establishment and per person. This is classified by industrial sector and broken down by region and company size.

Access to CSO Data

All CSO publications may be consulted in the CSO Libraries in Cork and Dublin, which are open to the public. Information may also be easily obtained by phone. Detailed information is published in the quarterly Statistical Bulletin, the annual Statistical Abstract and the reports on large-scale CSO inquiries. These may be purchased and are generally available in public and third-level institution libraries. The CSO also maintains a computerised data bank containing its principal economic and social statistics.

A huge variety of CSO data and information is accessible via the Internet. The Internet address is http://www.cso.ie. It also provides valuable linkages to other EU and related sites.

Provision of Special Analyses

Considerable volumes of *ad hoc* analyses not incorporated in published reports are provided on a fee basis on request.

CSO Library

The CSO Library contains an extensive up-to-date collection of statistical and economic publications, including those of international organisations (i.e. EU, OECD, UN, and ILO). A large selection of statistical publications and yearbooks of other countries (e.g. all EU member States, other European countries, Canada, USA, Australia, New Zealand, South Africa, Japan, China, etc.) is also available for consultation. A number of statistical, economic and other journals are stocked as are the annual reports of government departments and state-sponsored agencies.

The main library is located in the Cork office. A limited library service is being maintained in Dublin comprising mainly national statistical publications and the publications of the principal international statistical organisations (e.g. EUROSTAT, OECD, UN). Both Libraries are open to the public from 9.30 a.m. to 12.45 p.m. and 2.30 p.m. to 4.45 p.m., Monday to Friday.

Postal and Fax Delivery of Statistical Releases (StatsMail/StatsFax)

Copies of all regular monthly, quarterly, etc. statistical releases may be obtained by post. Copies of some statistical releases may be obtained through the StatsFax service.

Government Departments

At present, there are seventeen government departments, each charged with responsibility for policy in their respective areas. In the course of operations, much data is generated and published and can be utilised by a researcher. It is also worth noting that much of this information is housed within a departmental library.

For example, the Department of Agriculture, Food and Forestry is responsible for the operation and implementation of EU schemes and regulations, the provision of grants for farm improvements, the operation of measures to improve livestock and horticultural production, the control and elimination of animal diseases, ensuring quality control in marketing and processing, and the formulation and operation of land policy. Much information pertaining to these topics can be accessed in the Department of Agriculture library.

• State-sponsored Bodies

Many Irish state-sponsored bodies have a direct impact on the business world and so are important sources of information for marketing researchers. In addition to the regular and general releases and reports of state bodies, there are a number of special industry reports and occasional studies undertaken or commissioned on their behalf. For these reasons, state bodies can be classified as shown in Figure 4.5.

Figure 4.5 Classification of Irish state bodies

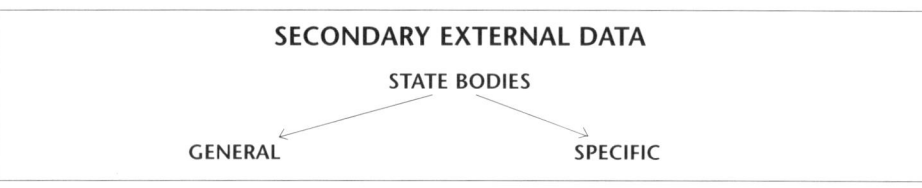

The most relevant state bodies for marketing/business purposes, Enterprise Ireland,[7, 8, 9] Bord Failte,[10, 11, 12] the IDA Ireland[13], Udaras na Gaeltachta[14] and Shannon Development[15, 16, 17] are detailed below.

Enterprise Ireland

Enterprise Ireland assists Irish firms in developing sustainable markets at home and overseas. Its market information centre contains the largest collection of market information in Ireland. It covers the Irish market, North and South, European, American, Japanese and other world markets. Enterprise Ireland can help by:

1. providing the information you need to identify market opportunities;
2. providing the knowledge and expertise you need to profit from these opportunities;
3. providing ways in which you can work together with other Irish companies to achieve a greater impact on the marketplace than you could on your own;
4. providing help to identify and evaluate the most appropriate sources of supply in Ireland (Professional Buyer Services);
5. its Market Information Centre.

Enterprise Ireland has a Market Information Centre, the largest of its type in Ireland, with extensive information on products, markets and companies in both printed and electronic sources. Types of information available include:

1. *Product and market information*: market size; trends and developments; distribution channels; country profiles and company information.
2. *Business news*: business environment; sectoral issues and developments; company activities; government programmes.

3. *Company information*: who makes what; who owns what; company profiles by sector, size and location; credit/financial reports.
4. *Trade information*: export/import procedures; documentation; tariffs and the Irish Exporters Handbook.
5. *European Union information*: one of over 200 centres in the EU providing information on legislation; funding; business co-operation and public procurement for small and medium enterprises.

All of this information is comprehensive, accurate and up-to-date. It can be accessed through the library at Sandymount in Dublin or via www.enterprise-ireland.ie. Information can be obtained from regional offices (information at this level reflects the general needs of companies in a given region). All offices are on-line to the Market Information Centre in Dublin, this houses a large marketing library which contains all marketing publications, overseas trade directories, industry directories, market statistics, specialist research reports, textbooks, booklets and information guides. Overseas offices, Europe: London, Manchester, Glasgow, Amsterdam, Berlin, Brussels, Copenhagen, Dusseldorf, Madrid, Milan, Paris, Stockholm, Budapest, Prague, Warsaw, Moscow; World: New York, Toronto, Riyadh, Tokyo, Singapore, Beijing, Hong Kong; these provide more specialist additional information, e.g. the New York office would have detailed information on North America.

Examples of reports published by Enterprise Ireland include:

Market Opportunities

- Profile of Irish Buyers of Process Equipment Services and Consumables.
- Selling to the Public Sector in Northern Ireland (Produced by Government Purchasing Service NI).
- Directory of Software Buyers in the Public Sector in Ireland — North and South.
- Directory of Key Industry Buyers in Northern Ireland.
- Directory of Industrial Product Distributors and Agents in Northern Ireland.
- Consumer Products Distribution in Ireland, North and South; Director and Development Guide.
- Supplying the Tourist Industry in Ireland.

Market Opportunities in Ireland — North and South

- Soft furnishings.
- Housewares.
- DIY/hardware.
- Toys.
- Stationery.
- Music/books.
- Sports goods.

- Leisure products.
- 'Opening the Door to New Profit'.

The Enterprise Ireland Market Information Centre is open at Merrion Hall, Sandymount, Dublin 4, from 9 a.m. to 5 p.m., Monday to Friday. Visitors require advance appointments. The centre also offers a customised enquiry service (£50 per hour). Recent enquiries include:

- Identification of potential distributors of catering equipment in Europe.
- Market information on sports goods in France.
- Duty and VAT rates on telecommunications equipment in Brazil.
- A list of major non-food retail outlets in Sweden.

Bord Failte: The Irish Tourist Board

Bord Failte's focus is to aggressively, professionally, and in close partnership with the Irish tourism industry, market the Irish tourism product world-wide. It is involved in every aspect of the promotion and development of tourism, from the procuring of tourists to the provision of plans and services. Fundamental to tourism planning is the identification of tourist requirements. Therefore, Bord Failte carries out an intensive research programme both within Ireland and in overseas markets. Following this research Bord Failte publishes various documents which may be very useful as a secondary source of information. These sources of potentially useful information are:

1. The Annual Report.
2. The Tourism Plan.
3. *Gulliver.*

The Annual Report and Accounts are published every year in the Dublin office of Bord Failte. The report contains information on:

1. Overseas tourism revenue and total revenue.
2. Tourist numbers (with a breakdown of country of origin) and regional distribution of revenue.
3. Tourism and the economy including the effects of inflation, exchange rates, etc.
4. Promotional campaigns.
5. Accommodation statistics.
6. Activities and services available for visitors.
7. Accommodation grants payments, names of recipients and amounts received.

Bord Failte's Tourism Plan is also published annually in Dublin. It outlines the marketing and development guidelines for the Irish tourism industry. The Tourism Plan gives projections for a five-year period. The principal sections of the report and the information contained in it are:

Objectives and background:
- Objective of the Irish tourism industry.
- World tourism trends.
- General assessment of the international economic situation.
- Current situation and outlook for Irish tourism.
- Summary of Aer Lingus flights to the US and Europe.
- Summary of B & I trips, numbers of passengers and cars carried.

Markets:
- Analysis of the principal markets: USA, Canada, Britain, Germany, France, Benelux, Australia, New Zealand, Northern Ireland and the home market.

Developments:
- Development of tourist resorts, parks, river and sea fishing, inland cruising and sailing, riding, water sports, historical tours, entertainment, availability of conference centres, coach tours and car rentals.

Accommodation:
- Numbers, category and capacity of hotels, guest houses, farm houses, town and country homes, youth hostels and camping sites.

Box 4.3 Examples of Bord Failte publications[18]

1. Tourism Facts and Figures (Free)

Outlines the key tourism statistics for previous year. It includes tourism performance, economic benefits, main sources markets, expenditure patterns, regional tourist numbers and revenue, and method of travel and market characteristics.

2. Marketing Intelligence Newsletter (eight issues annually, £35)

This newsletter reports developments in markets, advertising campaigns, enquiry and advance booking levels, changes in access services and tour operations and new research findings.

3. Marketing for Success (£75)

A five-part series, in modular form, is designed to build up step-by-step into a programme to assist in improving the marketing activities of a tourism business.

4. Know Your Markets (guidebooks, £25 each)

This report contains details of the motivations and experiences of overseas holidaymakers to Ireland. Topics include motivations for choosing Ireland, the holiday planning process, expectations and experiences, ratings of services and facilities in respect of quality, service and price.

5. *The Overseas Market for Seniors (£20)*

This report focuses on the size of the market, traveller characteristics and product requirements and promotional channels.

6. *The Potential for Health Tourism (£20)*

The potential for health tourism is discussed and tour operators listed.

7. *Perspectives on Irish Tourism (£10 to £20 each)*

A number of reports have been issued that summarise tourism between 1992 and 1997. The reports focus on four areas:

- Markets 1992—96.
- Regions 1993—97.
- The Product (activities and accommodation 1993—70).
- Visits to Tourist Attractions 1996.

8. *Hotel Survey 1997—98*

This is an ongoing survey of bed and room night sales throughout the country.

9. *Operational Programme for Tourism 1994—99*

This policy document, drawn up by the Department of Tourism, Recreation and Sport, describes how ERDF funding is being directed. The total funds amount to £652 million, the largest amount spent in Irish tourism ever.

10. *Developing Sustainable Tourism: Tourism Development Plan 1994—99*

This document sets out a strategy for the development of the Irish tourism product and identifies areas of opportunity. It includes highlights of the Regional Plans produced by each Regional Authority.

Gulliver is the name of the new computerised information and reservations system developed by Bord Failte. It is a vital element in Bord Failte's strategy to double tourism and achieve continued growth throughout the 1990s. *Gulliver* assists in getting information to potential customers. The information is held in a central database at Bord Failte headquarters in Dublin and is accessible throughout Ireland and internationally. The wide range of services available in the system including accommodation, places to visit, calendar of events and general information enables staff to provide a more efficient service in responding to queries. Travel agents can quickly call up information on services offered and match them to customer needs. *Gulliver* allows businesses to have information on facilities and prices updated as often as they wish. The system gives all operators in Ireland direct access to potential customers overseas.

The publications and services of Bord Failte can reduce the time needed to research a particular area quite significantly. For any new entrant to the tourism or related trade there is a comprehensive source of market information provided. From these it is possible to assess the market and the market variables. For example:

- the size the of market (in terms of revenue and numbers) can be determined from the Annual Report;
- the nature of competitors in the area and the services they offer can be easily sourced through *Gulliver*;
- current prices in the trade are also easily obtained;
- potential gaps in the market or opportunities may be spotted from the tourism plan;
- details of grants available helps the user to maximise on any assistance offered in their area;
- all promotions and events are listed in the Annual Report and this could be used to decide where a product or service is promoted;
- various companies already use such events to advertise their products, e.g. the Guinness Jazz Festival;
- the breakdown of the tourist market in the Annual Report can be used in deciding where to offer a particular service or product and to whom.

Bord Failte themselves have segmented the market by means of socio-economic groups and also by purpose of visit. Through continuous research they try to assess the optimum marketing mix for each market segment. This could provide guidelines to some businesses when planning their own marketing mix and eliminates the need for a lot of research when doing so.

The Industrial Development Agency, Ireland

The Industrial Development Agency, IDA, was established by the Irish Government to provide industrial development by attracting foreign investment into the country. The objective of the IDA is to continue to create the welcoming business environment, which has attracted over 1,000 overseas companies to set up in Ireland.

The agency has a network of fifteen international and nine regional offices, this helps them to combine the Irish strategic resources with a generous grant and tax incentive programme. It covers areas such as electronics and engineering, pharmaceuticals, healthcare and consumer products, international services and financial services.

Information provided by the IDA includes the following:

- Annual Reports — give detailed information on recent activities, regional performance, organisational resources, IDA accounts, output and exports, R & D, employment.

- Listing of manufacturing companies and financial services in each county — breakdown, by county of manufacturing companies in the region (names, addresses, types of business, numbers employed, etc.).
- Listing of manufacturing companies classified by sector — as above but by industry.
- Overseas companies in Ireland — a listing of the grant-aided overseas firms in production in the Republic of Ireland.

Údarás na Gaeltachta

Údarás na Gaeltachta is a regional development agency which addresses the specific language, social and economic needs of the Gaeltacht and its community. It places a lot of emphasis on companies improving research and development capacity and strengthening their technical and management capabilities.

The total Gaeltacht population is more than 83,000. Of a total workforce of 28,500, almost 7,500 are in full-time employment and a further 3,900 in seasonal employment in Údarás-assisted industries. The Gaeltacht comprises large parts of counties Donegal, Mayo, Galway and Kerry, all on the western seaboard, as well as smaller areas of counties Cork, Waterford and Meath.

An important aspect of An tÚdarás activities is the provision of support and assistance to Gaeltacht businesses in developing new markets, new technologies, new products and strategic relationships to increase profitability and enhance viability.

Shannon Development

Shannon Development has been Ireland's leading regional development company for more than three decades. In addition to its specific mandate, which embraces an area of some 10,000 square kilometers and a population of approximately 400,000 people, the company has been regularly charged by the Irish Government with responsibility for the pursuit of national development goals and the testing and establishment of better development models for eventual national application.[19]

The Shannon Region, within which the company operates, is comprised of counties Limerick, Clare, Tipperary North Riding, North Kerry and South West Offaly. There are 730 Irish-owned firms in the Shannon Region employing over 11,610 people. Employment is greatest in the food, engineering and electronic, and international services sectors.

Shannon Development works in close co-operation with other agencies, such as Enterprise Ireland, to ensure a comprehensive range of State services are accessed by Enterprise. Shannon Development works in partnership with trade and other interests to foster skills, develop new products, market the attractions of the region, grow business through all access routes and enhance the visitors' experience.

The company is now an integrated development agency responsible for:

- Shannon Free Zone — manufacturing and international service industry.

- Indigenous industry in the Shannon Region.
- Management and development of the National Technological Park in Limerick.
- Tourism development in the Shannon Region.
- Shannon World Aviation Park sector industries.
- Rural/local development in the Shannon Region.
- In conjunction with other agencies, promoting the Shannon Estuary as an international tourism and industrial location.

- **Directories** —look at most recent + use if certain it is most recent

Commercial directories provide profile data on companies, industries, manufacturers, organisations or individuals. They are always a good starting point in unfamiliar situations. They can be used to generate a list of company names, addresses and telephone numbers for promotional or research purposes; identify company personnel such as the finance or marketing director; to profile all manufacturers of a specific product; identify competitors; to locate companies, new outlets or new partners in a particular area.

Kompass Ireland

Kompass Ireland[20] is one of the most comprehensive sources of hard commercial information about companies and industrial products in Ireland. It provides:

- Lists of manufacturers, distributors, finance companies and other commercial organisations.
- Detailed information about a great range of products, and where they can be sourced.
- Product information to source both potential customers and suppliers.

Kompass uses an internationally recognised classification and cross-referencing system designed for detailed searches using well-defined headings. You can search companies on:

- Company name.
- Geographical areas.
- Type of business (manufacturer, exporter, etc.).
- Employee number.
- Executive role/department.
- Industry sector.
- Product sector.
- Year company founded.
- Executive name.
- Top 1,000/2,000 companies.

Similar criteria are used to locate industrial products, from process engineering equipment to computer printers. Kompass also supplies a wide range of related services for sales, marketing and product sourcing.

It is compiled in association with the Irish Business and Employers Confederation (IBEC), and the Northern Ireland Chamber of Industry and Commerce. The aim of bodies, such as IBEC, is to promote the development of business in Ireland and to ensure a favourable economic and administrative environment, which will encourage investment and enterprise — economic growth — in Ireland. The Northern Ireland Chamber of Industry and Commerce has a similar function. These industrial bodies believe that a key factor that will help businesses become competitive, is readily available access to information. It does this by providing the user with:

1. An alphabetical index of products and services.
2. An alphabetical index of companies.
3. Trade names, principles and agencies.

These profiles of Irish industry are derived from firms who supply:

1. Detailed company information including company names, addresses, telephone and fax numbers, executives, banks, office hours, share capital, date of establishment, complete product range and number of employees for 18,600 of the top Irish companies.
2. Products and services information covering 20,000 products and services and 1,000 trade names. Kompass also publishes sectoral directories on Irish industry and acts as Irish representative for other national Kompass publications, provides on-line access to European Kompass databases.

Kompass is a worldwide network of companies specialising in business-to-business information databases of products and services. This lets the user quickly pinpoint a product company from the wealth of raw data available. Users can locate precisely the suppliers of the product or component needed. It is also possible to search for companies by name or geographical location. There are Kompass directories for 29 other countries worldwide. These range from directories covering important trading countries such as Japan, to EC countries such as Belgium, France and Germany. Such a global directory is important in the Europe of a single market.

Kompass data is published as a printed book, on floppy diskettes, and on CD-Rom. The electronic products can be used to print out mailing lists or transfer data to the user's computer. Kompass on Disk comprises 18,600-plus top Irish companies in a Windows database. Users can search for companies, suppliers and products using eight criteria (e.g. location, company size, product type, industry, executive title), build mailing lists and export data to their own databases.

Kompass also publishes directories of specific industrial sectors (food, construction, engineering, electronics, computers, chemicals and pharmaceuticals etc.). Other directories include details of the top 1,000 and 2,000 firms, top finance and manufacturing firms. Products may be custom-designed for specific projects. Kompass will also help companies create their own computerised database using its information. Also available is a wide range of information on over 64 foreign countries and markets, compiled by the international Kompass network.

The information contained in the directory is also available on Minitel and there is also a European Kompass on-line (EKOL) service provided. The data is constantly up-dated and provides a source of information for directors, market research, direct mail, financial and credit companies. Access to over 300,000 major businesses is provided in just seven minutes. Virtually no training is required to use EKOL which can be accessed by the simplest personal computer.

Dun and Bradstreet's Marketing Guide to Ireland

This publication contains information on Irish firms in manufacturing, distribution and services. It has an alphabetical listing of firms within each category. Data includes names of directors, parent company where there is one, associated companies, number of employees, and telephone numbers. Importantly, this directory also includes company turnover — which others do not.

Thoms Register of American Manufacturers

Similar to the Kompass directory, Thoms provides detailed information about companies and the products offered. It is broken down into a number of volumes as follows:

- Volume 1–Volume 14: Products and services listed alphabetically. Product index included in Volume 14.
- Volume 15 and Volume 16: Company profiles listed alphabetically with addresses, zip codes, telephone numbers, branch offices, asset ratings and company officials. Brand names index included in Volume 16.
- Volume 17–Volume 23: Catalogue file bound alphabetically by company names and cross-referenced in the first sixteen volumes, inbound Traffic Guide included in Volume 23.

Thoms Commercial Directory

This lists businesses in 157 towns in Ireland. Separate classified listings are available of businesses in Cork, Galway, Limerick and Dublin as well as details of 1,300 principal private and public companies in Ireland.

MacMillan Dictionary of Marketing & Advertising

This dictionary provides concise but informative definitions for people who are exposed to marketing 'jargon' and need a clear explanation of their meaning.

Kelly's Business Directory

This is a comprehensive guide to British industry and commerce. The 1998 edition contains information on over 84,000 industrial, commercial and professional organisations in the UK. It can be used for checking names, addresses and telecommunication details and also for market research purposes.

Directory of European Industrial and Trade Associations

The *Directory* is designed to provide information on national industrial and trade associations (and, where appropriate, regional associations of national significance); it covers all the countries of Europe except Great Britain and the Irish Republic, which are covered fully by the *Directory of British Associations*.

• Trade Associations and Other Professional Bodies

Bodies that are organised to represent interests of their members on a trade and professional basis are another important source of information. Such associations publish or hold detailed information on industry sales, growth patterns, trade members and the like. Special studies relevant to the trade are conducted.

Generally speaking, trade professionals and associations publish an annual report, a regular trade journal and/or *ad hoc* research reports. These can provide the researcher with useful statistical and industry data. Some of the more relevant associations used by marketing researchers are presented below to illustrate their use in desk research. For example, in the tourism area, professional bodies include the Irish Hotel Federation, the Irish Hotel and Catering Industry (IHCI), the Irish Country Holidays, the Restaurant Association, the Hotel Sales and Marketing Association (HSMA) and the Vintners Association, to name a few.

Chamber of Commerce

The Chamber of Commerce came into effect on 16 November 1791, 'for the purpose of acquiring and disseminating useful information on the important subjects of agriculture, commerce, science and other sectors'. The Chamber of Commerce and Industry in its 200-year history has always fostered and promoted business growth and development in the interest of economic progress for the city and the region.

Most people join the Chamber in order to make contact with other business people in the city and to actively participate in the life of the business community. Members see the Chamber as a means of promoting business-to-business trade within the area and together to promote the city as a location for business — whether it be tourism, manufacturing, services, retailing, education, or culture. Services provided to members and of possible use to the researcher, encompass the following:

- In becoming part of this strong, active, local community group businesses achieve a certain credibility and recognition.

- The Chamber represents its members in matters such as rates and taxation through lobbying elected representatives and officials of the local authorities, state agencies and government or to the appropriate organisation on such matters.
- The Chamber is involved in the provision of information to individuals and groups through conferences and seminars, circulars to members, the European business centre, a trade reference library.
- The Chamber provides secretarial, fax and telex bureau services to both members and non-members.
- The Chamber is involved in promoting the source of goods and services locally.
- The Chamber establishes national and international links to keep towns in tune with developments and opportunities locally and worldwide.

The Marketing Institute of Ireland

The Marketing Institute is the representative body for the marketing profession in Ireland. The Institute represents over 5,000 marketing professionals in Ireland and abroad. It is a national organisation with regional councils in Athlone, Cork, Dundalk, Galway, Limerick, Sligo, Tralee and Waterford, and a national secretariat based in Leopardstown, Co. Dublin. The Institute is non-profit making and all income generated is spent on developing member services and the Institute's education programme.

Publications include *MII News; The Marketing Review; Programme of Events; Yearbook and Diary*, occasional publications. Marketing Institute Business Services provides a Consultants Register; Code of Practice; international affiliation with ESOMAR; European Marketing Confederation; information service; professional development in marketing — seminars and courses; in-company training.

The most effective way to keep abreast of marketing change is by attending the specialist MII seminars of the Professional Development in Marketing programme. Presented by top-calibre national and international practitioners and academics, these seminars are designed for busy professionals who need to keep abreast of developments in both theory and practice. Other services include in-company training, certification and FAS funding.

The Marketing Society of Ireland

The Marketing Society, based in Bray, provides a forum to keep marketing professionals up to date with the latest and most innovative developments in marketing and market research. The society issues and defends guidelines for marketing research practitioners. It publishes a list of Irish research firms and also represents the interests of members to state and international authorities.

• The Digital Age of Secondary Data — Databases and CD-Roms

The most dramatic development in desk research and secondary data has been the application of the computer to data collection, storage and transmission. This encapsulates CD-Roms, on-line and off-line databases, the Internet and WWW. Often referred to as the digital or new age of information, such secondary sources are transforming the world of marketing research[21].

Databases are computer-stored issues of journal articles, newspapers, and conference proceedings, trade statistics and other official publications on a wide range of topics.

Databases can be on-line or off-line. On-line refers to the fact that you connect up to computer, whereas off-line means the data is stored on a disk (CD-Rom). They can also be classified as national, international or global; full-text, numeric, statistical or abstracts. There can be a charge associated with the use of on-line databases, though many public libraries will provide access without charging. In special cases where a fee is payable, it is strongly advisable for a researcher to consult with a librarian who is familiar with the database, to minimise costs by using tightly defined search words.

It is also worth noting that many reference or sourcebooks exist, which compile lists of databases, CD-Roms and web-sites. *On-line/CD-Rom Business Sourcebook 1999* by Headland[22], *World Directory of Business Information*, 1998[23] and *The On-line Manual, A Practical Guide to Business Databases*[24] are some examples. A few of the most widely used databases include:

ABI Inform

A global business database on CD-Rom/Web covering the journal *Literature in Business and Management*. Over 800 journals are abstracted, and brief informative summaries are included.

Anbar Abstracts

A CD-Rom/Web based database covering the following six national areas: accounting and finance, information management and technology, marketing and distribution, operations and production management, personnel and training, and top management.

BOTIS

Specific on-line information on products, markets, agents, distribution, importers and promotional events worldwide.

DATA-STAR

This is Europe's largest database host. Set up in 1981, it hosts over 300 databases, but specialises in providing information about and for Europe. It is particularly good for: business information; international news; market research/comment; industry information; EC legislation; business opportunities; management; mergers and acquisitions.

Dialog

Based in Palo Alto, California, this is the world's largest data host, providing 24-hour access to over 450 databases in all subjects. Most of the on-line searches undertaken by the Library are done through Dialog. Examples of databases: Marketfull (full text of market research reports); D&B — Duns Market Identifiers; PTS International Forecasts.

Findex

Findex: The Worldwide Directory of Market Research Reports, Studies and Surveys is a reference guide to published, commercially available market and business research. It contains descriptions of consumer and industrial studies and surveys, syndicated and multi-client studies, audits and subscription research services, as well as published reports on general management and business topics. Individual reports may cover an entire industry, a specific segment of an industry, or an individual product or services of related products. Also includes full text of *Business and Finance* and other Irish publications; abstracts of business items from *Irish Times*, etc.; overviews of 2,200 companies; index to market research studies and report.

FT Profile

This is the on-line business information service provided by the *Financial Times* Group. It covers business reporting, specialist industry data, company information and market research from the UK, mainland Europe and further afield. Sources covered include: newspapers; newswires broadcasts and statements; company and industry reports; magazines and journals; reference and market research publications; opportunity notices; European Union information.

The Irish Stock Market Annual

This annual provides a window for those seeking historic performance data and other details of Irish quoted companies.

McCarthys

On-line database covering over 60 areas of industrial activity, with articles from over 70 international journals and newspapers, including articles on Irish industries and companies from *Business & Finance, Irish Times, Irish Independent* and *The Sunday Business Post*.

MAID

On-line USA/European/UK full text market research reports.

Major Companies of Europe

Volume 1 contains useful information on over 3,000 of the top companies in the European Union, excluding the UK, nearly 1,300 companies which are covered in

Volume 2. Volume 3 covers nearly 1,400 of the top companies within Western Europe but outside the EU.

Profile

Newspaper and business abstracts text retrieval system.

Spearhead

On-line information relating to the Single European Market.

TED

On-line information on public sector contract opportunities in the EC.

Textline

An on-line record of all major worldwide publications. It allows the operator to search for any reference to a person, company, market or product in any period over the last ten years.

Times Index

A monthly printed index with annual compilations to *The Times, The Sunday Times, The Times Education Supplement, The Times Scottish Educational Supplement, The Times Higher Education Supplement* and *The Times Literary Supplement*.

Tradstat

This is the most comprehensive on-line source for tracing global trade statistics. The statistics stored on Tradstat are provided by the official customs or national statistical office of each country. Countries covered include EU countries, USA, Canada, Japan, and Hong Kong.

Who Owns Whom

Who Owns Whom is designed to help anyone needing to know about company connections. Ownership of subsidiary and associate companies and how they fit into their parent groups are shown. It is available for Continental Europe; United Kingdom and Republic of Ireland.

Others

Examples of these include company accounts, case studies from business schools and stockbrokers' reports. Many of these can be accessed through Enterprise Ireland Market Information Centre or European Business Information Centres. Many of the commercial directories highlighted above are also available through databases, such as Dun & Bradstreet and European *Kompass*.

- ## The Digital Age of Secondary Data — the Internet and the World Wide Web

One of the very exciting and dramatic developments affecting marketing research is the Internet and World Wide Web, sometimes referred to as 'MRNet'.[25] The Internet is a worldwide information highway based upon information technology — a global network of computers and communication. It's a huge global electronic library that never closes and is available 24 hours a day. In effect, location and geography are suspended. Researchers from all around the world have access to the same information.

An enormous breadth and depth of information is available on a vast variety of topics, e.g. company/product information, competitive information, scientific, technological, medical and historical data. Access to business libraries, professional associations, newsgroups and marketing research sites is also possible. In fact, almost all of the sources discussed above are available on the Internet, as well as other traditional media, such as books and articles. The value of the Internet lies in its ability to combine nearly all data sources into one information source. This will continue as new sites are emerging every day and existing sites are being up-dated. Nevertheless the Internet, like all sources of information, has its limitations. It can appear disorganised on first encounter. As the old saying goes 'practice makes perfect' and there is no substitute for experience, especially when it comes to infosurfing the Net! When you do find a site of value, remember to *bookmark* it. What is now presented is a list of the established and generally useful sites, but be fully prepared to add to this yourself on a regular basis.

For a comprehensive listing of web-sites in Ireland visit *Irish Business on the Web* site (http://www.iol.ie/~aidanh/business/index.html). There is an alphabetical and category index along with a 'What's New' section. This site gives a comprehensive listing of web-sites including Forbairt, FAS, IDA, Irish Trade Board, Shannon Development and even the Revenue Commissioners!

The *Irish Trade Web* (http://www.itw.ie/itw) provides information on essential Irish statistics, Irish trade shows, Ireland's top 1,000 companies, together with a listing of other information sources.

Another site is *Marketing World* (http://www.marketing-world.com). This is an on-line marketing journal which is updated daily. It includes marketing/business news, a features section which gives a number of articles on various aspects of marketing, a directory of companies, marketing vacancies and even software (which you can download) which performs various marketing-related functions.

A good starting point for marketing information on the Internet is the *Sources of Marketing Information at Washington* page. This page gives a list of sites which contain marketing information. This list includes journals, magazines and general sites of interest and is located at the University of Washington at http://weber.u.washington.edu.

The *Internet Marketing Digest* is a bi-weekly electronic magazine, with articles on marketing and the Internet at: http:// www.i-m.com/search.html.

Mintel at www.mintel.com deals with marketing intelligence reports on industries, products and services around the world.

http://ciber.bus.msu.edu provides information on everything from world bank statistics to indices of companies on the www by country. The site also has links to a number of on-line business journals and periodicals, as well as news features and research papers.

Other useful business directories include the *Doras Directory*, a directory of Irish-related sites; *In2Ireland*, the top 101 Irish sites; and *Irish Business Masterfile*, a directory of Irish businesses on the web, searchable by county and product classification. These can be accessed through Enterprise Ireland's web-site, via the links page.

Newspapers
- *New York Times:* www.nytimes.com.
- *Wall Street Journal:* www.wsj.com.
- *London and Sunday Times:* www.the-times.co.uk.
- *Financial Times:* www.ft.com.
- *Irish Times:* www.irish-times.ie.
- *Irish Independent:* www.independent.ie.
- *Sunday Business Post:* www.sbpost.ie.

The following are links to marketing resources that are available on the World Wide Web. Many of the links that are detailed below are connected to many other places of interest to those involved in the marketing profession, including on-line publications, search facilities, commercial companies, library resources and so on.

Web-sites
- Dun & Bradstreet, Marketing Information Services: http://www.dnb.com/market/hmenu.htm.
- Nijdenrode Business School: http://www.library-nijenrode.nl.
- Yahoo Marketing Page: http://www.yahoo.com/text/Business_and_ Economy /Marketing.
- EINet Galaxy Marketing Page: http://www.galaxy.com.
- Marketing groups and associations:
  - Marketing Institute of Ireland: http://www.failte.com/mii/.
  - American Marketing Association: http://www.ama.org.
  - Marketing Science Institute: http://cism.bus.utexas.edu/ravi/marketing_science.html.
- *The Economist:* http://www.economist.com.

Searching Mechanisms

- Alta Vista: http://www.altavista.digital.com.
- Excite: http:/www.excite.com.
- SavvySearch: http://www.savvysearch.com.
- InfoSeek: http://www.infoseek.com/.
- Webcrawler: http://www.webcrawler.com/.
- Lycos: http://www.lycos.com/.
- Yahoo: http://www.yahoo.com/
- Galaxy: http://www.einet.net/galaxy.html
- Inktomi: http://www.inktomi.com
- Hotboot: http://www.hotboot.com
- Looksmart: http://www.looksmart.com
- Netscape: http://www.netscape.com
- Northern Lights: http://www.northernlight.com
- Search: http://www.search.com
- WebCrawler: http://www.webcrawler.com

• EU and European

The Statistical Office of the EU, Eurostat, publishes comparable statistics and figures for European countries. Figures are published under the following five headings:

- Directorate B — Economic statistics and economic and monetary convergence.
- Directorate C — General matters; international and inter-institutional relations; external and intra-union trade statistics.
- Directorate D — Business and energy statistics; research and development.
- Directorate E — Social and regional statistics and structural plans.
- Directorate F — Agricultural, fisheries and environmental statistics.

These figures (and other European data such as that of the OECD, UN, IMF and Council of Europe) are readily available from the CSO.

European Information Centres (EICs)

There are six European Information Centres (EICs) in Ireland. They were set up both in Ireland and throughout the European Union to improve the information flow to business sectors. They are based in and run by existing business organisations (mainly the Chamber of Commerce). There is a network of 210 centres in the Community. Access to information is freely available. Information at the centres comes under the following headings:

EU Legislation

Information is provided on directives, regulations, decisions, parliament reports, preparatory documents and opinions of EU committees.

EU Policy

This covers issues such as employment policy, social policy, competition policy, consumer policy, environment policy and tourism policy.

EU Programmes and Funding

The EIC can help with information on structural funds, community initiatives, R & D, exchange programmes, joint venture initiatives. (There is a system in place whereby Irish companies can search for joint venture partners, through the network of EIC centres.)

National Information

A selection of documents is held in the EICs such as government publications, *CSO Statistics*, *Statutory Instruments* and *Irish Business Procedures*. Publications such as *PESP* and the *Culliton Report* are also available.

Eurostat Yearbook

The *Eurostat Yearbook* is for and about Europeans. Published by Eurostat, the office for official publications of the European Communities, it compares significant features of each country of the European Union and, in turn, of other European countries, those in EFTA, the USA, Canada and Japan. For ease of comparison, all statistics in this publication are compiled in the same way or harmonised with other Eurostat publications. It covers:

1. *The people*
   Age, sex, population increases/decreases, life risks, family life, international migration, non-national citizens, education, people inside and outside the labour force, earnings and working hours, social protection, consumption and spending, housing and crime.
2. *The land and the environment*
   Population density, use of the land, emissions and pollutants, fertilisers and pesticides, waste and recycling.
3. *National income and expenditure*
   Economic growth, contribution to output by industry, consumption and spending, government receipts and spending, consumer prices and interest rates, balance of payments, trade in services, trade in goods, key figures on the labour market, research and development.
4. *Enterprises and activities in Europe*
   Agriculture, forestry, fishing, industry, manufacturing, construction, energy, water services, transport and tourism.

5. *The European Union*
   Institutions, budgets, the euro, the internal economy, the European market and external trade.

Eurostat — Basic Statistics of the European Union

This booklet compares the major aspects of all EU member states, other European countries, the USA, Canada, Japan and the CIS. The thirty-third edition contains for the first time, data from Cestat, Central Europe Co-operation in Statistics, covering the Czech Republic, Slovakia, Poland and Hungary. Topics include: general statistics; economy and finance; population and social conditions; energy and industry, agriculture, forestry and fisheries; foreign trade; services and transport and the environment.

Eurostat — A World Directory of Marketing Information Sources

Comprehensive global information on official sources of publication, major business information libraries, leading market research companies, on-line databases etc.

Organisation for Economic Co-operation and Development

OECD compiles data relating to Ireland, together with comparable figures for other countries. For example, 'Monthly Statistics of Foreign Trade', 'Energy Prices' and 'Financial Market Trade'. Irish firms exporting to other countries generally use this type of data.

Eurobarometer, Public Opinion in the EU

Eurobarometer public opinion surveys have been conducted on behalf of the Directorate-General for information, communication, culture and audio-visual of the European commission each spring and autumn since 1985. The Eurobarometer report includes:

- How Europeans feel about public life at the end of this millennium.
- People's expectations of the near future.
- Level of perceived knowledge about the EU.
- Level of awareness of current EU affairs.
- Public assessment of media coverage of EU offices.
- Support for the EU and its policies.
- Single currency, the euro and employment.
- Attitudes to enlargement and CAP.
- Attitudes towards the European Parliament.
- Attitudes towards people from outside the EU.
- Holiday destinations.

Euromonitor

A business information publisher providing over 200 off-the-shelf research reports annually, focusing upon fast-moving consumer goods worldwide. Areas covered: alcoholic and soft drinks; automotives; catering and vending; clothing and footwear; consumer electronics; cosmetics and toiletries; disposable paper products; domestic electrical appliances; food; healthcare; household cleaning; household products; leisure and lifestyles; publishing; packaging; personal finance; retailing; tobacco; and travel and tourism.

EIU, The Economist Intelligence Unit

The EIU produces forecasts of the political, economic and business environment in over 180 countries, as well as a range of reports on strategic industries and the latest management thinking.

- **Syndicated Services**

Some data is collected on a regular basis and sold by specialised firms on a subscription basis to manufacturers. Such data is known as syndicated data and is produced for the needs of a number of users. For example, confectionery manufacturers in Ireland buy industry data about product size, weight, price and promotions on a monthly basis to monitor competitive actions. Data supplied on a syndicated basis is generally about:

1. Product flows through wholesalers, known as wholesalers' audits.
2. Product flows through retailers, referred to as retail audits.
3. The effect of the marketing mix on the consumer, called panel data.
4. The number of people reading, listening or watching different media sources, labelled media data.

It is worth noting at this point that most researchers do not classify syndicated services as secondary data — however, given the small size of syndicated services in Ireland, relative to other European countries, such as the UK, Germany, France and the USA, we present syndicated services under the heading of secondary data. The best known in Ireland is AC Nielsen[26] for retail data and the JNRR[27] for media data, much of which can be accessed through reports in libraries. These are now discussed.

AC Nielsen

AC Nielsen Retail Measurement Services capture point-of-sale and causal information from all retail channels, highlighting incremental changes in market dynamics. Utilising both in-store scanning of universal product codes (UPCs) and store visits by professional auditors, AC Nielsen offers a complete portfolio of sample- and census-based information services[28].

AC Nielsen tracks measures including descriptive characteristics (e.g. flavour and size), sales volume, selling price, and observed promotion and merchandising execution, encompassing an organisation's own brands as well as competitive brands. This helps management gauge penetration among retailers, overall product performance, promotion effectiveness and more, supporting long-term strategic planning as well as tactical decision-making.

Maintaining a large-household consumer panel, AC Nielsen provides insights into consumer purchase behaviour across every outlet — from warehouse clubs to convenience stores, supermarkets to independent chemists and mass merchandisers to bookshops. Such consumer panel information helps organisations identify target audiences and quantify the impact of advertising and other promotional initiatives.

With panellists carefully selected and geographically dispersed, the AC Nielsen consumer panel is a demographically balanced representation of Ireland's population. Readable at national, regional, local-market and account levels, AC Nielsen represents an excellent source for understanding the link between product purchase/shopping behaviour and the varied consumer segments across the population. AC Nielsen covers the following industries: food; personal and household products; durables; services and commercial/industrial.

AC Nielsen also provide a Virtual Store on the Internet that provides a graphical means of locating relevant information. By clicking on departments and then categories, information can be accessed for millions of products. The web-site is located at http://acnielsen.com. Some sections of the virtual store include: dry grocery, alcoholic beverages, frozen foods, and health and beauty aids.

Joint National Readership Research (JNRR)

This research is conducted and published by Lansdowne Market Research, twice a year. JNRR publications provide information on who reads what and also contain a 'Special Interest Group' section. They also provide some very relevant lifestyle questions. Topics covered in JNRR include: books; business decision involvement; central heating; clothing; confectionery; department/major store; drinks; farming; finance; food items; grocery shopping; holiday/short breaks; home improvements; home purchases; household items and products; leisure activities; lifestyle; motoring; pet ownership; property; sports and activities; sports wear and equipment; telecommunications; tobacco; toiletries; and transport. Media measured includes Irish national newspapers, magazines and cinema attendance.

In order to enhance the amount of information collected on the Joint National Readership Research, this year's study included a 'Lifestyle' section. The objective of this lifestyle analysis was to look beyond basic demographics, using people's attitudes as a means of targeting different groups within the population.

Special interest groups: JNRR surveys provide a substantial amount of information regarding product and service information. In total, 450 different categories were covered — up from 210 last year. Some of these topics include:

- *Expenditure*: This includes questions covering expenditure on products and services. The survey covers some 80 items purchased recently for the home and establishes how much people have spent on their purchases for the home in the past three years.
- *Leisure activities*: The JNRR questionnaire asks about a large number of leisure activities, covering everything from eating in fast-food restaurants to visiting ploughing championships. It identifies different levels of involvement, detailing weekly, monthly, three-monthly and less often for each activity. This section on leisure also includes book purchasing and reading. It also deals with involvement in sports, covering 38 different sports/activities, and collects information on the following levels of participation:
  - Play or do.
  - Watch on TV.
  - Read in a newspaper.
  - Play or watch as a spectator.

  Purchasing of sportswear and sports equipment in the past year is also included in this section.
- *Motoring*: This section contains information on the makes of car motorists have bought in the past three years and the price ranges in which they buy their new or second-hand cars. The survey also provides information on car ownership — annual mileage, membership of motoring organisations and insurance coverage, the type of car people own (two- or four-door saloon, hatchback, etc.), as well as the engine size. The survey continues to look forward to identifying the types of car people plan to buy in the near future.
- *Wine*: This section monitors trends in the consumption of wine.

Other syndicated media data sources range from the Joint National Listenship Research (JNLR, undertaken twice annually by MRBI) to Poster Advertising Research (by IMS), and Business Readership Research (also by IMS).

Marketing Research Uses

Syndicated data such as that outlined above provides the researcher with the ability to: track sales performance; monitor price changes; manage distribution; analyse promotion execution and impact; and evaluate new item success. It pinpoints opportunities and trends, enabling researchers and managers to identify and capture new markets and product niches. Such valuable data assists the researcher in determining *who* buys *what*, *how much* they buy and *where* they shop. Additionally, advanced analytical and forecasting tools, based upon the data, can allow the researcher to provide insights into marketplace activities. In summary, syndicated data is well suited to both qualitative and quantitative research.

• **Grey Material**

There is a virtually endless array of books, leaflets, dissertations, newspapers and magazines that contain information relevant to marketing decisions. Grey material is so called as it tends to be a collection of miscellaneous printed items. An exhaustive attempt to list or describe these sources is beyond the scope of this section, though some of the more useful material includes:

IPA Administration Yearbook and Diary

The directory part of this publication is widely regarded as the most comprehensive source of information on Irish life.[29]

Because this publication is so all-embracing it is worthwhile spending some time looking through the contents pages, the different chapters and the index to get an idea of its scope.

Examples of sections likely to be of direct use to marketing people are those on communications — containing listings of all newspapers (both national and provincial), advertising agencies, market research companies, etc. — and statistics, which contains figures for agriculture, trade, industry, etc.

Examples of some, perhaps less obvious, uses of the directory are the ways it can be used to access sectoral data which leads us to the role of other types of yearbooks.

Checkout Magazine

Checkout Magazine provides information on the food trade in Ireland and is issued to food and associated manufacturers, suppliers and distributors, multiple outlets, wholesalers, cash and carrys, group and independent grocery stores.

The publishers of this magazine produce an annual *Checkout — Yearbook and Buyer's Guide*. Typical material from this is a comprehensive analysis of Ireland's major food and drink categories, critical forces shaping the future of European retailing, and detailed data on individual companies, listing such things as main products, brand names and relevant management contacts.

MAPS

Another yearbook is the *MAPS Directory* produced by the Association of Advertisers in Ireland. Primarily aimed at users of advertising services, this volume also details a wide variety of business and consumer publications which, in turn, can point to further sources of data for the marketer wishing to target customers in that segment.

In summary, trade publications, especially yearbooks, are an invaluable source of marketing information for those sectors that they serve.

The Irish Consumer Market

This is a guidebook for marketing professionals, written by Professor Mary Lambkin for the Marketing Society. It deals with: demographics, providing basic statistics on the current size and composition of the Irish market and likely future trends; sociocultural factors, which are the fundamental characteristics that distinguish this market from those of other countries; consumer spending, saving and credit, which influence the performance of all businesses operating in this country; Irish consumers' lifestyles which have and will continue to have a pervasive influence on the development of many significant markets; and changes in the marketing environment, including retailing and distribution, advertising, promotion and market research, with an emphasis on international trends that are and will continue to affect the practice of marketing in Ireland.

Professional marketing managers and market researchers will be familiar with much of the material already but they will find it helpful to have it organised in a compendium of this type for easy reference. Entrepreneurs developing business plans or grant applications, and small businesses wishing to extend their market knowledge should find it a helpful starting point and a good source of references for further investigation. It is also valuable for marketing students in supplying a solid base of local market knowledge to supplement the principles provided in international texts.

A Profile of the Irish Market

In a similar vein is *A Profile of the Irish Market*, written by Edel Foley, DIT and published by the Marketing Institute of Ireland. It gathers together all relevant information about the Irish market. There are twelve chapters covering topics such as the Region: Geography and Population; Communications and Transport; Social Statistics and Social Attitudes; Employment and Earnings; Production and Output; Household Expenditure; Shopping and the Distribution System; Lifestyles; International Trade; Marketing and Media; Doing Business in Ireland; and References.

The Irish Market: Facts and Figures, Wilson & Hartnell

Wilson Hartnell Advertising[30] produces *The Irish Market: Facts and Figures* on an annual basis. This free booklet, as well as giving statistics on advertising, also has information on population, employment, income, savings, consumer, retail, grocery and foreign trade statistics.

It draws on a wide range of sources, providing commentary on the facts and subjects it covers in its 28 pages. Its primary focus is the Republic of Ireland, while presenting a summary comparison with a number of countries in relation to population, employment, and key economic indicators. Northern Ireland is covered in a section of its own.

Media Facts

Another free booklet is McConnell's *Media Facts*.[31] Of use to all marketing people, it provides a summary of the relevant advertising statistics for Ireland, such as who reads which newspapers.

Business Information Centre, Central Library, Ilac Centre

In addition to the standard Irish business reference sources (*Kompass*, Dun & Bradstreet, MAPS), the Centre has a vast range of information on Irish companies or Irish subsidiaries of international companies. The national newspapers and the *Financial Times* are searched daily for any mention of Irish companies, markets or economic sectors (advertising, agriculture, banking, etc.). The Library receives many specialised directories.

Over 300 magazines and newspapers are received in the Library. There is an index of all Irish magazines for company and sectoral information. Many of these magazines are not indexed elsewhere and they often contain very valuable information on less well-known companies. The computerised index (DPLNET) can be searched in the Library or through Minitel. For example, the database could be searched for market surveys on breakfast cereals excluding Kelloggs, or for information on Aer Lingus and Air Cargo etc.

Information on the Business Environment

For information on the business environment in other countries there is a comprehensive range of international trade directories as well as telephone directories covering most countries. These directories are backed up by newspaper cuttings on each country. There is also the Extel Workstation (up-to-date financial information on companies quoted on all stock exchanges).

There is a range of national and international statistics (CSO, OECD, UN, EC) as well as a range of Irish Government publications, legislation and Dail reports. All areas of local and national government are covered in clipping files and the DPLNET.

Of particular interest to those working in marketing may be the extensive personality files going back twenty years. Included are articles which appear in the national newspapers on Irish people from all walks of life. Biographical information can be found there on some of those who didn't make it into *Who's Who* in Ireland. Services can be summarised as follows:

Irish Companies and Business Associations
- Trade directories (*Kompass*, Thoms, Dun & Bradstreet).
- DPLNET — Dublin Public Libraries' computerised index to business magazines which can be searched by company, subject-specific product. Also available on Minitel.
- Irish stock prices on Aertel.

Government Information
- Government publications, legislation, Dail Debates and Reports.
- Newspaper cutting files.
- Statistics.

- Bookstock — politics, administration and government.
- National Economic & Social Council and Economic and Social Research Institute publications.

International Links

- Telephone and trade directories for UK, Europe and the world (US Yellow Pages on computer).
- Computerised database — covers 47 international stock exchanges (Extel).
- Statistics.
- Yearbooks.
- Abstracts — information files.
- Maps and atlases.

While this concludes our discussion of 'grey material' and 'secondary data', remember that there are numerous more sources of potential use to a researcher, so be prepared to develop your own list and up-date it on a regular basis.

• Summary

Data collection begins with secondary data. Secondary data is data collected by another person for another reason. It is the opposite of primary data. Secondary data tends to be inexpensive, easy to access but may not be accurate or timely.

The two major types of secondary data are internal and external. Internal data is already in existence within the firm. It is typified by accounts, customer profiles, or sales reports. It may come in a form that lends itself to immediate use or it may need modification.

External data is data already in existence outside the firm. It encompasses government statistics (CSO), government information from the various departments, public and state bodies, trade associations and professional organisations, commercial directories, syndicated retail and media data, databases and CD-Roms, the Internet, EU and miscellaneous sources.

The most important development in recent years has been the computerisation of information, via CD-Roms, on-line databases and the Internet. This has given rise to the digital or new age of secondary data. The effect of the information age is twofold. First, organisations can make information more readily, easily and cheaply available by using the Internet as an alternative distribution mode. Second, the digital age has given birth to new information sources in their own right. These constitute a new category of secondary data.

Regardless of the source or type of secondary data pursued, the most important aspect of desk research is to be thorough, exhaustive and diligent. Remember, secondary data should always be completed before engaging in any primary research.

Questions

1. What is desk research?
2. What is the difference between primary and secondary data?
3. Secondary data has been called the 'first line of attack' for marketing researchers. Discuss this description.
4. What role do secondary sources of data play in the research process?
5. What criteria can be employed to judge the accuracy of secondary data?
6. What are some of the advantages and disadvantages of secondary data relative to primary data for a marketing research study?
7. Differentiate between internal and external secondary data. Which should be analysed first, and why?
8. How might internal data be helpful to the researcher?
9. What kind of data can be gathered through CD-Roms?
10. What are the main secondary information sources available in the Republic of Ireland? Outline the different types and give examples of each.
11. What is meant by a 'syndicated source'?
12. What types of data are available from syndicated data sources?
13. What is a computerised database? What use has it regarding secondary data?
14. Why is it desirable to use multiple sources of secondary data?
15. Describe three different methods research suppliers can use to collect syndicated data. Which do you consider to be most reliable?

Problems and Assignments

1. List some major sources of information for the following situations:
   (a) The marketing research manager of a national food chain has to prepare a comprehensive report on the fast-food industry.
   (b) Mr Murphy has several ideas for instant soda bread mixes and is considering entering this industry. He needs to find the necessary background information to assess its potential.
   (c) The current market size and profile for the Irish Alginate Market.
2. Select a company of interest to you and develop a competitive profile for that firm, indicating the source for each piece of data used.
3. Select an industry of your choice. Using secondary sources, obtain industry sales and the sales for the major firms in that industry for the past year. Estimate the market shares for each major firm. From another source, obtain information on the market shares for these same firms. Do the two estimates agree?
4. List the various sources of published secondary data in Ireland released by the CSO within the past year. Use a library and the Internet to identify this information.

5. What secondary sources in Ireland might be sourced to find information on the following:
   (a) Information on tourist numbers for Waterford county for last year.
   (b) Information on the importation of a certain product to Ireland from Spain.
   (c) Information on a certain company in your county.
   (d) Information on demographic profiles of the Irish population.
   (e) The amount of expenditure on a certain product/service in the past year.
6. Obtain data on beer consumption in your county for the latest available year. Calculate the *per capita* consumption for this area and compare to that for the country as a whole. What accounts for the difference?
7. What would be the best source for the following data:
   (a) Birth rates in your county.
   (b) Attendance figures for Lansdowne Road Stadium last year.
   (c) Annual sales in the top three fast-food chains in Ireland.
   (d) Median weekly earnings of full-time, salaried workers for the last three years.
   (e) Trends in automobile ownership.
   (f) Brands of laptop computers recently introduced to the Irish market.
8. You are opening a new retail store that will sell personal computers and software. What secondary data are available in your area to aid you in deciding where to locate the store? Would the same data be relevant to someone opening a convenience copying centre?
9. Use the Internet to see if you can find information to answer the following questions:
   (a) What is today's weather like in New York?
   (b) Is there information about China and its population demographics?
10. Suppose you are doing a project for Aer Lingus. Identify, from secondary sources, the attributes of factors passengers consider when selecting an airline.

Case Study
Foinse
The Challenge of Marketing an Irish Language Newspaper

Background to Foinse's Conception

Foinse, founded in October 1996, was the new Irish language newspaper that had come into publication after Anois had ceased operations in June 1996. *Foinse* is the first national weekend paper to be produced outside of Dublin. The paper's production takes place in Spiddal, Co. Galway, and with the benefit of ISDN lines, data is transmitted to Dublin for printing. The main motivation for its foundation was to create a newsworthy vehicle through the Irish language. *Foinse* aims to be well integrated into the local community, while presenting a national perspective through the contribution of journalists from all over the country. The intention is to appeal to a wide audience by targeting the 25,000 people who are interested in things Irish. Furthermore, the paper is designed to bring the Irish language to the common person by using Irish which is clear, simple, accurate and grammatically correct.

Foinse's main objectives are to: become a profitable enterprise given a competitive industry; provide a newsworthy vehicle through the Irish language; enhance the general use and understanding of the Irish language; enhance interest in the Irish culture; and appeal to a wide market at various levels, e.g. core of dedicated users of the Irish language; students learning Irish in secondary level and third-level institutions; adults interested in improving their Irish language capability etc.

Competition Within the Irish Newspaper Industry

Despite being what some may consider a specialised paper for a niche market, *Foinse* still competes with all other newspapers for readership and circulation figures. Ireland, in particular, has a varied and widely read press, from *The Irish Times* to the popular tabloid *Star*. The Irish people are avid and consistent newspaper readers. For example, it is not uncommon for people to purchase several newspapers on a Sunday. Thus, it is not surprising that Ireland is believed to have among the highest newspaper readership rates (as a proportion of population) within the EU.

In Ireland, people not only have a choice of a range of Irish titles, they also have the full range of English-based titles. Currently, there are six national and five imported dailies; and four national and seven imported Sunday papers. In addition, there is a variety of provincial papers. The price of newspapers ranges from 20p to 50p for the provincial papers; from 45p to 85p for dailies; and up to £1 for the Sunday editions.

The daily newspaper market is dominated by *The Irish Independent*, with 22% of the morning market, followed by the *Star* with 13%, and *The Irish Times* with 11% of readership. The Sunday newspaper market is dominated by *The Sunday Independent* with 40% of the market, followed by the *Sunday World* with 37%, and the imported *News of the World* with 15% of Sunday readership.

Overall circulation figures for the indigenous Irish press appear to have declined in the period 1990 to 1996. This decline may be attributed, in part, to increased competition within the Irish newspaper industry, due to the considerable presence of the British press.

Foinse's Format, Price and Distribution

Foinse is a tabloid format with marked use of colour printing. In fact, twelve of its 28 pages are printed in colour, a rate which is comparable with that of magazines. It is available for purchase in the shops on Saturdays and retails for 75p per paper; a price point which is slightly below that of other weekend papers available on Sundays. Most newspapers, given that they are published daily, have a one-day shelf life. However being a weekend paper, *Foinse* may be able to enjoy a shelf life which extends to more than one day.

Foinse is distributed throughout the country via a prominent, national distributor, Newspread, a firm in the Independent Group. In this respect, its distribution channel is similar to any other national paper, thus affording *Foinse* the same potential for market exposure. However, while there are over 8,000 shops that sell newspapers in the Republic, *Foinse* is only actively sold through about 1,400 of these shops. The rationale being that many of *Foinse*'s potential core market (i.e. those with a dedicated interest in the Irish language) are composed of a small number of readers across a wide geographical spread.

Currently, *Foinse* prints about 9,000 copies of the paper per week; 6,000 to 6,500 of which are typically sold. It appears that sales have settled around 6,000 copies per week. *Foinse*'s objective is to achieve sales of 7,500 copies per week by the end of the first year, 10,000 at the end of the second year, and 20,000 at the end of the fifth year in operation. Eventually, the idea may be to expand *Foinse*'s exposure and distribution to the Internet.

However, despite *Foinse*'s level of sales, it is worthy to note that Pádraig Ó Céidigh, *Foinse*'s managing director, has estimated current readership levels to be higher at around 25,000 persons. This indicates that for every paper bought, there are an additional four or five people reading the paper. Newspapers do not typically have such a large pass-along audience; the average readership for most newspapers is 2.8 people per copy. Even though *Foinse* could be considered a specialist paper, this level still seems particularly high. However, Ó Céidigh believes *Foinse* is extensively used as a teaching tool in secondary, third-level, and adult Irish language classes. In these classes the teacher buys one copy of *Foinse* and photocopies relevant sections for the class in question. However, Ó Céidigh has not yet conducted a readership survey, and in this respect his estimates cannot be accurately substantiated.

Objectives and Opportunities

Foinse is seeking to establish its presence as a credible national newspaper that addresses a wide readership base. The issues with respect to such a venture relate to the: identification, profile and size of various target market segments; evolution of the paper as a product which appeals to identified segments; development of a positioning strategy relative to competition; and development of a marketing strategy which will facilitate profitability.

Foinse's most pressing information requirements relate to segmentation of the market, as the achievement of subsequent objectives are dependent on the segments *Foinse* chooses to target. Once the target markets are identified and profiled, decisions regarding product development, positioning and strategy can be made. To date, *Foinse* has conducted little or no research regarding the marketplace, its readers and the competition.

Data and Information Needs

1. Given *Foinse*'s objectives, list the type of information that *Foinse* requires to achieve its objectives. How would you prioritise the items you have listed?
2. How would you suggest *Foinse* could obtain this data/information? List the secondary sources to which *Foinse* should refer before conducting any primary research.
3. What kind of (quantitative) analysis, if any, can be drawn from the information sources you have identified?
4. What information gaps exist, if any? How would you suggest *Foinse* obtain this data/information?

*This case was prepared by Ann M. Torres, National University of Ireland, Galway. It is intended to be used as a basis for class discussion rather than to illustrate either effective or ineffective handling of a business situation. The case is based on a real-life situation, but some figures may have been disguised.

Case Study
Thornton Readymix*

John Thornton was the owner and Managing Director of Thornton Readymix, which, as its name implies, was a supplier of readymix concrete within a radius of about twenty miles from his base in the west of Ireland. He was the only supplier of readymix in the area and was largely shielded from competition by the rugged nature of the terrain, except at the fringes of his area where he faced some competition from suppliers in neighbouring districts.

Readymix concrete cannot be transported more than twenty miles economically, as the value of a load at £250/£350 could not sustain the cost of transport to and from the customer's site.

For some time, John had been contemplating entering the market for concrete blocks. He had good knowledge of the economics of block production and distribution, but was totally unsure of the size of the market. Clearly, he needed some estimate of the volumes he could expect to sell if he was to enter that market.

The Market for Concrete Products

Readymix concrete consisted of sand, aggregate (stone chips), cement and water. The ingredients, in defined quantities, depending on the strength of concrete required, were loaded from silos into a truck-mounted mixer. They were constantly mixed *en route* to their destination to ensure a uniform standard of product and to prevent premature setting of the concrete. Readymix was normally delivered and invoiced to the customer in cubic metres.

Concrete blocks could be seen as complementary products for several reasons. They used the same ingredients, albeit with different configurations. Customers for concrete were also likely to be customers for blocks. Concrete was used for foundations, floors and driveways, blocks for wall construction. While different types of blocks were available, the standard block used in construction in Thornton's local area was a solid block 18 inches by 9 inches by 4 inches. These were normally laid to create a double skin with a layer of insulation between the two sets of blocks.

There were several ways of producing blocks, which varied in accordance with the volume produced. Thornton knew that he would be at the lower end of the scale of quantity produced. This would mean using his existing silos and loading the ingredients into a block-making plant. He had purchased such a plant relatively cheaply and had laid out a large concrete flat surface area. Blocks were produced in the plant and laid out on the flat surface in rows to dry. When dry, they were stacked ready for delivery.

Thornton had done his sums on the proposed new project. He knew the price of blocks from phone calls to the nearest suppliers, both of whom were more than twenty miles away. The price for blocks, delivered to site, was £300 per thousand, excluding VAT. Thornton estimated that the new project needed a turnover of about £300,000 per annum to generate a reasonable return. At £250,000 turnover per annum, the project would break even.

The Problem

'The very man' said Thornton, as he spotted Dave McCarthy striding purposefully towards the bar in his local pub one evening. 'I saw your photo in the local paper recently, something to do with marketing, and I need an expert in marketing to solve a problem for me.'

'Yes,' replied McCarthy, 'for my sins, I am the new Regional Chairman of the Marketing Institute and we launched our new programme last week.'

'Right,' continued Thornton, 'my problem is simple. I have been looking at expanding into concrete blocks. I would need to sell about 750,000 blocks per year to break even and one million blocks to make a reasonable profit, but I have no idea of the size of the market for blocks in this area.'

McCarthy thought for a few moments. 'How much readymix do you sell in a year and is there any correlation between sales of readymix and blocks?'

'It varies,' said Thornton, 'in a normal year I would sell 5,000 cubic metres. However, if there is a large project such as the new pier in the harbour, the runway extension or the big new factory up on the industrial estate, sales can go as high as 10,000 cubic metres in a very good year. And no, there is no correlation, as far as I can see, between the sale of readymix and blocks. For example, we lay a lot of driveways where no blocks are involved and if we have to lay a heavy-duty factory floor, the volume of blocks would be small.'

'OK, so that is one theory shot down. Let us approach it from a different angle. What is the main use of blocks in this area?'

'That's easy,' replied Thornton, 'house construction would account for the bulk of the business.'

'How many blocks are used to build the typical house?' asked McCarthy.

'Around 4,000 is standard' replied Thornton.

'And what about other uses?'

'House extensions, retail outlets, factories and other commercial premises would use most of the rest, and they are not major users. For example, that new factory extension which you built last year was about 10,000 sq. ft. wasn't it?"

'Yes,' said McCarthy, 'it is about 50 feet wide by 200 feet in length with a double skin of blocks 10 feet high. From 10 feet up it is metal cladded.'

'So that leaves you with two walls 200 feet by 10 feet and two walls 50 feet by 10 feet, both multiplied by two for the double skin. I am ignoring openings and internal walls which probably cancel each other out. Given that a block is 18 inches by 9 inches or 1.125 square feet; that suggests a total of about 9,000 blocks.'

'OK,' replied McCarthy, 'that seems reasonable. So based on your experience, what proportion of blocks might be accounted for by house construction and what proportion by other uses?'

'I would say that the proportion is 3:1 in favour of house construction,' said Thornton, after a brief pause.

'OK, leave it with me and I will contact you in the morning. Now how about a pint, market research is thirsty work.'

The Answer?

The following morning Thornton received the following fax.

John — A phone call to the Central Statistics Office (CSO) produced the information that 1,047 houses were built in this county last year. That figure is 5% up on the previous year, having been steady at about 1,000 units built for the past several years. Your catchment area accounts for almost exactly 33% of the county's population assuming you cannot sell blocks outside a twenty-mile radius. This is also based on CSO district population figures.

It seems to me reasonable to assume that the level of house building in this part of the country is, at least, as high as in the rest of the county. While you have no competitor manufacturing blocks in your catchment area, blocks are coming in mostly, I assume, from O'Reilly to the north and Greeley to the south, both about 30 miles away. I hope this information is of some help in reaching a decision.

Regards, Dave

Questions

1. Estimate the total market for blocks in Thornton's area.
2. What other factors should he take into account in deciding whether or not to enter the block manufacturing business?
3. What, in your view, is Thornton's best course of action?

*This case was written by Gerry Mortimer, Dublin Institute of Technology. It is intended to be used as a basis for class discussion rather than to illustrate either effective or ineffective handling of an administrative situation. The case is based on a real situation, though certain information has been disguised. © Gerry Mortimer, Dublin Institute of Technology.

Chapter 5

FOCUS GROUPS, IN-DEPTH INTERVIEWS AND PROJECTIVE TECHNIQUES

- **Chapter Overview**
- Introduction • Focus Groups • Types of Focus Groups • Planning and Conducting Focus Groups • Selecting the Moderator • Moderator Discussion Guide • Advantages and Disadvantages of Focus Groups • In-depth Interviews • Projective Techniques • Types of Projective Techniques • Advantages and Disadvantages of Projective Techniques • Summary

Introduction

In Chapter 3, the distinction was made between exploratory research and other research designs. It was pointed out that exploratory research was one way of generating qualitative data. While it is fair to say that exploratory research is carried out to collect information in order to provide insights into the management problem and to identify courses of action, it is also true to say that exploratory research is, on its own, capable of answering the research problem. Remember, the concept 'qualitative' refers to data collection methods that generate soft or attitudinal type data. Qualitative data collection methods can be used for either exploratory or descriptive research purposes as detailed in Chapter 3. In practice, most researchers use the term 'qualitative research' to denote qualitative data collection methods.

Qualitative research can be defined as the collection of data which is open to interpretation, for instance on attitudes and opinions, and which might not be validated statistically.[1] It produces what is frequently referred to as 'soft data'. Qualitative research does not provide statistical answers. The purpose is to assess the minds of consumers to discover their impressions, expectations and prejudices. Qualitative research is predominantly a diagnostic tool to find out what the issues are and what respondents feel about them. You cannot do qualitative research and then try to pour quantitative results out of it.[2]

Extensive qualitative research convinced Murphy Brewery in Cork that the brand's traditional burgundy coloured livery and counter mounts were too conservative, and did not appeal to drinkers in the important 18 to 25 age category. Murphy has now adopted a cream and black livery for all of its stout products.[3]

Qualitative research conducted by Green Isle, who produce Goodfella's pizzas, showed emotional aspects of fun, freedom, social and a cosmopolitan outlook associated with pizzas.[4]

Qualitative research is generally applied in customer satisfaction research, service quality research, and customer complaint analysis. Irish Distillers spent three years and £500,000 on researching their new Polo drink. Part of the research included qualitative product test studies. Among the nuggets of information the research threw up was that the young adults didn't want a long bottle, they were fussy on price and they believed they were already being bombarded by too many other products.[5] The principal factor which has led to the growth in qualitative research in Ireland is probably recognition of increased consumer sophistication leading to a much greater concentration on finding out *why* people do things (or don't) as distinct from *what* they do.[6]

In summary, applications of qualitative research include:

- generating ideas on new product development, packaging, design, strategy, branding or image;
- examination of advertising strategy, execution and pre-testing;
- exploring the purchasing decision-making process;
- as an exploratory study before quantitative research;
- after a quantitative study to add depth to issues.

Phelim O'Leary, a specialist in this area, has documented the development of qualitative research, and points out that qualitative research has developed from a fringe area of marketing to a widely used and sophisticated set of procedures.[7] He goes on to say:

> Throughout the past decade there has been a consistent growth in the volume of qualitative market research conducted in Europe. At home this has been driven by Irish companies which have a consumer marketing focus and more recently has been added to by a widening range of organisations and institutions somewhat outside the classical marketing field; this would include government agencies, voluntary charitable groups, schools, political parties and the churches . . . A renewed, and welcome, emphasis is the more frequent collaboration of qualitative research with quantitative methods in the pursuit of solutions and valuable market intelligence.

In this chapter we examine three qualitative research methods, namely focus groups, in-depth interviews and projective techniques. By the end of the chapter, you will be able to:

1. describe qualitative research;
2. examine the main qualitative research tools;
3. discuss the growing role of focus groups;
4. outline in-depth interviews;
5. explain projective techniques.

• Focus Groups

Focus groups had their beginnings in group therapy used by psychiatrists. A focus group consists of eight to twelve participants who are led by a moderator in an in-depth discussion on a particular topic or concept. The main purpose of the focus group is to gain insights by listening to a group of people from the appropriate target market. The group is generally selected so as to include people who have common backgrounds or experience regarding the topic at hand, e.g. householders who burn solid fuel or recent purchasers of life insurance. The objective of focus group research is to learn and understand what people have to say and why. Focus group sessions are used to explore and define the attributes and issues in customer terms.[8] The emphasis is on getting people to talk at length and in detail about the topic in question and provide discussion and debate, and hence new ideas.

Focus groups are useful in exploratory research where the goal is to develop ideas and insights before proceeding toward further investigation into the topic of interest. Before you even start working on a survey, Gerry Grehan of BOI advises organising some customer focus groups to identify what are the key issues for customers.[9] But this group interviewing approach can also be of more immediate value — for example, in identifying problems associated with existing products, in evaluating the attractiveness of new alternative products and their features, in probing the effectiveness of advertising and in determining customer attitudes, perceptions and behavioural patterns. Focus groups are widely used to consider the potential of alternative brand names.[10] One company carried out consumer focus groups to check reaction to the brand name but not to construct the name itself.[11] Green Isle Food Group used focus group research to monitor consumer response to its Goodfella's pizza TV advert depicting an Italian wedding scene.[12] Superquinn is a well-documented organisation that makes extensive use of focus group research on a regular basis to monitor customer perceptions of services offered. Bord Failte conducted seventeen focus groups around the world, which showed a low recognition factor of the shamrock.[13] Guardian Direct use focus groups with employees to help with decision-making.[14] Prior to launching its 'Big Pint' strategy, Guinness conducted 60 focus groups using skilled consumer psychologists. From this, and other research, it became apparent that Guinness needed to be lowered from a pedestal upon which many drinkers placed it and it had to be given a more accessible image.[15] Recently, focus groups have become popular in industrial organisations, government and even academia. Colleges now use focus groups to help them develop marketing plans.[16]

The value of the technique lies in the unexpected findings often obtained from a free-flowing group discussion.

In summary the main objectives of focus groups are:

1. to generate ideas;
2. to better understand customer language;

3. to uncover customer needs, attitudes, perceptions and motives;
4. to generate information helpful in structuring customer questionnaires;
5. to interpret quantitative data findings.

Growing Popularity of Focus Groups

Marketers are using numerous variations of the focus group and other qualitative techniques to gain an even better understanding of what motivates consumers and why they make certain purchase decisions. Focus groups are probably the most important qualitative research procedure. Few qualitative interview methods in marketing have received as much positive press as focus group interviews.[17] They are so popular that many market research practitioners consider this technique synonymous with qualitative research.[18] However, focus groups are but one aspect of qualitative research. Yet the growing popularity of the focus group technique has virtually overshadowed other qualitative tools. Focus groups tend to be used more extensively by consumer goods companies than industrial goods companies. This can partly be explained by the fact that it is probably much easier to assemble a group of ten consumers of a domestic household product than to assemble a group of ten organisational buyers.

Box 5.1 Bord Failte uses focus groups to . . .

Following on a preliminary study commissioned by the National Tourism Council, Bord Failte and its partners commenced the full process of brand development and repositioning in the latter part of 1995. An initial large-scale consumer research exercise involving focus groups in Britain, Germany, the Netherlands, USA and Ireland showed many positives about the existing Ireland brand image. Ireland was characterised by accessible and unspoilt nature, friendly engaging people and the opportunities for personal interaction which enhanced a holiday. There were nonetheless some important 'missings'. There was little spontaneous awareness of architecture or marine landscapes in a country which was seen primarily as an adult male destination where good food and sophistication were not often present.

(Source: *Link*, Bord Fáilte Publication, p.3, Jan '96)

• Types of Focus Groups

Focus groups can be classified into three major areas: exploratory, clinical and experiencing.[19] But in practice marketing research practitioners rarely make these distinctions.

Exploratory Focus Groups

Used at the exploratory phase of the market research process to help in problem definition, generating hypotheses, explaining ideas and preparing for quantitative research.[20] For example, a focus group may be used to decide the content of a future questionnaire. A research director once commented 'We use focus groups for fishing.'

Clinical Focus Groups

This is qualitative research in its purest form, and is based on the premise that a person's true motivations and feelings are subconscious in nature, and that what consumers say cannot be taken at face value. But this requires employing moderators skilled in clinical psychology, and with an ability to entice participants into revealing inner feelings and thoughts. Validating findings from clinical focus groups can also be a problem.

Experiencing Focus Groups

This approach is an opportunity for the market researcher to experience a 'flesh and blood' consumer of the product or service. It allows the researcher to relive the consumer's experiences when buying, using, reusing and disposing of the product. When conducting research, Japanese firms prefer to talk to people who have actually experienced the product or service.

Cadler adopts a similar classification. He suggests that focus groups can be used for three different types of purposes:[21]

1. *Clinical* — to uncover consumers' underlying feelings, attitudes, beliefs, opinions, and the subconscious causes of their behaviour.
2. *Exploratory* — to generate, develop and screen ideas or concepts.
3. *Phenomenological* — to discover consumers' everyday life experiences, such as their thoughts, feelings and behaviour.

• Planning and Conducting Focus Groups

The first step to planning a focus group is to establish the objectives of the marketing research project. This begins with a general statement of the management problem. What does management want to achieve? Following that, the objectives of the qualitative research should be clearly specified. These objectives can be set by asking the question 'What information is needed to meet the needs of management?' The research objectives will guide what questions to ask during the focus group. Research objectives have been discussed in Chapter 2. An example of how research objectives help formulate the focus group issues guide, is contained in the Bord na Mona Case Study at the end of this chapter.

Recruiting Participants (and Group Composition)

Researchers normally establish a screening profile for the group participants. A focus group should be reasonably homogenous in terms of demographic and socio-economic characteristics. Participants feel more at ease once they realise they share similarities such as age, job situation, leisure pursuits, family composition etc. Commonality among group members prevents interactions and conflicts about side issues among group members.[22] The session therefore does not become rife with too many arguments and different viewpoints stemming from diverse backgrounds. *e.g. similar demographic characteristics*. The participants should also have adequate experience with the object or issue being discussed. Initially prospective participants may be contacted by telephone first in order to qualify them and then to solicit their co-operation in the focus group. For this, inducements and rewards such as monetary compensation, free products or gift certificates may be used. To overcome the problem of 'no shows' the researcher may need to over-recruit or have replacement standbys.

The researcher should strive to avoid repeat or 'professional' respondents in focus groups. These are people who have already participated in numerous focus groups. It is highly unlikely that they are representative of the target market in question. Most participate simply to get the respondent fee.[23] Another issue in respondent selection relates to allowing people to participate in a group that contains a relative, friend or neighbour. Participants with these pre-established relationships may tend to talk to each other and not to the whole group.

Number of Participants

A typical group will consist of eight to twelve people, but there is no ideal number of participants. However, groups of fewer than eight are unlikely to generate the energy, momentum and group dynamics ('snowballing') necessary for a successful session. Having a higher number of respondents participate in the group gives rise to a broad spectrum of responses and encourages the 'domino' or 'snowball' effect — what one respondent says sparks off comments from others. Snowballing and inter-stimulation within focus groups may lead participants to feel more excited so that they cannot hide or relax their responses.[24] Likewise, groups of more than twelve may be too crowded and may not be conducive to a cohesive and natural discussion.[25] Focus groups normally run for an average of one and a half to two hours, with a maximum of two hours. This period of time is needed to establish rapport with the respondents and to explore in depth their beliefs, feelings, ideas and insights regarding the discussion topic. But, the more participants, the less time available for each to speak and air their opinions. Researchers who wish to collect information from different categories of people should conduct several focus groups; for example, one focus group may consist only of men and another only of women. Most focus group experts believe that four focus group sessions can satisfy the needs of exploratory research.[26]

The Setting

The physical setting for the focus group is also important. A relaxed informal atmosphere encourages spontaneous comments. Light refreshments should be served before the session and made available during the session. Purpose-built focus group facilities are rare in Ireland — Quota Viewing in Dublin is one such facility. Purpose-built focus group facilities consist of a conference room-style setting with a one-way mirror. This enables clients to observe the session through the one-way mirror from an adjacent room. Microphones are placed in unobtrusive locations to record the discussion. New video transmission technology enables the clients to observe focus group sessions live from a remote location (e.g. company headquarters). Videoconferences can broadcast sessions to a remote facility where a number of people can observe the proceedings live over a television monitor. With this technology, the clients observing from afar can move the camera to look at individuals in the group, the moderator, or the entire group. They can also communicate with the moderator through a direct telephone or fax line. While uncommon at present, focus groups using videoconference technology may become more popular in the coming years.[27]

In reality, most Irish focus group settings consist of booking a conference room in a hotel, arranging seating, and installing a tape recorder and possibly a video camcorder. A circular seating arrangement enables all participants to see each other. Videotaping the session allows for recording facial expressions and body movements. Some researchers may choose to use a living-room setting as an alternative to conference-room setting, believing that the informality of the living room will make the participants more at ease, as in a typical home-like setting.

• Selecting the Moderator

The key figure in the focus group interview is the interviewer, in this case referred to as the moderator. The moderator is a critical factor influencing the effectiveness and usefulness of the focus group.[28] He or she must be sensitive to the feelings and comments of group members, but also possess the firmness necessary to successfully direct the group along the intended path of discussion by the ability to maintain a high degree of interaction among group members. Unskilled moderators may end up conducting individual interviews with each of the participants rather than working the group's dynamics. One or more of the group participants may tend to be domineering. The moderator must reduce their effect by calling for the opinions of others. Qualifications required of the moderator depend on the type of groups being conducted. For a clinical focus group, it is advisable to have a trained psychologist. Disagreement exists among researchers as to the educational requirements for moderators of exploratory and experiencing focus groups. But at minimum, moderators need to have good interpersonal and communication skills and a knowledge of the discussion topic at hand.

> **Box 5.2 Ten traits of a good focus group moderator**
>
> 1. Be experienced in focus group research.
> 2. Provide sufficient help in conceptualising the focus group research design, rather than simply executing the groups exactly as the client specifies.
> 3. Prepare a detailed moderator guide well in advance of the focus group.
> 4. Engage in advance preparation to improve overall knowledge of the area being discussed.
> 5. Provide some 'added value' to the project beyond simply doing an effective job of conducting the session.
> 6. Maintain control of the group without leading or influencing the participants.
> 7. Be open to modern techniques such as visual stimulation, conceptual mapping, attitude scaling, or role-playing, which can be used to delve deeper into the minds of participants.
> 8. Take personal responsibility for the amount of time allowed for the recruitment, screening and selection of participants.
> 9. Share in the feeling of urgency to complete the focus group while desiring to achieve an excellent total research project.
> 10. Demonstrate the enthusiasm and exhibit the energy necessary to keep the group interested even when the hour is running late.
>
> (Source: Thomas L. Greenbaum, 'Do you have the right moderator for your focus groups? Here are 10 questions to ask yourself', *Bank Marketing*, Vol. 23 No.1 (1991), 43.)

• Moderator Discussion Guide

A discussion guide is an outline of the topics to be covered during the session. The discussion agenda is based on the research objectives and client information needs. It serves as a checklist and provides a detailed outline of the issues to be addressed during the discussion, including the approach, the types of questions to be raised, the sequence of issues, and any stimuli (e.g. alternative sample packaging) to be introduced. But inflexible formats and highly structured question sequences should be avoided, especially when attempting to find out the unexpected and new. The moderator's guide usually flows through three stages. Firstly rapport is established between the moderator and the participants. Individual participants may be asked to introduce themselves. This acts as an 'icebreaker', particularly for more timid participants. Also, at this stage the rules of group interaction are explained by the moderator and the objectives of the research are outlined (unless the purpose of the research and the name of the sponsoring organisation is purposely being hidden from the group). The second stage of the session consists of the moderator attempting to provoke intensive discussion in the relevant areas. The final stage is used to summarise the group's response to determine the extent of agreement.

Example of Focus Group Discussion Guide
The Evening B.Comm Degree, NUI, Galway

Introduction

This is a focus group session to explore your motivations and feelings about the evening B.Comm Degree at NUI, Galway. We want to find out your principal reasons for undertaking the course and your reactions and suggestions to what you've experienced.

Most of you already know the guidelines for focus groups. I'm a facilitator, not a judge. My role is to encourage members of the group to give their views and discuss and exchange ideas on the issues raised. To facilitate this I have a semi-structured questionnaire here to lead us through issues important in planning a course such as this.

There's one golden rule. Everyone is free to raise what they feel about each issue without criticism. Each of your views is as important as the next person's. The discussion should last about two hours. There will be a break for refreshments. Recording is for transcription purposes only. I hope nobody has any objections to this.

Here's another suggestion

Focus groups should be constructive. Therefore this one follows the structure of the questionnaire. It's easy to complete. But please do so in relation to the points raised and in a constructive way. At the very end there'll be an opportunity to raise any issues close to your heart.

Focus group checklist

Original decision
Let's go back to the beginning when you decided to take this course

What made/encouraged you to undertake the evening B.Comm?
Probe:	Spontaneous?
	Influences of friends?
	Change in lifestyle?
	Change in job?
	Encouragement at work?
	Other?
What other courses, colleges, if any, did you consider?
Probe:	Professional courses — accountancy?
	Marketing?
	Other degrees?
	RTC?
	Open University?

What was the clinching factor(s) for NUI Galway?

How important is the title B.Comm?
Probe: Enterprise and Management?

How would you feel if it had been called a BA?
Probe: Or BBS?

Had you considered an evening BA?

How significant was the Diploma being awarded after two years?
Probe: Reasons.

Expectations
What, if any, were your expectations about how the course would be conducted?
Probe: Had you a chance to attend university lectures before?
Compared to school/training events?
How much of the content did you expect to be covered in the lectures?
What were your expectations about home study?

Delivery
In the University, course delivery means the way the course is provided, e.g. duration, number of nights per week, form of examination or assessment, class content and structure, etc.

Let's get your feelings. What about setting off on a four-year programme? How did you feel?
Probe: Try it?
Diploma?
Knew others who did it?

There's a lot of material to cover so how else could the course be structured to cover the material in that or a shorter period?

Probe: Was there too much, or just about right amount of time in lectures?
Distance learning format?
How significant is being with the class? Support?
More at-home assignments/readings supported by less frequent tutorial-type lectures? Form? Frequency? For what subjects?
What about using IT for course delivery?
What subjects not suited to distance format?

Grading
In terms of grading, what's your reaction to the grading systems used in the course?

Probe: Individual assignments versus group ones?
Amount of continuous assessment versus final examination?

During the course
Take your mind back to during the course.
Tell us your impressions, feelings and mood as you went through the course.
What are your thoughts/reactions to the subjects you were doing each year?
What subjects should have been included/dropped?
What skills were covered or could have been covered?

End
Given all you've told us, has the course lived up to what you'd expected and hoped for?
If you had known what you know now, would you do it again? *Probe.*
What changes would you make, if any?
Finally — have we left anything out you feel is significant and which you'd like to talk about?
Probe:

Thank you for your time.

© Department of Marketing NUI, Galway.

Analysing the Results and Preparing the Report

While the purpose of focus groups can vary, the primary purpose is to build a foundation for the conclusive research phase of the project. Focus groups provide a wealth of insight into how and why buyers purchase products. This may, for example, be used later to formulate question content and sequence in questionnaire design. Often managers believe they can use qualitative research as a substitute for quantitative research. This is not necessarily so and may prove later to be an incorrect assumption. Because the number of participants is small, frequencies and percentages are not usually reported in a focus group's summary. Instead, reports typically include expressions like 'Most participants thought that . . .', 'Some members felt that . . .', 'Many agreed that . . .'

Before sitting down to write the report, the researcher attempts to pull together common themes or trends in response patterns by viewing and listening to the audio-visual recordings and referring to any notes taken during the session. With a well-planned discussion guide which has been properly adhered to, the analysis of focus group findings should be straightforward. The last step is to write the actual report. A liberal sprinkling of respondents' actual remarks (verbatim) can be used in the report to enforce or dramatise findings.[29]

Developments and Variations on Focus Groups
1. *Mini-groups* — typically four to five participants.

2. *Two-way focus groups* — consisting of two groups. The second group listens in on the first group, then holds its own discussion.
3. *Dual-moderator group* — two moderators share the responsibility of moderating the group.
4. *Client-participant group* — clients sit in on the focus group and are identified to the participants. They may also take part in the discussion and answer queries.

A more recent development is where specialist firms provide focus groups on the Internet. Net users can enter *chat rooms* where selected topics are identified. There they can submit their comments in a public forum.

• Advantages of Focus Groups

In comparison with other forms of research, focus groups offer the following specific advantages. These can be summarised as the **ten S's**.[30]

1. *Synergism*: Putting a group of people together will produce a wider range of information, insight and ideas than will individual responses secured privately.
2. *Snowballing*: A 'bandwagon' effect often operates in a group interview, in that one person's comment triggers a chain reaction from the other participants. (It should be noted that in practice, the snowball effect can also be a disadvantage. It can result in a 'follow-the-leader' approach, where one strong-minded individual may raise a point and persuade others to his or her line of thinking.)
3. *Stimulation*: Usually after a brief introductory period, the respondents want to express their ideas and expose their feelings as the general level of excitement over the topic increases in the group.
4. *Security*: Because the participants' feelings are similar to those of other group members, they feel comfortable and are therefore willing to express their ideas and feelings.
5. *Spontaneity*: Since participants are not required to answer specific questions, their responses can be spontaneous and unconventional and should therefore provide an accurate account of their views.
6. *Serendipity*: Ideas are more likely to arise out of the blue in the group than in an individual interview.
7. *Specialization*: Because a number of participants are involved simultaneously, use of a highly trained, but expensive, interviewer is justified.
8. *Scientific scrutiny*: The group interview allows close scrutiny of the data collection process, in that observers can witness the session and it can be recorded for later analysis.
9. *Structure*: The group interview allows for flexibility in the topics covered and the depth with which they are treated.
10. *Speed*: Since a number of individuals are being interviewed at the same time, data collection and analysis proceed relatively quickly.

Disadvantages of Focus Groups

Disadvantages include the possibility that people who submit to the interview process may not be typical of the population they are presumed to represent. This presents a problem when attempting to generalise upon the results of the session, which is why focus groups are frequently used as an exploratory technique or when statistical extrapolation to the larger population is not of critical importance. It can of course be said that if the focus group members are not typical of the population, then that is the fault of the sampling procedure, not of the credibility of the focus group methodology. A related problem is the inevitable small sample size when compared with the more statistically powerful survey research approaches. According to Gerry Grehan of BOI, 'focus groups can be quite good if you have a specific topic, you know the target market you're after and the target market is sitting in the room with you. But for broad brush issues, the focus groups are not great. You can get very conflicting views.'[31]

The quality of the research results depends heavily on the skills of the moderator. Another problem with the focus group interviews is the inherent subjectivity of the results. Results can be more easily misjudged than the results of other data-collection methods. Different researchers may reach dissimilar conclusions based on the same set of interview data. Also the unstructured nature of the responses makes coding, analysis and interpretation difficult. Finally, there is the danger that the decision-makers may consider the findings as conclusive evidence rather than exploratory information.

In-depth Interviews

Also known as individual extended interviews, in-depth interviews are another way of obtaining qualitative data. Like focus groups they are also an unstructured and direct way of obtaining information, and are used primarily for exploratory research. But unlike focus groups, in-depth interviews are conducted on a one-on-one basis. They are particularly appropriate when:[32]

1. intensively probing needs behaviour or attitudes, e.g. car purchase;
2. examining potentially embarrassing subject matters, e.g. sexual habits;
3. eliciting confidential personal data, e.g. use of off-shore banking accounts;
4. detailing socially acceptable norms, e.g. family planning or breast feeding;
5. understanding complicated decision-making patterns, e.g. mortgage purchase;
6. interviewing professional people, e.g. purchasing managers;
7. interviewing competitors who are unlikely to reveal information in a group setting, e.g. local hotel-owners.

The technique uses extensive probing in the context of a personal interview to get a single respondent to reveal motivations, beliefs, attitudes and feelings on a topic.[33] The purpose of the technique is to descend beneath the superficial answers that are often provided by respondents and to disclose the more fundamental reasons underlying the respondent's attitudes and behaviour.[34] In 1995, a survey of corporate purchasing and materials management was carried out by KMPG Stokes Kennedy Crowely on behalf on the Marketing Institute and the Irish Institute of Purchasing and Materials Management (IIPMM). The survey examined the constraints and barriers to developing better business-to-business relationships between purchasers and suppliers. One of the ways it did this was by asking those responsible for purchasing for their views on the marketing and selling capabilities of indigenous Irish companies. Qualitative research involving in-depth interviews was conducted with key purchasing managers in twenty organisations.[35]

The following are some key phrases that the interviewer may use to this end: 'What do you mean by that?' 'Would you elaborate on that?' 'Can you give me an example?' 'Can you be more specific?' 'What else?' Essentially the direction of the interview is determined by the respondent's initial reply.[36] In addition, the interviewer's mannerisms (such as nodding the head, smiling or other non-verbal expressions of approval), repeating the answer as a question ('So you thought the hotel staff were friendly?'), or interviewer silence can also be used to elicit more in-depth responses from the participant. While the interviewer may attempt to follow a rough outline, the actual wording of the questions and the order in which they are asked is determined by the subject's responses. Unlike focus group interviews, which often disguise the purpose of asking certain questions, in-depth interviews generally employ undisguised techniques, so that the purpose of the interview is clear to the subject. (See page 141 for an example of a in-depth interview guide.)

The interviewer must gain the confidence of the person being interviewed so that an honest, open discussion will take place. The success of the interview depends very much on the interviewer. He or she must develop a rapport with the interviewee, without passing judgment on what the respondent says. The interviewer must avoid the appearance of superiority and remain objective. Above all the interviewer must probe into attitudes, beliefs and feelings and not accept brief 'Yes' and 'No' answers. In-depth interviews may last for half an hour, an hour or up to two hours.

Normally the interviewer will take brief notes during the session, and it is advisable (with the permission of the interviewee) to tape record the discussion. This allows the interviewer greater flexibility when conducting the interview and also ensures that all important issues are recorded.

Application of In-depth Interviews

As with focus groups, the primary use of in-depth interviews is for exploratory research. But for several reasons, which we will look at later, in-depth interviews are probably used less frequently than focus group research. The disadvantages of the technique contribute to its limited use.[37] However, in-depth interviews may be used to address special problem situations such as those outlined earlier. A project undertaken for a leading firm of chartered accountants involved up to 50 interviews with their existing and prospective clients, as well as influential bankers, solicitors, senior management from state agencies and financial journalists. The principal objective was to investigate how these various well-informed business or professional people regarded the client firm *vis-à-vis* competition. Clients were questioned in great detail about the nature and perceived quality of the service they got from their accountants. They were probed about attributes they considered important in an accountancy firm. Was, for example, the concept of an accountancy firm providing a complete range of financial, legal, and business services (the so-called 'One-stop shop') appealing or not?[38]

Advantages and Disadvantages

In-depth interviews are versatile but they require careful planning, training and preparation.[39] The main strength of the in-depth interview is in its ability to uncover more complete answers to questions than might be answered at a more superficial level during survey research. The one-to-one in-depth interview also has the advantage of respondents revealing attitudes or motives that they may be reluctant to discuss in a group setting.

In-depth interviews have a number of weaknesses. First, because of the one-to-one nature of the research, sample sizes are small and statistical extrapolation of research findings becomes a problem. In-depth interviews are also much more expensive than groups to conduct. They are more physically exhausting for the interviewer to conduct than focus groups. Typically an interviewer may conduct four or five one-hour interviews in a day, whereas one focus group lasting one and a half hours can cover up to twelve respondents. Interpretation of the in-depth interview is subjective and dependent on the interviewer's view of what was said. Another problem is the difficulty of editing, coding and analysing the qualitative results.

The disadvantages of the technique contribute to its limited use.[40] Therefore, unless a situation demands a very high level of rapport on a one-to-one basis between interviewer and respondent, the focus group interview is generally capable of providing the same information at a lower cost.

Killarney All-Weather Centre. Local Tourism Experts Survey.

Depth Interview Guide

A. Introduction
Introduction
Purpose of the research

B. Tourism in Killarney
What are the principal reasons for visitors to visit Killarney?
What are the major attractions of Killarney town to the visitor (not including the Lakes)?
What do you think are the major weaknesses of Killarney town as a tourism centre?
Do you feel the town is weak in its ability to attract/keep visitors? Why?
What do you estimate the average length of stay of visitors to Killarney to be?

If accommodation is provided, could you estimate what percentage of your business are one-night stays:

- Under 30%.
- Between 30% and 50%.
- Between 50% and 75%.
- Over 75%.

Do tourists, in your experience, complain about the lack of things to do in Killarney? Are there sufficient activities for tourists in Killarney?

How do you rate existing tourism attractions in the region?

Is there a need for a large weather-independent visitor attraction in Killarney town? Why/Why not?

C. Reaction to the proposed attraction
Show proposed centre and explain . . .

What is your reaction to the proposed centre?
What central themes should it include?
What would you see as the key success factors of the proposed attraction?
Are there any successful attractions which the centre should/should not be modelled on?
Any other product/marketing suggestions (theme, facilities, etc.)?
Would you be willing to recommend this new attraction to your guests?

D. Impact on tourism in the town
Would such an attraction make it easier for you to attract more visitors to Killarney/aid the performance of your business?

Would the centre be beneficial to the long-term development of tourism in the Greater Kerry area/region? How?

Would such an attraction:

- make Killarney a more attractive place to visit?

- increase tourist numbers?
- increase tourism spend?
- affect length of stay of visitors to Killarney?

How and to what extent?

How do you feel a new attraction would fare as regards visitor numbers?

E. Other details

Is there an opportunity for tourist operators in the region to work more closely in selling their products?

Do you carry brochures/posters from various day attractions in the area?

Do you operate on a commission basis with any day attraction operators in the region?

F. Close

Thank you/any concluding comments.

Consent to follow-up, if necessary.

Agreement use of the information gained from the discussion/confidentiality.

© Envision Marketing Consultants, Galway.

• Projective Techniques

carried out by consumer psychologist

These techniques are often used in conjunction with individual in-depth interviews. Projective techniques are derived from the field of clinical psychology.[41] The objective of projective techniques is to delve below surface responses to obtain true feelings, attitudes or motivations. Both focus groups and in-depth interviews are direct approaches in which the true purpose of the research is disclosed to the respondents or is otherwise obvious to them. Projective techniques are different in that they attempt to disguise the purpose of the research. A projective technique is an unstructured, indirect form of questioning that encourages respondents to project their underlying beliefs, motivations and attitudes or feelings regarding the issues of concern.[42] People are often reluctant or cannot reveal their deepest feelings, or they may be unaware of those feelings because of psychological defence mechanisms. Projective techniques rely on stimulus ambiguity to obtain a more free and open response. Because the stimulus is ambiguous and has no true meaning, the respondent has to project himself or herself into the task, i.e. the respondents are provided with an opportunity to 'indirectly' express their feelings through a third party or by interpreting the behaviour of others.

As Oscar Wilde once said, 'A man is least himself when he talks in his own person; when he is given a mask he will tell the truth.'

• Types of Projective Techniques

The most common forms of projective technique used in marketing research tests are:

- word association;
- sentence completion;
- story completion;
- cartoon tests;
- picture response;
- role-playing;
- personification;
- third person;
- psychodrawing;
- time travel.

These techniques can be classified under four main headings[43] which are: association, completion, construction and expressive techniques.

Association Tests

A respondent is presented with a stimulus and asked to respond with the first thing that comes to mind. The most popular is that of word association. The respondent is presented with a list of words, one at a time, and asked to respond with the first word that comes to mind. The test words related to the subject of the research are dispersed throughout the list and are intermixed with some 'neutral' words so as to hide the purpose of the study. The words are read to the respondent in rapid sequence and the subject responds with the first word that comes to mind. Rapidity of response is crucial to the technique so as to avoid time for defence mechanisms to come into play. 'First-thought' responses are more likely to reveal the respondent's strongest feelings towards the stimulus. If a respondent does not respond to a stimulus word within a reasonable period of time (e.g. five seconds) the eventual response should be either disregarded or discounted. Hesitation in responding (sometimes referred to as 'response latency') may indicate that the respondent is emotionally involved with the word and possibly seeking an acceptable response. As an example of word association technique, consider the following (note: test words are identified by an asterisk):

Stimulus	*Word*
Bicycle	_____
Shop	_____
Canteen*	_____
Library	_____
Food*	_____
Smoking	_____

Seating*   _____

Staff*   _____

Word association tests are used to evaluate brand names, pre-test words for questionnaires, and to obtain top-of-mind reaction to companies, products, retail outlets and concepts. United Beverages launched the highly successful Finches brand in 1990. In deciding a name for the product, initial brainstorming sessions produced a list of 75 possibilities. From this, United Beverages initiated a screening process which narrowed the list to just six names. Those names were Simmons, Appian, Chase, Manns, Morgans, and Finches. Word association tests were then used to explore the perceived image of each of the brand names.[44]

A variation of the word association test is where respondents are asked to give the first two or more words that come to mind, rather than just the first word.

Completion Tests

The subject is required to complete an incomplete stimulus situation. Completion tests are also based on the principle of free association and can be used in conjunction with word association tests. The most commonly used in marketing research are sentence completion and story completion. The objective is for the interviewee to project themselves into the scenario presented.

Sentence Completion

An extension of the word association concept; but will probably produce larger responses than single-word answers, though one-word answers are acceptable. Again, it is important that respondents do not devote excessive time to the formulation of answers. With sentence completion the interviewee is presented with a more direct stimulus than is the case with word association. However, it is important that the purpose of the study remains disguised. For example:

As I was walking into Tesco I noticed . . .

Story Completion

An extension of sentence completion, story completion provides the respondent with the beginning of a story, then asks her to complete it. Story completion provides a more structured and detailed scenario for the respondent. The respondent is given enough time to direct attention to the particular topic of interest, but the ending is left open. The interviewee projects herself into an imaginary scenario. For example:

'It was a Saturday afternoon in November. Rachel parked her car in the car park opposite the shopping centre. It was raining and she had forgotten to bring an umbrella with her. Never mind, she thought. All I need to do is to collect my evening dress from the dry cleaners and then I can go home, light a fire and relax. As she approached the counter she handed the ticket to the attendant and waited. The attendant returned with the dress. Rachel noticed that the red wine stain was still visible on the dress. She . . .'

The story completion technique, because of its nature, tends to provide data which is even more qualitative than that resulting from word association or sentence completion.

Construction Techniques

While related to completion techniques, construction techniques require the respondent to construct a response in the form of a story, dialogue or description. Less initial structure is provided to the respondent than with a completion test. The most commonly used construction techniques are cartoon tests and picture response.

Cartoon tests

Cartoon techniques present cartoon-type drawings (similar to those seen in comic books) of one or more people in a particular situation. A typical cartoon test consists of two characters, one with a sentence in bubble form above its head, the other with a blank bubble above its head. The figures presented are vague and without expression so as to not suggest a response. The respondent is asked to fill in the blank bubble. The individual is allowed to project any subconscious or socially unacceptable feelings into the cartoon character. The settings can be used for discussions about products, services, packaging, store personnel, promotional activity etc.

Picture Response

Picture response (or interpretation as it is sometimes referred to) has its origins in clinical psychology where it is known as a 'thematic apperception test' (TAT). With picture response, respondents are asked to react to a picture or series of pictures in which consumers and products are the centre of attention. These pictures are usually relatively vague, so that the respondent must use his or her imagination to describe what is occurring and what might happen next. Hence, themes (thematic) are elicited on the basis of the perceptual interpretative (apperception) use of picture.

The TAT is probably the most ambiguous of commonly used projective research techniques, but is also probably the most flexible, since pictures can be constructed to depict nearly any type of marketing situation. However, interpretation should ideally be carried out by trained individuals.

An imaginative application of the picture response technique is where the researcher collects a wide variety and number of picture postcards. These can range from the abstract to the relatively straightforward. The postcards are spread on a flat surface such as the floor or a table. Respondents are asked to pick, for example, three postcards that best describe their thoughts, feelings, attitudes etc. towards the object in question and to explain why. The whole procedure can be extremely insightful and revealing. It is particularly useful in focus group settings, for not only does it provide a means for respondents to 'project' their feelings but it also serves as a very useful exercise to relax the group. After all, the sight of grown adults on their knees on the floor selecting postcards is enough to make any group feel at ease!

Expressive Techniques

The respondents are presented with a verbal or visual situation and asked to project the attitudes and feelings of *other* people onto the situation. There are two variations of this: role-playing and third-person technique.

Role-playing

In role-playing, the consumer is asked to assume the role of another person or an object. The researcher assumes that the respondent will project their own feelings into the role. The 'acting out' of brands, stereotypes, fantasies etc., may be an individual or group activity.[45] For example, the consumer may assume the role of a car salesperson. The role-playing consumer can then be asked to sell a given car to a number of different 'consumers' who raise varying objections. The means by which the role-player attempts to overcome these objections can reveal a great deal about his or her attitudes. Role-playing can be especially useful in exploring issues of gender. For instance, gender reversal can be employed to examine brands which are predominantly male or female, e.g. a group of men 'become' women buying bath oil.[46]

Third-person Technique

By asking the respondent how friends, neighbours or the average person would think or react in a given situation, the researcher can observe the respondent projecting his or her own attitudes onto this third person, rather than directly expressing personal beliefs and attitudes. By enabling the interviewee to respond in the third person, it reduces the social pressure to give an acceptable answer.

A frequently cited example of this indirect projective technique is a study which was conducted in 1950, when Nescafé Instant Coffee was new to the US market. Two shopping lists, identical except for the brand of coffee, were given to two groups of women:

> A pound and a half of hamburger.
> Two loaves of Wonder Bread.
> Bunch of carrots.
> One can of Rumford's Baking Powder.
> (Nescafé Instant Coffee) (Maxwell House Coffee, drip grind).
> Two cans Del Monte peaches.
> Five pounds potatoes.

Respondents were given the following instructions: 'Read the shopping list. Try to project yourself into the situation as far as possible until you can more or less characterise the women who bought the groceries. Then write a brief description of her personality and character. Whenever possible indicate what factors influenced your judgment.'

48% of the housewives given the list which included Nescafé described the Nescafé user as lazy and a poor planner. Other responses implied that the instant coffee user was not a good wife and spent money carelessly. The Maxwell House user, on the other hand, was thought to be practical, frugal, and a good cook.[47]

Personification can be looked at as a variation of the third person technique. It involves the respondent attributing human characteristics to inanimate objects. In focus group research on cars for example, the moderator may ask 'If a Toyota AVENSIS was a person, what sort person would it be?' Or, 'If this package were a person, what would it be like in terms of age, gender, likes and dislikes, and lifestyle?' A similar approach is to ask the respondent to write an obituary for, for example, a brand that has just 'died'. Respondents are asked to write an obituary giving reasons for death as well as for what the brand will be remembered for.

Two other projective techniques[48] include:

Psychodrawing

Respondents produce abstract paintings of their feelings about the subject, e.g. a brand or a company service. The painting is titled and personally signed. An art gallery is constructed, with each 'artist' explaining the emotions and meanings of his or her painting for the others in a small group.

Time travel

The respondent enters an imaginary time capsule and can move back or forward in time to defined years. 'It is 1937, we are in the bathroom of a suburban house in Dublin . . . picture this in detail . . .'

Time travel is useful for establishing historical contexts and future projections.

• Advantages and Disadvantages of Projective Techniques

The primary value of projective techniques is that they enable the researcher to get information that probably would not be available through direct questioning or by other means, e.g. observation. The types of data that these techniques generate are particularly important at the exploratory phase of a research project, especially when insights and ideas are important. The results of projective techniques can also be used directly for decision-making and may even eliminate the need for further study of the research problem.

On the negative side, projective techniques generally require trained interviewers, and responses need to be interpreted by qualified analysts. This can make them expensive to use. Also, reliance on small sample sizes (and usually non-probability selection procedures) makes it difficult to project the findings to a larger population. Non-response may also be a problem. Respondents may be required to engage in behaviour that may well seem strange to them (e.g. role-playing). Therefore, those who participate are likely to be different to those who do not. Despite these limitations, projective techniques are a very useful research tool and particularly suitable to exploratory type research.

Box 5.3 New techniques

By and large, qualitative research continues to have a similar basic function as ever it did. These are exploring the emotional nature of attitudes, motivations and decision-making; and an emphasis on answering the question 'Why?'

- A major Irish company observed that it was held in great respect, but that underneath this respect lay a syndrome of complex negative emotions directed at the company. There was a marked difference between 'public' and 'private' attitudes to the company. The long-term strategic problem was the possibility of ever-declining corporate status, and the operational difficulties that could ensue. The immediate problem was the potential 'secret' negative attitudes to the company hindering the development of the company's *products*. Here, research facilitated the development of strategic plans at both corporate and product levels and, as importantly, guided the implementation of these plans.
- A food brand continued to lose market share to a competitor, although the elements of its total marketing mix (product, packaging, price, advertising etc.) were deemed and found to be in good health. Answering the question 'Why?' became critical in the knowledge that refining elements of the mix would be unlikely to change the situation. (The most plausible answer, and most actionable insight, was found in the evidence that consumers had come to conceptualise the brand as being in a different product sector than that in which it was assumed to be, leading to fundamental re-thinking about the brand, and how it should behave and speak.)

This latter area has led to much contemporary interest in what are known as 'new techniques' in qualitative research, which are variously described as *projective* techniques, *non-verbal* techniques and *creative* techniques. In truth, these are not new at all, but have, as it were, been re-invented to meet demands of the current marketplace for deeper insight. I would like to sound a warning note in this context. It is obvious that use of these techniques can represent the sexy end of qualitative research, but their use is meaningless unless they further the objectives of the study. In unskilled hands, they are dangerous, insofar that analysis of findings becomes cock-eyed. There is also the considerable danger of an emphasis on *techniques* getting in the way of high quality qualitative research; a moderator who arrives in a focus group with a bag of verbal and non-verbal tricks can become more involved with the tricks than what is occurring in the group. If the techniques appear to be 'techniques' to respondents, an unwanted and distracting dynamic will be introduced.

With these caveats, projective techniques can facilitate examination of subconscious attitudes and emotions. They may be successfully used in circumstances where either high or low verbal articulation skills among respondents form barriers to exploration (for instance, highly articulate respondents can unwittingly employ their ability to intellectualise as a screen to truer and more fundamental emotions and feelings). Projective techniques are particularly useful in developing creative and innovative avenues for a brand, product or service; they can provide guidance on the symbolic nature of the subject, for example, where certain colours, shapes and visual codes are key elements of a brand's make-up.

There is now a great range of creative techniques which may be drawn upon. A more recent development has been the tailoring of specific techniques to illuminate very particular areas of interest.

At the end of the day, techniques are just that — techniques. They constitute nothing novel in the field of qualitative research, but their contemporary integration and judicious use indicates perhaps what is the most significant trend in the field for the future. This is the simple objective of higher quality, especially in a richer analysis which is itself geared towards action on the part of the research buyer.

(Source: *Qualitative Research: Where It's At, Where It's Going*. Phelim O'Leary, *Irish Marketing Review*, vol. 6, 1993, 23–8.)

• **Summary**

Qualitative research has developed from a fringe area of marketing to a widely used and sophisticated instrument. The chapter examined three qualitative research methods, namely focus groups, in-depth interviews and projective techniques.

Focus groups are probably the most important qualitative research procedure. They can be classified into three major groups: exploratory, clinical and experiencing. The main purpose of the focus group is to gain insights by listening to a group of people from the appropriate target market. A typical group will consist of eight to twelve people. A focus group should be reasonably homogenous in terms of demographic and socio-economic characteristics. The key figure in the focus group interview is the moderator. A discussion guide is used to outline the topics to be covered during the session. Most Irish focus group settings consist of booking a conference room in a hotel, arranging seating, and installing a tape recorder and possibly a video camcorder. The value of the technique lies in the unexpected findings often obtained from a free-flowing group's discussion.

In-depth interviews are another way of obtaining qualitative data. But unlike focus groups, in-depth interviews are conducted on a one-to-one basis. The technique uses extensive probing and aims to disclose the more fundamental reasons underlying the respondent's attitudes and behaviour. While the interviewer may attempt to follow a rough outline, the actual wording of the questions and the order in which they are asked is determined by the subject's responses. Above all the interviewer must probe and not accept brief 'Yes' and 'No' answers. The main strength of the in-depth interview is in its ability to uncover more complete answers to questions than might be answered at a more superficial level during survey research. In-depth interviews may last for an hour, an hour and a half, or up to two hours.

Projective techniques are derived from the field of clinical psychology. A projective technique is an unstructured, indirect form of questioning that encourages respondents to project their underlying beliefs, motivations and attitudes or feelings regarding the issues of concern. Projective techniques rely on stimulus ambiguity to obtain a more free and open response. These techniques can be classified under four main headings which are: association, completion, construction and expressive techniques. Examples of individual projective techniques include: word association, sentence completion, cartoon tests, role-playing and personification. Although they have limitations, projective techniques are a very useful research tool and particularly suitable to exploratory-type research.

Questions

1. Differentiate between qualitative and quantitative research techniques.
2. What are the basic uses for exploratory research?
3. Why would an organisation consider conducting a focus group? Why are focus groups becoming more popular?
4. What are the three types of focus groups and how do they differ?
5. How are the participants of focus groups recruited? What are some of the pitfalls that should be avoided during the recruitment process?
6. What are some of the difficulties that may be encountered during a focus group interview and what strategies can the moderator employ to avoid them or minimise their effect?
7. What key qualities should a moderator possess?
8. Why should one safeguard against professional respondents?
9. Should the members of a focus group be similar or dissimilar? Why?
10. What physical facilities and equipment are required to conduct a focus group?
11. Discuss the purposes of a focus group interview and describe how such an interview would be carried out. What are the advantages and disadvantages of this technique compared to the in-depth interview?
12. Under what circumstances would you suggest that a in-depth interview be conducted rather than a focus group?
13. What is the purpose of projective techniques? Under what circumstances would projective techniques be preferred over focus group and/or in-depth interviews?
14. Describe and illustrate the major types of projective interviewing techniques and when they should be applied.
15. Describe the word association technique. Give an example of a situation in which this technique is especially useful.
16. How do third-person techniques differ from sentence completion techniques?
17. What is meant by role-playing?

Problems and Assignments

1. How might exploratory research be used to screen various ideas for advertising copy in television commercials?
2. Develop a projective technique to determine students' attitudes towards cheating in exams. Would mini-groups or individual in-depth interviews provide better data on college students' attitudes towards cheating?
3. Following the methods outlined in the text, develop a plan for conducting a focus group to determine consumers' attitudes towards and preferences for imported automobiles. Specify the objectives of the focus group, write a screening questionnaire, and develop a moderator's outline.
4. If a researcher wanted to conduct a focus group with teenagers, what special considerations might be necessary?
5. What projective techniques would you use to help develop a campaign to reduce drinking and driving by college students? Why would you choose these methods?
6. Toothpaste manufacturers have found consistently that if they ask for detailed information on the frequency that people brush their teeth, and then make minimal assumptions as to the quantity of toothpaste used on each occasion as well as spillage and failure to squeeze the tube empty, the result is a serious overstatement of toothpaste consumption. How would you explain this phenomenon? Would it be possible to design a study to overcome these problems and obtain more accurate estimates of consumption? Describe how such a study would be conducted.
7. Most projective techniques attempt to assess a respondent's true feelings by asking indirect questions rather than using direct questions that could give a respondent a better idea as to the researcher's motives. Is this deception?
8. Discuss the issues involved in determining when and where a car tyre manufacturer should conduct focus groups to get feedback from customers on its line of wet-driving winter tyres. Give a brief description of customers who would be good candidates for this type of focus group.
9. Using the Internet, connect with a special interest bulletin board such as one for college students. Conduct an electronic focus group exploring what factors are used as criteria to choose destinations for the summer holidays.

Case Study
Growing in a declining market: Bord na Mona*

The Irish market for solid fuel declined by half over a period of ten years starting in the 1980s. For Bord na Mona's Solid Fuel Division this acute decline, replicating what had happened in other countries, posed a serious threat.

The growth of the natural gas network, decline in electricity and oil prices, as well as changing lifestyle patterns, such as increased numbers of working parent families, were identified as negative factors affecting the market for Bord na Mona's products.

Research objectives

Bord na Mona's Marketing Department carefully analysed future strategy for the company. How would the company maintain, or grow sales in a declining overall market? To help answer this question Bord na Mona commissioned a research company to undertake a programme of extensive market research.

Key issues to be addressed in the research included:

- the perceived role of solid fuel in the home;
- trends in usage patterns and expectations regarding future usage levels;
- comparative evaluations of different forms of heat and energy (e.g. oil versus solid fuel) as well as evaluations of the various solid fuel products and suppliers on the market;
- identification of the positive, as well as the negative aspects, of solid fuel;
- perceptions of Bord na Mona, in particular understanding the value of its image/brand in the marketplace.

These issues were to be addressed across a range of different consumer groups, including urban and rural dwellers, solid fuel users and non-users, socio-economic groups, etc.

The methodology

Consumers were recruited to field-test the new products in their homes and then attended a focus group to discuss their perceptions and evaluations post-usage. Participants were provided with consumer diaries. These were essentially folders containing pages where consumers could evaluate the various new products upon a range of scores for each lighting occasion and at different stages in the lighting of each test fire, provide evaluations of heat output, quality of flame, and so on, which could be explored in detail at the focus group discussions. The combination of focus groups along with diarying of product use ensured that the quantitative evaluations, as gathered through the consumer diaries, could be understood by the company in the context of qualitative perceptions about the products.

Focus group research was also undertaken with consumers who, as in the real market situation, would not have an opportunity to test the product before making a decision on purchase. These consumers were, therefore, asked to evaluate the product concept based on being shown draft sales literature on the products and inspecting a product sample in its proposed packaging.

A second phase of the research was aimed at obtaining consumer and distributor reaction to prototype new products, including the shrink-wrapped half bale of briquettes and the 'Firelog'. These products were designed to address consumer requirements for increased convenience and cleanliness from solid fuel.

The results of the research

As a result of the research Bord na Mona identified opportunities to target new consumer segments with its new prototype products which overcame many of the perceived drawbacks of solid fuel, while still providing the ambience and character associated with 'a real fire'.

The research highlighted important adjustments to the product prototypes, including packaging and name changes, revised formulation and shape. The research also drew Bord na Mona's attention to the strong market image of the company, suggesting opportunities for the company to further exploit its brand equity through the branding of related products/fuels (e.g. firelighters and coal).

A successful outcome

Bord na Mona has successfully launched a number of consumer goods through new channels (e.g. supermarkets and forecourts) in the 1990s, demonstrating the value of market information in shaping strategy and identifying opportunities to grow in a declining market.

Questions/exercises

1. Devise an issues list for the focus groups mentioned above. Would the issues list for consumers who undertook product trial be different from that for those consumers who were asked to evaluate the product concepts, without trial?
2. Outline one page of the consumer diary to evaluate the proposed 'Firelog' product on one of its trial usage occasions.
3. How would you recruit participants for Bord na Mona's focus group research? What groups would you be anxious to include in your sample (e.g. urban and ABC1)?
4. Would there be any advantages to conducting the focus group research in a home setting (i.e. a consumer's home), as opposed to a hotel venue? What might the practical disadvantages be and which, on balance, would you recommend?

*This case study was written by Ray Collis, Envision Marketing, Galway. It is intended to be used as the basis for class discussion rather than to illustrate either effective or ineffective handling of an administrative situation. The case is based on a real situation though certain information has been disguised. © Envision Marketing Consultants, Galway.

Case Study
A Global Player Intimate with the Irish Market: Smith and Nephew*

Smith and Nephew is a global player in the healthcare market, manufacturing an extensive range of specialised healthcare products, including bandages, casting supplies and equipment, patient hoists and so on.

Ray MacDermott joined Smith and Nephew Irish subsidiary in 1996. Ray was anxious to understand how the company was perceived by its customers and its share of the market as a first step.

Focus groups were conducted with occupational therapists and physiotherapists, both key groups of users of Smith and Nephew's products in hospitals, as well as community care and out-patient services.

The research made interesting reading, as Ray recalls:

. . . we learned that we were the main player in the market and that customers thought our products and our sales reps were great. However the most important things we learned were the opportunities for improvement. In particular, the speed of delivery and the availability of stock when required were areas which, like the competition, we could improve. With this information we instituted a system of stocking and delivery that has had a major impact on our business.

Reading the quotes from our customers in the research reports brought home to us what our competitive advantages were and how they could be enhanced even further. It both told us what to do and inspired us to act. We are now committed to ongoing research with our customers to ensure that we stay ahead of the many changes taking place in the marketplace.

Section D of the focus guide used by Smith and Nephew to evaluate occupational therapists' and physiotherapists' perceptions of Customer Service follows:

Section D: Customer Service

- How would you rate the service you receive from S and N?
- What in your opinion is 'good service'?
- What in your opinion is 'bad service'? (Going through each of the above, ask customers to evaluate S and N on each element of good/bad service.)
- How satisfied are you with delivery by S and N?
- Is delivery speedy enough for you?
- Do items arrive when promised? Are you informed if delivery is going to be late?
- Are the items you require always in stock when you request them?
- How much contact do you have with S and N:
  - Customer Service personnel.
  - Sales representatives/product specialists.
- What do you think is the role of these personnel? Do they help you/are they helpful? How?

- Is there any way in which they could be of greater assistance to you?
- What form does this contact take? Would you like to hear/receive visits from S and N personnel more often?
- Contact with sales representatives/product specialists — quality and frequency?
- Would an 1850 number be of value? What is an 1800 number?

Question

1. Evaluate the above focus group checklist. What changes, if any, would you suggest?

*This case study was written by Ray Collis, Envision Marketing, Galway. It is intended to be sued as the basis for class discussion rather than to illustrate either effective or ineffective handling of an administrative situation. The case is based on a real situation though certain information has been disguised. © Envision Marketing Consultants, Galway.

Chapter 6 — Primary Data Collection Methods

SURVEYS, OBSERVATION AND PANELS

- **Chapter Overview**
- Introduction • Survey Methods of Data Collection • The Personal Interview • The Telephone Interview • CATI • The Postal Interview • Reducing Non-Response in Postal Questionnaires • Methods of Estimating the Degree of Non-response Error • Combining Survey Techniques • Observation Methods • Advantages and Disadvantages • Summary

• Introduction

In the previous chapter we discussed qualitative research and examined three qualitative data collection methods, namely focus groups, depth interviews and projective techniques. We now move on to look at *quantitative* research by describing surveys, observation and panels in this chapter. These techniques are descriptive by nature. In the next chapter we will examine experimentation, which is associated with causal research.

The reader, upon completion of this chapter, will be able to:

1. discuss survey research;
2. outline the three survey methods;
3. examine personal interviews;
4. examine telephone interviews;
5. examine postal questionnaires;
6. describe observation research;
7. understand panels and omnibus surveys.

• Survey Methods of Data Collection

The survey process by which respondents are questioned may appear deceptively simple. The reality however is probably best summed up by the following quote: 'questioning people is more like trying to catch a particularly elusive fish, by hopefully casting different kinds of bait at different depths, without knowing what is going on beneath the surface'.[1] When evaluating the quality of information obtained from survey results, one must make some determination as to the accuracy of these results. This requires a careful examination of the research methodology used and an eye for the various forms of survey error that might occur. Primarily, in order to obtain meaningful results from the interview process, the following conditions must apply:

1. A correctly defined population.
2. Representative sample of the population.
3. Selected respondents are available and co-operative.
4. Respondents understand the questions asked of them.
5. Respondents have the knowledge, facts, attitudes or opinions to contribute.
6. Respondents are willing and able to respond.
7. The interviewer understands and correctly records the response.

There are two basic methods we can use to obtain information from individuals. We can ask them or we can observe them. Collectively they are known as descriptive research. Descriptive research has already been introduced in Chapter 2.

The first of these alternatives, an approach that is sometimes mistakenly equated with market research itself, is survey research. A survey methodically gathers information from respondents by communicating with them. A survey can be conducted in person, by telephone, or by post. It is probably fair to say that surveys are the most widely used method of data collection in marketing research. However there is no best method of data collection. Each research problem must be examined to determine the best way to collect the data.[2]

The most common marketing research surveys are 'cross-sectional', that is to say surveys of cross-sections of populations. One frequently hears the words 'survey' and 'questionnaire' being mentioned in the one sentence. Survey research relies on a questionnaire (or measuring instrument) of some sort to record responses. It should be stressed that the use of questionnaires is not intrinsic to surveys. One can have surveys based on observation where no questions are asked of any respondents. Questionnaires will be discussed later in the text.

Survey research is the systematic collection of data from a sample of respondents, usually involving the measurement of a large number of variables such as:

1. depth and extent of knowledge;
2. attitudes, interests and opinions;
3. behaviour — past, present or intended;
4. classification variables, demographic and socio-economic variables.

Survey research is usually conducted when the market researcher has already developed an understanding of the area to be researched. Therefore, other marketing research methods such as observational research (discussed later in this chapter) and secondary data analysis are more likely to be used to improve or supplement the

Surveys, Observation and Panels 159

survey method, than take its place. The popularity of survey research is due in part to its versatility.

Sources of Error in Survey Research

Broadly speaking there are three sources of error that impinge upon survey work:

Sampling Error

Error of this type occurs when selecting samples that are not representative of the population. In other words, it is the difference between the sample value and the true value of the population mean. Some degree of sample error will be present whenever we select a sample. Because sampling error is the result of chance, it is subject to the laws of probability. Sampling error is covered in more depth in Chapter 10.

Response Error

Response error occurs when respondents for whatever reason give an incorrect answer. Respondents can answer questions in a certain direction that consciously or unconsciously misrepresents the truth. Interviewer error can also give rise to response error. Response error is covered in Chapter 8.

Non-Response Error

Error of this type occurs when respondents refuse to be interviewed or cannot be contacted. Non-response is a problem because those who respond are likely to differ from those who do not respond. Item non-response (where respondents choose not to answer certain questions) is also a form of non-response. Non-response error is a particular problem in postal surveys. When attempting to manage non-response error, researchers can employ two strategies:

1. Pre-survey approach to non-response. This is dealt with later in the chapter, under the heading 'Reducing non-response in postal questionnaires'.
2. Post-survey approach to non-response. Five methods to deal with the effect of non-response error are also detailed later in this chapter.

Survey research can be classified based on the modes of communication and administration. There are three major survey methods:

1. Personal interviews.
2. Telephone interviews.
3. Postal interviews.

[handwritten annotation: can use all together]

Each method has its own advantages and limitations. Variations of each method also exist, e.g. rather than posting the questionnaire to the respondent, it may instead be distributed within the body of a magazine or newspaper, or attached to a product sample. It is also possible to 'mix' these survey methods in order to take advantage of their individual strengths and compensate for their respective weaknesses. For example, a combination of telephone interviews and personal interviews may be used to communicate with respondents. We will now look at each survey method in turn.

• The Personal Interview

Personal interviews are direct, face-to-face communications between the interviewer and a respondent. Personal interviews may take place in a variety of different locations, including the home of the respondent, a street corner or a shopping centre. They are sometimes referred to as face-to-face interviews.

The Procedure

The personal interview begins with the interviewer approaching the respondent. The first concern is to ensure the full co-operation of the interviewee. This is followed by a brief explanation of the study and how the respondent can help. Respondents must be made to feel that both the study and his or her responses are important. Having gained the respondent's co-operation, attention now turns to the data collection instrument. This helps standardise the data collection procedure. The researcher asks the required questions in the proper sequence and using the exact wording. The interviewer may encourage the respondent (e.g. by asking for clarification, repeating the question, pausing, nodding etc.) to provide additional information if an initial response is vague or overly brief. The interview ends with the interviewer thanking the respondent for his or her co-operation.

Advantages of the Personal Interview Method

Because there is greater interaction between interviewer and respondent, the personal interview has great flexibility. The interviewer can explain and clarify complex questions, probe for additional information, administer complex questionnaires, utilise unstructured techniques and present visual cues such as advertisements and product concepts to the respondent all as part of the questioning process.

The personal interview tends to have less non-response error than other survey methods. Refusal rates tend to range from about 10% to 30% on average. Interviewers rely primarily on their sales ability to convince individuals to co-operate. Most provide an introductory statement designed to secure co-operation: 'Good afternoon, I am conducting Marketing Research for . . .' It is more difficult for the respondent to say 'No' in a face-to-face situation. Also, respondents typically are required to do no reading or writing — all they have to do is talk. Another strength of this method is its ability to obtain more information. Once on board, respondents are generally reluctant to cut short a face-to-face interview by saying 'That's enough.' It is easier for respondents to hang up the telephone or return an incomplete postal questionnaire. The personal interview offers the best degree of sample control. The interviewer has greater control over who is interviewed (unlike telephone and mail).

Sampling procedures that do not require a list of the sampling units rely heavily upon the personal interviewer in the process of selecting the sample.

Limitations

Personal interviews are often impractical to conduct over wide geographical regions for reasons related to time and cost — the need to travel between interviews, set up appointments and schedule return visits to contact 'not at home' non-respondents, for example. Only one-third (30% to 40%) of the interviewer's time on the job is devoted to interviewing itself.[3] There is also the high cost of using trained interviewers in the field.

A second difficulty is the potential for interviewer bias. The rephrasing of questions, the interviewer's tone of voice or physical appearance may influence the response. Interviewers may unknowingly inject bias into the respondent's answers. Cheating can also be a problem. Interviewers may deviate from standardised procedures, cut corners to save time, falsify answers to sensitive or embarrassing questions, or fake all or parts of a questionnaire. Therefore interviewer ability and integrity are important to reducing response error. Interviewers should be properly trained, and procedures to discourage cheating established. One such technique involves contacting (or threatening to contact) a small number of the respondents to determine either the existence or quality of interviews conducted. A final difficulty with the personal interview is that the respondent is not anonymous and may therefore be unwilling to provide confidential information or answers to sensitive questions on a one-to-one basis.

Shopping Centre Intercepts

Increasingly, personal interviews are being conducted in large, high-traffic centres. Shoppers are intercepted in the public area of the shopping centre, or asked to come to a 'permanent' interviewing facility (room) in the centre. However, some shopping centres may not permit market research interviewing as they view it as an unnecessary nuisance to shoppers. The advantage of this method is that it is more efficient for the respondent to come to the interviewer than *vice versa*,[4] and thus many interviews can be conducted quickly.

It also allows the interviewer to show respondents (in the test facility) large, heavy or immobile products such as durable goods and have their reaction recorded. A major problem with shopping centre interviewing is that refusal rates tend to be high. People are usually in a hurry to shop. Also, some people shop at malls more frequently than others and therefore have a greater chance of being interviewed.[5] Furthermore shopping centres tend to attract a certain type of person, based on the shops they contain, and may produce an unrepresentative sample of the larger population (unless they are the population of interest).

• The Telephone Interview

Telephone interviews involve phoning a sample (unless it's a census) of respondents and asking them a series of questions. Telephone interviews are becoming increasingly popular and are probably one of the most efficient methods for collecting data quickly.[6] If proper sampling (including using computer-generated random numbers to account for those persons who may be ex-directory) and call-back procedures are employed, the telephone approach probably produces a better sample than any other survey procedure.[7] While telephone interviewing is also two-way conversation between interviewer and respondent, the fact that it is voice-to-voice and not face-to-face communication, means that it has its own unique problems, strengths and limitations.

Box 6.1

Taylor Nelson-Sofres, the parent company of MRBI Ltd, recently opened a new call centre in Dublin. MRBI is in the process of introducing a range of market research products based on telephone interviewing, both nationally and internationally. While the telephone approach has long been used for business-to-business research, household ownership of telephones — currently almost 90% — now makes it an appropriate medium for a wide variety of consumer research.

(Source: *Irish Times*, 15 June 1998, p. 16.)

The Procedure

While the telephone interview has many characteristics similar to that of the personal interview, i.e. respondent co-operation must be sought, questions can be clarified, respondents can be probed etc., it does not lend itself as much to the collection of lengthy and detailed information. The use of complex measurement scales is also restricted. Telephone interviews are more suited to concise and straightforward data collection.

Telephone interviewing depends on a representative sampling frame — a list of population units with their telephone numbers.[8] The telephone directory is the normal sampling frame used, but telephone directories are limited in that:

1. not everyone has a telephone;
2. there are many unlisted numbers;
3. new or recently connected telephones are not included.

There are two main approaches to overcoming the problem of unlisted or new numbers. One technique is the use of random digit dialling, in which the last four numbers of the telephone number used are selected randomly, using a random numbers table or a computer-based random-number generator. The second approach is called plus-one dialling in which a number is selected from the directory by means of systematic sampling. However, rather than dialling the number listed and selected, 'plus-one' is added to the final digit (e.g. 509492 becomes 509493). The revised number is then dialled. While these two techniques help overcome the problem of unlisted and new numbers, they do not distinguish between household and business telephone numbers. Secondly there may be a higher refusal rate than when surveying listed telephone numbers.[9]

Finally, as with personal interviews, it is recommended to use carefully selected and well-trained interviewers, and to validate their interviews by calling a small sample of numbers they claim to have called.

Advantages of the Telephone Interview Method

As the cost of personal interviews may be prohibitively high, the cost of telephone interviews is somewhat less. Travel time and cost of travel are eliminated. This is especially important when respondents are geographically dispersed or when callbacks are required. A second advantage is the speed of data collection. Of the three survey methods, it is the fastest way to obtain data. With a short questionnaire, an interviewer can complete up to ten interviews per hour. Because the interviews are being carried out from a central location, it is easier for the researcher to monitor and control the quality of the interviewing. Because of the absence of face-to-face contact, there is less opportunity for interviewer bias — that is not to say that interviewer bias is completely eliminated. The interviewer can still vary the tone of his or her voice, ask leading questions or misrepresent respondents' answers.

Limitations of Telephone Interviewing

Telephone interviewing has some limitations. Firstly, only a limited amount and detail of information can be collected. A good rule-of-thumb is to keep the interviews approximately fifteen to twenty minutes long; respondents are unlikely to stay on the phone for a longer period unless they are highly interested in the survey subject. In general, refusal to co-operate is directly related to interview length. It is easier for the respondent to terminate the interview by simply hanging up. Therefore telephone interviews must be relatively short, simple and interesting. As already mentioned, the telephone book as a sampling frame may not be representative of the population of interest. Random digit and plus-one dialling helps reduce this problem. It does not, however, compensate for households that do not have a telephone. This can be particularly so in rural and lower-income areas. A related problem is when a single telephone serves an entire block of apartments or flats.

Because visual aids cannot be used in telephone interviews, certain types of research such as packaging, print advertising, or some concept tests, cannot be conducted on the phone. This limitation can be overcome by sending the respondent the required visual material in advance. Because of the more impersonal nature of telephone interviewing, response error or interviewer bias, while still present, is probably less than in the personal interview method. Finally, ownership of telephone answering machines (and call answering service) is making access to consumers increasingly more difficult. However, if enough call-backs are made at different times and on different days, most respondents are contactable.

- **Computer-Assisted Telephone Interviewing (CATI)**

A recent development involves conducting telephone interviews using a computer to guide the interviews. Telephone interviewers, wearing headsets, are seated at computer terminals. The computer may or may not dial the number to be called. Monitors display the questions, one at a time. As the interviewer asks the question, he or she records the response directly into the computer, and it is automatically stored in memory. Therefore, the time-consuming steps of coding, editing and entering data are eliminated. Because the responses are entered directly into the computer, interim and update reports, or data analysis or results can be provided almost instantaneously. This type of computer-assisted interviewing works best when answers to the questionnaire are highly structured, i.e. pre-coded possible responses to the questions, with unacceptable answers being rejected by the computer. This may also help increase the accuracy of the data being collected. It is expected that voice recognition technology will be a standard feature of CATI in the future.

A variation of the above is the completely automated telephone survey (CATS). A computer dials a phone number. A recording is used to introduce the survey and ask the questions. The respondent uses the push buttons on the telephone to respond and interact with the computer.

Box 6.2 Computers and the telephone take over from pencil and paper

The image of market research as an industry whose main protagonists are people with clip-boards collecting information from passers-by in streets or from people at home is one that is changing rapidly. Pencil and paper have been the main tools of the industry for many years, ticking boxes and completing questionnaires. But as the information needs of industry become more complex, questionnaires are becoming longer and more complicated, putting severe strains on this method of data collection.

The telephone and the computer are also increasingly important as tools of the industry but the real revolution has now begun as their capabilities have been combined to produce the interview method used to an ever greater extent today — computer-assisted telephone interviewing. In fact there are two revolutions underlying this change. The computer is changing the way market research is undertaken, with new standards of accuracy being achieved and, alongside this, new skills required for scripting of questionnaires for off-screen delivery.

But perhaps more important has been the revolution in how we communicate. The telephone is now accepted as a standard tool of market research, with the resulting data standing alongside that collected face-to-face. This change in attitude to telecommunications is exemplified by our use of the fax. We no longer feel the need to ring to ensure that our fax message has been received. The medium has achieved a level of trust that would have been unheard of ten years ago and is now commonplace.

In the USA nearly all quantitative work is done by phone. With free local calls in many states and telephone penetration at almost 100%, the telephone is a very economic way to carry out research.

Across Europe the proportion of interviewing by telephone varies widely. In Scandinavian countries telephone interviewing accounts for at least one in four of all interviews. In the UK the telephone accounted for 20% of all interviews in 1995, an increase of 10% on 1994. Over 90% of this telephone interviewing in the UK uses computer-assisted telephone interviewing techniques. Pen and paper are becoming a thing of the past and this blend of telephone with computer technology has been embraced fully by the industry for much quantitative work. To put this in perspective, personal interviewing still accounts for 40% of all interviews in the UK but this figure is being steadily chipped away each year by the telephone. Naturally use of the telephone for market research is dependent on telephone ownership being at statistically acceptable levels. The internationally recognised norm of households is 80% penetration. Residential telephone ownership in Ireland passed this level late in 1995 and is expected to exceed 85% by the end of this year. It varies across the country as you might expect. In Dublin, the area with the highest level, it is almost 95%. Only in particularly remote pockets of the south east does it go below the international norm. And that is a factor that can be accommodated in any sample work. For business-to-business, where ownership is virtually 100%, the telephone has become a totally viable tool for research, contributing to the growth of this area.

As CATI is hardly known in Ireland, its advantages need to be stated:

- Increased speed of project turnaround.
- Greater quality control of interviews and interviewers.
- The ability to use more complex questionnaires.
- Reduced interview time.
- Automatic and clean data entry — elimination of error.
- No key punching.
- Reduction in costs.

Basically the programme takes care that data entry is correct, that rotations of questions are accommodated automatically, and that routings through questionnaires are followed. And because data is being entered directly to the computer there is no need for checking and editing questionnaires nor punching. The computer leads the interviewer though the interview and does not allow the wrong data to be entered. With interview times on the telephone set to be less than 25 minutes, interviewee fatigue is not a factor. The saving in time is substantial. What may take six to seven weeks by pen and paper can be achieved in seven to eight days. The set of questions agreed on Friday can produce results a week later with 1,000 or more interviews completed. Such timings as these are becoming standard in the UK. One company is now promising results at 9.30 in the evening from a questionnaire going into the field at 3.30 the previous afternoon.

It is becoming a positively Utopian state of affairs for marketing management. Reliable, usable information available very swiftly and at short notice. And has this wonderful state of affairs reached these shores? It has, because since January of this year, the market research agency MRC has been operating its Telephone Research Centre in the north of Dublin using the latest software available in Europe.

Built using state-of-the-art telecentre design and computer technology, the Centre has twenty workstations and can provide a research facility of up to twelve hours a day, seven days a week. The panel of interviewers now consists of around 100 individuals, fully trained to MRC's standards. As partners in the Euro-quest group of market research agencies, these standards are international. The question of language, or of regional accents if this arises, is not a problem because the panel has been recruited to provide this facility.

Sample management is a critical aspect of any telephone research unit. The computer system in MRC's Telephone Research Centre has been designed to accept samples from clients in a variety of formats. For random sampling the Centre is equipped to use the Irish telephone directory as the core universe, with a statistically valid methodology for 'capturing' non-listed numbers. 'Who gave you my number?' is a question that management at the Centre gets asked fairly often. The answer, entirely truthfully, is that no one did. It was arrived at on a totally random basis, increasing the statistical validity of the method. Another bugbear of the industry is the fear of refusals; in point of fact, the rate of refusals for telephone interviews, at around 10%, runs lower than for face-to-face.

In face-to-face interviewing a similar revolution is going on as lap-tops have begun to take over from pen and paper. CAPI (computer assisted personal interviewing) provides even more advantages for clients, but cost is not, yet, one of them. With a mission to be at the forefront of technological advance in the industry and raise quality standards, MRC are also providing this service to their clients with a 'fleet' of lap-tops now in constant use north and south of the border.

The atmosphere of innovation and technology at MRC, pushing at the boundaries of the possible, in this exciting development for the market research business in Ireland, has almost to be seen to be believed. It's far removed from pencil, paper and clipboard on Grafton Street.

(Source: from *IMJ*, 'Computers and the telephone take over from parcel and paper', pp. 12–13, November 1996.)

• The Postal Interview

The postal survey is a self-administered questionnaire sent to respondents through the post. It is very much a paper and pen method of collecting data.

There is no interviewer available to:

1. ask the questions;
2. probe for more information;
3. induce co-operation;
4. record answers;
5. clarify questions for the respondent;
6. guide the interview.

[Handwritten margin notes: envelope must strike person arouse curiosity • covering letter necessary to explain why you are doing interview • anonymity of respondent id. coded]

The questionnaire is administered to the respondent by the respondent, and the respondent completes and returns the questionnaire.

The Procedure

As mentioned previously, as there is no interviewer present to clarify issues or to encourage the respondent's co-operation, the construction of the questionnaire and related materials is crucial to the success of this survey method. The researcher must make decisions about the various elements of the postal interview package. It is composed of:

- the out-going envelope;
- the cover letter;
- the questionnaire itself;
- the return envelope;
- the incentives used.

Unless the curiosity and co-operation of the respondent are quickly aroused, it is likely that the respondent will 'shelve' the questionnaire. The cover letter that accompanies the questionnaire is an important means of inducing the reader to complete and return the questionnaire. The cover letter should at least:

1. Explain the purpose and importance of the study.
2. Say how and why the respondent was chosen for participation.
3. State who is sponsoring the study.
4. Indicate why the respondent's co-operation is important.
5. Detail what the respondent is being asked to do.
6. State how the information provided will be used.
7. Indicate whether the respondent will remain anonymous.
8. State what degree of confidentiality applies.

The cover letter, while not too long, may also indicate the amount of effort and time required from the respondent, mention a token incentive and refer the reader to a pre-paid reply envelope.

Advantages of Postal Interview Method

Postal surveys are particularly versatile in reaching all types of people (i.e. consumer or business), in all geographic areas, rural and urban areas, and at the same low cost. The postal survey method generally will have a cost advantage over other survey methods, though it is not cheap. It may necessitate follow-up mailings which require additional postage and printing costs.

The interviewer–respondent interaction is absent in the postal survey. Therefore this dimension of response error is eliminated. (However, as we will see in Chapter 8, response error can still occur in postal surveys.) Also interviewer bias in the selection of sample members is eliminated.

Another advantage of postal surveys is that the respondent has more time to formulate and record his or her answers. The questionnaire can be filled in at a time and pace convenient to the respondent. In some situations, for example business-to-business marketing research, postal surveys allow respondents to collect facts, such as sales or inventory figures, that they may not know off-hand. In consumer research the respondent may be able to give a more valid and accurate answer by having the time and flexibility to check in the fridge or consult other family members.

Postal questionnaires have been shown to be superior when collecting data on sensitive or embarrassing topics.[10] This can be attributed to anonymity of the respondent. Anonymity can also reduce the possibility of respondents giving socially acceptable answers, i.e. reduce social desirability bias.

Limitations of Postal Surveys

The primary limitation of this method is that of non-response error. Surveys that are boring, confusing or too complex get thrown in the bin. Response rate refers to the number or percentage of respondents that return the questionnaire. Mail surveys are usually plagued by low rates of return, typically 10%, and often drag over many weeks. Often the questionnaires received are either poorly filled out or incomplete, further adding to analysis problems.[11] However, although exceptional, it is not unknown for a properly planned and well-designed postal survey to achieve response rates of up to 70%. Much depends on the length of the questionnaire, content, group surveyed, incentives employed and other factors.[12]

A fairly high response rate can be achieved if certain techniques are used by the researcher to increase participation.[13] These techniques will be discussed later. However, non-response is only a problem if the respondents are different to those who do not respond. Certain types of people — people with more education, higher-level occupations, women, students and others have been shown to have a greater probability of not responding.[14] People who have a particular interest (e.g. a hobby) in the topic of the research have a greater probability of responding. A general rule-of-thumb, the questionnaire should not exceed six pages in length. An over-lengthy questionnaire will most likely be discarded by the respondent.

Sequence bias is also a threat in postal surveys — respondents can change their answers after seeing later questions, and there is no control over the order in which questions are answered. There may also be problems with open-ended questions in postal surveys, whereby responses from less articulate and less literate participants may be very brief or non-existent. Postal questionnaires are therefore often highly standardised with structured questions and clear-cut instructions. Another problem with the postal survey is the turnaround time required. A time lag of two to three weeks is common for receiving the majority of responses. The researcher needs to factor in time for follow-up mailings, leading to a total turnaround time of up to five weeks. For BOI, it takes about four months from sending out the questionnaire, putting all the scores together and getting results.[15]

This makes postal surveys unsuitable for measuring certain characteristics, e.g. changes in political opinion leading up to an election. It also makes the responses vulnerable to external events taking place during the study.

There is no guarantee that the intended respondent, i.e. the person's name on the envelope, will be the actual person who fills out the questionnaire. This is a particular problem with business-to-business research. A busy director or financial controller may request a subordinate to fill in and return the questionnaire.

Postal surveys also require suitable mailing lists. An Post has a customer database called 'Targetpoint' which it rents to other companies. This is one of the largest databases in Ireland containing 1.2 million consumers.[16] *Kompass* Ireland publishes a range of directories for business use, including *Register of Industry and Commerce*, listing details of 16,000 Irish companies' contact names, addresses, phone and fax numbers and product information.[17] Regardless of its source, a mailing list should be current and closely related to the population of interest. In some instances a suitable mailing list may not exist.

Finally, like telephone interviewing, it is not possible for the market researcher to make concurrent observations (e.g. physical appearance and non-verbal cues) as is the case with the personal interview.

With all these limitations, one might easily wonder why postal questionnaires are ever used. Bank of Ireland is planning to phase out paper questionnaires in favour of the telephone to survey its customers.[18] They are, nonetheless, a frequent and popular choice among market researchers.

• Reducing Non-response in Postal Questionnaires

As we have already mentioned, non-response is always a potential hazard when conducting postal survey research. In fact, whatever the survey mode used, those who respond may be different to those who choose not to. Those who respond may be more involved with the product, they may have more education, or they might be more satisfied with the service provider than the target population of interest.[19] Researchers have developed a number of techniques to influence the response rate of postal respondents. These are dealt with in summary form in Box 6.3 and Box 6.4. It should be noted that some of these techniques could also be applied to other survey methods. There is evidence that with the main types of survey methods, the inclusion of some monetary incentive or product promotion will increase response rates.[20] To encourage people to fill in and return postal questionnaires, BOI promises a donation to a group of charities for every response it gets back.[21]

Box 6.3 Methods used to increase postal survey response

Inducement	*Examples*
Preliminary notification	Advance letter or postcard, telephone pre-notification.
Foot-in-the-door	Use of small initial incentive and then a larger subsequent incentive to those who comply with the small incentive. *eg free draw entry*
Personalisation	Hand-addressed envelope, personal signature, individually typed/addressed cover letter.
Anonymity	Assurance of anonymity, use/non-use of ID number.
Response deadline	Different due dates following receipt of questionnaire.
Appeals	Social utility, help the sponsor, egoistic.
Sponsorship	Company, trade association, university researcher.
Incentives	Non-monetary (for example, ballpoint pens, summary of findings), monetary (for example, given to sample member, donated to charity).
Questionnaire length	Printing of both sides of sheet, white space related to perceived length.
Questionnaire size, reproduction and colour	Standard A-sizes, printed, mimeographed, various colours.
Type of postage (out-going)	Commemorative stamp, metered postage, first class, third class.
Type of postage (return envelopes)	Business reply permit, regular stamps, metered postage.
Follow-ups	Different intervals, postcard, letter, replacement questionnaire

(Source: Jeffery Connant, Denise Smart and Bruce Walker, 'Mail survey facilitation techniques: an assessment and proposal regarding reporting practices', *Journal of the Marketing Research Society*, Vol. 32 No. 4 (1990), 569–80.)

Improving Returns

There are many examples in the research literature of studies which examine the difficulties of improving postal survey returns. A number of helpful ideas on improving response rates are available.[22]

Follow-ups

Follow-ups, or reminders, are very sucessful in increasing response rates. Since each successive follow-up results in added returns, the very persistent researcher can potentially achieve an extremely high total response rate. However, the value of additional information thus obtained must be weighed against the costs required for successive contacts.

Preliminary Notification

There is evidence that advance notification, particularly by telephone, is effective in increasing response rates; it also serves to accelerate the rate of return. However, follow-ups are a better investment than preliminary notification.

Concurrent Techniques

1. *Questionnaire length.* Although common sense suggests that short questionnaires should obtain higher response rates than longer questionnaires, research evidence does not support this view.
2. *Survey sponsorship.* There is little experimental evidence concerning the influence of survey sponsorship on response rates; however, the sparse evidence that does exist suggests that official or 'respected' sponsorship increases response rates.
3. *Return envelopes.* A study that tested the hypothesis that return envelopes increase reponse rates suggests that the inclusion of a stamped, return envelope does encourage response because it simplifies questionnaire return.
4. *Postage.* Many tests regarding postage are reported in the literature, but few studies have tested the same variables. The existing evidence shows that special delivery is very effective in increasing response rates. Findings do not show a significant advantage for first class over third class, for commemorative stamps over ordinary postage, for stamped mail over metered mail, or for multiple, small-domination stamps over single, larger-dominational stamps.
5. *Personalisation.* Empirical evidence suggests that personalisation of the mailing has no clear-cut advantage in terms of improved response rates. Neither personal inside addresses nor individually signed cover letters significantly increased response rates; personally typed cover letters proved to be somewhat effective in most but not all cases cited. The one study that tested the use of titled signature versus one without a title did show a significant advantage in favour of the title.
6. *Cover letters.* The influence of the cover letter on response rates has received almost no experimental attention, although the cover letter is an integral part of

the mail survey. It is the most logical vehicle for persuading individuals to respond, yet the few studies that are reported offer no insights as to its formulation.
7. *Anonymity.* Experimental evidence shows that the promise of anonymity to respondent — either explicit or implied — has no significant effect on response rates.
8. *Size, reproduction and colour.* The few studies that examined the effects of questionnaire size, method of reproduction and colour found no significant difference in response rates.
9. *Money incentives.* A monetary incentive sent with the questionnaire is very effective in increasing response rates. Larger sums bring in added response, but at a cost that may exceed the value of the added information.
10. *Deadline dates.* The few studies that tested the impact of deadline dates found that they did not increase the response rate; however, they did serve to accelerate the rate of questionnaire return.

Box 6.4 Types of appeals used in survey research

Appeal	*Wording of appeals*
Social utility	'Your assistance is needed!! Your attitudes and opinions can provide information that contributes to understanding how consumers can be better served by local retail shopping facilities . . . Your co-operation is truly appreciated.'
Help-the-sponsor	'We need your assistance!! Your attitudes and opinions are very important to our successful completion of this study . . . We truly appreciate your co-operation.'
Egoistic	'Your opinions are important!! It's important for you to express your opinion so Madison's retailers will know the types of products and shopping facilities you would like to have available . . . Thanks for expressing your opinions.'
Combined appeal	'Your opinions are important and useful!! Your attitudes and opinions are important for three reasons: (1) they can provide information that leads to an understanding of how consumers can be better served by local retail shopping facilities; (2) they will enable Madison's retailers to know the types of products and shopping facilities you would like to have available; and (3) they will help us successfully complete this study . . . thank you for your co-operation.'

(Source: Michael J. Houston and John R. Nevin, 'The effects of source and appeal on mail survey response patterns', *Journal of Marketing Research*, August 1977, pp. 347–87, published by the American Marketing Association.)

• Methods of Estimating the Degree of Non-response Error

Despite all efforts, it is next to impossible to totally eliminate non-response in survey research, be it postal, telephone or personal interview. Five methods to deal with the effect of non-response error are briefly presented below:

1. Sensitivity analysis

This approach requires the researcher to determine how different each successive call-back group is from the previous respondent group. If the research decision is insensitive to this difference, no further call-backs are necessary. The central question here is how different the non-respondents would have to be in order for this difference to have an effect on our decision.

2. Trend projection

If, from successive call-backs, a trend emerges on the variables under study, this trend can be utilised to estimate the characteristics of the non-respondent group.

3. Sub-sampling of non-respondents

A separate study is conducted with a sample of the non-respondents. This data is then used to make generalisations about *all* of the non-respondents.

4. Subjective estimate

The researcher uses judgment and past experience to estimate the proportionate effect of non-response.

5. The 'ostrich' approach

Here the researcher merely assumes that non-respondents are the same as respondents, i.e. there is non-response but no non-response bias. This is obviously a risky approach to deal with non-response in survey research.

• Combining Survey Techniques

[margin note: it may be necessary to amalgamate the approaches to get sufficient results]

Since each of the basic methods of data collection has its own strengths and limitations, it may be necessary to combine two or more approaches to survey research. For example, in a tourism research study, personal interviews may be carried out with tourists visiting the area, telephone interviews conducted with regional tourism information offices and postal questionnaires sent to tour operators.

Alternative Means of Administration

The preceding discussion covered the traditional and primary methods of collecting survey data. There are however also variations of the above and emerging survey approaches.

- Restaurants, hotels and service providers frequently have short questionnaires available for guests and customers to fill out after they have experienced the service, e.g. Mother Hubbards, Bewleys, Statoil etc. However, it is interesting to note that only 1% of most hotel guests complete their questionnaires.[23]
- Self-administered questionnaires are left on a table/counter with instructions, pens and deposit box at the exit point of, for example, a tourism attraction or bookshop seeking customer feedback. UCI introduced a 'viewpoint' box in the cinema for people to air their views. It also provides a freepost facility for those who want to take the questionnaire home.[24]
- Using the drop-off method, questionnaires are hand-delivered to the respondent's home or place of business and are collected at a later date (e.g. census of population research). A variation is where the respondent returns the completed questionnaire by post.
- Questionnaires are distributed via print media such as magazines and newspapers. Completed questionnaires are returned to a 'freepost' address.
- Fax surveys have emerged as an alternative means of collecting information from business markets. While having some of the features of the postal method, fax surveys have the advantage of speed. A variation is the computer-based faxing of a questionnaire to the respondent who returns it via the fax machine or post.
- Use of an automated interviewing line can eliminate some of the problems associated with postal and telephone interviewing. It can work as follows: an appropriate mailing list and sample are developed and a package is mailed in the typical way. The package contains a unique ID number, stimulus materials, and instructions to call an 800- number. The 800- number is available 24 hours a day, seven days a week. Respondents call at their convenience. Participants key in their responses using their telephone key pads.
- Computer interactive surveys and interactive kiosks (see Box 6.5) are becoming popular at trade shows, exhibitions and conferences. The respondent interacts directly with an on-site computer. The questions appear on a computer screen and the respondent replies using the keyboard or touch screen. It is probably best to use only dichotomous or multiple-choice type questions.
- E-mail questionnaires will probably become increasingly more popular in the future. Decisive Surveys is a Windows-based computer program that allows the researcher to create a questionnaire, send it to any number of e-mail addresses, receive the responses, perform simple tabulations and make graphs of findings. Decisive Survey may be viewed at http://www.decisive.com. As Internet access by and to households is limited, such surveys are at the moment primarily used in business-to-business research.
- Laptops have begun to take over from pen, paper and clipboard of personal interviews — CAPI (computer assisted personal interviewing). Ci3 is an example of a software package for creating and administering questionnaires by PC.

- Surveys can also be conducted by sending a computer disk (in the post) to the respondent. The questionnaire and instructions are contained on the disk. It requires the respondent to have access to a computer. Completed disk-questionnaires are returned to the researcher in the post.

Box 6.5 Using interactive kiosks for retail research

Traditionally, researchers have used phone and exit interviews, shop intercepts and postal surveys to study retail shopping experiences. Although these methods have their strengths, there is an alternative, and that is kiosk-based research. Kiosks are multimedia touch-screen computers contained in free-standing cabinets. They can be programmed to perform complicated surveys, show full colour scanned images (store layouts, products), play high quality stereo sound clips and show video segments. With little need for instruction, most people enjoy these interviews and 'play' them with little reservation. Kiosks can also be used at trade shows and exhibitions. Kiosks, like exit interviews, score high in terms of capturing recent experiences and are useful for interviewing low-incidence respondents because they are on site. At the same time kiosk-based research tends to be less expensive than exit interviews, allowing a higher number of stores to be included in the survey. A bonus is that people tend to give more honest answers to a computer than to another human being. Kiosks have several other advantages. Internal control, for example, is much higher with kiosks than with other methods. Because the survey is preprogrammed, the researcher doesn't have to worry about whether the correct visual stimuli were shown or whether the right skip pattern was followed. Although kiosk-based research does not replace the more traditional ways to capture the shopping experience, it should be considered a less expensive, easily implemented alternative, especially when evaluating hard-to-reach populations.

Source: Adapted from *Marketing News*, 2 January 1995, Vol. 39 No. 1, 'Using interactive kiosks for retail research', Beth Schneider.

Box 6.6 Internet marketing research

Consumers now live in a multimedia world. They are bombarded with sights, sounds and motion that subtly communicate a product's benefits. Multimedia is one new emerging method of conducting marketing research among the youth market on topics such as music, fashion and entertainment. Multimedia represents a new and powerful method of channelling information from teenagers to marketers. But today's computer-based techniques don't interact well with all consumers. Respondents need at least some level of comfort with a keyboard or mouse.

Marketing researchers, as they strive to find increasingly efficient design solutions for their clients, are attempting to keep pace with on-line technology. These efforts have led to on-line focus groups and surveys as well as greater interest overall in research and idea generation. On-line research can provide the researcher with a solution that is sensitive to both budget and time constraints. Now thanks to innovations in technology, researchers know in real time what is happening in the marketplace.

There are three electronic primary data collection methods. These are: the World Wide Web, e-mail, and on-line discussion groups. HTML forms (also called web questionnaires) are accessible via the WWW or via an Intranet. E-mail questionnaires are essentially questionnaires which are written in ASCII format, or alternatively an e-mail with an attached HTML form. Unlike e-mail questionnaires which are quite restrictive in their potential size, format and design, web forms or questionnaires can potentially integrate colour, graphics, sound and video. On-line discussion groups are text based and controlled by moderators. Only specified users are permitted to take part and the discussions are moderated in order to initiate dialogue from respondents.

For certain types of research (on-line focus group discussions) the Internet has some fervent supporters. With an on-line discussion you have an immediate transcript, already in computer form, and the respondent can get involved from anywhere in the world. If the topic is about a sensitive subject the respondents don't have to sit in front of other people and say what they are thinking. Sensitive topics such as birth control, health care and personal finance sometimes can be researched more candidly on-line than in person. However, it should also be noted that e-mail provides less anonymity to the respondent in that the receiver can in most cases identify the respondent.

In conventional surveys, the initial contact is made via telephone, post or person-to-person meeting. However, the principal method of communicating over the Internet is e-mail. With on-line surveys, respondents can choose either to answer the questionnaire on their screens and return it electronically, or print out paper copies, fill them out and return them by mail or fax.

Coupled with developments in software (e.g. SNAP which combines questionnaire design, data collection and analysis), web surveys remove any errors that typically occur in surveying techniques that rely on human encoding of the collected data. Also a more recent development is that, instead of scrolling down a web page to answer a survey, questions will be shown to the respondent individually (or in sections) and the actual responses to questions will determine which questions will follow thereafter.

To date, many studies have looked at electronic primary data collection compared with conventional research methods such as postal or face-to-face interviewing. There is very little evidence which proves that electronic survey methods enjoy higher response rates when compared to other methods. However there is evidence to show that a quicker response can be obtained from e-mail as opposed to postal surveys. There is also some evidence (although to a lesser extent) to show that responses to open-ended questions in e-mail surveys are higher than that of conventional postal surveys.

As a way of reaching certain target groups, such as anything to do with IT and technical people, business people, academics, early adopters and youth markets, the Internet can be quite useful. Yet because household e-mail penetration is still low, it cannot be considered as a representative sample of Joe Public. A parallel is to be found in terms of the development of telephone interviewing in Europe, where twenty years ago a number of countries were waiting for the household penetration of telephones to reach critical mass before CATI was both viable and representative.

The sampling frame for electronic surveys is restricted to members of the population who have access to computer networks and to those who feel comfortable using them. As more and more organisations and individuals have access to and rely on computer-mediated communication, the opportunity for network, electronic, or on-line surveying will increase. When TVs and computers converge we will become a truly 'wired' generation.

And as the on-line use population continues to rise and the profile more closely matches that of the general population, the results of these methods will be useful in extrapolating results to form conclusions about the general population.

(Source: Adapted from: 'Electronic surveys — new methods of primary data collection', Competitive Paper, 27th EMAC Conference, May 1998; 'Fishing by the Net', *Marketing*, 22 August 1996, pp. 25—6; 'Online technology creates research tools', *Marketing News*, Vol. 30 No. 6; 'Virtual research exists, but how real is it?', *Marketing News*, 3 June 1996, Vol. 30 No. 12; 'Fountain of youth', *Marketing*, 14 September 1995, pp. 39—41; 'Multimedia research can improve NPD today', *Marketing News*, 3 June 1996, Vol. 30 No. 12; 'Technology forces changes in marketing research', *Marketing News*, 23 October 1995, Vol. 29 No. 22.)

Box 6.7
Virtual reality shopping and market research are still in their early stages, but the implications are far-reaching and will affect many companies

"A shelf full of washing powder stares you in the face. Every conceivable brand is there, row upon row. They are brightly coloured and neatly stacked. They could be yours. Just press a button. This is not a dream. This is virtual reality shopping with a vengeance. Neat pictures of supermarket shelves are depicted on the screen. Each shelf displays a different sort of product. You move from one to another with ease and choose what you would like to buy.

Visionary Shopping is a system developed by Harvard academics and is providing what is described as 'a virtual-reality computer simulation of a supermarket'. Its main use currently is as an alternative market research tool. In Britain, two companies have tried it out — one a snacks manufacturer and one a producer of soft drinks.

Virtual reality techniques have significant potential in new product development (NPD) research. Virtual shopping can reduce the NPD timescale and assist consumers in examining new concepts.

It is 10% to 20% cheaper than conventional market research and it takes two weeks rather than six months. If respondents are interested in something, they simply touch it and it emerges from the shelf. Closer inspection can be achieved by touching a magnifying glass at the side of the screen. If it looks worth buying, simply touch the article again and it drops into a screen trolley.

'We have three basic types of market research — price of goods, promotions of goods and package testing. These work particularly effectively because consumers can actually look at a shelf on the screen to make their purchasing decisions rather than read options from a list' says Dr Stephen Needel, President of VS.

One of the most obvious ways in which companies can benefit from virtual reality is in the area of packaging. 'The new design does not even need to be made up. We can put it in the system just using the artwork and test it out. This can save manufacturers hundreds of thousands of dollars', explains Needel.

A criticism of VR-based techniques is that they generate an unusually high level of interest in shopping due to their novelty. More research is needed to assess how these techniques affect consumer behaviour."

Source: Adapted from: *The Evening Standard*, 'Couch potatoes in the supermarket', MCC95, February 02 (765) by Joanne Hart, and 'VR techniques in NPD research', *JMRS*, October 1995, Vol. 37 No. 4, p. 345 (11), Philip Rosenberg and Leslie Chernatony.)

Table 6.1 Strengths and weaknesses of principal survey methods

	Mail	Telephone	Personal	Internet
1. Flexibility	Poor	Good	Excellent	Fair
2. Quantity of data that can be collected	Good	Fair	Excellent	Good
3. Control of interviewer effects	Excellent	Fair	Poor	Excellent
4. Control of sample	Fair	Excellent	Fair	Fair
5. Speed of data collection	Poor	Excellent	Good	Excellent
6. Response rate	Poor	Good	Good	Poor
7. Cost	Good	Fair	Poor	Excellent
8. Sample frame	Good	Excellent	Fair	Poor

(Source: *Principles of Marketing*, Chapter 8, p. 328, European edition 1999, Philip Kotler *et al.*)

Panel Research

A panel or longitudinal survey is a form of sample survey from which comparative data from the sampling units are taken on more than one occasion. It is a form of continuous research reporting on the behaviour of the same respondents over time. Panels can be made up of individuals, households, firms or retail outlets and are a convenient method of obtaining continuous information over a period of time.[25] A longitudinal study that gathers data from the same sample of individuals over time is called a consumer panel. Households are commonly selected on the basis of random sampling.

Most panels use some form of 'diary' which members fill in with details of purchases or product usage. Diary data that is recorded regularly over a period of time allows the researcher to track repeat-purchasing behaviour and changes in purchasing habits. Completed diaries are posted back to the researcher or collected at regular intervals.

Panels are by nature longitudinal. This makes them different to regular surveys which are typically cross-sectional, i.e data is collected at a single point. Continuous research can be equated to a motion picture whereas one-off survey research is akin to a snapshot.

The advantage of panel research over one-off surveys is the ability to measure changes in the behaviour of individuals. A continuous panel is one way of conducting quasi-experiments, that is to say that the effect of changes in price, advertising and packaging etc. can be monitored through panel research. Experimentation is dealt with in the next chapter. Because there is an on-going relationship between the panel members and the research company, there is also more opportunity to collect attitudinal and classification information to help better understand the observed changes in behaviour.[26]

A major drawback with panels is the problem of mortality. For one reason or another panel members may choose not to continue and drop out. Incentives are offered to encourage continuing participation. There is always the possibility that those who drop out will differ from those who remain on the panel. Replacements should be as representative as possible. There is a tendency for newly recruited panel members to initially change their behaviour because of the novelty of the reporting responsibility. It may be therefore advisable to exclude the results from these households until the novelty has worn off and their behaviour has returned to normal. This may take a week or two.

There can also be the problem of selection bias. Many individuals or households may refuse to participate, thereby raising the question of how representative are panels of the population of interest.

The following section outlines the two major types of panel techniques in Ireland.[27]

1. Nielson operates a retail audit service. It monitors the performance of Fast Moving Consumer Goods (FMCGs) by collecting data in a sample of retail outlets spread throughout the country. The sample outlet data is grossed up to the total number of outlets in the country to give estimates on volume of sales, market share, average retail selling price, distribution and out of stocks. A number of different services, or Indices, is provided. For example, food, on-licence, chemists, and confectionery are all separate services. Nielsen is the larger of the two market measurement panels.
2. Attwood sends diaries to a continuous sample of housekeepers who provide information based on their household purchases. The consumer records type, size, price and place of purchase for each item printed in the diary. The data is used to estimate total market size and share. Attwood, however, is able to say what type of consumer is buying the product where Nielsen shows information relating to performance in the shop. Other analyses can also be run by Attwood data such as brand switching, repeat buying and consumer loyalty.

Overall, panels are not as commonly used in Ireland as in the UK, Europe and USA. Abroad they are frequently called syndicated services. This is dealt with in Chapter 4.

Omnibus Surveys

Omnibus surveys are shared surveys. Like panels, they are a form of continuous research. This means that measurement is conducted on an ongoing basis and is designed to monitor and track changes in the marketplace. Omnibus surveys are good at tracking consumer purchasing, awareness and attitude trends. Omnibus surveys are run by research companies. Clients buy space in the questionnaire by adding questions to meet their requirements.[28] For the client company, it can be a quick and cheap method of collecting information at short notice. Such surveys consist of several sections, each dealing with a different topic and conducted confidentially for an individual client. Individual client companies share the costs but not the results. Questions can be directed to all adults or to particular groups — such as housewives, young people, car owners, alcohol drinkers, or simply to people who use the company's product.[29]

Interviewing and other administrative costs of each survey are shared collectively by the participating clients. Omnibus surveys can therefore provide a very economical facility for obtaining national and regional survey data on products or services.[30] Questions can cover many areas of interest to individual clients, e.g. brand awareness, price awareness, frequency of purchase, place of purchase, media exposure etc.[31]

In Ireland, Irish Marketing Surveys and Lansdowne Market Research are two companies which offer an Omnibus service. The following are some of the marketing issues recently covered by Lansdowne Omnibus surveys:[32]

- Measure trial and consumer acceptance, following the launch of a new snack food.
- Monitor brand switching activity in the beer market to identify recruitment and defection levels for individual brands.
- Track housewives' shopping patterns and customer satisfaction with multiple and symbol group stores.
- Annually monitor the corporate image of major public companies.
- Identify emerging niche sectors within the alcoholic drinks market.
- Evaluate performance of advertising for a wide selection of branded products before, during and after advertising campaigns.
- Measure attitudes to editorial content of newspaper, radio and TV programmes.
- Determine awareness, comprehension and reactions to new services in the financial sector.
- Measure public opinion on a wide range of social and political issues.

• Observation Methods

We have already looked at surveys as a methodology for conducting descriptive research. Observation research is the second way to conduct descriptive research. There is a long tradition of observational research in the social sciences, especially amongst those researchers influenced by social anthropology. The term observation is usually used to refer to methods of generating data which involve the researcher immersing himself in a research setting, and systematically observing dimensions of that setting, interactions, relationships, actions, events, and so on.[33] In this section we restrict ourselves to observation of ongoing and current behaviour. Observation involves systematically recording the behavioural patterns of people, objects and occurrences without questioning or communicating with them. Information may be recorded as events occur or completed from records of past events. It can be a source of low-cost research information. Yet it is probably one of the most under-utilised approaches to collecting marketing research data. However it is rare for a research design to rely entirely on observational research. In practice observational research is used with other data collection methods. Some retailers use a mixture of survey and observational research. Retailers use a data collection technique called 'super walks', where a researcher walks with a shopper through the store recording the shopper's comments while observing their buying behaviour and decision-making.

Mystery shopping is a technique that is becoming increasingly popular. This is where the researcher poses as a customer to find out what happens in the normal interaction between the customer and salesperson. Mystery shopping has changed dramatically in the past ten years from a hiring-and-firing technique used predominantly in restaurants (and mainly in the US) to a 'nurturing' learning tool. Researchers are now beginning to use it more as a means of evaluating the shopping/buying process. Traditionally it was confined to banks and fast-food outlets and petrol stations but now it is used almost everywhere that a service is delivered.[34]

Box 6.8 What makes an effective mystery shopping programme?

- Defining clear objectives is essential. These objectives should take into account existing training and operational procedures and desired standards of customer service and sales performance.
- Questionnaires should be designed to record objective observational feedback. There should be a mixture of closed and open questions and plenty of opportunity for assessor comments and suggestions for improvement.
- Some issues of front-line performance are more important than others. To reflect this, individual questions, and questionnaire categories, should be weighted. Appropriate weighting is critical to the overall framing of the evaluation.
- Assessors should receive comprehensive training and clear written instuctions. All evaluations should be completed over a similar period of time, with assessors provided with specific scenarios and instructions to ask for the same or similar products/services.
- Completed questionnaires should be quality checked for validity, accuracy, consistency and objectivity.
- Reporting on timely basis. Turnaround time should be kept to a maximum of 30 days.
- If possible reports should be location-specific and also provide summary information. Questionnaire category statistical results should be outlined in depth, backed up with adequate qualitative information. This qualitative information is important as it improves the actionability of the findings by providing the reasons behind the various category scores.
- Mystery shopping should not be used as a once-off audit. Ongoing programmes are more effective and objective and also allow companies to make real positive changes to front-line performance.

(Source: 'Taking the mystery out of mystery shopping', *Marketing Institute News*, July/August 1998. Aidrian Bushnell.)

The same scientific approach should be used when carrying out observational research, as is applied to other types of research. If proper hypotheses, objectives and sampling procedures are followed, the results may be generalised to a larger population. Observational research is frequently used as an exploratory research tool. In some instances, observation may be the only way to obtain the desired information, e.g. toy manufacturers may provide young children with prototype or a competitor's toys and observe how they play with them. After all, very young children cannot communicate verbal responses.

> **Box 6.9 Look and learn!**
>
> 'We often ask too many questions when all we really need to is observe what people are doing. I don't think that the Japanese car companies asked people in this country if they wanted a cup holder in their car. I believe that they observed people getting into their cars first thing in the morning holding a cup of coffee and looking for a flat surface on which to put the cup.'
>
> (Source: 'Changing demands', *Journal of Advertising Research*, January/February 1996, Vol. 36 No. 1, p. 31(4), by Watts Wacker.)

Observational techniques fall into five different classifications as follows (most observational research will possess two or more degrees of these classifications).

1. Natural versus Contrived Observation

Natural observation involves observing behaviour as it takes place naturally in the environment, for example, as people are shopping in a supermarket or availing themselves of bank services. A cereal company may conduct observational research in the cereal aisle of a supermarket. They may wish to know how the in-store purchase decision appears to be made for adult versus children's cereal. Contrived observation on the other hand involves creating an artificial environment and observing behaviour patterns. An artificial environment may include a simulated supermarket aisle or a test kitchen. Contrived observation allows the researcher to control extraneous variables and is often more efficient than waiting for the same situation to occur of its own accord. However, behaviour that is observed in an artificial environment may be different to what would occur in a real-world situation.

2. Open versus Disguised Observation

In observation research the respondent may or may not be aware that he or she is being observed. Disguised observational research enables respondents to behave naturally, since people tend to behave differently when they know they are being observed. Research can be disguised by using hidden cameras, one-way mirrors, or researchers dressed as sales staff or posing as shoppers.

There are two schools of thought as to how much the presence of the observer will affect people's behaviour patterns. One viewpoint is that the observer effect is small, the other is that the observer can seriously bias the behaviour patterns.

3. Structured versus Unstructured Observation

Observation can be structured or unstructured in much the same way as surveys. For structured observation, the researcher specifies in detail what is to be observed and how the measurements are to be recorded. Structured observation requires using a structured questionnaire-like data collection instrument. Structured observation is appropriate when the decision problem has been clearly defined, the information needed has been specified, and the behaviour patterns to be observed are not overly ambiguous. Structured observation reduces the potential for interviewer bias, increases the reliability of the data, and is most suited to conclusive research. In unstructured observation the researcher is free to note whatever he or she deems relevant. It is most suited to exploratory research, when flexibility is required to identify key components of the problem and to generate hypotheses.

4. Direct versus Indirect Observation

In direct observation, researchers directly observe current behaviour. Much of the observation done in marketing research is of this type. Behaviour is observed as it actually occurs. Indirect observation refers to observing some record of past behaviour, i.e. the effects of the behaviour are observed rather than the behaviour itself. Sherlock Holmes could be considered as an expert in indirect observation. Likewise with archaeologists and forensic scientists. One approach to indirect observation is called the analysis of physical traces. Two examples come to mind. One is where the researcher (with permission) studies the refuse of households in an attempt to determine buyer or usage behaviour. Alternatively, the researcher may conduct a pantry audit. The observer inspects the respondent's cupboards or fridge for the pre-determined products or brands.

Other innovative applications of trace analysis include:

1. Erosion of floor tiles around an exhibit or painting in a museum or art gallery as an indicator of relative popularity.
2. The position of car radio dials in cars brought in for service to determine which national or local radio station is best for the garage to advertise in.
3. An analysis of the cars in the parking area of the Point Depot as an indicator to the target audience for a Murray Raphael Seminar.
4. Brand preference studies and relative store emphasis on different brands is noted by observing the size of the inventory displayed, i.e. number of facings.

Analysis of secondary data and other published sources is another application of indirect observation. Content analysis is an observational technique used to analyse written material (usually advertising copy). Content analysis can be used to measure the change in the content of advertising over a time period. The frequency of appearances of African Americans and other minorities in USA mass media has been a topic of content analysis.

5. Human versus Mechanical Observation

In mechanical observation, mechanical devices rather than human observers record the behaviour being observed. Compared to human observation, such devices may offer increased accuracy, lower costs, and the ability to tackle special measurement requirements and the recording of ongoing behaviour for later analysis. The major mechanical devices used in observation include:

(a) Traffic counters used to measure vehicle or people flow over a stretch of roadway or street. At its simplest it may consist of the observer pressing a button on the counter every time an object passes, e.g. street people-counts used to determine a suitable retail shop location. A more sophisticated application, which reduces or eliminates the necessity for the observer to be present, is the use of laser or electronic-based traffic counters.

(b) Video cameras are used to record shopping behaviour in supermarkets, car showrooms, banks etc. Video cameras can be used to assess traffic flow patterns, in-store promotional material, package designs and floor displays etc. The primary advantage of this approach is repeat viewing and the ability for a number of analysts to view the behaviour sequences at the one time.

(c) The audiometer, which was developed by AC Nielson, is used to record television viewing and radio listening behaviour. This technology is used to measure TAM ratings of a representative sample of the population.

(d) Eye tracking equipment such as oculometers and eye cameras are used to record gaze movements of the eye. It can be used to assess the effectiveness of TV and print advertising, promotional material and packaging design by determining how long the respondent looks at various parts of the stimulus. To determine the relative strengths in colour in advertising, an eye movement recorder was used to study how people actually read. The study was used to ascertain how advertisements are read in the context of the total newspaper, and a separate study looked specifically at the reading of advertisements themselves.[35]

(e) A Pupilometer measures changes in the diameter of the pupils of the respondent's eye as it is exposed to marketing stimuli. The assumption is that increased pupil size reflects positive cognitive activity.

(f) A Psycholovometer measures changes in perspiration rate. The respondent is shown stimuli such as brand names, advertisements, packages and slogans. The device measures the person's emotional reaction to these stimuli. The general principle involved is not unlike the lie detector. It is assumed that involuntary physiological changes such as increased perspiration accompany emotional reactions.

(g) Voice pitch analysis measures emotional response by monitoring normal voice frequency. Changes in the respondent's voice can be used to interpret response to marketing stimuli.

Note: Items (d) to (g) measure physiological reactions to stimuli. Yet there is no strong evidence to support the argument that a physiological change is a valid measure of future sales, attitude change or emotional response.

(h) Electronic scanning is an observational method that is rapidly increasing in popularity. Those little glass screens at the checkout over which goods are passed to a beep of a bar code recognition are the hottest thing to hit retailing since the old pop-up cash register.[36] Laser scanners at supermarket checkouts 'read' the UPC codes on products, and the store's central computer can produce instantaneous information on sales. With a better knowledge of what to stock, how to display it and how to price and promote the brand, retailers can improve profit margins and depend less on price-cutting promotions. Among the information contained in the code are such descriptors as brand, size or weight and flavour. Store inventory data is automatically reduced to reflect the purchase. Analysis of the purchases may reveal brand share and other relevant marketing information, such as tracking sales with advertising and promotions. However, the potential applications of scanner databases have been relatively unexplored in Europe when compared with the USA.[37]

Box 6.10 Scanner-based data

The availability of Electronic Point of Sale (EPOS) data from retail store scanners has led to major changes in monitoring and changing marketing effort for fast-moving consumer goods (FMCGs). EPOS data provides information on sales volumes (litres, units etc.) and value (pounds and pence) for all products scanned in a store. This data is linked to trade promotional efforts. These promotions may include secondary stocking locations (in-store displays), retailer promotion materials, consisting of feature advertising in newspapers, coupons and other in-store promotion activities such as shelf-talkers (retail shelf-mounted cards which highlight product features and/or promotion offers) and temporary price reductions. Here the goal is to identify how a promotion impacts sales for the product on promotion. Comparisons can be made between baseline sales and incremental business that the promotion generated. Baseline sales are the sales that we would expect to see based on past history and market conditions for a product, and exclusive of its trade promotion efforts. These promotion indicators, along with historical sales and pricing trends for each product, trends in other stores and seasonal patterns of consumption can be used to better assess sales performance.

Source: Adapted from 'Scanner-based data applications for improving FMCG sales and marketing efforts', ESOMAR 1995, Thomas Harris.

> **Box 6.11 Loyalty cards — 'High stakes in the big card game'**
>
> Loyalty cards are about much more than enticing customers to stick to a particular retailer. They give an opportunity to learn about shoppers' wants and needs. But the key test will be if the company can exploit its database detailing customers' behaviour more successfully than its rivals.
>
> The objective is to identify a store's most profitable customers and maximise their spending. Every time the customer goes to the checkouts, their cards are swiped and information about the contents of their trolleys is transmitted to a computer database. The retailer can then pinpoint customers who spend heavily on highly profitable items, as well as those who go for cut-price offers. Making use of this information can take a number of different forms. The profitable customers can be sent special offers and news of store improvements. Spending habits can be analysed in order to revise the products on offer or alter the store layout. And as well as using checkout counter scanners, some retailers, such as Superquinn, are offering customers a self-scanning service. This service equips shoppers with a handheld bar-code reader which allows customers to scan goods as they select them.
>
> As one retailer explains, 'A loyalty scheme is purely a means of identifying the customer when they come into the store and in exchange for that information, you have to give them something back, which is usually points they can spend. A retailer without such information is like an army fighting with bows and arrows against laser guns and night vision goggles.'
>
> Source: Adapted from 'High stakes in the big card game', *The Observer*, 12 May 1996, p. 5, Alexander Garrett.

• Advantages and Disadvantages of Observational Research

Observational research permits the measurement of actual behaviour, rather than reports of preferred or intended behaviour. Certain types of data can only be collected by observation. These include behaviour patterns which the respondent is unaware of or unable to communicate. For example, observation is a very effective form of research when the subjects are children or animals. Observation allows the researcher to obtain information on attitudes or behaviour that people may be unwilling to provide.

The potential bias caused by the interviewer and interviewing process is reduced or eliminated. Observation may be combined with other data collection methods at relatively low cost, for example, using a traffic counter to measure street or store traffic. The primary limitation of observational research is that while behaviour can be observed, no information is obtained concerning the factors which motivate that behaviour. Underlying beliefs, feelings, attitudes and preferences cannot be observed. A particular brand selected in a supermarket may not be the respondent's preferred choice. Perhaps the preferred brand was not in stock or the item was being purchased for another member of the family or as a gift. Observational research requires drawing inferences that may not necessarily be true.

Observing the purchase of a product in a supermarket tells very little about how the product is actually used or consumed. It is also difficult to observe certain behaviours such as personal hygiene (e.g. using a deodorant) that occurs within the home. Also, most observation requires some degree of subjective judgment on the part of the observer. Observation may be time-consuming and expensive if the behaviour to be observed is not reasonably predictable or occurs infrequently (remember the panda bears in the Kit-Kat TV ad?).

Finally, observation raises ethical issues. Is it inappropriate for researchers to collect information on individuals without their permission as this directly conflicts with the ethical responsibility that a professional researcher adheres to?

• Summary

Survey research is the systematic collection of data from a sample of respondents.

A survey methodically gathers information from respondents by communicating with them. It can be conducted in person, by telephone, or by post. Survey research is usually conducted when the market researcher has already developed an understanding of the area to be researched. It is probably fair to say that surveys are the most widely used method of data collection in marketing research. Survey research usually relies on a questionnaire (or measuring instrument) of some sort to record responses.

Survey research can be classified based on the mode used to administer the questionnaire. There are three major survey methods: personal interviews, telephone interviews, and postal interviews. Each method has its own advantages and limitations. Variations of each method also exist.

Personal interviews are direct, face-to-face communications between the interviewer and a respondent. Personal interviews may take place in a variety of different locations, including the home of the respondent, a street corner or a shopping centre. The researcher asks the required questions in the proper sequence and using the exact wording. The interviewer can explain and clarify complex questions, probe for additional information, administer complex questionnaires, utilise unstructured techniques and present visual cues such as advertisements and product concepts to the respondent all as part of the questioning process. The personal interview tends to have less non-response error than other survey methods. However personal interviews are often impractical to conduct over wide geographical regions. There is also potential for interviewer bias to occur. Increasingly personal interviews are being conducted in large high-traffic shopping centres.

Telephone interviewing involves phoning respondents and asking them a series of questions. Telephone interviews are becoming increasingly popular and are probably one of the most efficient methods for collecting data quickly. As the cost of personal interviews may be prohibitively high, telephone interviews are relatively inexpensive. Because of the absence of face-to-face contact, there is less opportunity for interviewer bias. It does not, however, lend itself as much to the collection of lengthy and detailed information. The use of complex measurement scales is also restricted. Telephone interviews are more suited to concise and straightforward data collection. Telephone interviewing depends on a representative sampling frame. Because visual aids cannot be used in telephone interviews, certain types of research such as packaging, print advertising, or some concept tests, cannot be conducted on the phone. This limitation can be overcome by sending the respondent the required visual material in advance. A more recent development involves conducting telephone interviews using a computer (CATI).

The postal survey is a self-administered questionnaire sent to respondents through the post. It is very much a paper and pen method of collecting data. The questionnaire is administered to the respondent by the respondent and the respondent completes and returns the questionnaire. The construction of the questionnaire and related materials is crucial to the success of this survey method. Postal surveys are particularly versatile in reaching all types of people (i.e. consumer or business), in all geographic areas, rural and urban areas, and at the same low cost. The postal survey method generally will have a cost advantage over other survey methods, though they are not cheap. The respondent has more time to formulate and record his or her answers. The questionnaire can be filled in at a time and pace convenient to the respondent. The primary limitation of this method is that of non-response error. A fairly high response rate can be achieved if certain techniques are used by the researcher to increase participation. Despite all efforts, it is next to impossible to totally eliminate non-response in postal surveys. Five methods to deal with the effect of non-response error were briefly presented.

Observation research is another way of conducting descriptive research. Observation involves systematically recording the behavioural patterns of people, objects and occurrences without questioning or communicating with them. It can be a source of low-cost research information. Yet it is probably one of the most under-utilised approaches to collecting marketing research data. Observational techniques fall into five different classifications. Observational research permits the measurement of actual behaviour, rather than reports of preferred or intended behaviour. Certain types of data can only be collected by observation. These include behaviour patterns which the respondent is unaware of or unable to communicate. The primary limitation of observational research is that while behaviour can be observed, no information is obtained concerning the factors which motivate that behaviour.

Questions

1. What conditions must apply in order to obtain meaningful results from the interview process?
2. Distinguish between sampling error, response error and non-response error.
3. Outline the type of variables survey research can be used to measure.
4. What is the purpose of survey research? What type of variables does this type of descriptive data collection method measure?
5. What factors should you consider when choosing among mail, telephone, personal and shopping centre-intercept interviews and what are their limitations?
6. What is meant by random digit dialling?
7. Which of the four interview methods mentioned in Question 5 is the most common, and why?
8. How has computer assisted telephone interviewing (CATI) revolutionised the way in which market research is undertaken?
9. What should be included in the cover letter that accompanies a postal questionnaire?
10. What techniques are available to the researcher to reduce non-response in postal questionnaires?
11. Outline the four methods for dealing with non-response error.
12. Differentiate between response error and non-response error in a survey. How can these difficulties be minimised when conducting survey research?
13. Why is it sometimes necessary to combine two or more data collection methods?
14. What are the trends in questionnaire administration? What methods are becoming increasingly popular?
15. Name the types of mechanical observation and explain how they work.
16. When are observational techniques used and what are the relative advantages and disadvantages of using this technique?
17. Name and outline the five classifications of observational techniques.
18. Why is it sometimes advantageous to conduct observational research by means of exerting control over the observational setting (i.e. contriving to ensure that the situation you would like to study does, in fact, occur) instead of relying on natural situations to occur on their own?
19. What are some of the most commonly used mechanical and/or electronic observational devices and what advantages and disadvantages do they have compared to human observation?
20. What is the difference between direct and indirect observation? How could one employ indirect observation in identifying the relative popularity of various cigarette brands among spectators at a college football game?
21. What is trace analysis and what are some innovative applications of this observational technique?
22. What are some of the major mechanical devices used in observation?

Problems and Assignments

1. How would you decide if a shopping centre-intercept interview approach is appropriate for a particular research project?
2. Which survey method is best for the following situations:
   (a) Administration of a complex attitude scale to measure the impact of a major new product launch by a competitor?
   (b) Administration of a questionnaire on the viewing of 'X-rated' movies on VCRs?
   (c) Administration of a questionnaire to determine the number of people that read a feature article in a Sunday paper?
   (d) Administration of a questionnaire by a university to determine students' attitudes towards a proposed change in the core curriculum?
3. Describe a marketing research problem in which both survey and observation methods could be used for obtaining the information needed.
4. How might one go about setting up an observational study to determine the incidence of car-pooling among faculty versus commuter students at your college or university?
5. What are some of the commonly used mechanical and/or electronic observational devices and what advantages and disadvantages do they have compared to human observation? Discuss.
6. What biases, if any, might be introduced by offering to give respondents £10 upon receipt of the questionnaire? The purpose of the payment is to ensure a high response rate. Will it work?
7. Even with the use of expensive gifts and call-backs all three interview methods can sometimes produce low response rates — under 30%. What are some ways to increase these response rates?
8. How would you overcome some of the problems you might anticipate in designing a survey to establish the kind of paint used by the 'do-it-yourself' market when members of this sample group last redecorated a room?
9. You decide to take a telephone survey of 40 families in the 021- exchange area. You want an excellent representation of all subscribers in the exchange area. Explain how you would carry out this survey.

Case Study
Teilifis na Gaeilge*

Tracking Performance and a Growing Audience

Teilifis na Gaeilge (TnaG) commenced broadcasting in autumn 1997 and through a creative mix of Irish language and other programming has steadily grown its share of viewers to 1.4% nationally, based on its 60 plus hours of broadcasting weekly.

TnaG's management regarded the station as having two equally important sets of customers, or clients. The first group was its viewers and potential viewers, both nation-wide and in Irish language-speaking areas. The second group, advertisers and potential advertisers, would be necessary to enable the company to fund its ambitions to provide viewers with a new approach to programming.

In order to meet the needs of both sets of clients, or customers, TnaG committed itself to ongoing research with viewers and making such information available to advertisers. Since its launch the station partook in AC Nielson research, as well as regular omnibus research.

In mid-1997, TnaG, conscious of a resurgence of interest in the Irish language and support from two-thirds of the population for Irish language broadcasting, sought to establish how successfully the station had established itself as a part of life in the Gaeltacht areas.

Given the minority nature of the Gaeltacht-speaking areas and their disparate location, the station was concerned that the nation-wide research available to it did not provide an insight into the important Gaeltacht audience for its programming.

TnaG commissioned a programme of viewership research in Gaeltacht areas. The survey to be undertaken with a representative sample of the Gaeltacht population would establish viewing patterns, as well as satisfaction with various aspects of the station's broadcasting.

Proportionate stratification was undertaken to ensure that the different demographic criteria (location, age, income, etc.) which might influence viewing patterns and preferences could be easily discerned.

Research was undertaken by a mix of telephone and personal interviews with almost 300 Gaeltacht residents. Personal interviews were undertaken on a door-to-door basis, in areas selected on the basis of systematic random sampling. Field-work supervisors undertook follow-up research with a selected number of those interviewed in order to validate the field work undertaken and tabulated the numbers surveyed in each category to ensure the requirements of proportionate sampling were met.

The research with Gaeltacht viewers was greeted with delight by TnaG, as Cathal Goan, the station's Chief Executive recalls: 'Our level of viewing in those Gaeltacht areas where TnaG is available emerged as a major success for the station in its first year of broadcasting, while the reaction to our key programmes, such as Ros na Run, was superb.

'While we do not see the station as catering only for the Gaeltacht population, but rather having a national appeal,' says Mr Goan, 'we do plan to analyse national viewership and other survey findings on a regular basis, so that we know our position in each of our target audiences.'

Questions/exercises

1. Contrast the advantages and disadvantages of telephone and personal interviews for TnaG.
2. In the TnaG viewership survey, researchers used a standard opening statement to elicit participation in the station's survey. Outline what you feel should be contained in such an opening statement.
3. Should TnaG consider using postal questionnaires in subsequent viewership research? Outline the advantages and disadvantages associated with this research technique.
4. How many questions do you think could be answered in each of TnaG's telephone interviews, or how long, on average, do you think such an interview would last?
5. Should TnaG send something in advance, by letter, to those whom it plans to interview in forthcoming viewership research? What would be the advantages and disadvantages?

*This case was written by Ray Collis, Envision Marketing Consultants, Galway. It is intended to be used as a basis for class discussion rather than to illustrate either effective or ineffective handling of an administrative situation. The case is based on a real situation, though certain information has been disguised. © Envision Marketing Consultants, Galway.

Chapter 7
EXPERIMENTATION

19-10-01

- **Chapter Overview**
- Introduction • Experimental Terminology • Causality and Causal Explanations • Validity and Experimentation; Internal Validity; External Validity; Field and Laboratory Experiments • Experimental Designs; Pre-Experimental Designs; True Experimental Designs; Quasi-Experimental Designs and Advanced Experiments • The Selection of an Experimental Design • Test Marketing; Standard Test Marketing and Controlled Test Marketing • Simulated Test Marketing • Summary

---

- **Introduction**

So far, the data collection methods discussed generate either exploratory or descriptive data. In this chapter, we turn our attention to causal research and the associated data collection method, experimentation.

Experiments measure cause-and-effect relationships. To do this, experiments create an 'artificial' situation to allow the researcher to test the effect of one or more variables, such as advertising or a price decrease on another variable, say, the level of sales. This artificiality is the very essence of experimentation and causal research. It explicitly permits the researcher to control factors that may confuse the relationship between the variables. It enables the researcher to proactively participate in the testing process. These two reasons make experiments a very powerful data collection method. However, as we will see later, issues such as costs, security, and ethics mean that, in practice, experimentation has not been as popular as one would expect. This is changing though, with techniques such as simulated test markets set to bring about a significant growth in this area over the years to come.

Against this background, our discussion begins in this chapter with the terminology of experiments. We then consider the basic principles of causality and their role in experimentation. This leads us to the concept of validity and to the question of field versus laboratory experiments. The various experimental designs are then detailed. We conclude our discussion by examining test marketing and simulated test markets. Upon completion of this chapter, the reader will:

1. understand the nature of experiments as a data collection method;
2. learn about the concept of causality and causal research;
3. examine the role of validity in experimentation;
4. be able to detail potential threats to internal and external validity;
5. be able to select and conduct experiments;
6. gain an insight into test marketing;
7. appreciate the development of simulated test marketing.

The discussion presented in the chapter surrounding causality and the advanced experimental designs is, by nature, abstract and theoretical. To this end, readers may wish to confine themselves to the sections on validity and true experiments for a general broad insight into experiments.

• Experimental Terminology

To fully understand experimentation and causality within the data collection phase of any research project an appreciation of the standard experimental terminology is needed, together with a knowledge of the accepted symbols used. Some of the more important terms[1] include:

(a) Experiment

This is a data-collection tool, method or technique where the researcher consciously and explicitly controls and manipulates one or more independent variable(s) to determine the effect(s) it has on a dependent variable, under controlled circumstances. It asks the question 'Did X cause Y'? An experiment has three elements:

1. the factor being acted upon, namely the dependent variable;
2. the factor causing the imposed change, the independent variable;
3. the results or outcome of the change.

(b) Independent Variable

This term refers to a variable causing the effect. The independent variable is manipulated by the researcher. It can also be referred to as the experimental or treatment variable (these terms are used in the text to acquaint the reader with them). It is denoted as X. If there is more than one independent variable, these are shown as X_1, X_2, X_3, and so on. Examples of independent variables include price changes, new brand names, packaging changes, product variations and alternative advertising themes. Different levels of an independent variable can be tested; for example, the effect of income levels on the purchase of shares. The different income levels are represented as X_1, X_2, X_3, and are referred to as treatment levels of an independent variable, income. The term 'treatment levels' is generally reserved for discussion of advanced or statistical experiments.

(c) Dependent Variable

The dependent variable is the factor being influenced or affected by the independent variables. Sales levels, market share, brand preferences and awareness levels are traditional dependent variables. A measurement of the dependent variable is taken — this is referred to as an observation or measurement. It is represented as O. More than one measurement of the dependent variable is shown as O_1, O_2, O_3. Measurement of the dependent variable can occur either before or after the application of the independent variable. This is traditionally labelled as either a pre- or post-measurement observation. It is denoted by:

$$O_1 \quad X \quad O_2$$

and reads, a pre-measurement of sales at time period 1, followed by, X, the application of an independent variable, e.g. a 5% price increase and O_2, a post-measurement of sales at time period 2. The physical measurement or observation of the dependent variable can take several forms, e.g. observational techniques, surveys, use of scaling techniques such as the Likert scale, and physiological measures. (These are described and detailed in the forthcoming chapters.)

(d) Extraneous Variables

Extraneous variables are any other variables other than the independent or dependent variable(s). They can be controllable (e.g. price) or uncontrollable variables (e.g. competitor's price) and are external to the experiment. They are factors outside the researcher's control or knowledge that may alter the value of the dependent variable, e.g. competitors' price changes or pack alterations. Extraneous variables therefore confuse and confound the results of an experiment. Much of the researcher's energy is exercised over minimising or, better still, eliminating extraneous factors. Such variables can seriously hinder a researcher in answering 'Did X cause Y'?

(e) Test Units

These are individuals, groups of people, objects, shops or items which participate in the experiment. These test units are also known as experimental subjects — showing that they (products, people, stores) are participating in an experiment. Measurements are taken from the test units to describe the effects, if any, of the independent variable on the dependent variable. If there is more than one test group we classify these as either an experimental or control group.

The experimental group consists of test units or members who receive the independent or treatment variable, i.e. they are the group of subjects exposed to the independent variable. EG can be used to denote the term experimental group.

The control group is a group of test units who do not receive the independent variable. They reflect the normal environment before, during and after the treatment. The control group has to be similar in composition and nature to the experimental group so as to enable us to measure the true effect of X, the independent variable. CG is sometimes used as an abbreviation to represent the notion of a control group.

When test units do not know if they are receiving the independent variable (i.e. they do not know if they are in the experimental or control group) we say they are blind. When the test units and researchers do not know which group is the control or experiment group, we refer to this as a double-blind test. These terms are commonly used in the medical profession and pharmaceutical industry when conducting experiments.

(f) Randomisation

Randomisation, R, is the random assignment of test units to either the control or experimental group. It eliminates any subjective bias on the researcher's part with regard to the selection of experimental subjects. The purpose of random assignment is not to ensure identical groups as one might expect, but rather to disperse differences between test units randomly between the groups.

Additional Comments

The time occurrence of events in experimentation is always written and read from left to right. That is, symbols to the left represent activities that occurred first. Hence:

$O_1 \quad X \quad O_2$

reads pre-measurement (or pre-test) of dependent variable, then application or manipulation of the independent variable and post-measurement (post-test) of the dependent variable. From a practical perspective, the pre-measurement, O_1 could be a questionnaire measuring a person's attitude towards a product, say a beer. X could be the showing of a new TV advertisement about the product and O_2 would be the same questionnaire measuring the person's attitude towards the product.

X's and O's vertical to each other demonstrate stimulus and measurement are taking place simultaneously.

$O_1 \quad X_1 \quad O_2$
$X_2 \quad O_3$

The presence of parallel rows indicates that randomisation has been used to equalise the groups, such as that shown above. Alternatively, some researchers will use the notation of (R) to denote the use of randomisation. A dashed line is used by some researchers to denote the absence of randomisation.

$O_1 \quad X_1 \quad O_2$
$X_2 \quad O_3$

• Causality and Causal Explanations

To understand experimentation as a data-collection method, we must first explain the concept of causality. Our approach here is from the scientific perspective as opposed to the everyday commonsense stance. From the scientist's view — causal statements are tentative by nature as all causal explanations are more or less probable. Causality states that a change in one variable causes a predictable change in another variable. Such inferences are difficult in marketing and the social sciences as, generally speaking, a variety of variables explain a probable outcome. It is difficult to predict the outcome due to the complexity of factors and units involved. As a result, many marketing explanations are descriptive in nature. They take the form 'X and Y occur together in a pattern'. In the scientific sense, to say 'X causes Y' implies each of four types of evidence have to be demonstrated by the researcher. These are:

1. concomitant variation;
2. temporal sequence;
3. theoretical support;
4. non-spurious association.[2]

1. Concomitant Variation

Sometimes referred to as associative variation, concomitant variation demonstrates a correlation between X and Y, i.e. the presence of X is associated with the presence of Y or technically speaking, the independent variable X is associated with the dependent variable Y. This suggests that a rise in X will give rise to a predictable rise or decrease in Y. The relationship between X and Y can be positive or negative, i.e. a positive relationship means that the two variables move in the same direction, an increase in X will give rise to an increase in Y or a decrease in X will equate with a decrease in Y. Alternatively, a negative relationship means that a change in one direction in the independent variable gives rise to an opposite change of direction in the dependent variable. So, a price increase results in a drop in sales.

So, concomitant variation, implying a consistent pattern, is one type of scientific evidence needed to demonstrate a causal relationship. However, while concomitant variation is necessary, it is not sufficient.

2. Temporal Sequence

Time precedence is concerned with the time order of occurrence of events or the sequential occurrence of variables. It refers to the fact that a researcher has to be able to show that X occurred in time before Y. This enables the researcher to measure a change in Y due to a change in X. If changes in X occurred after changes in Y, then we do not have sequential variables or a necessary condition for causality. For example, to demonstrate that a change in advertising had an effect on awareness levels, you have to be able to show that the change in advertising happened before changes in awareness levels.

3. Theoretical Support

The third type of evidence required for causal explanations is theoretical support, i.e. the claim that X causes Y is expected to fit with the body of knowledge already in existence or into a known conceptual model. However, caution is advised in rigidly applying this rule, as the story of Galileo classically illustrates.

4. Non-Spurious Association

To infer a causal relationship between X and Y, a researcher must be able to account for, or eliminate, all other possible explanations. That is, that observed changes in Y were not caused by factor(s) other than X. To take the preceding example, a change in awareness levels can happen because a competitor launches a new media campaign; a government report draws attention to the product or consumers actively pursue an information search. Essentially, this type of evidence focuses the researcher's attention on possible explanations other than the one being investigated, so as to rule them out.

In conclusion, the nature of causality requires that to determine that X causes Y, four criteria be fulfilled: concomitant variation, temporal sequence, theoretical support, and non-spurious association. Given this scientific stance, a causal explanation between X and Y is always inferred from the presenting evidence. Causality cannot be only one of a number of factors giving rise to a change in Y. In other words, causality and causal explanations demand, more than any other data collection method, an absence or elimination of error or sources of error. We now turn our attention to such a discussion.

• Validity and Experimentation

Recall that validity is about measuring what we really wanted to measure. With respect to causality and experiments, this means measuring changes that the independent variable, and only the independent variable, brings about in the dependent variable, i.e. did X really cause Y? To answer such a question, there are two main types of validity to be considered in any causal study or experiment. These are internal validity and external validity.

Internal Validity

Internal validity asks 'Did X really cause the difference in Y?' It is concerned with establishing that X was the sole cause of changes in Y and not outside factors, Z, A or B. So, internal validity rules out alternative explanations and aims to control for errors which may detract from establishing and measuring a causal relationship. There are seven threats to internal validity that concern a researcher. These are: history; maturation; testing (a) the main effect and (b) the interactive effect; statistical regression; instrumentation; mortality; and selection bias.

History

History errors occur due to specific events external to the experiment that happen between the pre- and post-measurement (O_1 and O_2), which affect the dependent variable, thus confounding the estimation of the treatment variable. Typical examples include competitive changes in pricing or promotional spend; government; media story; food scare; new competitive products — all of which are outside the control of the researcher. In marketing, the longer the time span or duration of the experiment, the greater the threat to internal validity from history. Note, the term 'history', as used here, does not relate to historical events or past events prior to the running of the experiment.

Maturation

Maturation denotes changes within the test units that occur over time between O_1 and O_2, i.e. the pre- and post-measurement times. These changes are not due to the independent variable, but due to the passage of time itself. For example, when the test units are people — hunger, tiredness, degree of concentration can alter with the time of day or even year and so alter the pre- or post-measurement. Organisations that are test units can also change. Stores can increase in size, shop traffic can fluctuate and shops can be renovated. A further corollary to this arises — the greater the time period between O_1 and O_2, the more likely an experiment will suffer from maturation error.

The Testing Effect

This threat to internal validity focuses upon the possible effects of a measurement taken before the experiment, which can alter the experimental results. An alternative way to think about the testing effect is to think about the effect that running an experiment has on subjects. There are two such effects: the main testing effect, and the interactive testing effect.

The *main testing effect* is said to have occurred when a measurement influences following measurements, e.g. respondents are asked as part of an experiment if they have seen an Oscar-winning film, *Titanic*. 10% say they have. As a direct result of the questions in O_1, the pre-measurement phase, many respondents decide to go to the film. Upon the next measurement two weeks later, 70% say they have seen the movie. The dramatic attendance increase between O_1 on O_2 could be a direct result of being asked the question about the film in the first place. This is the effect of O_1 on O_2 and is the main testing effect.

The *interactive testing effect* happens when the pre-measurement, O_1, influences the test unit reactions to the independent variable, X. For example, in asking consumers about the effect of BSE, consumers may be more sensitive to BSE news afterwards or even actively look for information. A further measurement, O_2, could result in greater changes in attitudes and knowledge, beyond that expected. This elevated result reflects the treatment variable plus the interactive effect of O_1. The use of a control group can counteract the testing effect.

Instrumentation

Instrumentation error takes place when there are changes in the measuring instrument or measuring process between the pre- and post-measurement time, i.e. O_1 and O_2. For example, a hand-made chocolate firm is considering introducing a new line of white chocolates. Consumers are approached before the launch of the chocolates and are asked if they love white chocolates. After the launch, consumers are asked if they like white chocolate. The alteration of the question from loving chocolates in O_1 to liking chocolate in O_2 will result in instrumentation error. O_1 is not comparable or compatible with O_2. So any change to the wording, layout or scales within the measuring instruments can poise a threat to internal validity. Hence, it is recommended to keep the measurement instrument as constant as possible, to avoid instrumentation error.

Mortality

When respondents leave or drop out of an experiment, 'mortality' has occurred, i.e. those subjects lost to the experiment may be different to those who remained. Suppose, in an experiment to test a new vitamin, those leaving the experimental group were people who do not believe in vitamins. Thus, the results may be a reflection of the group composition and their attitudes to vitamins, rather than the independent variable itself. Careful selection and screening of respondents can counteract possible mortality threats.

Statistical Regression

When respondents are chosen to participate in an experiment due to an extreme score or position on a variable, there is the possibility of their further scores gravitating to the population mean. If this threat materialises, statistical regression is said to have occurred. Consider the following hypothetical situation.

A researcher specifically chooses ten drivers who failed their driving test first time round.

- O_1: Drivers fail driving test for the first time.
- X: Each driver receives a complimentary course of driving lessons.
- O_2: All drivers pass the test on the second sitting.

The results show dramatic improvement for all experimental participants. However, it is possible that the participants failed their driving test first time for some reasons other than their lack of driving skills. Perhaps they had to use a new car for the driving test, one which they were not used to. Perhaps some of them were sick before the first test, or extremely nervous, or just having a bad day. Hence, it is possible that the failure to pass the test obtained in the pre-measurement phase was due to other random factors rather than the participants being really poor at driving! Given such a result, when a group is purposely chosen because of its extreme score on a variable, statistical regression may affect the experiment.

Selection Bias

The final threat to the internal validity of an experiment is selection bias. It happens when participants are assigned to the experimental or control group by means other than randomisation. That is, a bias is introduced because respondents have a different propensity to react to the independent variable. Suppose the respondents are members of a political group opposed to hare coursing. Some participants may purposely choose the control group to avoid seeing hurtful or unsettling pictures, while others may select the experimental group to strongly voice their opposition to hare coursing. In both situations, the participants are reacting differently to the independent variable. This can arise as the respondents were not equivalent in their attitudes towards hare coursing.

The best methods for preventing selection bias is the use of both *matching* and *randomisation* of respondents. Matching refers to the procedure which ensures that groups of respondents are comparable on the dependent variable, i.e. like is compared with like. For example, in an experiment to test the effectiveness of a new flea spray for domestic animals, the animals could be matched according to type, i.e. all cats are grouped together, while dogs constitute another group and budgies the third group. Randomisation refers to respondents being randomly assigned to the control and experimental matched groups, so as to distribute or scatter the effect of extraneous factors among all groups. As previously noted, random assignment eliminates any subjective selection bias on behalf of the researcher.

External Validity

Having established that X really did cause Y (and not some outside factor) we now pose the question 'So what, can we generalise the results?' We are querying the external validity of the experiment, given that we are satisfied with the internal validity. External validity is required if the results of an experiment are to be applied to the whole population in the real world. Much of the difficulty in generalising to the real world can be attributed to the artificial nature of the experiment, i.e. to the control which a researcher actively pursues. Thus, the threats to external validity often become an issue in whether to use a laboratory or field setting for the experiment.

In a laboratory experiment, the test units are placed in artificial surroundings so as to increase the researcher's control over extraneous variables and ensure a high internal validity content to the experiment. However, the use of a laboratory approach can induce reactive error. The 'Hawthorne Effect'[3] is a classic example. In a 1920s experiment to study the effect of different working conditions on workers' productivity, the results showed that regardless of the combination of working conditions used (rest periods, lighting and length of shifts), productivity continuously increased. It transpired that the productivity increase was due, not to the working conditions, but to the presence of the researchers and the experiment itself. Workers were aware they were part of an experiment, which of itself induced a higher level of morale, regardless of the working conditions. The artificial nature of the experiment resulted in a threat to the external validity of the experiment.

In a field experiment, the test units remain in their natural setting, perhaps their home, in supermarkets, in their office or a factory. In this life-like or market setting, test units are less likely to react to the experiment (the opposite holds true for laboratory settings) but they are more open to errors from outside events. Competitors are well known for their ability to 'scuttle' an experiment — they purposively increase their advertising rate in the experimental area or decrease their price, so as to confuse the results of the experiment. If not anticipated or managed, such actions can threaten the external validity of most experiments.

So, generally speaking, external validity requires the researcher to control for respondents reacting to the experiment, the experimental setting, and the independent variable. This reactive error and surrogate threat to external validity demands a balance between the advantages and disadvantages associated with field and laboratory experiments, as presented in Table 7.1 below. These advantages are relative and not absolute, as the controls for one type of validity (internal or external) often conflict with the other. At this point we'll note that there are two main types of field experiment, test marketing and simulated test marketing. Our discussion of these is left to the end of the chapter as these are best understood when you have an appreciation of experimental designs.

Table 7.1 A comparison of field and laboratory experiments

	Field experiment	*Laboratory experiment*
Internal validity	Weaker	Stronger
External validity	Stronger	Weaker
Cost	More	Less
Time	More	Less
Place	Shop/store/home	Research centre/office

Box 7.1 summarises the different types of validity threats to experimentation.

> ## Box 7.1 Summary of validity threats to experiments
>
> ### Internal validity threats
>
> *1. History*
> The effect of outside events that occur between O_1 and O_2.
>
> *2. Maturation*
> The effect of changes within the test units between O_1 and O_2.
>
> *3. Testing*
> The main testing effect is the effect of O_1 on O_2. The interactive testing effect is the effect of interaction between O_1 and test units reactions to experimental treatment, X.
>
> *4. Statistical regression*
> The tendency for groups initially chosen because of their extremely high or low scores on a variable to gravitate toward the mean.
>
> *5. Instrumentation*
> Changes in the measuring instrument or process between O_1 and O_2.
>
> *6. Mortality*
> The effect of test units dropping out of the experiment and changing the composition of the experimental and control groups.
>
> *7. Selection bias*
> Assignment of subjects to experimental and control groups such that test units are initially different on the dependent variable being measured, or differ in terms of their responsiveness to the experimental treatment, X.
>
> *8. External validity*
> A question of field versus laboratory setting. Often referred to as reactive error and surrogate error.

So far, we have examined the issues of experimental terminology, causality, internal and external validity and the question of field or laboratory experiments. We are now ready to turn our attention to the various types of experimental designs and the different methods to deal with threats to the validity of experiments.

• Experimental Designs

The term 'experimental design' refers to the testing procedure where the researcher manipulates an independent variable to specifically measure the effect on a dependent variable. To this end, four conditions have to be met. There has to be:

1. An independent variable to be manipulated.
2. Test subjects to experience the independent variable.
3. A dependent variable that is measurable.
4. A method for controlling extraneous factors.

If these conditions are met, there are four main categories that experimental designs can fall into. These are:

1. Pre-experiments.
2. True experiments.
3. Quasi-experiments.
4. Advanced (statistical) experiments.

This categorisation of experimental designs reflects the degree of control they afford the researcher over threats to both internal and external validity. Pre-experimental designs, by definition, provide little protection against validity problems, whereas true and statistical designs explicitly control for such errors. We will now examine each category of experimental designs, starting with the weakest category of experiments and progressing to the strongest.

Pre-experimental Designs

These are not real experiments insofar as they offer minimal control to the researcher over the experimental situation. Internal and external validity are not managed. However, they present an oversimplified insight into the more complex experimental designs and therein lies their value. The first of these pre-experimental designs is the 'after only' design.

The 'After Only' Design

This is the most basic of all experimental designs. As suggested by its name, this design involves a measurement or observation of the dependent variable after test units have experienced the independent or treatment variable. This is represented as:

X   O

A typical case is the use of a new promotional tool, by a south-east food manufacturer. In an effort to increase sales, a special offer is advertised in all local supermarkets and shops — a free loaf of bread with every home-making marmalade kit. The conclusion drawn is that the loaf of bread caused the sales of marmalade-making kits. While logic would suggest we agree with this conclusion, any good marketing manager would ask a number of questions. What were the level of sales before the promotional offer? What were competitors doing? What was happening in the market? Any of these issues could also explain the sales of the marmalade kits.

Thus, serious threats to validity abound with this design, so much so that the 'after only' design is best thought of as an exploratory case study method or a useful technique for establishing a hypothesis, for further testing.

The 'Before-After' Design

In this design, the dependent variable is measured before and after the independent variable is administered to the experimental subjects. This design was used to evaluate a large fee increase for doctors, by using multiple observation points before and after the fee increase.[4] The following notation represents the before and after experimental design:

$$O_1 \quad X \quad O_2$$

The difference between this and the previous design is the use of the pre- or before measurement of the dependent variable. Returning to the design above, an example illustrates. All students of a college in north-west Ireland are asked to express their first choice of daily national newspaper. A week later, a competition is held in the college by one daily paper offering students a free return air ticket to anywhere in the world. After the end of the competition, the same college students are again asked to express their first preference in daily national newspapers. The results read as follows:

O_1 The before measurement = 10% gave *The National* as their first preference.

X Fly Anywhere Competition

O_2 The after measurement = 80% gave *The National* as their first preference.

The effect or result of X, the Fly Anywhere Competition, is O_2 minus O_1. In this case, 80%–10% = 70% increase in first preference.

The results, O_2–O_1, can be attributed to the independent variable. But it is still evident that other uncontrollable variables, such as price increases of competitors, out-of-stock alternative newspapers or lecturers' recommendation of the *National* paper could have interfered with or influenced the experiment, thus rendering the results questionable. To this end, the 'before-after' design is threatened by internal validity errors; history, maturation, instrumentation and the testing effect. These threats suggest the need for an alternative experimental design.

True Experimental Designs

True experimental designs empower the researcher with control over the experimental situation, thus eliminating or minimising serious internal and external validity threats. Control is achieved through the use of control groups and random assignment of test units to either the experimental or control group(s). It is these two factors which differentiate the pre-experimental designs from true designs, as the major deficiency of equivalent groups is overcome. Furthermore, statistical analysis is enhanced by the use of random assignment (in conjunction with probability sampling as discussed in Chapter 10).

The 'Before-After with Control Groups' Design

Known as the classic experimental design, the 'before-after with control group' is depicted as follows:

(R) O_1 X O_2
(R) O_3 O_4

The effect of independent variable, X, is

$$E = (O_2 - O_1) - (O_4 - O_3)$$

This has all the elements of the 'before-after' design plus two significant and critical additions. First, there is the use of a control group — a group of test units, similar in nature and profile to those who experience the experimental treatment, except for the fact that the control group are not exposed to the independent variable. This enables the researcher to assume that both groups (experimental and control) are equally affected by extraneous factors, such as history, maturation, testing and instrumentation. Second, the test units are randomly assigned to the various groups, thus selection bias is managed.

Take the area of sales promotions. Sales promotions are a popular promotional element of the marketing mix of Irish breweries. High levels of competition within this market call on the breweries to come into direct contact with their consumers and communicate with them at the point of sale, in the pub. To this end, the 'before and after with control group' design has been used to good effect in the Irish breweries industry,[5] to test the effects of Guinness in-pub sales promotion. The design consisted of two pre- and post-measurements.

(R) O_1 O_2 X O_3 O_4
(R) O_5 O_6

Two pre-tests were conducted with the experimental group before the in-pub promotion, to measure consumers' perceptions of the brand image of Guinness. The pre-tests used a questionnaire specifically constructed to measure the different components of brand image. One further pre-test was completed by consumers, using the same brand image questionnaire, who were part of a control group and therefore would not be exposed to the in-pub promotion. All participants were matched and randomised prior to any pre-measurements. The in-pub promotion was run over a week-long period. Two post-measurements (consumer's brand image) were taken of the experimental group; one post-measurement was taken from the control group. The results were positive — the in-pub promotion led consumers' evaluation of the brand image of Guinness to increase, though only to a small extent.

However, in practice, such experimental designs can suffer from validity threats, e.g. if participants dropped out, the design would suffer from a mortality error. On external validity, the design does not perform so well — it is open to reactive error emanating from the experimental setting, the experiment itself or the selection of respondents from the population. So, while several major threats to internal validity are dealt with by this design, replication of the experiment several times may be needed to deliver external validity. This poses huge cost and time constraints.

In addressing the need to provide marketing education and training to the owner/manager of the small firm, FAS (then AnCO)[6] tested an open-learning programme in marketing by using a variation of the 'before-after' design. It incorporated two phases: a pre-measurement and post-measurement, to control for the interaction effect — a particular threat to this study.

(R)   CG O_1
(R)   EG   X O_2

The pre-measurement phase consisted of a survey of all small firms in Ireland, to establish a baseline of their marketing knowledge. Then, a survey was conducted among those small firms who completed the course, to test their marketing knowledge. The results of two surveys were compared, with the improvement in marketing knowledge being attributed to the open-learning package.

However, the problems of history and statistical regression still remain with this design. Take the situation where the government or a state agency was to launch a marketing grant to assist small firms with their marketing. Such an outside event, if occurring at the same time as the experiment, could leave managers more interested in marketing, more willing to learn about marketing and thus more receptive to a marketing learning package. To specifically control for these threats, an alternative experiment is required.

The 'After-Only with Control Group' Design

This true experimental design, the 'after-only with control group', is the same as the 'before-after with control group', without any pre-measurement. It is depicted as follows:

(R)   X O_1
(R) O_2

The effect of the independent variable is calculated as

$$E = O_2 - O_1$$

In our college newspaper example, we would randomly assign two similar colleges to the groups, and measure sales in both colleges after the competition was run. The effect of the competition would be: the sales of the newspaper in the experimental college minus the sales of the newspaper in the control college, as shown by the equation above.

Internal validity threats from history, maturation, selection and statistical regression are controlled for by the random assignment. The big advantage of this design is its ability to control for the interactive effect (as there is no pre-measurement, there can be no interaction between the pre- and post-measurement), as well as controlling for other threats to internal validity such as history and maturation. The assumption is that the 'before' measurement is the same in both cases. In practice, this assumption should be confirmed by using secondary data. Since the subjects are only measured once, the threat of testing effect is also managed for. However, different mortality rates between the experimental and control groups could pose a threat to the design, as can external validity threats.

The simplicity of the 'after-only with control group' design lends itself well to many marketing mix situations. For example, price changes, new packaging and promotional tools plus new advertising campaigns can be assessed and analysed.

The Solomon-Four Group

The Solomon-Four Group is a true experimental design that combines the best of the two preceding designs ('after-only with control' plus the 'before-after with control') and for this reason can be regarded as the Rolls Royce[7] of classic designs available to a researcher. It is symbolised as follows:

(R)EG	1	O_1	X	O_2
(R)CG	1	O_3		O_4
(R)EG	2		X	O_5
(R)CG	2			O_6

Several measures of the independent variable are possible, e.g. $(O_5 - \frac{1}{2}(O_1 + O_3)) - (O_6 - \frac{1}{2}(O_1 + O_3))$.[8] The advantage of this design is that it caters for the isolation, quantification and control of specific internal validity threats, and is the least susceptible to sources of error. For example, it enables the investigators to capture the effect of the before measurement on the experimental and control group. Since all groups are pre-selected to be equivalent, the pre-measurement should be the same for all except for random factors. Despite the Solomon-Four Group being the ideal design, it is, nevertheless, rarely used in marketing research practice, due to its complexity and the extreme costs associated with conducting such an experiment.

Quasi-Experimental Designs

Quasi-experimental designs are classic designs adapted for ease of use. These involve periodic measurements (pre- and post-) and adopt the term 'Quasi' because there is no randomisation, i.e. subjects are not pre-assigned to either an experimental or control group. In reality, it is not always possible or practical to implement a true experimental design. Given this, quasi-experiments appear to be like true designs. To some extent this is correct as they can control for some extraneous factors, e.g. maturation, testing and instrumentation. However, the absence of randomisation limits their ability to deal with threats such as history, the interactive effect and specifically, selection bias. Nevertheless, they offer a practical alternative to true experimental designs. Some of the more popular quasi-designs are the times-series design and multiple time-series.

The Time-Series Design

This is an extended before-after design, with multiple observations taken before and after the experimental treatment. It is depicted as:

$$O_1 \quad O_2 \quad O_3 \quad O_4 \quad X \quad O_5 \quad O_6 \quad O_7 \quad O_8$$

It is often used when introducing a price change, a package alteration or new advertising theme. The multiple pre- and post-measurements reflect the reality in the marketplace where marketing mix changes could take six to eight weeks. The effect of X is calculated by taking the mean of the post-measurements minus the mean of the pre-measurements. Say, for example, you are a biscuit manufacturer. You are planning to include the 'Made in Ireland' logo on all your biscuit lines next July. To measure the effect of this pack change on sales, you decide to monitor sales of all your brands for the year, let's say on the last day of every month.

Figure 7.1 Measuring the effect of a pack change

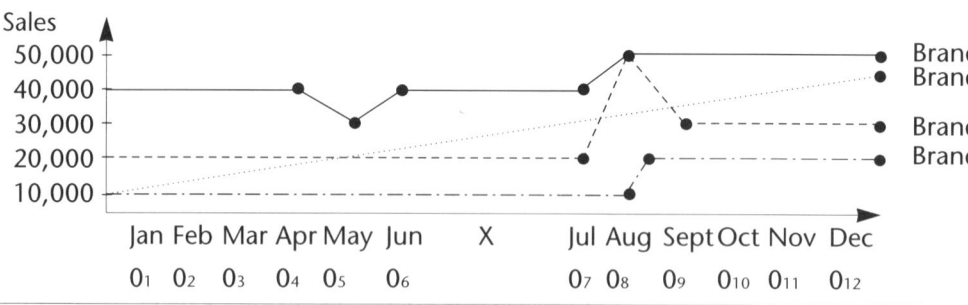

The effect of the pack change is the result of the mean sales, O_7–O_{12}, per brand minus the mean sales, O_1–O_6, per brand.

The pre- and post-measurements can all come from the same sample (test units) over time, (secondary source — syndicated services data). This is often referred to as panel data (refer to Chapter 4). The alternative is for the pre- and post-measurements to come from separate population samples and is often the case for firms who monitor sales. This time-series quasi-experiment is useful when records are naturally kept at set time periods in the natural environment, as is the case in the retail trade. It is also a useful adaptation when reactive error is unlikely in the natural environment.

The Multiple Time-Series Design

This is the same as the time-series design, with the addition of a control group. It is symbolically represented as:

$$O_1 \quad O_2 \quad O_3 \quad O_4 \qquad X \qquad O_5 \quad O_6 \quad O_7 \quad O_8$$
$$O_9 \quad O_{10} \quad O_{11} \quad O_{12} \qquad \qquad O_{13} \quad O_{14} \quad O_{15} \quad O_{16}$$

Under the auspices of this design, we use a control city, town or store where sales are monitored over time, but there is no treatment variable introduced as there is in the experimental city, town or store. This approach gives the researcher more control, minimising the effect of errors, e.g. history.

However, the groups are not randomly assigned. The groups are assumed to be comparable. To this end, the researcher must carefully select the control group to be equivalent to the experimental group. It is also advisable that a log or journal be kept of external happenings to afford some control over history. Another threat can arise from the interaction testing effect — but this is minimised if frequent record-keeping is a natural part of the environment. So, in practice, this design is well suited to marketing mix changes, as opposed to attitudinal or behavioural changes in the consumer.

Advanced (Statistical) Experimental Designs

So far, the discussion of experimental designs is based on two assumptions. Firstly, that both the control and experimental groups are similar with respect to the variables of interest; and secondly, we are testing the effect of one, and only one, independent variable. Of course, many occasions arise in marketing when these conditions are not met. We often want to control for the effect of one or two extraneous variables, such as a competitor's price or store size. It is reasonable for a manager to want to test different levels of an independent variable, e.g. a price increase of 5%, 7% or 10%, or four different advertising campaigns. In such circumstances, the researcher will opt for a statistical or advanced experimental design.

In essence, these designs (four in total) are an extension of the true experimental designs previously examined. These designs can measure different experimental stimuli simultaneously, i.e. different treatment levels can be measured within the one experiment, such as different price increases or different advertising themes.

Furthermore, these advanced designs can cater for the test units being classified according to a known factor. This is referred to as a blocking factor. So, these statistical designs provide a framework for testing the impact of different treatment levels and other factors. The statistical designs in question which exhibit these characteristics are: the Completely Randomised design; the Randomised Blocks design; the Latin Square design; and the Factorial design.

1. The Completely Randomised Design

Consider a situation where a shampoo manufacturer wishes to increase the price of his product. He is unsure whether to increase the price by 1%, 3% or 5%. To test the effect of the various price increases on sales he could utilise the completely randomised design. Such a design allows for the measurement of different levels of the independent (or treatment) variable, in this case, price. Test units are randomly assigned to different experimental treatments at the same time (X_1 equals one price increase, while X_2 equals another level of the price increase, and so on). The assumption behind this design is that extraneous factors will not unduly affect one group of test units more than another, as the test units are similar.

Table 7.2 Completely Randomised design

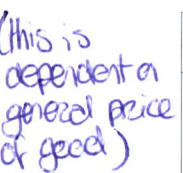
(This is dependent on general price of good)

		Different levels of the independent variable price increase		
		X_1 1% increase	X_2 3% increase	X_3 5% increase
9 shops (a – i)	(R) (R) (R)	sales a sales d sales c	sales e sales g sales h	sales b sales f sales i
		Average sales X_1	Average sales X_2	Average sales X_3

As Table 7.2 shows, the test units are randomly assigned to different levels of the independent variable, over an agreed time period. The average sales levels for each level of the independent variable are analysed, using a statistical technique known as analysis of variance. Analysis of variance is dealt with in Chapter 13. Given that it is used to analyse all four of the statistical designs, it is worth noting that analysis of variance measures the variance occurring between treatments, known as the treatment effect. It compares the average result (say sales) for the treatment groups to determine the probability that the observed differences (in sales) occurred by chance. If the differences in sales did not occur by chance, then the treatments brought about the differences, and the results are said to be significant. In our case, it enables the manager to calculate the effect of the different price increases on sales. From the results of this analysis, the shampoo manufacturer can infer which price increase to use.

Of all the four advanced designs, the completely randomised design is the least expensive. It is also the easiest to administer. It is used when the test units are known to be identical or very similar to each other, and thus randomisation of the stores to the different treatment levels assumes the groups of stores are equivalent. Of course, the main problem is this matching of groups or test units. In reality, test units are rarely identical. A further problem arises, especially if this design were used in a field experiment, i.e. the real world. Extraneous factors, such as store type or size, might play a role in the level of sales. If these problems cannot be satisfactorily solved, then an alternative design must be chosen.

2. The Randomised Block Design

This design is well suited when the researcher wishes to isolate the influence of one extraneous factor. It takes the notion of stratification and applies it to experiments. It 'blocks' the effect that an important extraneous variable may have on a dependent variable; hence the name 'randomised block design'. Common extraneous variables that marketing managers may wish to block include age, store size, store type, educational level or competitive price. This 'blocking effect' essentially means that test units are grouped into similar clusters or blocks, before random assignment of the independent variable. As an example, consider the previous example of a shampoo manufacturer who wishes to determine the effect of price increases on sales. He may be worried about the various distribution channels and their reaction to the price increases. In such circumstances, he will want to control for any variance that channel types may have on sales. This gives the researcher a precise picture of the treatment's impact on the dependent variable. It does so by isolating one key extraneous variable. That is to say, the advantage of the randomised block design lies in its ability to measure the effect of the treatment variable at different levels of the blocking variable.

Table 7.3 shows the randomised block design in operation. The extraneous variable has to be identified prior to the experiment. This and the different levels of the treatment variable are all measured at the same time, during the experiment. Analysis of variance is used to determine the treatment effects.

Table 7.3 Randomised Block design

	Different levels of the independent variable price increase		
	X_1	X_2	X_3
Blocking factor Store type	1% increase	3% increase	5% increase
National chains (R)	sales	sales	sales
Corner shops (R)	sales	sales	sales
Health food shops (R)	sales	sales	sales
	Average sales X_1	Average sales X_2	Average sales X_3

3. The Latin Square Design

To control or block for the effect of two or more extraneous variables, e.g. the type of outlet and store size, the Latin square design is used. The name is derived from the two extraneous variables, being used as blocking factors to form the rows and columns of a square table. Treatment effects are then randomly assigned to the cells within the square. This requirement is central to the Latin square and because of it, there must be equal numbers of rows and columns, i.e., 2 X 2 X 2 or 3 X 3 X 3 or 4 X 4 X 4. The Latin square is therefore a natural extension of the previous design.

An example best illustrates; let's return to our shampoo manufacturer. As well as being concerned about the types of distribution outlets having different reactions to the proposed price increases, the manager is seriously concerned about the store size. He knows from past experience and historical sales records that sales are influenced by the size of the store. So, to determine the best price increase, 1%, 3% or 5%, he also needs to control for, or block the influence of, store type and size.

Table 7.4 Latin Square design

		Blocking factors — store types and size		
		National	Corner stores	Health shops
Small	(R)	X_1	X_2	X_3
Medium	(R)	X_2	X_3	X_1
Large	(R)	X_3	X_1	X_2
		Average sales	Average sales	Average sales

As with previous designs in this section, over an agreed time period, treatments (recall, these are the different price increases, where 1% increase = X_1, 3% increase = X_2 and 5% increase = X_3) are randomly assigned, subject to the restriction of each treatment appearing once and once only in each row and column. (This restriction rule does not apply to the randomised block design.) So, each treatment is tested in each store type and store size. The sales results are noted and the average treatment effect (average sales in this case) is calculated, using analysis of variance. From this, we can determine the main effect of the different price increases for the various store types and sizes.

What we cannot do with this design is measure the interaction between the two extraneous factors. Thus, the Latin square design suffers from one notable limitation — the assumption that there is no interaction between the treatments and the blocking factors. Hence, we are unable to calculate the inter-relationship between the store types, store sizes, price level increases and sales. Coupled with this is the 2 x 2 x 2 or 3 x 3 x 3 requirement, making this an expensive and complex design in practice.

4. The Factorial Design

If our shampoo manufacturer wants to know about the simultaneous effects of two or more independent variables, then a factorial design must be utilised. A factorial design measures the effect of interacting variables on a dependent variable. So, it moves away from the blocking approach of the previous designs, and focuses upon a number of independent variables.

To continue with the shampoo example, any changes in sales could be attributed to both the store type and size and the price increases. With such a design, the manufacturer can estimate the main effects of the two independent variables and the interaction between them. He can measure the *main effects* of each independent variable and the *interaction effects*, when their combined effect does not equal the sum of their individual effects.

The design looks like the figure below. The three variables and their treatment levels are as follows:

X_1 = Price increases
 level 1 = 1%
 level 2 = 3%
 level 3 = 5%

X_2 = Store type
 level 1 = national chains
 level 2 = corner shops
 level 3 = health food shops

X_3 = Store size   new factor
 level 1 = small, under 5,000 sq. feet
 level 2 = medium, 5,001 to 10,000 sq. feet
 level 3 = large, over 10,001 sq. feet.

Figure 7.2 Factorial design

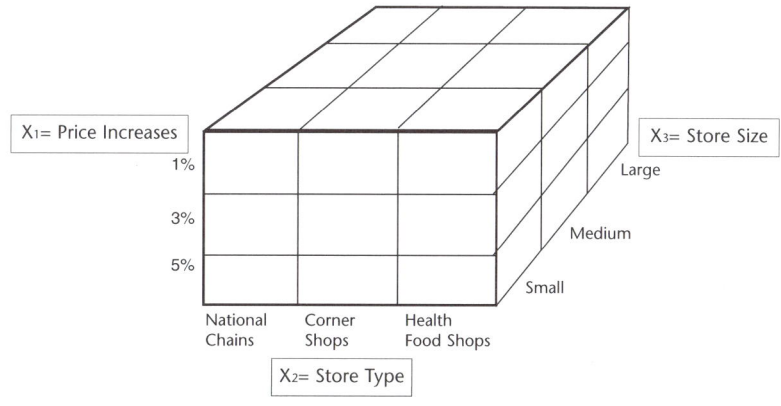

This is a 3 x 3 x 3 factorial design. In the case of store type, we might want to consider national chains versus all other outlets. This would result in a 3 x 2 x 3 design, with 18 cells, as the first independent variable has three treatment levels, the second variable has two treatment levels and the last independent variable has three treatment levels. Thus, in the factorial design, a cell is required for each possible combination of independent variables. A full factorial design, consisting of 32 product combinations or cells, (4 brands x 4 prices x 2 bundling features) was effective in estimating the unit demand for a new product in a relatively new product category. It enabled management to explore a range of product, pricing and promotional support alternatives to develop a realistic guide for the marketing strategy.[9]

In conclusion, while the factorial design undoubtedly is the best experimental design, it can be very expensive, demanding relatively large sample sizes and extensive measurement processes.

• Selection of an Experimental Design

An important question for any researcher at this point is the selection of the best design for a study. In choosing the most appropriate experimental design, the researcher balances two issues, the potential threat to internal validity against the pragmatics of the project, e.g. cost, test units, and the time dimension. By way of summary, the various experimental designs are presented in Table 7.5 together with the potential validity threats or errors, as one method to select the most appropriate experimental design for any given project.

Table 7.5 Experimental designs and their ability to combat validity threats

Experimental designs	Validity threats						
	History	Maturation	Testing Effect	Instrument-ation	Mortality	S/Regression	S/Bias
Pre-experimental designs							
After-only	No	No	Yes	Yes	No	No	No
Before-after	No	No	No	No	Maybe	No	Maybe
True experimental designs							
Before-after with control	Yes	Yes	Maybe	Yes	No	Yes	Yes
After-only with control	Yes	Yes	Maybe	Yes	No	No	No
Solomon-Four	Yes	Yes	Maybe	Yes	Yes	Yes	Yes
Quasi-experimental designs							
Time-series	No	Yes	No	No	Maybe	No	No
Multiple time-series	Maybe	Yes	No	No	Maybe	No	No

As can be seen from Table 7.5, a general rule of thumb is that the more formal and statistical the design, the more control the researcher has over validity threats. Against that, the more complex the design, the more costly and time-consuming the experiment.

Another way to select the most appropriate design is to consider the independent and dependent variables, coupled with the desired levels of control, as depicted in Figure 7.3.[10]

Figure 7.3 Which experimental design can be utilised?

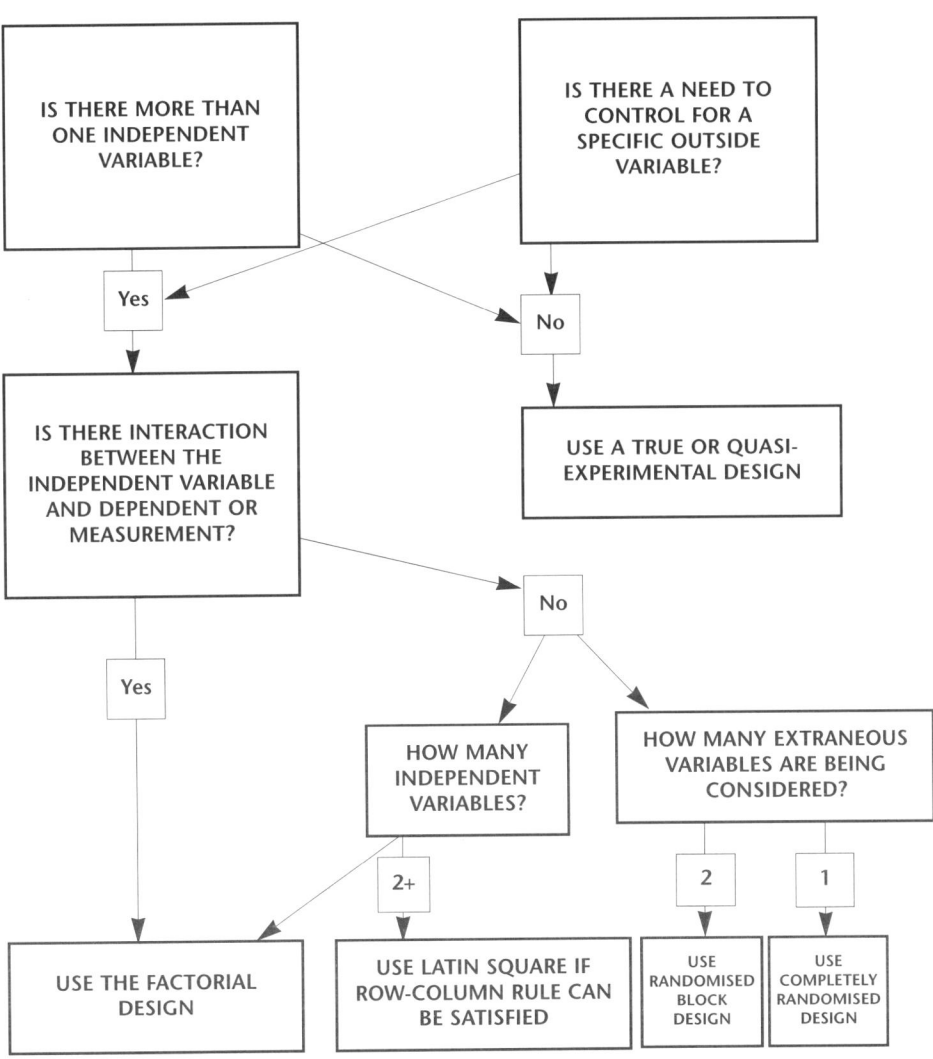

Essentially, the researcher uses the number of independent variables (one, two or more), the number of levels of the independent variable(s) (treatments, one or two or three or more) and the degree of main and interaction effect to select the best design.

From all of the preceding discussion, it is evident that experiments are a very powerful method for collecting data. Yet, the survey approach is generally regarded as the most popular tool for marketing researchers. This apparent anomaly arises because of the expensive nature of experiments, the complex nature of the marketplace and difficulties with implementing experiments, e.g. competitors becoming aware of marketing plans before full product launch.

Experiments cost significant time and money when compared with other data collection methods, but more importantly, managers may perceive the cost of running an experiment as outweighing the benefits of the supplied information. Consider, for example, the cost of testing three different advertising campaigns in three different countries. The ads, with three different languages, have to be produced and aired in three different countries, possibly on three different TV channels. Meanwhile, sales have to be measured before, during and after the advertising campaigns. A host of factors, varying from country to country, have to be controlled for, before one can consider the analysis stage.

In the preceding example, another problem is the advance knowledge competitors can glean about a marketing plan or some key factor within, as a result of running an experiment. The advantage of being the first mover can be lost as competitors are given time to react and respond. It has been known for concepts to be stolen in this manner and militates often against the use of experiments.

Finally, it may be administratively impossible to implement the conditions necessary to run an experiment. For example, retailers may not be willing to co-operate, a control group may not be feasible and there are moral and ethical concerns when the test units are humans.

This use, or non-use, of experiments leads us to the final topic before finishing our investigation of experimentation — that of test marketing and the development of simulated test marketing.

• Test Marketing

Traditionally the most popular form of field experiment, test marketing involves the use of representative areas, e.g. towns or television regions, some as test areas, others as control areas, to derive a sales estimate of the effect of an independent variable, like a new product or advertising campaign. Within these test areas, all other factors are kept constant and the independent variable is introduced with changes in the dependent variable monitored. In this manner, a company can gain experience and knowledge of what is likely to happen at a national launch. Test marketing allows the researcher to use experiments as a 'toe in the water'.

In Ireland, Guinness test-marketed a new range of premium taste beers in twenty Dublin pubs, aimed predominantly at male lager and ale drinkers, aged 28 to 40.[11] Mars Ireland test marketed their Celebrations chocolates and achieved 40% of the test market; moreover, 97% of the research respondents said they would purchase the product again — resulting in a successful national launch.[12] Stella Artois, from the Guinness Ireland Group, was test marketing in the Temple Bar and Grafton Street areas of Dublin[13] while McDonald's asked people if they would like to 'McOrder' while waiting at the petrol pumps as part of their on-the-go eater test market.[14] Finally, Beamish Red Irish Ale was launched on a test market basis in a number of Dublin and Cork outlets.[15]

To conduct a test market, a number of steps have to be undertaken. First, the objectives of the test market need to be articulated. These generally include determining sales levels and volume, frequency of purchase, repeat purchase rates, awareness levels, and effect on other sales of related products. Once completed, the next decision is to choose between a field or controlled (laboratory) test market. Then, an appropriate experimental design is selected, based upon the desired control over validity threats, cost and time constraints. The question as to how long a test market should last is important, as it has to be long enough for consumers to become aware of the product and buy it again. Next, the issue of the actual test markets, cities or regions is confronted. The selected areas must be representative of the whole population. In practice, it can be hard to achieve this in a miniature sample. That done, the treatment variables are applied, all the necessary observations are made and the results are analysed. Management is then in a position to make decisions about the national launch and marketing strategies to employ, should they wish to proceed.

The procedure, as described above for test marketing, can take the form of either a *standard test market* or a *controlled test market*. A standard test market is where the firm selects a number of cities, TV areas or other test units to market the product (and marketing mix) as it would do in a national launch. Sales forecasts are based upon audits of retailers, stores, distribution paths and consumers. This enables the company to evaluate the optimum marketing mix and make any necessary changes. The advantage of such a test market is the high degree of external validity given to the results. Using the 'real world', in every sense of the word, truly allows the firm to gauge the market reaction to the new product launch. Against this, the chosen locations have to be fully representative of the population at large. Coupled with this, sufficient time has to be allowed for the market and customers to respond to the new product, whilst guarding against competitors interfering with the launch.

On the other hand, controlled test marketing is where the company chooses the outlets through which to release the product, uses its own sales force and tests different marketing strategies (the firm is not confined to testing one particular strategy in all outlets in one area). This approach is cheaper and easier to implement than the standard test marketing procedure, but it is not as realistic.

Standard test marketing and control test marketing, two forms of test marketing, have historically been confined to the larger or multinational firms, due to cost and time demands, and the noted problems of experimentation highlighted above, such as competitive reaction, or inability to match towns or areas. In more recent years, one of the most interesting experimental developments (and an answer to many of the historical difficulties of test marketing mentioned above) has been simulated test marketing.

• Simulated Test Marketing

Simulated test marketing is the third type of test marketing available to a researcher. In general, this test marketing experimental method generates probability data about awareness levels, purchase levels and consumption likelihood. 'Mock' computer situations (simulated test marketing in a laboratory or virtual experiments, as opposed to standard or controlled which are in the field) are created to determine 'consumer reaction to marketing initiatives prior to their market entry'.[16] These reactions are combined with marketing plan information to predict the likelihood of usage, sales volume and probability of repeat purchase.[17, 18, 19, 20] Lyons successfully used STM to identify round teabags as a differentiating factor to arrest a decline in their market share for Tetley tea.[21]

Simulated test marketing is made possible as a result of technological advances. Essentially consumers are exposed to a new product or marketing programme in a simulated shopping environment. In this way, the manufacturer's products can be shown alongside competitive offerings in a photograph or slide presentation. The alternative is to allow consumers to purchase from shelves stocked with the products in question. Those consumers who choose the test product are asked to use a free sample at home and provide feedback. In this way, the new product with its price and the competitive products with prices can be shown in a photograph, slide presentation, computer simulation or video presentation. The type of consumer exposure is chosen to represent the dominant marketing vehicle which will be used in the product launch. In some cases, no consumer advertising is used with the launch of a new product, the consumers are exposed to a picture of the shelf set or an actual shelf set with prices. After exposure to the new product, most simulated test market designs use an attitudinal question concerning the probability of purchase, such as that in Box 7.2, to identify consumers who are likely to purchase the new product. Those consumers who are likely to purchase the test product are given the test product in its actual size to use at home and provide feedback.

Box 7.2 Sample attitudinal measurement often used in STM

Certainly will purchase	90% chance
Almost certainly will purchase	80% chance
Very probable will purchase	70% chance
Good possibility will purchase	60% chance
Fairly good possibility will purchase	50% chance
Fair possibility will purchase	40% chance
Some possibility will purchase	30% chance
Slight possibility will purchase	20% chance
Very slight possibility will purchase	10% chance
No chance will purchase	0% chance

Behavioural measures of purchase interest are also used in simulated test market designs; however, they are used less frequently than attitudinal measures due to the cost of conducting the research. Behavioural measures are obtained by allowing respondents to actually purchase the test and/or competitive products in the study. Respondents are exposed to the new product and competitive advertising. Next, consumers are exposed to actual shelves in the test product category. This methodology allows consumers to purchase from actual shelves stocked with the products in question. Consumers use their own money to purchase the test product in some cases, in other cases they use coupons provided by the research company. The consumers are called for feedback concerning the new product after they have used it at home.

These trial, retrial, and purchase and repeat rates (probabilities) are transcribed into advanced analytic software packages, to predict sales levels and market share. Variables, such as estimated advertising spend, shelf space, pricing and other promotional expenses are also included.

The accuracy of the simulated test marketing forecasts are tracked by the research companies generating the forecasts. All products actually launched into the marketplace are investigated after the launch year. The sales forecast and actual year-one sales are compared. The success of each forecast is included in the accuracy record for the particular simulated test market model. Since simulated test marketing models have been successful in forecasting the sales of the new products, the methodology has grown in use over time.

There are many other benefits to be had from utilising simulated test marketing. One key advantage is the realism offered by STM over and above other data collection methods and traditional test marketing. It sets products in a competitive context, positioning the test product against other valid options. Secondly, consumer purchase behaviours and reactions are measured, linking the consumers' attitudes to actual behaviour. This is difficult in typical test marketing. Thirdly, simulated test marketing allows a company to test their proposed marketing plan or mix before committing themselves to a full launch, in a cheaper and quicker manner than test marketing. Finally, STM provides accurate quantitative estimates of possible sales levels, marketing share and product cannibalisation. The noise and clutter of actual stores are recreated. Management and researchers have a large degree of control and flexibility over the independent and dependent variables, different price levels can be easily tested. As a result, today most consumer packaged goods companies are using STM to screen their new ideas early in the development process, so they can identify the better ideas and allocate more effort and resources to them.[22]

These benefits, alongside developments in software packages, EPoS, scanning and analytical models, such as those already in use, e.g. LTM, BASES and ASSESSOR, all suggest that simulated test marketing will continue to grow in popularity over the coming years.[23]

• **Summary**

Causal research establishes that a change in an independent variable causes a predictable change in a dependent variable. To demonstrate such an effect, the experiment is used as the data collection method for causal research. Experiments are defined as studies to manipulate an independent variable to measure the effects on a dependent variable. Four factors are required: concomitant, temporal sequence, theoretical support, and non-spurious association.

Experiments pay particular attention to internal and external validity. Threats to internal validity include history, maturation, the testing effect (main and interactive), instrumentation, mortality, statistical regression, and selection bias. External validity translates into a question of field versus laboratory experimental setting.

Experimental designs can be classified as pre-experiments; true experiments; quasi-experiments or advanced statistical experiments. This categorisation of experimental designs reflects the degree of control they afford the researcher over threats to both internal and external validity.

Test marketing is the experimental testing of a new marketing development, e.g. a new product, new promotional theme or a new marketing mix. It can be a standard, controlled or simulated test market to provide estimates to likely sales levels, consumers' reactions, and potential problems with proposed marketing mix strategies. As technological advances continue in both hardware and software applications, it is inevitable that experimentation, in the form of simulated test marketing becomes more widely used.

Key Terms

Causal research
Experiment
Independent variable
Dependent variable
Test units
Control group
Experimental group
Randomisation
Internal validity
History
Maturation
Testing
Main effect
Interaction effect
Instrumentation
Selection bias

Statistical regression
Mortality
Matching
External validity
Reactive error
Field experiments
Laboratory experiments
Pre-experimental designs
True experiments
Quasi-experiments
Statistical experiments
Test marketing
Standard test marketing
Control test marketing
Simulated test marketing

Questions

1. How do the scientific notions and commonsense notions of causality differ?
2. Describe some independent and dependent variables that could be used in consumer goods experiments.
3. What is the purpose of randomisation and matching in experimental design?
4. Indicate the kind of evidence needed to demonstrate the existence of a causal relationship.
5. Describe, and give an example of, each of the following error types:
   (a) testing effect;
   (b) interaction error;
   (c) maturation;
   (d) history;
   (e) selection bias;
   (f) mortality;
   (g) instrumentation;
   (h) main effect.
6. How can the statistical regression effect exert an influence on the results of an experiment? Provide a real or hypothetical example of a situation in which this effect is likely to be present.
7. Is it possible for a marketing experiment to have high internal validity, but very low external validity? If so, provide an example of a situation in which this would be likely to occur.

8. Experiments may be conducted in a variety of settings that are usually classified as laboratory or field.
   (a) What differences distinguish laboratory from field settings?
   (b) What concerns should the experimenter be particularly aware of in each setting?
9. What are the distinctions between pre-experimental, true experimental and quasi-experimental designs?
10. Explain how various measurements of the experimental effect in a Solomon-Four group design can provide estimates of the effects of certain extraneous variables?
11. What is the key characteristic that distinguishes true experimental designs from pre-experimental designs?
12. What is a time-series experiment? When is it used?
13. Suggest at least three specific situations in marketing, in which you think an experiment would be an appropriate research design. Which of the various designs would you recommend for each of the situations? What specific internal and/or external validity threats would you face with your suggested designs?
14. What ethical problems do you see in conducting experiments with human subjects? In your answer, refer to a 'Code of Conduct' from a recognised body at either national or international level.
15. Explain:
    (a) controlled test marketing;
    (b) simulated test marketing.
    How are they different from traditional test marketing?
16. Which of the following products or marketing strategies are likely to be test marketed? Why or why not?
    (a) a computerised robot lawn mower;
    (b) a line of eight-ounce servings of vegetarian dishes for senior citizens;
    (c) a forklift truck;
    (d) a new brand of eye-drops especially for brown-eyed people;
    (e) a new, heavy-duty kitchen mixer;
    (f) an advertising campaign to drink a cola drink in the morning.

Problems and Assignments

1. A leading manufacturer of frozen food products decided to test the effectiveness of an in-store display. Eight large supermarkets, near the company's head office, were selected for the experiment. The display was set up in four of the stores, and sales were monitored for a period of two weeks. The sales of the other four stores were also recorded, but no displays were used. Sales volume for the frozen food products increased by 1% in the stores that used in-store displays compared to the stores that did not.

(a) What type of design was being used? Justify your answer.
(b) Diagrammatically represent the design.
(c) Discuss the threats to internal and external validity for the design.

2. The product development team at Bord na Mona has been working on several modifications of their highly successful fireplace log. The most promising development is a new log that comes prepacked and burns an hour longer. At a recent strategy meeting, the marketing director suggested a test market before a national launch of the new log. He pointed out that a test market would be a good way to evaluate the effectiveness of two alternative advertising and promotional campaigns that have been proposed by Bord na Mona's advertising agency. He felt that effectiveness should be evaluated in terms of the trial and repeat purchasing behaviour. He also wanted to assess Bord na Mona's current distributor's acceptance of the new product. The Bord na Mona CEO is not very enthusiastic about the idea of test marketing. He is concerned that Bord na Mona's competitors could easily duplicate the new log; and that the seasonal nature of log sales makes it imperative to reach a decision on the new log by early April, only four months away.
    (a) What information should be obtained from the test market in order to satisfy the marketing director?
    (b) What constraints must the test-marketing operate to satisfy the CEO?
    (c) What test market approach should be pursued? Why?

3. A manufacturer of gas cookers has designed an improved model that will reduce gas usage and decrease cooking times. However, this new model will increase the product's price by 15% because of new components and design changes. The company wants to assess to what extent the new model will affect sales of its existing gas ovens. Suggest an experimental design, justifying your choice, that will enable management to make a decision as to whether to launch the new cooker.

4. The student union at your university or college is considering three alternative brands of burgers to be offered in the student restaurant. Design an experiment to determine which brand of burgers students would prefer.

5. Bord Bia, in conjunction with Bord Iascaigh Mhara and a group of mussel farmers, has developed a new frozen mussel dinner — one heats it and serves it in the tray. The group overseeing the development are not considering test marketing the product. They are planning to go with a national launch. What are the advantages of doing so, given that the group already had five successful food launches in the Irish market over the past three years? What are the disadvantages of not test marketing?

6. What experimental designs would you advocate in the following circumstances? How would you recruit the test subjects? What treatment would you apply to the subjects? How would you measure results?

(a) The acceptability of a prepackaged custard.
(b) The response to an addition to a confectionery counter-line popular with primary schoolchildren.
(c) The response of the Irish public to a new Irish drama on RTE 1;
(d) The awareness of males, 18–35, to a new line of shoes by Dubarry.

8. 'Drimavoughane' is a goat's cheese sold locally in the south-east of Ireland, where it is popular with restaurants. The firm feel that Drimavoughane is losing market share among restaurants to the national brands. However, no exact measures of the restaurant's attitudes or consumption patterns exist. Management is considering placing an advertisement in the local newspapers and/or local radios. However, they are not sure how effective this would be. Design a study to test the effectiveness of the advertisements.

9. State the type of experiment being conducted in the following situations. In each case, identify the potential threat to internal and external validity.
   (a) A major distributor of telecommunications equipment is considering a new sales pitch for its salespeople. The sales territory with the largest sales figures for the past year is selected, the new sales strategy is implemented, and the effect on sales is measured.
   (b) Procter & Gamble wants to determine if a new package design for Fairy washing-up liquid is more effective than the current pack. Ten supermarkets are randomly selected throughout Ireland. In five of them, randomly selected, Fairy is sold in the new packaging. In the remaining shops, the old package is used. Sales are recorded for both groups of supermarkets for three months.

10. The Marketing Society of Ireland has asked you to design an experiment to measure the effect of compensation on response rates when conducting Internet surveys among Irish businesses. This involves 600 firms who will be assigned to one of the following conditions: no compensation; £1 compensation; and £3 compensation. Describe how your design would work if it were:
    (a) a Completely Randomised design;
    (b) a Randomised Block design;
    (c) a Latin Square; or
    (d) a Factorial design (suggest another independent variable to use).
    Which is the most appropriate design? Why?

11. Connor McWilliams, the newly appointed marketing manager of a highly popular and successful pottery shop in Temple Bar has requested a larger budget for shop window displays.

    McWilliams thinks that continuous changes in the shop window display, to reflect local events such as St Valentine's Day and St Patrick's Day, will attract customers. Specifically, he expects customers to come into the shop more often, increase their purchase amount and develop a more positive image of the shop and products. The owner is not convinced and has asked McWilliams for proof to justify the increased expenditure on displays. Identify the independent variable(s), the dependent variable(s) and the likely extraneous variables to impact on the dependent variable.

12. A manufacturer has developed a new food product to test marketing stage. Previous experience suggests the appeal of this type of product to customers may vary both across regions of the country (Dublin, other urban and rural) and in the type of outlet (small local shops, Centra/Spar-type co-ops, and large supermarkets). So, in addition to attempting to estimate the overall sales of the new product, the manufacturer wishes to determine whether sales vary across region, across type of store and also whether there is some interaction between store type and region. Describe briefly how an experiment could be designed to answer the manufacturer's question. (Adapted from a Marketing Institute of Ireland examination paper, 1996.)

Case Study
Broccoli Quick, A New Product Introduction*

Background

Connolly Produce of Clifden, Co. Galway, has been importing fresh produce products since 1973 from the United States, France, Italy and Israel for sale in grocery stores in Ireland. In 1995 one of Connolly produce's suppliers from the United States, T&J Growers, suggested that Connolly Produce import one of their products which was very successful in the United States, Salad Quick. Salad Quick is a ready-to-eat salad product. It includes iceberg and romaine lettuce, carrots, and red cabbage which have been washed and cut. It is packaged in a re-sealable bag and it is priced 25% above head lettuce. It is a value-added produce product.

Catherine Connolly, President of Connolly Produce, did not want to risk importing such a premium product without using simulated test marketing to examine its market potential. A simulated test market was used instead of a test market because a simulated test market:

- provides results in a shorter time period;
- provides confidentiality;
- is less expensive than a test market;
- is an empirically validated methodology.

A simulated test market was conducted for Salad Quick using a representative sample of produce purchasers in Ireland. The simulated test market methodology used by Connolly Produce exposed consumers to an advertisement of the new product. The purchase probability was forecasted using an attitudinal response to a purchase probability question administered to consumers after the advertising exposure.

Consumers who indicated a 70% chance or higher purchase probability were sent home with the new product. The consumers were called on the phone one week later to evaluate the repurchase probability, anticipated purchase volume, and product performance.

The results of the simulated test market predicted strong consumer acceptance. The purchase probability forecasted for Salad Quick was 40%. Therefore, 40% of consumers exposed to the print advertisement of the new product were willing to purchase it. The repeat purchase rate and anticipated purchase volume among likely purchasers were at normative levels after an in-home use phase. The strong consumer response generated a sales forecast within the target range. The new product was imported and distributed throughout Ireland in 1996. Actual sales were within 5% of the sales forecasted using the simulated test marketing methodology.

Simulated Test Market Results for Line Extension

Since Connolly Produce achieved success with importing Salad Quick from T&J Growers, they examined the potential of importing another item in the T&J Growers' value-added line which was a success in the United States, Broccoli Quick. The unique new product, Broccoli Quick, is a package of fresh broccoli, fresh pasta, and an alfresco sauce sold at a retail price of £2.34 in grocery stores. It can be cooked within ten minutes.

A simulated test market was conducted for Broccoli Quick using a representative sample of produce purchasers in Ireland. Consumers were exposed to a print advertisement of the new product. Consumers who indicated a 70% chance or higher purchase probability were sent home with the new product. The consumers were called on the phone one week later to evaluate the repurchase probability, anticipated purchase volume, and product performance.

The results were disappointing. Broccoli Quick generated a purchase probability of only 10% and a sales forecast below the target. However, the product performed well during the in-home use phase. The repurchase interest among likely purchasers was at above normative levels and the product performed higher than expected before use in the home.

Connolly Produce was not willing to abandon the new product without further analysis because it performed well in the home. Catherine Connolly understood that if she could manipulate the marketing mix to encourage trial of the product it would be successful. Trial is achieved through a generation of consumers' perceptions of a product based on advertising and promotion. An analysis of consumers' perceptions of a new product is achieved through positioning analysis.

Evaluation of Low Purchase Probability Using Positioning Analysis

The print advertisement used in the simulated test market positioned Broccoli Quick as a fresh, fast and nutritious meal. Positioning analysis was included as part of the simulated test market research. Respondents rated Broccoli Quick on nine product attributes and benefits using a 100-point scale after they were exposed to the advertising, but before they took it home and used it.

A comparison of the mean ratings of Broccoli Quick between likely purchasers and non-purchasers in Table 7.6 indicates that the advertisement did not effectively communicate the positioning. Likely non-purchasers rated Broccoli Quick significantly lower on all attributes and benefits than likely purchasers. Likely non-purchasers did not understand that the product contained fresh ingredients and rated it low on value.

Table 7.6 A comparison of mean brand ratings for Broccoli Quick between likely purchasers and likely non-purchasers of Broccoli Quick

Attribute/benefit	Likely purchasers[1] (N = 50)	Likely non-purchasers (N = 450)
Contains fresh ingredients	91*	78
Has fresh vegetables	90*	78
Is nutritious	88*	73
Is fresh tasting	88*	72
Is easy to prepare	87*	81
Has fresh pasta	86*	74
Tastes homemade	81*	65
A good value for the money	78*	68
Is low priced	65*	59

[1] Note small base size.
* Significantly different at the 0.05 level.

Table 7.7 shows a comparison of Broccoli Quick with a frozen product, Pasta Pronto, which is currently in the market priced at £1.75. The results show that although Broccoli Quick is a fresh product and Pasta Pronto is a frozen product, respondents evaluated them similarly on the characteristics pertaining to freshness. Broccoli Quick rated lower than Pasta Pronto on value.

Table 7.7 A comparison of mean brand ratings between Broccoli Quick and Pasta Pronto

Attribute/Benefit	Broccoli Quick (N = 500)	Pasta Pronto (N = 500)
Contains fresh ingredients	81	78
Has fresh vegetables	80	78
Is easy to prepare	82	81
Has fresh pasta	77	74
Is nutritious	76	72
Is fresh tasting	75	72
Tastes homemade	68	65
A good value for the money	70*	80
Is low priced	61*	69

* Significantly different at the 0.05 level.

Questions

1. What is the dependent variable in the experiment?
2. What is the independent variable(s)?
3. After reviewing the results of the positioning analysis, what changes would you make to increase the purchase probability of Broccoli Quick?
4. Design an experiment which would evaluate the impact of those changes on the purchase probability of Broccoli Quick.
5. Describe the sample that would be used in the experiment.
6. Evaluate the validity of the experimental design.
7. Are there main effects in the experiment? Explain your answer.
8. Are there interaction effects in the experiment? Explain your answer.

*This case was written by Professor Marianne McGarry Wolf, Agribusiness Department, California Polytechnic State University, San Luis Obispo, California. She also works with Yankelovich partners in the USA as a senior consultant on experimental designs and simulated test marketing. It is intended to be used as a basis for class discussion rather than to illustrate the effective or ineffective handling of an administrative situation. The case is based upon a real situation, though certain information has been disguised. © Marianne McGarry Wolf.

Part 3

DATA COLLECTION AND ACQUISITION

Chapter 8

QUESTIONNAIRE DESIGN AND FIELD WORK

> - **Chapter Overview**
> - Introduction • Guidelines for Questionnaire Development
> - Preliminary Considerations • Question Content • Response Format
> - Question Wording • Question Sequence • Physical Characteristics
> - Pre-test • Field Work • Selection of Field Workers • Training of Field Workers • Supervision of Field Workers • Validation of Field Workers
> - Evaluation of Field Workers • Summary

• Introduction

The two main methods of collecting primary data are asking questions and observing. Survey research (in whatever form — personal interview, telephone or postal) relies on the use of a questionnaire. The heart of a survey is the questionnaire,[1] which is a formalised means of collecting data from respondents. The primary purpose of a questionnaire is measurement. There are a number of ways to apply survey questionnaires: personal interview, telephone, postal or self-administered. Questionnaires can be used to measure customers' behaviour, their attitudes, awareness and characteristics. By using a questionnaire the researcher provides standardisation and uniformity in the data-gathering process. If researchers go out and ask people somewhat different questions, they will get answers that are not directly comparable. A questionnaire standardises the wording and sequencing of the questions and allows the field workers to achieve speed and accuracy in recording the data. Because the data are collected in common form a questionnaire enables the recorded information to be edited and summarised more quickly and with less error.

A questionnaire has three objectives.[2] First, it must translate the information needed into questions that the respondent can and will answer. Secondly, a questionnaire must uplift, motivate and encourage the respondent to co-operate and complete the interview. Thirdly, a questionnaire should minimise response error.

Given this, at the end of this chapter the reader will be able to:

1. discuss questionnaire design;
2. describe the seven steps of questionnaire design; and
3. explain fieldwork issues.

• Guidelines for Questionnaire Development

Questionnaire design is a major source of non-sampling error. Questionnaire design is more of an art than a scientific undertaking and is beset with potential pitfalls. It is a skill that the researcher learns through experience. The design of an appropriate questionnaire involves no firm set of foolproof procedures. There are, however, a number of rules or guidelines that can be followed. These rules have emerged from the accumulated experience of researchers. While these rules are useful in preventing serious errors, the fine-tuning of a questionnaire requires the creativity of a skilled researcher. Ultimately, a sound questionnaire requires the application of guidelines, commonsense, concern for the respondent, a clear understanding of the information needed, and extensive pre-testing. But the best data collection instrument is not necessarily the one that is perfect. Rather than attempting to develop the 'ideal' questionnaire, the practicality of conducting marketing research may require developing a questionnaire that is both workable and adequate for the task at hand. After all, out-of-date information collected through use of a perfect questionnaire is of little use.

Questionnaires can be classified according to their degree of structure and directness. The type of questionnaire used is, to an extent, dependent on the method of survey. Highly structured questionnaires consist of a series of structured formal questions which limit the responses of the respondent, whereas unstructured questionnaires are made up of more open investigative-type questions. Structured questionnaires tend to incorporate more multiple-choice, dichotomous and scale-type questions. Unstructured questionnaries lend themselves more towards open-ended-type questions as in an in-depth discussion guide. In practice most questionnaires are a mix of both the structured and unstructured type. Directness, on the other hand, refers to the degree to which the respondent is aware of the purpose of the study. While any combination of structure and directness is possible, the use of unstructured indirect questionnaires is more akin to applying projective techniques.

The discussion of questionnaire design will be presented as a series of seven steps. While the steps are presented sequentially, they are, in fact, inter-related. Not only do decisions made during the early stages influence choices later in the sequence, but decisions made during the final stages may compel the reconsideration of earlier choices. For example, decisions on question sequence will often influence the wording of the questions involved. The seven steps can be summarised as shown in Figure 8.1.

Figure 8.1

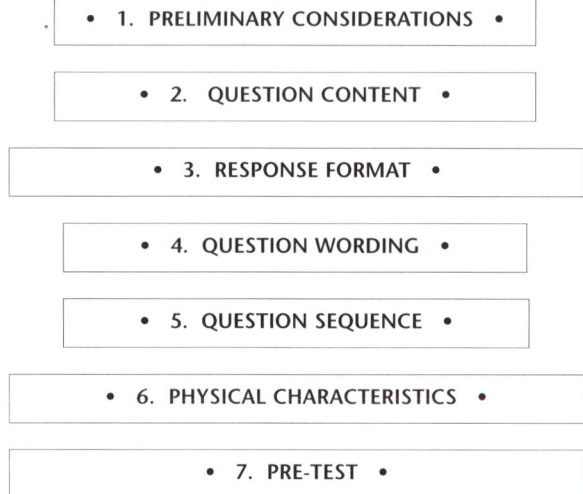

The major part of this chapter will be devoted to the problems encountered in constructing good questionnaires. Some of this will also be pertinent to observation forms.

①• Preliminary Considerations

The researcher must make decisions regarding:

1. What information is required?
2. Who are target respondents?
3. What method of communication will be used to reach these respondents?
4. How will the resulting data be processed and analysed?

1. What information is required?

Decisions made during the early stages of the research process will influence the questionnaire design. The preceding chapters stressed the need to have good problem definition and clear objectives for the study to deal with the management problem at hand. Research objectives (listing of information needs) should be spelled out as clearly and precisely as possible. The questionnaire is the link between the information needed and the data to be collected. The questions from the questionnaire should flow logically from the list of information needs. It is helpful to write each question number opposite the objective that the particular question will help accomplish. A questionnaire is relevant if no unnecessary information is collected and only the information needed to solve the marketing problems is obtained. The collection of data that is not required increases the cost of the project — more about this later.

2. Who are the target respondents?

The characteristics of the respondent groups have a great influence on questionnaire design. Questions that are appropriate for a group of college graduates may not be appropriate for respondents with a second-level education. If, for example, CERT wished to conduct a survey with summer workers in the hospitality industry, it may choose to design one questionnaire for third-level students and have another designed specifically for sixth-year secondary students. Likewise, a questionnaire designed for use on children would require much simpler language than that designed for use on adults. A questionnaire must 'speak' to respondents in an understandable language and at the appropriate intellectual level. The more heterogeneous the groups, the more difficult it is to construct a single questionnaire that is appropriate to everyone. Marketing jargon and business terminology should be avoided where possible (unless that is your respondent group). It is best to use simple, everyday language, as long as the result is not insulting or demeaning to the respondent.

3. What method of communication will be used?

The method of administering a questionnaire (personal interview, telephone, postal etc.) will also have a bearing on its structure and content. In personal interviews, respondents see the questionnaire and interact with the interviewer. More difficult and complex questions can be asked of the respondent. In telephone interviews the respondent does not see the questionnaire, whereas postal questionnaires are self-completing. This poses its own problems for the type and style of questions that may be asked of the respondent. In general, a more conversational style of writing is appropriate for personal and telephone interviews. These factors and others were discussed in Chapter 6, where we examined the characteristics of different approaches to collecting marketing research data. In all such cases the decision as to which survey method is used will affect the types of questions to be asked and the general nature of the questionnaire design.

4. How will the data be processed and analysed?

Consideration must also be given to the latter stages of the research process. Decisions regarding editing, coding, processing and statistical analysis of the data need to be factored in to the design of the questionnaire; for example, where statistical analysis is to be employed, highly structured questionnaires are needed.

keep thinking why am I asking this question?

- **Question Content**

When evaluating possible questions for inclusion in the data collection instrument, the following issues must be considered:

1. Is the question really necessary?

Although it seems obvious that no question should be included in a questionnaire unless it is necessary, there may be a tendency to include interesting questions that have no particular contribution to the research objectives. The answers to these questions may be 'nice to know' but convey no managerially useful information. If there is no satisfactory answer to the question 'How am I going to use the data generated by this question?' that question should be eliminated. Unnecessary questions add to the expense of the survey and increase the demands made on the respondents, thereby possibly decreasing the chances of their co-operation. In certain situations a 'dummy' question is included at the beginning of, or strategically throughout, a questionnaire in order to obtain respondent involvement and rapport prior to asking more sensitive or controversial question; or questions may be asked in order to disguise the true purpose or sponsorship of the study. For example, questions may be asked about competing brands merely to hide the identity of the brand under study.

2. Does the respondent have the information requested?

Once we are sure that our question is necessary and addresses the information needs, we must consider the respondent's ability to provide an accurate answer. Certain factors limit the respondent's ability to provide the desired information. The respondent may not know the answer, may know the answer but have forgotten it, or may be unable or unwilling (due to confidentiality) to articulate the answer.

3. The respondent may not know the answer

Respondents are often asked questions on topics that may not fall within a given respondent's experience. They are 'uninformed' in the sense that they have never known the answer to the question. Asking a respondent about a brand or store that they have never encountered is an example of this problem. Respondents will often be more than willing to answer questions they do not know the answer to. Although uninformed they may be reluctant to admit a lack of knowledge on a topic. This is especially so when a question is worded in such a manner that implies that a respondent should know the answer. Uninformed respondents are a source of measurement error.

Respondents who falsely report awareness of marketing stimuli such as brand names, logos, product promotions, advertisements etc. are guilty of 'bogus recall' or 'spurious awareness'. The researcher should be wary of continuous 'yea-saying' respondents. Where there is doubt, filter questions should be used to determine familiarity and past experience with a product category. Filter questions are asked before questions about the topic itself. They are essentially screening questions that are used to filter out respondents who are not sufficiently informed. Filter questions can be indirect ('What brands of deodorant are you familiar with?') or direct ('Have you ever used Fiacla toothpaste in the past year?').

4. Can the respondent remember the information?

Not only should the individual have the information sought, but he or she should remember it. However, in many situations respondents cannot recall the answer to a question. Can *you* answer the following questions?

- What products were advertised before the nine o'clock news last Sunday?
- What did you have for lunch five days ago?
- What brand of petrol, if any, did you purchase two weeks ago?

We may have known the answers to these questions once, but do not remember when questioned specifically. Our ability to remember various events is influenced by the event itself, its importance, the length of time since the event, and the amount of recall stimuli provided to jog our memory. Three aspects of forgetting are of concern to the researcher:

- *Omission,* which is the inability to recall an event that actually took place.
- *Telescoping,* which occurs when a respondent remembers an event as occurring more recently than it actually occurred.
- *Creation,* which occurs when an individual 'remembers' an event that did not actually occur.

Researchers cannot easily change the ability of an individual to remember things. They can, however, try to ask the person most apt to remember, e.g. recent purchasers. If the event could be considered relatively unimportant to the respondents, they can limit their questions to events that have happened recently. In fact, when memory is involved, researchers must be cautious not to overestimate the accuracy with which respondents will remember the information they want.

Consumers are particularly poor at remembering quantities of products. Classification of users into heavy users and light users of a product on the basis of reported use has been found to misclassify up to 75% of respondents in some product categories.[3] Another factor which affects our ability to remember is the stimulus we are given. An unaided recall approach does not provide the respondent with cues. Questions like 'What brand of coffee do you remember being advertised on TV last night?' rely on unaided recall. The aided recall approach attempts to stimulate the respondent's memory by providing cues; for example 'From the following list of coffee brand names, which one do you remember being advertised on TV last night?' Aided recall is an attempt to overcome the memory problem.

5. Ability of the respondent to articulate

When respondents are unable to articulate their responses on an issue, they are likely to ignore that question and/or refuse to co-operate with the remainder of the survey. This may be particularly so for open-ended questions — 'Why do you use this dry cleaning service?', where respondents may have difficulty in verbalising the issue.

Closed-ended questions, lists of alternatives to choose from, and pictures etc. may help respondents to better articulate their response. Projective techniques is another method researchers use to help respondents to verbalise answers.

6. Willingness to respond accurately

Assuming that the respondent can answer the question, he or she may be unwilling to do so. Unwillingness to respond accurately can be manifested in:

- a refusal to answer a specific question(s), i.e. item non-response error;
- deliberately providing an incorrect answer. This distortion results in measurement error.

Non-response or distorted answers can result from any of the following reasons:

- The situation or context may not seem appropriate for disclosure. For example it may be inappropriate for a family planning clinic to carry out on-street personal interviews to determine the public's family planning activities. Such questions are perhaps better asked by a nurse or GP.
- The information requested may be considered personal or embarrassing to the respondent. Questions on topics such as sexual behaviour and orientation, purchase of personal hygiene products, consumption of alcohol, theft and car accidents, readership of certain magazines etc. may result in refusals or distortions.
- Requests for 'prestige' or 'normative' information.

Questions that have a bearing on prestige or adherence to social norms include education level obtained, income earned, amount of time spent reading quality newspapers or watching educational TV, purchase of high prestige magazines, etc. typically produce answers with an upward response bias. Likewise, ownership or usage of low prestige or less socially acceptable products or services is typically understated by respondents.

How to deal with respondents who are unwilling to respond accurately

Intuitively, it would seem that anonymity would increase the likelihood of respondents providing accurate answers to sensitive questions. However, in many instances, assurances of anonymity are not sufficient to encourage unwilling respondents. A number of techniques have been developed to seek out potentially embarrassing or sensitive information.

1. Placing of sensitive topics at the end of the questionnaire. By then rapport has been created, any initial mistrust has been weakened and the legitimacy of the survey established.
2. Counter biasing statement. Begin with a statement that suggests the behaviour in question is relatively common. For example, if we anticipate that responses will

tend to be distorted in the 'Yes' direction we can preface the question with a statement that makes the 'No' response more acceptable for the respondent, i.e. the question is intentionally biased in the opposite direction. For example, 'For various reasons people delay in paying their TV licence on time. Have you ever delayed from paying for your TV licence on time?' Ideally, the prefacing statement should contain an amount of counter bias, equal to the response bias resulting from the question itself. There is a danger that too much or too little counter bias will be introduced. Some respondents may admit to behaviour they did not engage in because it may suddenly seem embarrassing to have not engaged in the behaviour in question. Also, unethical researchers who use counter biasing statements could arrive at findings that are purposely distorted to suit their own agenda.

3. Use an indirect statement.
4. Phrase the sensitive question so that it refers to 'other people' and allow respondents to reveal their attitudes by expressing them indirectly through a third party. As an example:

   'Q9. For one reason or another most people find it difficult to attend Mass every week on at least one occasion. Do you think this is improper?'

5. Another approach is to hide the potentially sensitive questions within a group of other more innocent questions. The entire list of questions can then be asked quickly. Respondents may be more likely to respond than might be the case if the question was asked in a vacuum.
6. Provide response categories rather than asking for specific figures. For example, 'What is your age?': a. 20–29 b. 30–39 c. 40–49 d. 50–59 e. 60+.

   Using age categories, e.g. 45–54 has an advantage in that people can get over the psychological barrier of being, for example, in their fifties.

If the sensitive information is being sought by means of personal interview, the interviewer can provide the respondent with a card containing labelled response categories such as:

(a) under £15,000
(b) 15,001–20,000
(c) 20,001–25,000
(d) over 25,000

and ask them to respond with the appropriate letter, e.g. (c).

Another approach to overcoming non-response and measurement error caused by sensitive questions is the 'randomised response technique'. The respondent is presented with two questions, one sensitive or potentially embarrassing, the other a neutral question with a known probability of 'Yes' response, e.g. 'Were you born in February?' The respondent, depending on the outcome of a random procedure (e.g.

flip of a coin) is asked to answer the question that is associated with the random outcome, which he alone observes. As a result the researcher receives only a 'Yes' or 'No' response, but does not know what question the respondent has answered. The proportion of respondents who answer 'Yes' to the neutral question is determined through secondary sources (e.g. Census of Population) or through another research survey. The proportion of respondents who answered 'Yes' to the sensitive question can then be determined by means of a formula. For example:

- Sensitive question: 'Have you ever used drugs?'
- Neutral question: 'Were you born in February?'
- P ('Yes' to sensitive question)

$$= \frac{P(\text{yes}) - P(\text{neutral question}) \, P(\text{yes to neutral question})}{P(\text{sensitive question})}$$

If the proportion of respondents who answered 'Yes' is .20, the proportion born in February (obtained from census data) is .10 and the probability of answering each question is .5, the estimate of the proportion of respondents who answered 'Yes' to the sensitive question is as follows:

P(yes to sensitive question)

$$= \frac{.20 - (.5)(.10)}{(.5)} = 0.3$$

The result of our finding is that 30% of respondents have used drugs.

However, the researcher cannot determine which respondents have answered 'Yes' to the sensitive question. This would preclude any opportunity to determine, for example, if drug-taking behaviour was associated with any particular demographic characteristic.

- **Decide on Response Format**

Once the content of an individual question has been determined, the researcher needs to decide what type of question to use. In the development of a questionnaire three basic types of questions may be utilised:

1. Open-ended. *least structure*
2. Multiple-choice (multichotomous).
3. Dichotomous *most structure*

Each poses a different degree of structure on the person's responses, and has its own particular uses, advantages and disadvantages. In terms of the amount of structure involved, open-ended questions have the least, and dichotomous questions the most, structure.

1. Open-ended Questions

Open-ended questions are those in which the respondent can reply in his or her own words. The researcher does not limit the response choices. In postal or self-completing questionnaires space is provided in which the respondent can write the answer. In the personal or telephone interview, the respondent verbally reports the answer to the interviewer, who records it on the questionnaire. Open-ended questions are useful in the following circumstances:

- At the beginning of a questionnaire or as a lead in to a section or topic to establish rapport and gain the respondent's co-operation.
- When there are too many possible responses to be listed, or the researcher is not sufficiently aware of all possible responses.
- When verbatim responses are required to give a flavour of people's answers or to cite as examples in the report. This 'real world' terminology (as different from laboratory or marketing jargon) can be later useful for designing promotional and advertising material.

Examples of open-ended questions include:

'Why do you shop here?'
'What do you think of Irish vegetables?'
'How do you eat yours?'

Open-ended questions are easy to formulate, and elicit a wide variety of responses. Because there is no fixed set of response alternatives from which to choose, respondents are less likely to be swayed toward a response that does not reflect their true opinion regarding the subject of the question. This makes them particularly suitable for exploratory research or problem identification research. Open-ended questions are also often used to probe for additional information.

Certain weaknesses limit the usefulness of open-ended questions. A principal weakness is the large amount of interviewer bias they permit. Interviewers rarely record respondents' answers *verbatim*, or summarise them accurately. Much depends on the speed and skill of the interviewer. The result is a mixture of interviewer and respondent rather than respondent alone. Tape recorders should be used if verbatim reporting is important. Secondly, the depth of responses to open-ended questions depends, to a great extent, on how articulate the respondent is in an interview or the willingness to compose a written answer to a postal survey. Another problem with unstructured questions is the time and cost associated with coding responses.[4] Classifications must be established to summarise the response, and each answer assigned to one or more categories. As each answer is, to an extent, unique, this involves subjective judgments that are prone to error, and the danger of forcing data into a category. Pre-coding can overcome some of the disadvantages of open-ended questions. Essentially, a multiple-choice question is presented to the respondent as open-ended. The response alternatives are not read to the respondent. Instead, the interviewer selects the appropriate response category based on the respondent's reply to the open-ended question. It does, however, require sufficient familiarity with subject areas to anticipate respondents' answers.

2. Multiple-choice Questions

Also known as multichotomous questions. The multiple-choice format typically presents the respondent with a question and a set of alternatives that will be mutually exclusive (no overlap occurs and only one alternative can be selected) and collectively exhaustive (the alternatives include all possible responses). From the list of possible answers provided, the respondent must select the one that expresses his opinion. The check list is a variant of the multiple-choice approach and asks the respondent to select all alternatives that apply to him.

For example:

'How would you rate the quality of this product'?

Very good ☐   Good ☐   Average ☐   Poor ☐   Very poor ☐

'Which of the following factors do you consider important when choosing a restaurant? Please tick as many as apply.'

Location ☐
Good food ☐
Friendly staff ☐
Decor ☐
Reputation ☐
Prices ☐
Signage ☐
Atmosphere ☐

Several of the issues discussed in Chapter 8 with respect to itemised rating scales also apply to multiple-choice answers. Multiple-choice questions overcome many of the disadvantages associated with open-ended questions. They are generally easier for both the interviewer and the respondent. They ensure greater ease of data recording and tabulation, thus eliminating interviewer bias and editing subjectivity. Multiple-choice questions are easier for the respondent to answer in both an interview and a postal survey. Indeed, they are almost essential for securing adequate co-operation in self-administered surveys. Likewise, respondents who are more articulate are less likely to be over-represented. However, there are limitations to the multiple-choice question format. First, good multiple-choice questions require time and effort. Exploratory research may be necessary to ensure that all potentially important response categories are included. If important response alternatives are not included, significant bias can be introduced to the findings. Also, showing the respondent a list of response categories can cause distortion in the resulting data. The researcher may be providing answers that the respondent might not have considered. The respondent may end up choosing a 'responsible' alternative. Similarly, if the respondent does not agree with any of the response categories, he may select one anyway. This problem can be somewhat overcome by providing an alternative such as 'Other — please specify', 'None', 'No opinion', or 'Don't know'. Even so, there may still be a strong tendency for the respondent to choose from the alternatives. For example:

Which of the following reasons is most important in your choice of fridge freezer?

Price ☐
In-store service ☐
Brand name ☐
Guarantee ☐

Other (please specify) _____

A further problem with multiple-choice questions is the respondent's tendency to select an alternative purely because of order or position bias. We will look at this next.

Position Bias

Multiple-choice questions tend to bias results by the order in which the alternatives are presented. When statements or ideas are involved, there is a bias towards the first or last item on the list, particularly the first.[5] This position bias can be minimised by using a split-ballot technique, i.e. alternating the order in which the alternatives are presented. This will require multiple versions of the questionnaire to be prepared, unless the alternatives are being presented on separate cards as outlined earlier. In that instance it is only necessary to have differing forms of the card which is shown to the interviewee. When the alternative response categories are numbers (e.g. prices or quantities), there is a bias towards the central position of the numbers array. Central positions are chosen more than either extreme. Unfortunately, it is not easy to rotate most numbers since they logically should appear as a sequence; for example, increasing or decreasing order. Even if the numbers are presented out of order the respondent will tend to mentally sort them into a sequence before making a choice.

How Many Response Categories?

Ideally, the response categories should be mutually exclusive and collectively exhaustive. However, it is frequently impractical to include all possible alternatives. As a general rule of thumb, the range of opinion on most issues can be captured best with five to seven categories. A list of brands might include twenty or more names. Rather than listing all twenty names, perhaps only the top five to seven names are listed, with the remainder confined to an 'Other, please specify' category. As well as the number of alternatives presented, consideration must be given to the range of the alternatives. This was previously discussed when we considered the issue of balanced and unbalanced attitude scales. An unethical researcher could intentionally bias the survey results to his favour, for example:

'Compared to Brand X, how do you rate our company's product?'

Excellent ☐   Very good ☐   Good ☐   Poor ☐

'Do you think that protection of the ozone layer is important?'

Extremely important ☐   Very important ☐   Important ☐   Not important ☐

Unless there is a specific reason to do otherwise, e.g. evidence that the vast majority of candidates will report on one side of the issue, a balanced set of alternatives should be presented.

Dealing with Uncertainty and Ignorance

When drafting multiple-choice questions, it is necessary to consider respondents who genuinely do not know the answer, have forgotten the answer or have no opinion on the issue. A neutral response category such as 'Don't know, no opinion', 'Neither like nor dislike', 'None' etc. should be provided to cater for the above. If there is a likelihood of both ambivalence and ignorance, then both a neutral category and a 'Don't know' category are appropriate.

3. Dichotomous Questions

The dichotomous question is an extreme form of the multiple-choice question, and allows for only two response categories, e.g. 'Yes' and 'No', male or female, agree or disagree. In practice however, the two alternatives of interest are often supplemented by a neutral alternative, such as 'Don't know', 'No opinion', 'Both' or 'Neither'. While this may allow respondents to avoid taking a position on the issue, not to do so would force respondents to choose one of the dichotomous alternatives. As a rule, it is best to include a neutral category, if a substantial proportion of respondents can be expected to be neutral. However, a source of bias can occur when respondents who are not neutral select the neutral category for reasons of convenience or embarrassment. Because both multiple-choice and dichotomous questions represent closed-ended questions, much of our discussion on the advantages and limitations of multiple-choice questions also apply to dichotomous questions and will not be repeated here. For example dichotomous questions also suffer from position bias. In fact dichotomous questions can often be framed as multichotomous questions and *vice versa*. Consider the following:

'Do you intend to go abroad for Christmas?'

Yes ☐
No ☐
Probably will ☐
Probably will not ☐
Definitely will not ☐
Undecided ☐

Dichotomous questions are best suited for determining points of fact, e.g. 'Did you go on a foreign holiday last year?', and other clear-cut issues on which the respondent has a well-developed viewpoint.

Concluding Words on Question Format

Most questionnaires mix open-ended, multiple-choice and dichotomous question formats. While the expense of editing open questions militates against their use, if it is at all possible, avoid them. Answers to open-ended questions can help to interpret closed-end questions. In addition a change of pace can eliminate respondent boredom and fatigue.

• Question Wording

Once the marketing researcher has decided on the desired question content and structure, the next task is the actual writing of the questions. It is critical that researcher and respondent assign the same meaning to the questions asked, otherwise the results will be seriously biased.[6] Poor phrasing of a question can cause respondents to refuse to answer it or to answer it incorrectly, either on purpose or because of misunderstanding. The first condition, known as item non-response, can increase the complexity of data analysis.[7] The second condition produces measurement error, in that it does not reflect the respondent's true score on the issue. Even small changes in wording can shift respondent answers. While there are no clear 'right' or 'wrong' ways of asking questions, it is important for the researcher to be sensitive to the effect of question wording and the answers obtained.

> **Box 8.1 Asking the right question is crucial!**
>
> A stranger arrived in a small town and he wanted to get to know the locals. So he went over to the village square where an old-timer was standing with 'a kind of mean-looking German shepherd'. Looking at the dog fairly tentatively, the stranger asked 'Does your dog bite?' The old-timer replied 'Nope'. So the stranger reached down to pet the dog. The dog lunged at him, nearly taking his arm off. The shocked stranger turned to the old-timer and said: 'I thought you said your dog doesn't bite.' He replied 'Ain't my dog.'
>
> The moral: it's important to ask the *right* question.
>
> Source: Buffett: *The Making of an American Capitalist*, by Roger Lowenstein.

How do we ensure that the words we select are likely to be clear to our respondents? A good first step is to consult an up-to-date dictionary and thesaurus and ask the following six questions of each word.[8]

1. Does it mean what we intend?
2. Does it have any other meanings?
3. If so, does the context make the intended meaning clear?
4. Does the word have more than one pronunciation?
5. Is there any word of similar pronunciation with which it might be confused?
6. Is a simpler word or phrase suggested?

While it is sometimes hard to develop good phrasings of questions, the following guidelines should be considered in designing the wording of a question.

1. Define the issue

A question should clearly define the issue being addressed. Junior newspaper reporters are trained to define the issue in terms of who, what, when, where, why and which (i.e. how) — the six W's.[9] These can also serve as a guide to the researcher preparing a questionnaire. Each question should be checked against those points to be sure that the issue is clear. Who, what, where and when are particularly important. The why and how may be applicable in some questions.

Consider the following example: 'Which brand of coffee do you use?' By subjecting the above question to a who, what, where, when analysis the meaning of the question becomes less clear. Does the 'who' refer to the respondent alone, or does it also refer to other members of the respondent's household? 'What' is the brand of coffee. But perhaps more than one brand of coffee is being used. Does the 'what' refer to the brand used most recently, the brand used most frequently or the preferred brand? 'When' is also not clear. Does the interviewer mean last month, last week or the last time. Does 'where' refer to at home or at work? A better wording for the question is: 'Which brand, or brands, of coffee did you personally consume at home during the last week?'

2. *Use simple, clear and unambiguous words*

The challenge is to choose words that can be understood by all respondents, regardless of education level, but do not sound patronising. If in doubt it is best to err on the side of simplicity. There is always great potential for respondents to misunderstand what they are being asked, even when simple words are used. The most common pitfall is to use jargon or specialised terms.

Consequently the questionnaire must use terminology native to the target respondent group. Questionnaires designed for children must use a simpler vocabulary than those designed for third-level students.

Use clear and unambiguous words and questions. Not only should the words used be simple, but they also should be unambiguous. The same is true for questions; for example, care must be taken to avoid words which have different meanings across socio-economic groups. A TD recently referred to his supporters as 'people who eat their dinner in the middle of the day'. Other socio-economic groups refer to a meal at this time of day as lunch, and have dinner (or supper) in the evening. A better solution might be to use 'mid-day meal' and 'evening meal'. But even those may be subject to misinterpretation. The words used in a questionnaire should have a single meaning which is known to the respondents.[10] Researchers have found that words such as 'usually', 'regularly', 'normally', 'frequently', 'kind', 'about', 'always', 'ever', 'often', 'occasionally', 'sometimes', 'many', 'good', 'fair', and 'poor', lack an appropriate time reference, so respondents choose their own, with the result that answers are not comparable.

For example, try to avoid asking the following:

'In a typical fortnight, how often do you listen to local radio?'

1. Never.
2. Occasionally.
3. Sometimes.
4. Often.
5. Regularly.

These words have different meanings to different respondents. Response bias is inevitable, e.g. does 'regularly' mean always, almost always, more than any other, or what? Thus, while the question would get answers, it would generate little real understanding as to the frequency of listenership. A much better approach would be to provide concrete alternatives and to ask about the most recent instance of the behaviour. For example:

'In the last two weeks, how often have you listened to local radio?'

1. Not at all/never. ☐
2. One or two times. ☐
3. Three or four times. ☐
4. More than four times. ☐

This provides respondents with a consistent frame of reference. Respondents are no longer free to superimpose their own interpretations on the response categories.

Problem words in questionnaire design

All, always, any, anybody, bad, best, could, daily, ever, every, everybody, everything, fair, few, just, know, like, might, more, most, much, never, none, now, own, quite, see, should, today, where, you.

Box 8.2 A Questionable Question

'"Most people are willing to pay a small entrance fee to a museum." To what extent do you agree with this statement?'

There are three flaws in this:

- The phrase 'most people' makes it difficult for respondents to do anything other than agree — who knows what the rest of the population thinks?
- What is meant by 'a small entrance fee'? Small is a relative term which different people will interpret in different ways.
- The question itself asks the extent to which the respondent agrees — it doesn't suggest that people might disagree.

Source: *Creative Arts Marketing*, Elizabeth Hill, Catherine O'Sullivan and Terry O'Sullivan, 1997, p. 87, Butterworth-Heinemann.

---

3. Avoid Leading Questions

Leading questions suggest or imply certain answers, or indicate the researcher's own point of view. A leading question causes a constant measurement error in the research findings. Consider the following question: 'Do you own a Whirlpool dishwasher?' This question will result in more reports of ownership of Whirlpool dishwashers than will the question: 'What, if any, brand of dishwasher do you own?' Another example of a leading question: 'Do you think that men's shoes priced at £90 are over-priced?' An unbiased statement can be easily biased by prefacing it with 'Don't you think' or 'Don't you agree'. Bias may also occur when respondents are given cues about the sponsor of the project. With the use of a brand or company name in a question, there is a tendency for respondents to respond favourably towards the sponsor, e.g. 'Is Dawn your favourite brand of orange juice?' produces more measurement error than 'What is your preferred brand of orange juice?'

4. *Avoid Loaded Questions*

Loaded questions suggest social desirability or are emotionally charged. A loaded question introduces a more subtle bias than a leading question, and suggests a feeling of approval or disapproval. Examples of loaded questions include:

- 'How do you generally spend your free time — watching TV, or what?'
- 'Should the government increase income taxes in the next budget in order to improve our children's education system, or should they keep income tax unchanged?'
- 'Last year, a greater number of people than ever were injured at work. Do you think the government is doing enough?'

Yes ☐
No ☐
No opinion ☐

Also, the suggestion that an attitude or position is endorsed by a prestigious organisation, group or individual, can bias the response, e.g.:

'The Irish Medical Organisation has suggested that Irish people do not include enough fibre in their diet. Do you agree?'

Yes ☐   No ☐   No opinion ☐

'In your opinion, should the Alzheimer Society of Ireland have more than one national fundraising tea day per annum?'

Yes ☐   No ☐   No opinion ☐

> **Box 8.3 Row flares over Bord Failte survey**
>
> "London-based consultants Arthur D. Little were appointed in April 1994 to review the structures and functions of Bord Failte. However, it is understood that Bord Failte considered some of the questions in the seven-page questionnaire to be loaded against them. One of the questions, dealing with Bord Failte's relationship with tourism groups, asked respondents to indicate what help the Board had given them by choosing one of three responses:
>
> A lot / A little / None.
>
> A source sympathetic to Bord Failte criticised this selection as inadequate because it contained two negatives versus one superlative, and provided no outlet for those who believed that Bord Failte was doing a reasonable job."
>
> Source: *Sunday Tribune*, 26 June 1994.

5. Avoid Double-barrelled Questions [one of biggest pitfalls]

A double-barrelled question is one in which the wording calls for two responses. Making the mistake of asking two questions instead of one is easy, for example, 'Do you like the taste and aroma of the coffee?' When multiple questions are asked in one question, the result may be exceedingly difficult to interpret. A respondent may feel torn between a 'Yes' to one part of the question and a 'No' to the other. As a rule, when the question includes 'and' review it to see whether two responses are required. If yes, split the initial question to two separate questions. According to Payne — 'since question marks are not rationed, there is little excuse for the needless confusion that results [from] the double-barrelled question'.[11]

6. Avoid Generalisations and Estimates

Questions should always be asked in specific rather than in general terms. Questions dealing with estimates of volumes of product used or frequency of store visits should be designed in such a way that the respondent does not have to answer by giving an estimate or making a generalisation. Consider the following question: 'How many litres of milk do you purchase in a year?' To provide the answer requires that the respondent compute how many litres per day and multiply that by 365 (or by 4 and 52). This burden should not be placed on the respondent. The results would be more accurate if the question asked 'How many litres of milk did you purchase in the last week?' with the researcher doing the calculations later to estimate annual consumption. A related problem is asking burdensome questions that may tax the respondent's memory. Questions relating to prior behaviour should be kept relatively recent.

7. Avoid Implicit Alternatives

An implicit alternative is one that is not expressed in the options. As a rule it is best to state clearly all relevant alternatives to a question, unless there is a special reason for not doing so. Further, as the order in which explicit alternatives are presented can affect the response, the split-ballot technique should be used to rotate the order in which the alternatives appear.

8. Avoid Implicit Assumptions

Questions should be worded so that the answer is not dependent upon implicit assumptions about what will happen as a consequence. Implicit assumptions are assumptions which are not stated in the question — for example:

Q1. 'Do you favour legislation requiring all new cars to be fitted with an air-bag?'
Q2. 'Do you favour legislation requiring all new cars to be fitted with an air-bag, even though it will require a small increase in the retail price of the car?'

Q2 is a better way to word this question. Q1 fails to make its assumptions explicit and may result in an inflated estimate of respondent support for mandatory car air-bags.

9. Consider Using Both Positive or Negative Statements

Questions designed to measure attitudes and lifestyle are frequently worded as statements to which the respondents indicate their degree of agreement or disagreement. However, the response obtained can be influenced by the directionality of the statements; whether they are stated positively or negatively. If this problem is anticipated, it is better to use dual statements, some positive, others negative. Two different questions, incorporating the alternative statement, could be used. For example:

'Do you think TV advertising should be increased during Christmas?'
'Do you think TV advertising should be decreased during Christmas?'

Another approach would have been to state both alternatives, the positive and the negative:

'Do you think TV advertising should be increased or decreased during Christmas?'

A Final Word on Questionnaire Wording

When all is said and done, there is however no one correct wording for a question. It is possible that different wording may get different answers, yet no one can say one wording is right and the others wrong. One way to resolve this is by using the 'split-ballot' technique. Whenever there are two wordings from which to choose, and if there is no basis on which to pick one over the other, one of the words can be used on half of the questionnaires and the other on the other half. Comparison of the two

Try not to exceed 20 words in q

halves of the questionnaire will permit a better interpretation of the results than would be possible where only one wording is used.¹² A word on question length — short questions are not always best, but if at all possible the number of words per question should not exceed twenty.

⑤ Question Sequence (Questionnaire Flow and Layout)

While there are no rules cast in stone regarding the optimum sequence in which questions should be asked, there are however some general guidelines. Mostly it is common sense. To an extent the flow of questions will be somewhat influenced by the research objectives set earlier.

After a brief initial explanation regarding the nature and purpose of the survey, what is required of the respondent, and perhaps offering assurances regarding confidentiality, the first few questions are normally screening (sometimes called filter) questions. These are used to determine whether the respondent fits the predetermined selection criteria and qualifies to participate in the survey.¹³ Examples of screening questions include:

'Are you visiting Killarney on holidays?'
'Have you stayed at this hotel before?'
'Do you own a car?'

The next questions should be simple and interesting. They are referred to as warm-up questions and are designed to put the respondent at ease and to encourage co-operation. These questions may not be of primary concern to the researcher and may or may not relate to the research objectives. Within the main body of the questionnaire the researcher should:

- Use transition statements to inform the respondent of what is ahead, particularly with regard to moving on to a new topic or section, e.g. 'Next I will ask you questions regarding your leisure activities'. This helps respondents switch their train of thought.
- Group related questions (topics) together, e.g. Section A, Section B and so on.
- Within a section move from the general to the specific. This is known as the funnel approach.
- Ask questions about present behaviour before examining past behaviour.
- Record behaviour before asking attitude questions, as this helps focus the respondent's mind on the topic in hand before expressing an opinion.
- If possible try to place together questions that are similar in format. Yet attempt to avoid boring sequences in the questionnaire, e.g. too many rating scales or too many multiple-choice questions one after the other.
- Use 'skip' questions (also called 'branching' questions) where appropriate; e.g. 'If NO please go to Q7'. The researcher may also choose to incorporate directional

lines and arrows to guide the respondent through the questionnaire.
- Complicated and difficult-to-answer questions are best placed deep in the questionnaire. Sensitive questions are best placed near the end of the questionnaire.
- Place questions of a classificatory nature, e.g. demographic information such as age, income, occupation, gender, education level, etc. in a final section at the end of the questionnaire. Tick Box
- Thank the respondent for their co-operation.

6. Physical Appearance of Questionnaire

The final matter to be dealt with in designing the questionnaire, before submitting it for pre-testing, relates to its physical appearance and layout. While certain changes may have to be made following the pre-test, the researcher should test the questionnaire in as close to final form as possible. The format, spacing and positioning of questions can have a significant effect on the results.[14] The appearance and layout of a questionnaire is a major determinant of the response rate. The physical appearance of the questionnaire is especially important in postal or self-administrated questionnaires. That is not to say that it is not important to have a good layout in questionnaires designed for personal interviews and telephone interviews. Much of the discussion which follows in this section, while particularly important for postal and self-administrating questionnaires, is also relevant to other survey methods. The objective of good questionnaire appearance and layout is to ensure that the tasks of the interviewer and respondent are as clear, logical and simple as possible. Several key considerations of layout and design follow:

1. Questionnaires should be designed to appear as short as possible. If it is more than three pages, it may be advisable to use a booklet form of questionnaire rather than stapling a large number of pages together. Booklets are easier to use, look professional, allow the use of double-page format, and minimise the problem of lost pages.
2. The questionnaire should be as professional-looking as possible. It should be printed on high quality paper, and have a 'typeset' appearance.
3. While it is advisable to have the questionnaire 'appear' short, the researcher should avoid the temptation to crowd questions together to make the questionnaire look shorter.
4. The questionnaire should allow for plenty of open space. A crowded questionnaire appears complex, difficult and can lead to errors in data collection. Ultimately, it is better to allow the questionnaire to be one or one and a half pages extra rather than using a crowded one.
5. Each question should be reproduced on a single page. Split questions and response categories can mislead the interviewer and respondent into thinking that

the question has ended at the end of a page. Rows and columns of answers should spread far enough apart, so that the interviewer or respondent can easily pick the proper row or column. Decent margins and white space should be used to separate questions. Columns of multiple boxes should be kept to a minimum. Multiple-question formats, if used properly, can make the questionnaire look interesting and inviting. If possible, response categories for a question should be listed in a single column rather than multiple columns. It is easier for the respondent to read downwards than sideways.

6. Directions and instructions for individual questions should be placed as close to questions as possible. Instructions for questions should be distinguished from the question itself, by using a different type (or capital letters). It is a good idea to divide the questionnaire into different sections with heading or subtitles for groups of questions. This helps the respondent follow the nature and logic of the questionnaire. Numbering is especially important if branching questions are used. Numbering of questions is also required if responses are to be coded. Clear instructions will be helpful to both respondent and interviewer, especially directional advice and 'skip question' instructions which will ensure that the questionnaire is used properly.

7. Each questionnaire should be numbered sequentially. This makes the field control of questionnaires, coding and analysis easier. However, numbering of postal questionnaires may make the respondent suspicious of loss of anonymity.

8. Consideration must be given to the amount of space required for open-ended questions. Researchers have found that the more lines or space left for recording the response to open-ended questions, the more extensive the reply. Likewise, it has been found that giving respondents more detailed information, through the use of larger questions, improves reporting behaviour.[15] This however has implications for questionnaire size. As a rule, three to five lines is probably sufficient for open-ended replies. Researcher judgment is required. In some instances it may be necessary to colour-code the questionnaire by printing on different colours of paper. For example, if panel research is being conducted which requires respondents to complete three separate questionnaires (contained in a folder) over a three-day period, it is a good idea to colour-code questionnaires to be completed over the period of time.

9. It is a good idea to spend some time phrasing the title of the questionnaire. A well-worded title can arouse interest among respondents, indicate the importance of the study, e.g. 'Awareness Study for Croi', gain their co-operation, or even appeal to their ego — for example 'Study of Top Executives'. A decision will have to be made whether or not to include the name of the sponsoring organisation. Realising that this can bias respondents' answers, it may be necessary to use a fictitious name, for the sponsoring organisation.

10. As mentioned earlier, reproduction of the questionnaire should be neat and make use of good quality paper. Otherwise the respondent will perceive the study as of little importance and not deserving of their time and effort.

Computer-aided design is now beginning to replace word processing packages in the preparation of questionnaires. Professional researchers, in particular, are now beginning to adopt specialised computer software, e.g. SNAP, to help simplify the process of questionnaire layout. Apart from creating a questionnaire complete with response categories, it can also code the questions, perform data analysis and graphically present the results. Software programs like this are also capable of linking to other software packages. Tabulated results can, for example, be exported to other packages such as SPSS for further analysis. An important feature of packages like SNAP, is their ability to deal with sequence bias. It is possible to randomise question order in a scale, giving each respondent a unique question order. Response categories can also be randomised, which prevents question format effects (e.g. recency effects).[16]

Pre-coding of questionnaires

Pre-coding of questionnaires, in order to speed up the process, is common given that most surveys are now tabulated by computer. The objective of pre-coding is to associate each possible response with a unique number. Codes that will be entered in the computer are printed on the questionnaire. Usually the code identifies the column number(s) in which a particular response will be entered. Pre-codes are placed alongside each response and in parenthesis.

While it is recognised that coding is very much an issue which needs careful consideration at the questionnaire design stage of the research project, we have decided to delay our discussion of coding until Chapter 12.

• Pre-testing the Questionnaire

After a first draft of a questionnaire has been finalised, it should then be pre-tested. No survey should be taken without a pre-test. The pre-test, which is a trial run of the questionnaire, should simulate as closely as possible the actual research conditions under which it will be administered. Pre-test respondents should be similar in aspects to those respondents who will form the actual survey, i.e. pre-test respondents must be taken from the 'population of interest'. All aspects of the questionnaire should be tested. Misinterpretations, lack of continuity, poor skip patterns, question content, wording, sequence, instructions, sufficient response categories, etc. are all open to scrutiny in the pre-test.

While it is a good idea to administer the pre-test questionnaire in person, a pre-test should also be conducted using the same survey mode as the actual survey. Pre-testing of postal questionnaires places additional demands on the timing of the survey. Such pre-tests help reveal problems peculiar to the chosen survey method. The pre-test provides the *real* test of the questionnaire and the mode of administration.

There is no set answer as to the number of respondents that should be involved in the pre-test; it is very much dependent on the final number and variety of target respondents, the complexity of the questionnaire and the time available. One author suggests five to ten respondents as being sufficient for a pre-test.[17] If the pre-test resulted in extensive design and question alterations a second subsequent pre-test with a different sample of respondents is necessary. While pre-testing is very important, excessive pre-testing in order to develop the 'perfect' questionnaire is a temptation to avoid. One pre-test is the bare minimum, and is probably as much as most questionnaires get. If a pre-test suggests only minor changes, once these changes have been made, the questionnaire is ready to go to final draft and distribution to field operators.

Finally, the researcher should consider coding and tabulating the pre-test research findings. Tabulating the results of a pre-test helps determine whether the questionnaire will meet the objectives of the research. Simple cross tabulations and other statistical analysis should be carried out where possible. Analyses of pre-test data helps to ensure that all data collected will be put to use and that all necessary data will be obtained.[18]

Considerable time and effort must be devoted to the end stage of questionnaire development to ensure that the questionnaire, or interview guide, is free from errors. It is too late once the survey is in the field to find out that a word is spelt incorrectly or that a response category has been omitted. Typing, spacing, numbering and pre-coding must be given rigorous proof-reading.

• Field Work

This section of the chapter focuses on field operations. This phase of the research project refers to what type of contact is made with respondents, how the data collection instrument is administered, and how the data is recorded and returned for processing. The market research project is no better than the data collected in the field.

The success of field operations requires investment in the selection, training, supervision and evaluation of field workers. Field personnel must clearly understand what is expected of them and how this performance will be measured. Marketing research data is not always collected by the person who designed the research. It is frequently collected by a field force that have little training in marketing research. The nature of fieldwork varies with the mode of data collection. A distinction can be made between field-based data collection (e.g. personal interviews and observation) and office-based data collection (e.g. telephone interviews and postal surveys). This section focuses on the interviewing process conducted by personal interviewers. However, many of the issues apply to all field workers when translated into their specific settings. The field-work data collection process will be presented under five headings:

1. Selection of field workers.
2. Training of field workers.
3. Supervision of field workers.
4. Validation of field work.
5. Evaluation of field workers.

1. Selection of Field Workers

One frequently sees job advertisements in national and local newspapers for market researchers. While every research firm will have their own selection criteria it is probably fair to say that at least some or all of the following criteria will be considered to be desirable when selecting field workers:

- Pleasant appearance.
- Outgoing personality.
- Good communication and listening skills.
- Accuracy and attention to detail.
- Patience and tact.
- Integrity and honesty.
- Resilient and energetic (stamina).
- Well organised.
- Efficient and reliable.
- Reasonable standard of education.
- Previous interviewing experience an asset but not essential.

Applicants may be asked to carry out a dummy interview to assess their ability. Interviewers who are similar to respondents tend to work well, that is to say, interviewer age, social background and education level should fit, as much as is practical and feasible with that of the respondent. In some instances specifically male or female interviewers may be the preferred choice of respondents, for example interviewing of female respondents regarding personal hygiene products.

2. Training of Field Workers

Training of interviewers is required at two levels. On one level interviewers need to be trained in the art of interviewing, i.e. approaching the respondent, gaining the respondent's co-operation, handling objections and refusals, asking questions, probing, recording the data, and terminating the interview. On another level interviewers need to be trained and briefed on the particular study at hand. Interviewers are not provided with too much information about the purpose of the study, thus ensuring they will not transmit any preconceived notions. Interviewers may not, for example, be provided with the name of the client firm.

Asking the questions and probing

Training in the art of asking questions is an important aspect of the above. Interviewers should:

1. Ask the questions using the exact wording.
2. Read the question slowly.
3. Ask the questions in the order they appear in the questionnaire.
4. Ask every question contained in the questionnaire.
5. Repeat questions that are misunderstood.
6. Carefully follow all instructions and skip patterns.

Question probing is commonly used when respondents' answers are overly brief. Probing encourages respondents to enlarge, clarify or explain their answers. Probing also helps respondents to focus more clearly on the content of the interview. It is not uncommon for individual questions to have written abbreviated probing instructions to guide the interviewer. Frequently-used probing techniques include nodding, repeating the question, pausing or silence, repeating the respondent's answer, asking for clarification or additional information. Regardless of which probing technique is used, care should be taken so as not to bias the respondent's answers.

Field workers also need to be trained on how best to record responses. Some practical advice here is to:

- Write legibly.
- Record responses during the interview.
- Use the respondent's own words.
- Avoid summarising or paraphrasing respondents' answers.
- If a question is not answered note why.
- Complete all interviewer identification data, e.g. time, date, id number, etc.
- Carry out field editing as soon as is possible (see Chapter 12).

Terminating the Interview

Having acquired all the necessary information, the interviewer is ready to close the interview. Before signing off it may be necessary to answer any final questions the respondent may have and to record any end-of-interview spontaneous comments and remarks. The interviewer should then thank the respondent for their time and effort. Ideally the respondent should exit the interview with positive feelings about what has occurred.

3. Supervision of Field Workers

A certain amount of supervision of field workers is advisable, especially when interviewing is widely dispersed. The purpose of supervision is to ensure that field workers are following the correct procedures. Elements of field supervision include quality control and editing, sampling control, and control of cheating. Misbehaviour by survey interviewers includes actions forbidden either explicitly or implicitly in codes of ethics, interviewer training, or interviewing instructions. As examples of misbehaviour, interviewers can reword questions, answer questions when interviewees refuse to respond, or fabricate answers to entire questionnaires.[19] Quality control refers to checking to see that field procedures are being followed. Field workers may require additional training or clarification. It can be helpful if the supervisor also does some interviewing. This helps the supervisor better understand or appreciate problems that field workers may be having. The field supervisor is also responsible for collecting completed questionnaires from the field workers at the end of each day. The supervisor should edit completed questionnaires to ensure that all relevant questions have been filled in, that there are no obvious omissions, that quotas are reached, and that the writing is legible.

Sampling control is also an important aspect of supervision. Sampling control ensures that the sampling plan is being adhered to and that the correct sampling units (e.g. male, over 30 years with college education) are being selected for interview. Quota samples are often seen as time-consuming and the interviewer may stretch the requirements to obtain seemingly qualified respondents.

4. Validation of Field Work

Validation of field work is carried out by the supervisor to ensure that interviewers are submitting authentic interviews. The most glaring example of cheating is when the interviewer fills out questionnaires without carrying out interviews. Frequently cheating is confined to falsification of certain data within the questionnaire. This type of cheating is more difficult to detect. Study-design and implementation influence the predisposition to cheat. If respondents are difficult to locate and interview, cheating increases. Other 'motives' for interviewer cheating are unreasonable deadlines and difficult-to-complete questionnaires. Interviewers may also fake answers to questions they find embarrassing to ask because of sensitive subjects. Or an interviewer might be tempted to go to the household next door for an interview rather than recording that the sampling unit was not at home, which would require a call-back. Careful recording of the number of completed interviews will help ensure that the sampling procedure is being properly conducted. Cheating can be minimised through proper training, supervision and validation of field work.

In order to validate field work the supervisor calls a percentage of all respondents (e.g. 10%). Anything over this would be more rigorous but time-consuming. In most instances this will require the supervisor to call upon a subsample of the sample to determine whether the interview actually took place and to verify the respondent's answers, including demographic details recorded. As an alternative to repeating the whole interview, the supervisor may instead re-ask the respondent a portion of the questionnaire. This, however, is not a foolproof recheck. Responses and demographic details are cross-checked against the data recorded on the questionnaire by the interviewer. Field workers should be made aware of supervisory verification call-backs.

This forces interviewers to be more conscientious about their work.

5. Evaluation of Field Workers

Field interviewers' performance can be evaluated across a number of criteria. More specifically:

- the quality of interviewing;
- the quality of data obtained;
- response rates;
- cost and time per completed interview.

- **Summary**

A questionnaire is a formalised means of collecting data from respondents. The primary purpose of a questionnaire is measurement. Survey research (in whatever form — personal interview, telephone, or postal) relies on the use of a questionnaire. Using a questionnaire provides standardisation and uniformity in the data-gathering process. Questionnaire design is a major source of non-sampling error. The design of an appropriate questionnaire involves no firm set of foolproof procedures. There are, however, a number of rules or guidelines that can be followed. The discussion of questionnaire design was presented as a series of seven steps, namely: preliminary considerations, question content, response format, question wording, question sequence, physical characteristics, and pre-test.

The researcher must make decisions regarding:

1. what information is required;
2. who are target respondents;
3. what method of communication will be used to reach these respondents;
4. how the resulting data will be processed and analysed.

When evaluating possible questions for inclusion in the data collection instrument, the following issues must be considered: Is the question really necessary? Does the respondent have the information requested? The respondent may not know the answer, or the respondent may not remember the information. Assuming that the respondent can answer the question, he or she may be unwilling to do so. A number of techniques have been developed to seek out potentially embarrassing or sensitive information from respondents who are unwilling to respond accurately. Once the content of an individual question has been determined, the researcher needs to decide what type of question to use. Three basic types of questions may be utilised. These are open-ended, multiple-choice, and dichotomous. Each of these poses a different degree of structure on the person's responses, and has its own particular uses, advantages and disadvantages. In terms of the amount of structure involved, open-ended questions have the least and dichotomous questions the most, structure.

Having decided on the desired question content and structure, the next task is the actual writing of the questions. Poor phrasing of a question can cause respondents to refuse to answer it, or to answer it incorrectly. A question should clearly define the issue being addressed. The challenge is to choose words that can be understood by all respondents. Not only should these words used be simple, but they should be unambiguous. The same is true for questions. A loaded question introduces a more subtle bias than a leading question, and suggests a feeling of approval or disapproval. Double-barrelled questions and questions involving generalisations or estimates should be avoided. Questions should be worded so that the answer is not dependent upon implicit assumptions about what will happen as a consequence.

While there are no rules cast in stone regarding the optimum sequence in which questions should be asked, there are however some general guidelines. Mostly it is common sense. To an extent the flow of questions will be somewhat influenced by the research objectives set earlier. The final matter to be dealt with in designing the questionnaire, before submitting it for pre-testing, relates to its physical appearance and layout. The objective of good questionnaire appearance and layout is to ensure that the tasks of the interviewer and respondent are as clear, logical and simple as possible. The pre-test, which is a trial run of the questionnaire, should simulate as closely as possible the actual research conditions under which it will be administered.

The success of field operations requires investing in the selection, training, supervision and evaluation of field workers.

Questions

1. What is a 'questionnaire'? What is its purpose?
2. Outline the seven stages to questionnaire development.
3. The preliminary considerations of questionnaire design requires the reader to make four decisions. What are they?
4. Discuss the issues to be considered when evaluating possible questions for inclusion in the data collection instrument.
5. How does the respondent affect the phrasing of the questions?
6. What are the reasons why respondents may be (a) unable to answer the question asked, and (b) unwilling to answer the question?
7. Describe some techniques which might be used to extract embarrassing or sensitive information from respondents.
8. What is the randomised response technique? How does it work?
9. What is telescoping error? What does it suggest about the period to be used when asking respondents to recall past events?
10. What is a multichotomous question? A dichotomous question? What are some of the key things researchers must be careful about in framing multichotomous and dichotomous questions?

11. Under what circumstances would dichotomous questions be inappropriate?
12. Do open-ended questions have any weaknesses?
13. What are the advantages and disadvantages of multiple-choice questions?
14. What is an ambiguous question? A leading question? A question with implicit alternatives? A question with implied assumptions? A double-barrelled question?
15. What are the key considerations regarding layout and physical appearance of a questionnaire?
16. How can the physical features of a questionnaire affect its acceptance by respondents and its handling and control by the researcher?
17. Why is it so important to pre-test the questionnaire? Discuss the issues involved.
18. What criteria might the researcher use when selecting field workers?
19. Discuss supervision and validation of field work.

Problems and Assignments

1. Construct a set of five structured, indirect questions to measure what might be 'communicated' by males wearing jewellery, such as neck chains, rings and bracelets.
2. Provide an example of a multiple-choice question:
   (a) In which the alternatives are unbalanced.
   (b) In which the possible responses are not mutually exclusive.
3. List ten ambiguous words that should not be used in framing questions.
4. Design a questionnaire suitable for assessing the market for home insulation products among householders.
5. Do the following questions define the issue? In each case explain why or why not:
   (a) What is your favourite lager?
   (b) How often do you go out drinking?
   (c) Do you consume vodka?
      1. Yes 2. No
6. Provide an example of a survey question that would have an upward bias — that is, people would be likely to give a 'Yes' response.
   (a) Rephrase the question so that there would be a downward bias — that is, people would be likely to give a 'No' response.
   (b) Rephrase your original question so that respondents would be likely to provide a truthful response.
7. Develop a series of questions for determining the proportion of households where one parent of the family abuses alcohol. Use the randomised response technique.
8. Design a short questionnaire to measure your classmates' knowledge of, and attitudes to, laptop computers.
9. Based on the following list of research questions, determine the research objective(s) of this questionnaire: are any of the questions unnecessary and, if so, why?

(a) How many hours per week do you work on average?
(b) What type of magazines do you read?
(c) Do you feel you have enough 'free time' away from work?
(d) What kind of hobbies do you have?
(e) Would you describe yourself as a well-rounded person?
10. Evaluate the following questions and suggest improvements:
    (a) When you eat dinner out, do you sometimes eat at the same place?
        Yes?   No?
    (b) Is the current level of government regulation on environmental protection adequate or inadequate?
        Adequate?   Inadequate?
    (c) Where do you buy most of your clothes?
    (d) Please indicate how much of an average issue of *Woman's Own* magazine you usually read:
        1. Less than one-third?
        2. One-third to half?
        3. Over half?
    (e) Do you often attend the theatre?
    (f) What kind of hobbies do you have?
    (g) Everybody knows that teenagers and their parents have lots of arguments. What are some of the things you and your parents have argued about lately?
11. Use the randomised response model to estimate the percentage of respondents who indicated they did not report all their income to the tax authorities in a survey in which a total of 16% answered 'Yes', and given 10% of the sample were estimated to have their birthdays in June (and so would have answered 'Yes' to the innocuous question) and a coin toss was used to choose which of the two questions to answer.

Case Study
The Cara Sports Centre

The Cara Sports Centre is located in a medium-sized town in the south of Ireland. The town has an urban population of approximately 16,000 inhabitants. Cara Sports Centre is located adjacent to a new shopping centre complex at the western side of the town. The complex, which was opened twelve months ago, has a major supermarket as its anchor tenant. Also contained in the complex is a diverse range of shopping units including clothes shops, an electrical outlet, bookstore, fast-food restaurant, and many others.

The sports centre is owned and managed by Mr Pat Williams, a qualified sports instructor who returned to Ireland having spent a number of years in Australia. Business is brisk and the number of members has grown steadily. Recently however,

Mr Williams has noticed that the number of new members joining is beginning to slow. Because of this he is considering an increased marketing effort to attract new members and to retain existing customers of the Centre. To date, Pat has undertaken little to no marketing research. At an aggregate level he knows very little about the attitudes and perceptions of his customers to his facilities. Also he wonders if it would be possible to attract new members from outlying rural areas. One of the centre's part-time weekend employees is a marketing student at the local Institute of Technology. Perhaps now, he thought, would be a good time to conduct some market research. He has asked Sarah, the marketing student, to design a questionnaire to measure how existing customers view his facilities. He has also asked her to examine the potential of attracting new members from rural areas.

1. What variables should the questionnaire measure?
2. What question response format should be used? Why?
3. Design a questionnaire to suit Pat Williams' information needs.
4. Should Sarah decide to design a questionnaire aimed at non-users of the complex? If so, how would it differ from the questionnaire directed at existing users of the complex?
5. Advise Pat Williams of any other issues he needs to be aware of that are relevant to the study.

© Department of Marketing, NUI, Galway.

'attitudes are learned predispositions to respond to an object, or class of object, in a consistently favourable or unfavourable way'

Attitudes

Attitude Components

three main components

Corrib river. Jim *likes* playing golf at Glenlo Abbey. He *intends* to play golf there every Saturday'. This short statement has identified the three components of an attitude which are:

1. the cognitive component;
2. the affective component;
3. the behavioural (or conative) component.

Cognitive   ⟶   Beliefs
Affective   ⟶   Liking
Behavioural   ⟶   Intention

The link between these three components illustrates what is known as the high involvement hierarchy of effects, i.e. the buyer passes through the stages of: awareness, knowledge, liking, preference, intention to buy, and purchase (see Figure 9.1). However, these stages can occur in different sequences, depending on the degree of buyer involvement with the purchase and the degree of differentiation among the alternatives.

Figure 9.1

Attitude components	Hierarchy of effects model
Cognitive	Awareness Knowledge
Affective	Liking Preference
Behavioural	Intention to buy Purchase

We will briefly look at each of these components in turn.

Cognitive: 'I think or I know . . .'

The cognitive component refers to the respondent's awareness of and knowledge about an object. A researcher may conduct an attitude measurement study to determine, for example:

- Whether consumers view an Irish-made cereal being of equal quality to Kelloggs.

- If customers are aware that a particular brand of soft drink is now available in lemon and lime flavour.

Affective: 'I like or I dislike . . .'

The affective component refers to the respondent's positive or negative feelings with regard to an object. It is sometimes referred to as the 'feelings component'. Under this component, an attitude measurement study may attempt to analyse the following:

- A local environmental group may wish to determine how many residents are not in favour of a new sewage treatment plant in a particular location.
- A local radio station wishes to find out if listeners are satisfied with a new breakfast show format.

Behavioural: 'I intend to . . .', 'I purchased . . .'

The behavioural component refers to buying intentions and actual purchase behaviour. It reflects a predisposition to action. The 'evoked set' is that set of brands from which we are predisposed to purchase. Examples of behavioural attitude measurement include:

- A financial services company may wish to know how many of its existing customers intend to use its new pension planning service.
- A cable TV operator wishes to determine what percentage of its subscribers have rented a movie video in the past week.

• Attitudes and Behaviour

Reinforcing, changing or modifying attitudes is often an important part of marketing strategy. Most marketing research studies contain questions designed to measure a respondent's attitudes. It is generally assumed that there is a link between attitudes and behaviour. Attitudes are assumed to be an important predictor of behaviour, i.e. having a positive attitude toward a product, service or retail outlet means we are more likely to purchase or use it. However, the student should note that attitudes alone are not an absolute guarantee that behaviour will occur, nor does intended behaviour, because of situational influences, always translate into actual behaviour.

• Measurement and Scaling

Before addressing the subject of attitude measurement, it is necessary to define measurement and to discuss the types of scales that can be used in measurement. We also need to examine marketing variables and concepts.

Marketing Variables

When we speak of measuring marketing variables, we are attempting to measure one or more of the following:

(a) *State-of-mind variables*. These refer to variables such as attitudes, personality and brand awareness which are internal to the individual and are therefore difficult to measure.
(b) *State-of-being variables*. Examples of variables of this kind include age, income, gender, marital status, number of children and product ownership. These are external to the respondent and are easier to measure than state-of-mind variables.
(c) *Behavioural variables*. Behavioural variables are concerned with past, present or future courses of action. Measurement of product purchase, usage and intention to buy fall into this category.

Measurement and Concepts

Before we can examine *how* to measure something we must first consider *what* it is we want to measure; that is to say we must first identify and define the relevant *concept* involved. A concept (or 'construct' — the terms concept and construct have similar meanings and are frequently used interchangeably) can be defined as a symbol that we attach to some aspect of reality. Thus the concept 'lawnmower' refers to the generalisation of the characteristics that all lawnmowers have in common. In marketing research we are required to address concepts such as attitude, brand loyalty, personality, channel power, low-involvement purchasing, market segmentation and product positioning. Many of these concepts are not directly observable and exist in the minds of individuals. Some concepts are easier to define than others. For example, the concept 'chair' is perhaps easier to define than 'brand loyalty'. The concept 'chair' is closely related to a physical reality and there will be little disagreement as to what is meant by the term. 'Brand loyalty' on the other hand is a more abstract concept and more difficult to define in a physical sense. It is therefore more difficult to measure. In a marketing research study, concepts must be precisely defined and measured, otherwise the usefulness of the information collected is questionable. In fact the researcher should define the relevant concepts in such a way that allows for practical measurement and ensures consistency by avoiding disagreement over its meaning. There are two approaches to defining a concept: a conceptual definition and an operational definition.

A conceptual definition defines an object in terms of other concepts. This approach is similar to that used in a dictionary where words are used to define other words. A good conceptual definition attempts to delineate the main characteristics of the concept as it differs or compares to other concepts, for example, brand loyalty versus habitual purchasing behaviour.

An operational definition on the other hand specifies how a concept is to be measured. It describes the meaning of a concept by outlining the procedures necessary to measure it. The operational definition translates the concept into one or more observable events. Thus a conceptual definition logically precedes and directs the development of an operational definition. It is possible to have several operational definitions of the same concept. The researcher must choose the operational definition that fits best with the objectives of the research. However, while operational definitions of a particular concept may vary across different research studies, the definition should be consistent within any given research study.

Box 9.1

Examples of concepts and possible operational definitions

Concept	Possible operational definition
Customer	Based on company warranty card records, any individual or group who has purchased one or more of our company's products within the past twelve months.
Small sailboat	Sailboats manufactured in Ireland that are less than 13 feet 7 inches in length and have a manufacturer's suggested retail price of £5,000 or less.
Exposure to point-of sale display	Stopped and visually examined display for five seconds or more as determined by hidden observer with stopwatch.
Brand loyalty	Based on consumer panel data, number of consecutive months in which a reporting household purchased our brand one or more times.
Product awareness	When asked to mention five brands of beer, subject mentions our brand in a personal interview situation.
Product attitude	When asked to mention five brands of beer that taste good, subject mentions our brand in a personal interview situation.

Source: Adapted from *Marketing Research*, Ronald M. Weiers, Prentice-Hall, 1988, pg. 151.

Measurement can be defined as a standardised process of assigning numbers or other symbols to certain characteristics of the objects of interest, according to some predetermined rules. Note that we measure the attributes of objects, and not the objects themselves. We do not measure a person, for example, but we may choose to measure the attributes of a person, i.e. income, social class, education, height, weight, attitudes etc. In marketing research, numbers are usually assigned because mathematical and statistical analyses can be performed only on numbers and they can be communicated throughout the world in the same form without any translation problems. An important aspect of measurement is the specification of rules for assigning numbers to the characteristics. This assignment process must be isomorphic, that is to say, there should be one-to-one correspondence between the symbol and the characteristic in the object that is being measured; and the rules for assigning numbers should be standardised and applied uniformly. They must not change over objects or time.

Scaling, which can be considered an extension of measurement, is the process of creating a continuum on which objects are located according to the amount of the measured characteristic they possess. An example of a scale that is often used in research is the dichotomous scale for gender. The object with male/female characteristics is assigned a number 1 and the object with the opposite characteristic is assigned the number 0. This scale meets the previous two requirements of the measurement process, i.e. that it is isomorphic. Measurement and scaling are basic tools used in the scientific method and are used in almost every marketing research situation. Scaling is commonly used in the process of measuring attitudes. There is no clear point from which to start measuring an attitude. Attitudes are something akin to temperature in this respect. Zero has been arbitrarily assigned on the thermometer (at different places for Fahrenheit and Centigrade), but this leads to difficulties such as the one defined in the conundrum: 'How cold is twice as cold as zero?' There is no agreed 'zero' at which to start measuring attitudes. The most common procedure is to measure in two directions from some neutral point. Attitude scaling is the process by which respondents are classified as having an unfavourable, neutral or positive attitude.

- **Scales of Measurement**

As previously stated, measurement in marketing research frequently deals with numbers. There are four characteristics of the natural (counting) number system 0, 1, 2, 3, 4, 5, 6, 7, 8, and 9. First, each number in the series is unique. Second, the ordering of the numbers is given by convention, for example $2 > 1$ and $1 > 0$. Third, we can define equal differences, for example, $4 - 3 = 2 - 1, 9 - 7 = 5 - 3$. Fourth, we can define equal ratios, for example, $8/4 = 6/3$. The manipulation of numbers using mathematics or statistics involves one or more of these four characteristics of the numbering system. It is traditional to classify scales of measurement on the basis of the mathematical comparisons that are allowable with them. There are four basic levels of measurement, which are nominal, ordinal, interval and ratio. Each represents a different kind of number assignment rule, or 'scale' of measurement. As we proceed from the weakest (nominal) to the strongest (ratio), two things happen. First, the numerical requirements for scale membership become more stringent. Second, the permissible modes of data expression and analysis become more liberal, that is to say more types of statistical operations are permissible. Also, because the higher levels of measurement contain all the properties of lower levels we can convert higher-level scales into lower-level ones (i.e. ratio to interval or ordinal or nominal; or interval to ordinal or nominal; or ordinal to nominal). Therefore, it is very important to understand the different types of scales, and to be able to identify them in practice, for their properties put significant restrictions on the interpretation and use of the resulting measurements.

Nominal Scale

Nominal scales are very common in marketing research. It is the simplest type of scale. A nominal scale partitions data into categories that are mutually exclusive (every individual or object must belong to one of the categories), and collectively exhaustive (the categories don't overlap). The numbers assigned to objects or phenomena serve as labels for identification or classification. The numbers themselves have no mathematical value. They cannot be ordered, added or divided. Examples of nominal scale numbers include RSI numbers, student id numbers or numbers on football jerseys. Application of the nominal scale to marketing measurement is generally for the purpose of coding questionnaire responses in which the data collected place the respondent into a particular category. Numbers assigned to represent the categories (1 for male, 2 for female) cannot meaningfully be added, subtracted, multiplied or divided. The only permissible operation on the numbers in a nominal scale is counting. Only a limited number of statistics (all of which are based on frequency counts) are permissible. These include frequency, percentages, mode and chi-square statistical test, plus some other non-parametric tests.

Please indicate your gender.   Male ☐   Female ☐

Have you visited *this branch* in the
last six months?   Yes ☐   No ☐

From the list below please tick all the brands of tea you would consider purchasing

_____   Barrys
_____   Lyons
_____   Tetley
_____   PG Tips
_____   Punjama
_____   Capital

Ordinal Scale

The ordinal scale goes beyond the simple identification capabilities of the nominal scale, and allows the possibility of 'greater than' and 'less than' as additional descriptors of marketing phenomena. However, the scale does not provide information on how much more or less of the characteristic various objects possess. Ordinal numbers are used strictly to indicate rank order. The object ranked 1 has more of the characteristic in question compared to the object ranked 2, and the object ranked 3 has less of the characteristic than 2 or 1. Ordinal scales indicate relative position and not the magnitude of the difference between the objects. We cannot say that the difference between 1 and 2 is the same as that between 2 and 3. Likewise we cannot say that the difference between 1 and 3 is twice that of the difference between 1 and 2. A typical ordinal scale in marketing asks respondents to rate brands.

'Please rate the following five brands in terms of value for money, in order of preference, 1 being the most preferred and 5 being the least preferred.'

Brand name	Bill — Respondent No. 1	Jane — Respondent No. 2
A	2	1
B	1	3
C	5	5
D	4	4
E	3	2

In the above example we cannot say that Bill preferred Brand B twice as much as Brand A. Nor can we say that both respondents preferred Brand D over Brand C by the same amount. For Bill, it may have been a close call between C and D. Jane may have much more preferred D over C. A scale such as excellent, good, fair, poor is also ordinal by nature. Excellent is higher than good but again we do not know by how much. Because we do not know the amount of difference between the objects, the permissible arithmetic operations are limited to statistics such as the median or mode (but not the mean) and rank-order correlation.

Example of Ordinal-scaled Questions

'Please rank the following Irish Sunday papers according to preference. 1 for your first choice, 2 for your second choice, and so on.'

_____ Sunday Independent

_____ Sunday Tribune

_____ Sunday Business Post

_____ Ireland on Sunday

_____ Sunday World

Interval Scale

Interval scales possess all the requirements of an ordinal scale, plus the 'equality of difference' characteristic of the number system. They make use of a constant unit of measurement or equal interval between scale value. The difference between 1 and 2 is the same as between 2 and 3, but is only half the difference between 2 and 4. However, this unit of measurement is arbitrary. Interval scale has no fixed or absolute zero point where none of the characteristics being measured is present, i.e. zero does not denote absence of the attribute. The most common examples of interval scales are the Fahrenheit and Celsius scales used to measure temperature. The freezing point of water is assigned a different numerical value on each scale, 32 on Fahrenheit and 0 on Celsius. Both scales use constant units of measurement, but the degrees on the Fahrenheit scale are 5/9 as large as those on the Celsius scale. Equal differences in temperature are measured by equal-volume expansion in the mercury used in the thermometer. The arbitrary zero point of interval scales restricts the statements that a researcher can make about the scale points. Multiples may not be expressed as if they refer to absolute values; one cannot say that 60°F is 'twice as hot' as 30°F. We can however say that 60°F is hotter than 30°F or that 65°F is 5°F cooler than 70°F; or that the difference between 60°F and 50°F is equal to the difference between 50°F and 60°F. The use of interval scales in marketing research is common. Attitudinal, opinion and willingness to buy are often treated as interval data. As an example, consider the following.

Toyota cars are:

	Strongly disagree			Neutral		Strongly agree	
	-3	-2	-1	0	1	2	3
Stylish	☐	☐	☐	☐	☐	☐	☐
Reliable	☐	☐	☐	☐	☐	☐	☐
Well engineered	☐	☐	☐	☐	☐	☐	☐
Economical	☐	☐	☐	☐	☐	☐	☐
Safe to drive	☐	☐	☐	☐	☐	☐	☐
Sporty	☐	☐	☐	☐	☐	☐	☐
Value for money	☐	☐	☐	☐	☐	☐	☐

As the possible responses are physically located at equal intervals on the questionnaire, they are assumed to represent equal intervals in terms of the measurement process. Most researchers treat the data from such scales as if they were equal interval in nature, since the results of most standard statistical techniques are not affected greatly by small deviations from the interval requirement.[2] The use or assumption of interval scale data means that interval scales are amenable to computation of an arithmetic mean, standard deviation, and correlation co-efficient. However, ratios calculated on interval data are not meaningful. A ratio, e.g. three times as much, 10% more than, etc. requires a ratio measurement scale.

Ratio Scale

A ratio scale has all the properties of an interval scale plus a meaningful absolute zero point and equal intervals of measurement. At the zero point, none of the characteristics being measured is present. Unlike the Fahrenheit and Celsius scale, the ratio measurement of temperature is known as the Kelvin scale. The Kelvin scale has an absolute zero point and represents the absence of heat (–273.15°C). Because there is universal agreement as to the location of the zero point, comparisons among the magnitudes of ratio-scaled values are acceptable. All arithmetic operations are possible including multiplication and division. Not only is the difference between 3 and 6 the same as the difference between 12 and 15, but also 12 is four times as large as 3 in an absolute sense. A great many important marketing phenomena possess the properties of a ratio scale. These include sales, market share, costs, ages, usage, income, number of purchases etc. The entire range of statistical techniques can be applied to the analysis of ratio-scaled data. However this produces only a minimal gain in analytic technique beyond those available for interval data. While the ratio scale is the 'ultimate' scale of measurement, ultimately, quite a lot of marketing research information will be in nominal, ordinal or interval (sometimes by assumption) form.

Examples of Ratio Scales

Please allocate 100 points among the following five brands of mineral water according to your degree of preference for each:

_____   Galway
_____   Perrier
_____   Tipperary
_____   Evian
_____   Kerry

On average, how many times a week do you listen to a local radio station?

0 ☐   1 ☐   2 ☐   3 ☐   4 ☐

more (specify _____)

Table 9.1 Summary of the four primary levels of measurement

Level	Description	Number system	Marketing examples	Typical methods for describing	Analyzing
Nominal	Uses numerals to identify objects, individuals, events, or groups	Unique definition of numerals (0, 1, 2, . . . 9)	Brand numbers, store types, sex classification	Frequency Percentage Mode Cross-tabulation	Chi-square test
Ordinal	In addition to identification, the numerals provide information about the relative amount of some characteristic posed by an event, object, etc.	Order of numerals (0<1<2 . . . <9 . . .)	Preference rankings, market position, social class	Median Mode Percentile	Rank order Sign test Non-metric multi-dimensional scaling
Interval	Possesses all the properties of nominal and ordinal scales plus the intervals between consecutive points are equal	Equality of differences (2 −1 = 6 − 5) Equality of ratios (1/4 =2/8)	Attitudes, opinions, index numbers	Range Mean Standard deviation	Correlation analysis Discriminant analysis Analysis of variance Metric multi-dimensional scaling
Ratio	Incorporates all the properties of nominal, ordinal, and interval scales plus it includes an absolute zero point		Age, income, costs, sales, market share	Geometric mean Harmonic mean	Coefficient of variation

Source: Adapted from S. S. Stevens, 'On the Theory of Scales of Measurement', *Science* 103, 7 June 1946), pp. 677–680.

• Validity and Reliability Concept

To have confidence in the results of a marketing research study, the researcher must be concerned about two characteristics of the measures being used to collect information. These two concepts are called *validity* and *reliability*. They can be defined as follows.

Validity: a measuring instrument is valid when it measures what it is supposed to measure. The instrument is valid to the extent that its measurements are free from systematic error (bias).

Reliability: a measuring instrument is reliable when the results it delivers are consistent. The instrument is reliable to the extent that its measurements are free from non-systematic (random) error.

The researcher, therefore, must be concerned with whether we are measuring what we wish to measure and whether our measurement is accurate. Ideally, it is desirable that the marketing information we collect have both validity and reliability. A necessary precondition for validity is that the measuring instrument is reliable[3]. But a reliable instrument may not be a valid one. A bent ruler will provide consistent results but it is not a valid measure. Or if you forget to put your watch forward one hour in summer time it will still be a reliable measure (it will say seven every twelve hours) but it will not be valid (incorrect time). Of the two, validity is probably the more important than reliability. This is especially so for a once-off study. However, if the research instrument is to be used repeatedly (e.g. consumer diary research), the role of reliability in the research findings becomes more important. A measuring instrument that could be considered low in validity was that which was used to research the market for 'New Coke'. It failed to measure customer loyalty to traditional coke.

Most practising marketing researchers probably do not spend a great deal of time measuring the validity and reliability of a research instrument. Often the issue of validity and reliability is left to those conducting academic research projects. Nonetheless, they are important concepts and deserve attention.

Validity

Validity can be examined from a number of different perspectives. The major approaches to the assessment of validity are as follows.

Content Validity

Content validity (also called face validity) is the weakest form of validity. It concerns the extent to which the measurement instrument 'appears to be measuring' what it is intended to measure. Content validity involves a subjective judgment by the researcher, or by asking another expert professional whether in his or her opinion the instrument is measuring what it purports to measure. The emphasis is on the expert's critical eye. For example, a questionnaire designed to measure a retail outlet's level of customer service that does not contain references to friendliness of staff, car parking facilities, opening hours and delivery service, cannot be considered to have content validity. After all, these are important aspects of customer service that are not being measured. Some writers distinguish between face validity and content validity as follows. Does, say, a scale measuring attitudes to something, seem to the person taking the scale to be as they would expect such a test to be? Content validity is taken to refer to the extent to which the test items cover the entire range, or domain, of what the test is supposed to measure.

Predictive Validity

Predictive validity refers to the ability of our measuring instrument to predict some future event. Predictive validity is most often associated with 'intent-to-purchase' measurements. A measure of buying intentions is valid if it can be shown through sales records to predict future sales. If the predicted results are highly correlated with the actual results, then the measurement is deemed to have predictive validity. The GMAT is used to predict how well a student with a particular score on the test will do in an accredited MBA programme. The wide use of this test by colleges attests to its predictive validity. Measurement instruments that are low in predictive validity are either not measuring intent to purchase, or there is a weak relationship between intent to purchase and actual future purchasing behaviour.

Concurrent Validity

Concurrent validity involves correlating two different measurements of the same marketing phenomena which have been administered at the same, or about the same point in time. The findings of a new measurement technique may be compared against the findings of an established measurement technique. Until recently, engineers relied on tape measures to measure the physical distance between objects. Suparule is a Shannon-based company which markets an alternative measuring technique that uses laser technology. The traditional and new technology methods of measuring distance both produce similar results. It can be said that there is concurrent validity between the new method and the established measurement technique. Likewise, a new measurement technique for measuring service quality levels could be compared against the well-established SERVQUAL method. If the new technique produces similar findings, it is assumed that concurrent validity exists.

Construct Validity

Construct validity is present when a logical argument can be advanced to defend a particular measure. Establishing construct validity occurs during the statistical analysis of the data. The empirical evidence should be consistent with the theoretical logic behind the concepts. A measure has construct validity if it behaves according to the underlying theory. It is present whenever our measure of a particular concept is related to measures of other relevant concepts in a theoretically expected way. For example, a measure of brand loyalty may be considered valid if consumers, who are loyal to a particular brand, also record very favourable attitudes towards that brand. The difficulty of this kind of validation is in the unobservable nature of many of the constructs (e.g. personality, attitudes, involvement, lifestyles) which we use to try to explain marketing behaviour (e.g. purchase behaviour) related to these constructs, in that we cannot observe the constructs themselves. Construct validity is the most difficult type of validity to establish.[4] If the construct exists, it is also true that it should be measurable by several different methods. If, for example, the following question was asked of the population by means of the three main survey methods: 'Are you in favour of extending pub opening hours?', a common measurement value, e.g. postal 42% in favour, telephone 44%, and personal interview 47%, may be evident. It is of course recognised that each of these survey methods has its own strengths and limitations.

Convergent Validity

The use of two or more independent measuring techniques should produce a common (but not necessarily equal) measurement value. Convergent validity exists if, for example, the following questions were asked of the population by means of the one survey method: 'What time should pubs close at?' Or 'What time should pubs stay open until?' Both questions, though worded differently, should, all other factors being equal, generate similar responses, e.g. Closing time 11.30 p.m.; Open until 11.30 p.m.

Discriminant Validity

While construct validity is the degree of correlation among different measures that purport to measure the same construct, discriminant validity is the lack of or low correlation among constructs that are supposed to be different. It involves demonstrating a lack of correlation among differing constructs. In other words, questions that measure different objects should yield different results. Supposing, in a survey of school principals regarding school security, a seven-point scale was used: 1 denoting 'Not concerned' and 7 denoting 'Very concerned'. When analysed, the average for the question dealing with fire safety was 6.2, whereas the average for a question dealing with theft of school equipment was 3.8. Therefore, school principals were found to be more concerned with fire safety than theft. This seems reasonable. In the above example two different constructs were being measured. The difference between the averages demonstrates discriminant validity.

Reliability Assessment

Reliability refers to the extent to which a scale produces consistent results, if repeated measurements are made.[5] If you step on and off a bathroom scales repeatedly over a two-minute interval it should show the same measurement value. If not, it is unreliable. In marketing research a reliable measurement scale should be relatively free from the interference of transient or situational influences. If we measure the same marketing phenomenon over and over again with the same measurement instrument we should get the same or highly similar results. Therefore, reliability is the degree to which measures are free from random error. Even if a study is undertaken just once, it is important that the measurement is free from random error. Otherwise, how can we be confident that the findings resemble the actual value? There are several approaches to the assessment of reliability.

Test-retest Reliability

Test-retest (also known as stability) estimates are obtained by repeating the measurement using the same instrument at two different times, and under as nearly equivalent conditions as possible between the two measurements. Assuming that the objects or individuals have not changed in the interim, the two measurement scores should correlate. The higher the correlation coefficient, the higher the reliability. There are several problems associated with the test-retest assessment of reliability. First, it may be difficult to locate and gain the co-operation of respondents for a second testing, or the research question may require the person's initial reaction to a new product. Second, the first measure may sensitise the respondent's response to the second or subsequent measurements. Equally, respondents may attempt to remember answers they gave the first time. Thirdly, the likelihood of a true change in attitude (versus a random fluctuation) or other form of maturation of the subject, is increased further if the time interval between the test and the re-test is too long. Environmental and personal factors may change, causing the second measurement to change. Therefore, a very short time interval will bias the reliability estimate upwards, whereas longer periods have the opposite effect. Thus, if a particular measuring instrument does not show a high degree of consistency between observations recorded during the first and second measurements, we are not certain whether the instrument is unreliable or whether the changes are due to some of the above-mentioned factors. An alternative means of reliability assessment may be required to overcome the problems of the test-retest method.

Split-half Reliability

The split-half approach to reliability assessment is concerned with the internal consistency of the measuring instrument rather that its stability over time. It involves two measurements taken at the same point in time. The theory of internal consistency is based on the idea of equivalence. Equivalence relates to the amount of error that may be introduced by different samples of items used to measure a phenomenon. At its simplest, split-half reliability works as follows, e.g. a list of twenty items are on a summated scale (a summated scale is where a number of items are summed to form a total score). Each item on the scale measures some aspect of the construct measured by the entire scale, and the items should be consistent in what they indicate about the characteristic. If, for example, hotel image was believed to consist of fourteen independent items, and we wished to measure hotel image on a single favourable or unfavourable image dimension, each item is assumed to independently measure this composite single dimension. The split-half approach randomly divides the fourteen items into two groups of seven. The research takes the results obtained from one half of the scale items and checks them against the results from the other half. High correlation between the halves indicates high internal consistency, which means that the items can be split into halves randomly or based on odd-and-even numbered items. A problem with the split-half reliability assessment approach is that the results will depend on how the scale items are split. To overcome this, an average split-half measure of similarity — coefficient alpha — can be obtained from a procedure that has the effect of comparing every item to every other item.

Equivalent Forms Reliability

The equivalent forms method is used when two alternative measuring instruments are designed to be equivalent but not identical. For example, two equivalent questionnaires can be constructed to measure store loyalty. Although the questions used to measure store loyalty are different in each questionnaire, the number of questions used to measure store loyalty should be approximately equal. The two equivalent forms are administered to the same groups of subjects, at two different times, usually two to three weeks apart, although in some cases they are given one after the other. The results are compared to determine the degree of discrepancy, as in the test-retest approach. A high correlation between the two forms would suggest that the scale is reliable. A low correlation reflects either low reliability or non-equivalent forms. There are two problems with this approach. First, is the difficulty of designing forms that are truly equivalent. Second, is the expense and time delay. Even if equivalence is established, it may not have been worth the effort.

A final word on reliability. Reliability is a necessary condition for validity. However, a reliable instrument may not be valid. A reliable but invalid measurement will yield consistently inaccurate results.

• Measurement of Attitudes

A variety of techniques have been developed to measure attitudes. The measurement techniques in this chapter tend to be of the self-administered variety, i.e. self-reporting, in which the consumer responds to questions posed. Self-administered techniques are by far the most widely used techniques for measuring attitudes, and are the most appropriate for conclusive research studies. Other means of measuring attitudes include observation and projective techniques (see Chapters 5 and 6). These methods are more appropriate for measuring attitude in exploratory research situations.

Measurement of attitude is much more difficult and uses less precise scales than these found in the physical sciences. Attitude is not observable, nor is it defined by any single, agreed-upon definition. It is a construct (i.e. not directly observable, but measurable through indirect measures) that exists in the mind of the consumer. Often, attitudes are measured at the nominal or ordinal level. There are, however, more sophisticated scaling procedures that enable the researcher to measure attitudes at the interval level. Conclusions obtained from attitude scale measurements are strictly limited by the properties of the scale that is used. It is not possible to attribute the more powerful properties of the interval scale to the lower level nominal or ordinal scales. Failure to recognise these limits can lead to serious misinterpretations; for example, assuming a ratio scale, where there was in fact only an interval scale.

The attitude measurement techniques discussed in this book can be grouped under two headings:

1. Attitude rating techniques.
2. Attitude scaling techniques.

We will look at each in turn.

• Attitude Rating Techniques

Rating scales are widely used to measure consumer attitudes, and many types of rating scales exist. The more popular rating scales will be discussed here.

Graphic Rating Scales

The respondent is asked to indicate the position on a continuum that corresponds to his or her attitude. The continuum runs from one extreme of the attitude in question to the other. A theoretically infinite number of responses are possible and the respondent indicates his or her attitude toward a concept by placing a mark at a point on the continuum. At its simplest, the graphic rating scale would look like this:

| Unreliable | ——————— X ——— | Reliable |
| Inconvenient | — X ——————————— | Convenient |

Variations of the above might include providing hatch marks, with or without accompanying numbers. As well as at the extremes, verbal descriptions may be included along the continuum. The scales can be arranged horizontally or vertically.

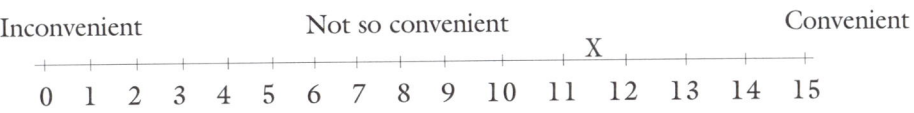

If the scale does not contain numeric intervals, analysis can be carried out by using a ruler, or superimposing a marked template on the scale. When designing the scale, it is better not to make the ends of the continuum too extreme, nor to have too many hatch marks or numeric intervals. If the anchors are too extreme it tends to force the respondent into the centre of the scale. Instead of hatch marks and/or numbers, the researcher may use any one of several graphic techniques to record the responses. These graphic techniques are particularly helpful for recording the response of children or if a language barrier exists. Examples include using happy/sad face scales and thermometer scales

Non-Comparative or Comparative

Graphic rating scales can be either non-comparative or comparative. The preceding examples were all of the non-comparative type, whereby the respondent is free to choose his or her own frame of reference. At this point, it is important to point out that some authors choose to discuss the measurement of attitude under the broad heading of comparative and non-comparative scales. In this book, we use this heading as it applies to the individual measurement scales; preferring instead to detail attitudes under the heading of Attitude Rating Techniques and Attitude Scaling Techniques. An example of a comparative graphic rating scale could be:

Compared to the *Irish Times*, the *Irish Independent* is:

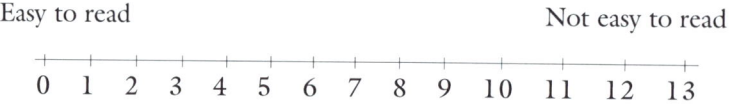

Graphic rating scales are easy to construct and simple to use. Numerical data obtained from the scales is usually treated as interval data. However, while graphic rating scales are used in marketing research, they are generally not considered as reliable as itemised rating scales.[6]

Itemised Rating Scales

The itemised rating scale is similar to the graphic rating scale except that the respondent is asked to choose from a limited number of identified categories, rather than placing a check mark on a continuous scale. Many of the more widely used scales in attitude measurement fall into the category of itemised scales. Itemised scales are easy to construct and administer, but do not allow for the fine distinctions that can be achieved in a graphics rating scale. This limitation is compensated for by the fact that the definitive categories of itemised rating scales probably produce more reliable ratings. Examples of itemised rating scales include:

Drying ability of a Whirlpool dryer is:

Very good	Good	Neither	Poor	Very poor
1 ☐	2 ☐	3 ☐	4 ☐	5 ☐

Shopping at Dunnes Stores is:

Very boring					Fun	
☐	☐	☐	Somewhat boring ☐	☐	☐	☐
-3	-2	-1	0	+1	+2	+3

The Cork Jazz Festival is well organised:

Strongly agree	Agree	Neutral	Disagree	Strongly disagree
☐	☐	☐	☐	☐

When developing itemised scales, the following issues must be considered:

1. Whether to have an odd or even number of categories.

Some researchers may believe that respondents should not be provided with a neutral category. Their reasoning is that everybody has some degree of an attitude and that by not providing a neutral category it forces the respondent to come down off the fence. Other researchers argue that respondents may be genuinely ambivalent or have a neutral attitude on the subject in question, and should therefore be provided with a neutral category. This can be achieved by having an odd number of categories with the central position neutral.

As well as providing a central neutral position it may be advisable to have another category for the 'Don't know' or 'No opinion'. After all, it is possible that a certain percentage of respondents may never have heard of or used the object in question. Uninformed responses like this should not be 'forced' into a neutral category. By not doing so, they are not included in the calculation of measures of central tendency, i.e. by providing a 'No opinion' response category you get a more accurate measure of the average response to the item.

2. Whether to use balanced or unbalanced scales.

In a balanced scale, the number of favourable response categories equals the number of unfavourable responses. An unbalanced scale will have more positive or negative categories. However, there may be instances when an unbalanced scale is the way to go. For example, it would be reasonable to assume that responses to a statement like 'Protection of the ozone layer is important for future generations' would be skewed to the positive or favourable response categories:

Disagree	Neutral	Agree	Strongly agree	Very strongly agree
☐	☐	☐	☐	☐
–1	0	1	2	3

3. How many categories should the scale have?

As a rule of thumb, a five- or seven-scale category is probably sufficient. More than that is likely to be confusing to the respondent; however, the greater the number of response categories, the greater the precision of the scale. In some instances a two- or three-category scale will be sufficient, i.e. 'Agree, Neutral, Disagree'. There is no correct answer to the number of categories to use. The researcher must use judgment.[7]

4. To what extent should responses be labelled and identified?

When providing guidance to respondents, the researcher may choose to provide: numbers versus no numbers; label only the end points of the scale; or provide verbal descriptions for all categories. The labelling of responses is an important issue as the presence of labels can affect responses.[8] Also, a combination of equally spaced categories and ordered numerical designations increases the possibility of assuming that the data obtained is by nature interval. It is common practice to treat rating scales as interval scales and to compute mean and standard deviations. The researcher should exercise caution in making such an assumption, as potential for measurement error exists.

It should also be noted that the verbal descriptions provided throughout the scale may not concur with the respondent's. By providing only extreme verbal descriptions, the respondent may feel that he or she is being forced less into a particular category on the scale.

Rank-Order Rating Scales

These scales require the respondent to arrange a number of objects with regard to some common criterion, e.g. product features in terms of importance, advertisements in terms of awareness or services with regard to liking. Ranking is widely used in surveys. The rank-order method is comparative in nature and the result is a purely ordinal scale that describes the objects from most favoured to least favoured. The respondent assigns a rank of 1 to the most preferred brand, 2 to the second most preferred and so on. Nothing is said about the distance between the objects. For example, the distance between 1 and 2 is not necessarily the same as the distance between objects 3 and 4. Also, perhaps none of the items on the list is the respondent's preferred first choice. The respondent may actually dislike, in an absolute sense, the brand ranked 1. The ranking technique may force respondents to make choices they might not otherwise make. In practice, respondents should not be expected to rank more than six items, otherwise it becomes arduous. Despite its limitations the rank-order scale is a popular choice of researchers; mostly because it resembles the shopping environment where the consumer is required to make direct comparisons among competing alternatives. An example follows.

'Please rank the following brands of washing powder according to whiteness. No. 1 should be the most preferred brand, no. 6 the least preferred. No two brands should receive the same rank number.'

Daz ☐
Bold ☐
Persil ☐
Tide ☐
Omo ☐
Radion ☐
Surf ☐

Paired-comparison Rating Scales

The previous technique required the respondent to consider all objects simultaneously. When using paired comparisons, the objects to be ranked are presented two at a time, and the respondent has to choose between them according to some criterion.[9] The data obtained is ordinal by nature. Paired-comparison overcomes the problem, as in rank-order, of ranking a large number of objects: it is easier for the respondent. Before a ranking of all objects can be obtained, all possible combinations of pairs have to be presented. This means that for n objects, $(n(n-1)/2)$ paired comparisons include all possible pairings of objects.[10] For example if there are six objects to be evaluated, $n = (6(6-1)/2)$ or fifteen paired comparisons. For five objects, the number of comparisons is ten. But the more objects, the more comparisons required. With ten brands, for example, there are 45 paired comparisons. This geometric expansion means the number of objects to be evaluated should be confined to a relatively small number. It should be noted that the comparison of two objects at a time is seldom the way choices are made in a retail situation. Thus, an item may do very well in a paired comparison test, but not perform as well in an actual market situation.[11] Also, respondents may prefer one object over another, but they may not like it in an absolute sense.

Example of paired comparison rating (Fanta, Coke, Lilt, 7-Up, Club)
Please evaluate the following brands of soft drink according to taste:

_____ Fanta versus _____ Coke
_____ Fanta versus _____ Lilt
_____ Fanta versus _____ 7-Up
_____ Fanta versus _____ Club
_____ Coke versus _____ Lilt

	Coke	versus		7-Up
	Coke	versus		Club
	Lilt	versus		7-Up
	Lilt	versus		Club
	7-Up	versus		Club

Constant-sum Rating Scale

The constant-sum rating scale requires respondents to allocate a fixed number of rating units (usually 100) among several objects, to reflect the relative preference for each object or attribute. The units used can be points, pennies, chips etc. If an object is considered unimportant, the respondent allocates it zero points. If an object is twice as important as some other object on the list it receives twice as many points. The data obtained is considered closer to interval scale. The technique is best used for relatively small numbers of objects, otherwise respondents may misapply points such that the total is more than, or less than 100. For example, a respondent may allocate 106 or 94 points. This can be adjusted for by dividing each point allocation by the actual total and multiplying the result by 100.

'Please divide 100 points among the following soft drinks according to your degree of preference for each.'

Coke _____
Fanta _____
7-Up _____
Pepsi _____
Lilt _____

Fractionation-rating Scale

This rating scale can be considered a variation of the previous scale. Respondents are required to rate an object by comparing it with a reference object. As an example:

'If NUI, Galway scored 100 points in terms of being a "fun" university, how would you compare each of the following universities to NUI, Galway.'

NUI, Galway   100
UCC   _____
UCD   _____
TRINITY   _____
UL   _____
DCU   _____

With a scale of this nature there is always the danger that a respondent will assign an outrageously high number of points to an object, that in no way reflects his or her preference or perceived value of the object. A solution would be to put a ceiling on the number of points the respondent can assign to any one given object. The constant-sum approach provides much the same information, but avoids the problem of extreme ratings. The researcher may therefore choose to not use the fractionation scale.

• Attitude Scaling Techniques

The rating scales methods outlined earlier require the respondent to react to a stimulus that typically consists of a single statement or question. However, attitudes toward complex objects such as health insurance, financial institutions, cars, educational establishments and pension funds have many facets. Thus it is often unrealistic to attempt to capture the full picture with one overall attitude scale question. The techniques in this section involve a battery of questions or statements in order to provide a more complete view of the respondent's overall attitude. These techniques measure a sample of beliefs towards the attitude objects (such as agreement or disagreement with a number of statements about the attitude object) and combine the sets of answers into some form of average score. The more popular scaling techniques employed in marketing research are Thurstone, Likert, semantic-differential and Stapel scales. Since these are versions of the itemised rating scale, we must keep in mind the various issues and problems associated with itemised rating scales, as discussed earlier in the chapter.

Thurstone's Scale

In the late 1920s, Louis Thurstone developed the concept that attitudes vary along continua and should be measured accordingly. The construction of this Thurstone scale is a complex process that requires two stages. The first stage is a ranking operation performed by judges who assign scale values to attitudinal statements. The second stage consists of asking subjects to respond to the attitudinal statements. Thurstone scales can be adapted to measure attitudes towards any type of object using the following procedure:

1. A large number (75 to 100) of statements or adjectives (favourable and unfavourable) relating to the attitude object(s) are collected by the researcher.
2. Then, a group of judges (15 to 20) classify these statements into eleven nearly equal piles. This eleven-category bi-polar scale represents the judgments of the panel members as to which statements are most favourable, and which are least favourable, about the subject. The sixth or middle pile is the neutral position.
3. Mean scores for each of the original 75 to 100 statements are determined on the basis of the piles in which they were placed by the judges.
4. The 20 to 25 statements with the smallest variance are chosen to be included in the survey.

5. The selected items are incorporated into the questionnaire in random order and the respondent is asked to select all the items with which he agrees, and his score is calculated as the average of the values (medians) of the items selected.

For example:

Attitudes towards a restaurant are being assessed using a Thurstone scale. A respondent indicates three statements with which they agree.

Statement	Value assigned by judges
1. The restaurant has a homely atmosphere	2.8
2. The restaurant provides a good selection of wines	1.7
3. The restaurant has consistently good quality food	2.4
Average	2.3

Because of the two-stage procedure, a Thurstone scale is both time-consuming and expensive to construct; however, the scale itself is easy to administer and requires a minimum of instructions. Some critics question whether the judges are representative of the ultimate respondents. The attitudes of those who judge the original collection of statements may bias the selection of those used in the test. It would be unwise to deliberately include judges with extreme views about the matter under survey.

Likert Scale

Rensis Likert published 'A Technique for the Measurement of Attitudes'[12] in 1932, in which he described a new method of attitude scaling known as Likert scales. Sometimes referred to as the summated rating scale, the Likert scale is one of the most widely used attitude scaling techniques. It is simple to administer and overcomes some of the criticism associated with the Thurstone scale. This makes the technique particularly useful for mail surveys and personal interviews with children.[13] The Likert scale usually consists of two parts, the item part and the evaluative part. The item part is essentially a statement about a certain product, service, attitude or event. The evaluative part is a set of response categories ranging from 'Strongly agree' to 'Strongly disagree'. Likert scales differ from Thurstone's scales in that respondents are presented with a series of statements and asked to indicate their degree of agreement or disagreement by selecting a point on a 3, 5, 7 or 9 point scale. Typically, each scale item has five response categories ranging from 'Strongly agree' to 'Strongly disagree'. In reality, the number of response alternatives may range from three to nine.[14] Consider the following example from a study of food shopping behaviour.[15]

'When buying food for my family, price is no object.'

Disagree	Neutral	Agree	Strongly agree	Very strongly agree
☐	☐	☐	☐	☐
−1	0	1	2	3

Note: Some researchers use 'Neither agree or disagree' as the midpoint.

The various degrees of agreement are assigned scale values, although the particular values differ from researcher to researcher. Thus, for example, for a five-point scale, a statement can be assigned a numerical score ranging from –2 to +2 or 5 to 1, or 1 to 5. The weights shown would not be printed on the questionnaire. The data collected by using Likert scales may be presented on an item-by-item basis (profile analysis), or a total (summated) score can be calculated for each respondent, as a measure of the respondent's overall attitude towards the object of the survey. If a summated approach is used, the scoring system for each item statement must be consistent across high and low scores. This is known as directional consistency (see below). While a summated score has its advantages as a summary statistic, its main disadvantage is that it loses the richness and detail which are obtained if one analyses the responses individually. Because each statement is a rating scale in its own right, such analysis is possible with Likert scales but not with Thurstone scales.

In constructing Likert scales it is important to use items which invite the respondents to express a clear opinion, i.e. to avoid neutral statements and to vary the presentation between positive and negative statements in order to avoid the respondents getting into a mind-set and automatically ticking the same box. The procedure for developing summated Likert scales is now described.

Constructing Likert Scales

Likert scales are developed in a manner similar to that used for Thurstone scales. The following section summarises the major steps, as proposed by Rensis Likert, in the development and administration of the Likert scale instrument.

1. The researcher identifies the concept to be scaled.
2. The researcher collects a large number of statements relevant to the attitude in question, that can be clearly identified as either favourable or unfavourable. The number of statements at this stage will be relatively large — perhaps 50 statements or more. The key is to develop *attitude revealing* statements and to avoid universally accepted statements of fact.
3. The next step is to administer the collected statements to a group of people reasonably representative of eventual respondents. At this stage, the purpose is to eliminate statements that contribute very little to the eventual attitude score a respondent receives. In the pre-test, the respondent indicates agreement or disagreement with each statement by checking one of the following direction-intensity descriptors (assuming a five-point scale).

Strongly agree	(+2)
Agree	(+1)
Neutral	(0)
Disagree	(–1)
Strongly disagree	(–2)

The numbers in brackets are for scoring purposes and need not be shown to the respondents.

4. Next, compute each respondent's score by summing the scores of responses to each question. In the scoring process, weights are assigned so that the direction of attitude — favourable to unfavourable — is consistent over items. This directional consistency can be achieved by either multiplying each individual's responses to unfavourable statements by –1, or by reversing the rating of the responses for unfavourable statements.

	Strongly agree	Agree	Neutral	Disagree	Strongly disagree
Positive +	5	4	3	2	1
Negative –	1	2	3	4	5

5. Following the pre-test it is necessary to eliminate those statements that do not discriminate between high and low scores on the total test. Selecting respondents with extreme scores (high or low) according to total score can do this. Then, determine the average score on each statement among those in the high quantity and similarly among those in the low quantity. Those statements on which these averages differ by the largest amount are the most discriminating.

6. Administer the refined test with the population or sample of interest. Each item response is algebraically added to provide a total attitude score for that respondent. Alternatively, individual statements can be profiled across respondents by computing the mean or median value for each item statement for the total group, or for each group that one wishes to compare with each other or with some 'ideal' profile.

It is possible that two individual respondents could have the same summated score but yet have rated various statements differently, i.e. specific attitudes towards components of their overall attitude could differ markedly.

Marketing research practitioners rarely follow the exact textbook-like process prescribed by Likert. The scales are often created by the client and researcher or following the completion of a focus group. As mentioned earlier, the main advantage of Likert scales is the ease of construction and administration. It does, however, take longer for the respondent to complete than other itemised rating scales. While output of the Likert is of the ordinal type, practitioners frequently treat the Likert total attitude score as an interval-scale result.

Figure 9.4

Profile analysis of two restaurants

Factor	Rating Excellent	Very good	Good	Average	Poor
Food	—	—	—	—	—
Service	—	—	—	—	—
Staff	—	—	—	—	—
Value	—	—	—	—	—
Decor	—	—	—	—	—
Variety	—	—	—	—	—
Atmosphere	—	—	—	—	—
Wine list	—	—	—	—	—
Management	—	—	—	—	—
Hygiene	—	—	—	—	—

———————— Restaurant No. 1
·················· Restaurant No. 2

Semantic Differential

A special type of rating scale borrowed from another area of research (semantics), this scaling technique was originated by Osgood, Suci and Tannerbaum[16] who discovered that the perceived meaning of a variety of words and concepts could be stated in terms of three components:

1. Potency, e.g. strong-weak.
2. Activity, e.g. fast-slow.
3. Evaluation, e.g. good-bad.

In marketing research, the semantic differential is widely used to describe the set of beliefs that comprise a person's image of an organisation or brand. It is also a revealing procedure for comparing the images of competing brands, stores, or services.[17] In general, only the evaluative, e.g. good/bad component, of the attitude is measured. In this technique, the respondent is asked to express his or her feelings on an object by selecting a position along a five- or seven-point rating scale bounded by bipolar adjectives or phrases that have semantic meaning. In the original work of Osgood *et al.*, only single-word bipolar adjectives, not phrases, were used. However, common practice in marketing research applications is the adjectival phrases (e.g. a bank study might use the phrase 'low interest on savings' and 'favourable interest on savings'. These phrases are not bipolar opposites). Some researchers prefer unipolar scales, while others use bipolar scales. However, the midpoint of the scale has two different meanings. With unipolar scales, the midpoint is simply a step on the scale from 'warm' to 'cold', whereas on a bipolar scale it is a neutral point. The scoring of the semantic differential can be illustrated by using a seven-point scale bounded by the anchors 'fast' and 'slow'.

Fast — — ✓ — — — — — — — — Slow

Respondents are asked to mark the blank that best indicates how best one or the other term describes the attitude object. Each position on the scale is assigned a numerical value, e.g. –3 to +3 or 1 to 7. The words (adjectives, phrases) should be carefully selected. Exploratory research generally is required to ensure that important attributes are represented and described in words that are familiar to respondents.[18] Semantic differential scaling may include as many as ten or fifteen different adjective pairs. Some adjective pairs will be quite concrete, others may be adjective pairs that are more abstract yet quite revealing (similar to projective techniques). For example:

Budweiser beer is:

sweet	—	—	—	—	—	—	—	bitter
weak	—	—	—	—	—	—	—	strong
colourless	—	—	—	—	—	—	—	colourful
angular	—	—	—	—	—	—	—	rounded
beautiful	—	—	—	—	—	—	—	ugly
masculine	—	—	—	—	—	—	—	feminine
old fashioned	—	—	—	—	—	—	—	modern
tasteful	—	—	—	—	—	—	—	tasteless
elegant	—	—	—	—	—	—	—	plain
undependable	—	—	—	—	—	—	—	dependable

In the past supermarkets have been surveyed using semantic differential scales. These were designed to give profiles of them as seen by consumers. The following bipolar scales were considered to be most relevant in one study.[19]

Example of a five-point semantic differential scale which was used to measure attitude towards supermarkets:

good	—	—	—	—	—	bad
friendly	—	—	—	—	—	unfriendly
modern	—	—	—	—	—	old fashioned
pleasing	—	—	—	—	—	annoying
convenient	—	—	—	—	—	inconvenient
clean	—	—	—	—	—	dirty
neat	—	—	—	—	—	disorderly
large	—	—	—	—	—	small
sincere	—	—	—	—	—	insincere
reliable	—	—	—	—	—	unreliable
active	—	—	—	—	—	passive
low prices	—	—	—	—	—	high prices
roomy	—	—	—	—	—	crowded

The bipolar adjectives in a semantic differential scale should ideally be randomised in order to avoid positive bias. The phrases are randomly flipped to avoid having all the good ones/positive ones on one side. Randomly assigning favourable and negative ends of the descriptors in a semantic differential scale minimises what is sometimes referred to as the 'halo effect'.[20] Also if respondents are likely to be ambivalent to the survey topic, it is better to use a balanced set of negatively and positively worded questions.[21] Before the researcher can begin to assign codes and summing occurs, he must reverse the individual scale items where necessary so that each attitude continuum ranges from unfavourable to favourable or *vice versa*.

Earlier we said that semantic differential can be used to compare images of competing brands, stores and services. Competing brands can be subjected to the same test and their profiles compared. In the supermarket example respondents could be asked to rate two or more supermarkets on the same scale and profile presented for each (as in restaurant example cited earlier).

Semantic differential data are typically analysed using the profile analysis approach. Profile analysis involves computing the arithmetic mean or median value for each set of bipolar adjectives, or verbal phrases for each object evaluated. The values calculated are compared by plotting or statistical analysis. It is possible that two or more brands compared would have similar aggregate scores yet their profiles be quite different. While the mean is most often used as the summary statistic, there is controversy as to whether the measurements can be treated as interval data. Critics argue that the data obtained will have only ordinal properties because the weights are arbitrary. Depending on whether the data are assumed to be interval or ordinal, the mean or median will be used to compare the profile of competing brands. An alternative to profile analysis is aggregate analysis. It requires that the scales across all adjective pairs be summed for each individual. Each individual is assigned a summated score. Individual scores can then be compared as the basis of total scores. However, profile analysis is the more preferred approach for marketing decision-making.

Stapel Scale

A derivative of the semantic differential scale is the Stapel scale. It was originally developed in the 1950s by Jan Stapel to measure the direction and intensity of attitudes simultaneously. The adjective pair of the semantic differential is replaced by a single adjective or phrase, i.e. unipolar. This is particularly helpful when it is difficult to create pairs of bipolar adjectives. Points on the scale are numerically identified with typically ten categories numbered from −5 to +5, without a neutral point(zero). In reality, any even number of numerical values can be used, e.g. −3 to +3. The scale is usually presented vertically. Respondents are asked to evaluate how accurately the adjective or phrase describes the object to be evaluated. In the second example below, +5 is very expensive; −5 is very inexpensive. The higher the numerical response category, the more the term describes the concept.

An example(s) of the Stapel scale is shown next in Figure 9.5.

Figure 9.5

+5
+4
+3   +3
+2   +2
+1   +1
Fast service Friendly staff
-1   -1
-2   -2
-3   -3
-4
-5

Alternative presentation

	Jurys	Fitzpatricks	Ryans	Best Western
	+5	+5	+5	+5
	+4	+4	+4	+4
	+3	+3	+3	+3
	+2	+2	+2	+2
	+1	+1	+1	+1

Expensive
```
   -1          -1          -1          -1
   -2          -2          -2          -2
   -3          -3          -3          -3
   -4          -4          -4          -4
   -5          -5          -5          -5
```

Results can be analysed the same way that semantic differential data are treated. Figure 9.6 presents Stapel scale comparative profiles of two hypothetical fast-food restaurants.

Figure 9.6 Stapel scale comparative profiles

Comparison of two fast-food outlets

Modern	
Friendly	
Fast service	
Attractive decor	
Tasty food	
Broad menu	
Convenient location	
Convenient hours	
Clean restroom	

Outlet No. 1 ———
Outlet No. 2 ·········

The Stapel scale produces results similar to the semantic differential.[22] It is particularly suitable for administration over the telephone.[23] Neither is there any need to pre-test bipolar adjectives or phrases to ensure true bipolarity. Despite this the Stapel scale is little used in commercial research. Semantic differential and Likert scales remain more popular. A problem with the Stapel scale is that descriptor adjectives can be phrased in a positive, negative or neutral way. The choice of phrasing could be said to affect the scale results.

• **Summary**

Attitudes towards brands are consumers' learned tendencies to evaluate brands in a consistently favourable, or unfavourable way. Attitudes are generally viewed to have three main components, which are the cognitive component, the affective component and the behavioural component. The cognitive component refers to the respondent's awareness of and knowledge about an object. The affective component refers to the respondent's positive or negative feelings with regard to an object. The behavioural component refers to buying intentions and actual purchase behaviour. Most marketing research studies contain questions designed to measure a respondent's attitudes. It is generally assumed that there is a link between attitudes and behaviour. Attitudes are assumed to be an important predictor of behaviour.

There are four basic levels of measurement, which are nominal, ordinal, interval and ratio. Each represents a different kind of number assignment rule, or 'scale' of measurement. As we proceed from the weakest (nominal) to the strongest (ratio), two things happen. First, the numerical requirements for scale membership become more stringent. Second, the permissible modes of data expression and analysis become more liberal, that is to say more types of statistical operations are permissible.

To have confidence in the results of a marketing research study, the researcher must be concerned about two characteristics of the measures being used to collect information. These two concepts are called validity and reliability. The researcher, therefore, must be concerned with whether we are measuring what we wish to measure and whether our measurement is accurate. Validity can be examined from a number of different perspectives. There are six major approaches to the assessment of validity. Reliability refers to the extent to which a scale produces consistent results if repeated measurements are made. There are three approaches to the assessment of reliability, test-retest reliability, split-half reliability and equivalent forms reliability.

A variety of techniques have been developed to measure attitudes. Self-administered techniques are by far the most widely used techniques for measuring attitudes. The attitude measurement techniques discussed in this book can be grouped under two headings: attitude rating scales and attitude scaling techniques. Rating scales are widely used to measure consumer attitudes, and many types of rating scales exist. The rating scales methods require the respondent to react to a stimulus that typically consists of a single statement or question. Attitude scaling techniques, on the other hand, use a battery of questions or statements in order to provide a more complete view of the respondent's overall attitude. The more popular scaling techniques employed in marketing research are Thurstone, Likert, semantic-differential and Stapel scales.

Questions

1. Define 'attitude'. What are the components of an attitude?
2. Distinguish between the cognitive component and behavioural component of an attitude.
3. What is meant by measurement, and why is this process important to marketing research?

4. What are the primary scales of measurement?
5. Differentiate between a nominal and an ordinal scale.
6. Why is a ratio scale more advantageous than an interval scale?
7. Distinguish between the validity and the reliability of a measure.
8. Discuss the major ways in which the validity of measurement is assessed.
9. What are the three methods of assessing reliability?
10. Outline the main attitude rating scales.
11. Give an example of the following rating scales: (a) graphic; (b) rank order; (c) constant sum.
12. What are the important decisions involved in constructing an itemised rating scale? How many scale categories should be used in an itemised rating scale? Should an even or odd number of categories be used?
13. What is the difference between balanced and unbalanced scales?
14. Distinguish between attitude scaling techniques and attitude rating scales.
15. How does one construct a Likert scale?
16. What is a semantic differential scale and how is a person's overall attitude assessed with this type of scale?
17. How does a Stapel scale differ from a semantic differential scale? Which is more commonly used?

Problems and Assignments

1. Mary says she'd be willing to pay £1,000 more for a used '94 Opel than for a used '92 Mercedes Benz. This comparison between the two cars represents what scale of measurement?
2. Identify the type of scale (nominal, ordinal, interval, or ratio) being used in each of the following:
   (a) I think there are too many stray cats in my neighbourhood.

   Disagree   **Agree**
   1   2   3   4   5

   (b) How many brothers do you have?
   (c) Please rank the following activities in terms of your preferences by assigning ranks 1 to 5.

   i.   Knitting   _____
   ii. Eating out   _____
   iii. Going to the movies   _____
   iv. Shopping   _____
   v.   Watching videos   _____

(d) What is your bank account number? _____

(e) On an average weekend, how much beer do you consume? _____

    i.   Less than 1 pint   _____

    ii.   2 to 4 pints   _____

    iii.   5 to 7 pints   _____

    iv.   8 to 10 pints   _____

    v.   More than 10 pints _____

3. Having read Chapter 8, design a questionnaire that includes a Stapel, Likert and a semantic differential scale for measuring the loyalty of a brand of your choice.
4. Develop a battery of attitude scales to predict whether or not people who currently smoke will try to quit smoking within the next year.
5. How would you select a set of phrases or adjectives for use in a semantic-differential scale to evaluate the image of banks and other consumer financial institutions? Would the procedure differ if you were going to use a Likert scale?
6. Advertising is an expenditure that ultimately must be justified in terms of an effect on sales and profits, yet most evaluations of advertising are in terms of the effects on attitudes. How do you account for this apparent mismatch?
7. You receive the results of a paired-comparison preference test of four soft drinks from a sample of 200 persons. The results are as follows:

	Coke	Fanta	7-Up	Lilt
coke	X	50*	115	35
Fanta	150	X	160	70
7-up	85	40	X	45
Lilt	165	130	155	X

* Read as 50 persons preferred Fanta over coke.

(a) How do these brands rank in overall preference in this sample?
(b) Develop an interval scale for these four brands.

8. Below is a Likert type scale that might be used to evaluate your opinion of the educational programme you are in. There are five response categories: 'Strongly agree' through 'Neither agree nor disagree', to 'Strongly disagree'. If 5 represents the most positive attitude, how would the different items be valued?

(a) This programme is not very challenging.
    SA   A   N   D   SD

(b) The general level of teaching is good.
    SA   A   N   D   SD

(c) I really think I am learning a lot from this programme.
    SA   A   N   D   SD

(d) Students' suggestions are given little attention here.
       SA   A   N   D   SD
   (e) This programme is below my expectations.
       SA   A   N   D   SD
9. One of the problems in developing rating scales is the choice of response terms to use. Below are samples of some widely used scaling codes. Do you see any problems with them?
   (a) Yes ___   Depends ___   No ___
   (b) Excellent ___   Good ___   Fair ___   Poor ___
   (c) Excellent ___   Good ___   Average ___   Fair ___   Poor ___
   (d) Strongly Approve ___   Disapprove ___   Strongly Disapprove ___
10. A researcher thinks many respondents will answer 'Don't know' or 'Can't say' if these options are printed along with agreement categories on the attitude scale. The researcher does not print either 'Don't know' or 'Can't say' on the questionnaire because the resulting data will be less complicated to analyse and report. Is this appropriate?

Case Study
Measuring Service Quality at the Bridge House Restaurant*

The Bridge House, award-winning restaurant and bar 'in the heart of Dublin', welcomes its guests to an elegant decor and offers an intimate and friendly atmosphere. The background music will charm the customers and complements the ambiance and the quality and freshness of food.

The restaurant is a well-established and up-market establishment which has been operating in Dublin for the last twenty years. It began by offering simple, straightforward cuisine to the regular patrons consisting of mostly local business people in winter and attracting additional tourists in summer. It is open from Monday to Saturday from 11 a.m. to 3 p.m. for lunch and 6.30 p.m. until 11 p.m. for dinner. From June to September the restaurant also opens every Sunday for dinner.

The Bridge House held the reputation as the 'best restaurant in Dublin' for a decade. It focuses on delivering good quality food in a relaxed atmosphere with efficient and friendly service. The restaurant offers a variety of food, with dinner costing approximately £19.50, and provides a four-course meal with dishes such as local seafood. The Early Bird menu costs £11.95 and is available from 6.30 p.m. to 7.30 p.m. The à la carte menu ranges in price from £8.95 to £16 and contains mouth-watering dishes and a wide selection of seafood.

The owners, Theresa and Barry O'Leary, feel that their mission is to deliver quality food and service in a friendly atmosphere. However, this is getting increasingly difficult. Several new restaurants have opened in Dublin in the last year, offering new 'cuisines', trendy atmospheres, sleek decor, and attract a trendy clientele. The restaurants are spending heavily on promotional activities including grand openings and thus receiving much publicity. However, their staff are mainly students and have received no official training and receive minimum wages.

Theresa has not noticed a reduction in sales as a result of this competition and their restaurant appears to be holding on to market share and sells 400 lunches a week and 250 dinners; Theresa feels that their core competence is service. Comments cards have revealed that the food still scores high but service has dropped from 'very good' to 'good'. Theresa knows that providing good quality service on a consistent basis will mean that customers will be continually satisfied, will want to return and use the service again and they will want to recommend the service to those around them. It costs five times more to get a new customer than to keep an old one. By retaining existing customers and gaining new customers through positive word of mouth, Theresa feels that the restaurant's customer base will continually grow without the need for expensive and unpredictable advertising. A growing customer base, in line with increased sales turnover, will enable the restaurant to become more efficient in its activities and avail itself of economies of scale. This in turn will enable the restaurant to increase its profits and offer attractive pricing structure to its customers, especially in the quieter 'shoulder' and winter months.

Theresa has decided to carry out a more extensive survey on patrons to identify their deeper perceptions of the quality of the service. She feels that the best approach is the comparison of expectations to perceptions regarding the actual service encounter. The problem is to identify what research method to use and what aspects of the service to research, e.g. is friendliness more important than speed? Theresa decides to carry out some focus-group interviews which consisted of informal discussions with eight to ten customers. The participants expressed their views with regard to the aspects of the service that *they considered important to them*. From this initial exploratory research Theresa learns that some of the most important aspects are:

- Dependability and accurate service performance.
- Promptness and helpfulness.
- Competence, courtesy, credibility and security.
- Good communications and good customer understanding.
- Atmosphere and ambiance, appearance of physical elements of service.

Theresa now wishes to set up an informal service-quality information system that will provide relevant data on an ongoing basis which can be used for decision-making purposes. She wants to use a quantitative method that can be administered on a regular basis and comparisons made. Luckily she has all her regular clients (250) on a database that she uses for direct mail and from them she chooses a random sample of 25. The main problem she feels is how to measure the important attributes of service as identified from the focus groups perhaps some type of attitude scales could help?

Theresa ponders these problems as she shuts the restaurant door late Sunday evening, tomorrow (she hopes) will reveal the best approach to solving the service-quality measurement task.

Assignment

1. Describe the non-comparative scaling techniques that Theresa could use to measure service quality in the restaurant (include Likert and Semantic differential scales in your answer).
2. Draw up a questionnaire that includes rating scales to measure service-quality using the attributes identified in the case study.
3. Discuss the criteria used for scale evaluation and explain how to assess reliability, validity and generalizability.

* This case was written by Monica Nielsen, Galway-Mayo Institute of Technology. It is intended to be used as a basis for class discussion rather than to illustrate either effective or ineffective handling of an administrative situation. The case is based on a real situation, though certain information has been disguised. © Monica Nielsen, Galway-Mayo Institute of Technolgy.

Chapter 10
THE SAMPLING PROCESS
(STAGE 4)

- **Chapter Overview**
- Introduction • Sampling Terminology • Basic Sampling Concepts
- Census versus Sample • The Sampling Process • Defining the Population • Selecting a Sampling Frame • Choosing a Sampling Method
- Selecting a Sample Type • Sample Size Determination • Selection and Validation of a Sample • Summary

---

- **Introduction**

Sampling is about taking a small portion of the larger part and drawing conclusions about the larger part from our experience of the smaller part. Put simply, sampling is finding out a lot from a little, in a scientific way. Sampling enables us to study some cases instead of all the cases, while still enabling us to draw conclusions about all the cases. From a practical marketing application, sampling asks the questions: who do we want to talk to? Who has the needed information? The aim of sampling is to make inferences about a population within acceptable margins of error. Finding the right person (object, item, shop, product or entity) to talk to is one of the signs of good market research.

The instinctive reaction for some people is to react negatively to the very words 'sampling' and 'statistics'; that is, to have a mental block or switch off (a sort of statistical seizure).[1] If you can add, subtract, multiply, divide, and calculate a square root, then there is no logical, rational reason for such an emotional reaction. As a researcher you can certainly grasp the concepts of sampling and statistics, with a small amount of effort. Researchers don't have to be statisticians to use sampling and basic statistical principles. The aim is to be comfortable with the general use, interpretation and analysis of data. Essentially, an investigator should be competent and able to collect data from a small group or set of items, persons or objects and use this group to reflect upon the larger group or population, make recommendations and therefore assist management with decision-making.

This chapter presents the principles of sampling and the related statistics. The reader is assumed to have a limited knowledge of mathematics. For further, more in-depth analysis of the topic please refer to Churchill.[2] Upon completion of this chapter, you will be able to:

1. define basic sampling terminology;
2. outline the general principles of sampling;
3. detail the steps necessary to conduct sampling;
4. define a population;
5. discuss the practical use of sampling frames in Ireland;
6. differentiate between the different types of sampling and sampling methods;
7. design a sampling procedure for a marketing problem.

• Sampling Terminology, Basic Sampling Concepts

Sampling is one of the few areas in marketing research that at first glance appears to have a vocabulary of its own. The terminology of sampling is that of the statistician and mathematician. It provides an appropriate starting point to an understanding of the concepts and ideas behind the marketing use of sampling. The more detailed statistical terminology, closely affiliated with sample size determination and derivation, is dealt with in the next chapter. The basic concepts which appear frequently in this chapter are as follows.

Population

The population is the total set of people, shops, items, members and/or objects of interest. The term 'population' refers to every, and all members from whom information is needed. It can also be referred to as the universe. A population member or element is one individual case from the total. A population has to be defined, according to designated specifications. Examples of possible populations or universes could be:

1. all housewives in Ireland in 1999;
2. all third-level, full-time students in Dublin city, as of October 1999;
3. all registered charities in Europe, as of January 2000;
4. all multinational corporations operating in Munster during the financial year 1999/2000;
5. all five-star hotels in Ireland as of August 2001.

Thus, the concept of population can be applied to people, firms, retailers, accountants, teenagers, students, doctors, stores and products alike. The symbol, N, denotes the size of a population. The population is what we make inferences about, based upon information from a sample.

> Q3 - Should a sample be taken?
> If so, what process should be followed?
> What kind of sample should be taken?
> How large should it be?
> What can be done to control + adjust for non-response error?
> *Keep refering back to Prob def

Sample

This term denotes a smaller group of items, members or objects, taken from a particular population, that we measure or observe. It is a sub-set of the population or universe. A sample should be the miniature or mirror of the population under examination. The symbol, n, refers to the number of elements in a sample. The aim of a sample is to enable the researcher to draw inferences or conclusions from the sample about the population. *small no. of units chosen at RANDOM from a total universe to reflect that pop-*

Census

A census is where all members or cases of a given population are observed/measured. Talking with every working urologist in the Republic of Ireland would qualify as a census, if the population of interest were defined as qualified, practising urologists in the 26 counties in 1999 (note, this excludes retired urologists).

Parameter

A parameter is a numerical dimension, measure, value or characteristic of the population we are interested in. It is better referred to as a population parameter. Sampling is used to estimate a population parameter. Parameters tend to be unknown at the time of conducting the study and actual information is needed about their value. Examples of parameters include the average amount spent on shoes by men; the number of female smokers in Ireland, or the number of married couples owning their own home.

Estimate

An estimate is a sample statistic. It is paired with the population parameter and taken as a measure of the population parameter. A common estimate is the sample mean, the average of the sample, e.g. the average length of time (days) a patient spends in hospital or the average amount spent per car (£s) in 1999.

Probability Laws

Mathematical laws governing the likelihood of a certain event occurring. As used in sampling, probability theory says that sample units have a known chance of selection, and so estimates can be made to determine how close the sample mirrors or reflects the population. Thus, a correctly selected sample will be, within measurable limits, representative of the population of interest.[3]

Sampling Error

Sampling error is the probable measurement of difference between the actual population parameter and the observed sample estimate of it. Sampling error is a result of taking a sample rather than a census. Sampling error is inherent in the sampling process.

• A Census or a Sample?

In wishing to learn about a particular population and describe its characteristics, one of the first issues to arise is the question of whether the researcher should be concerned with *all* members or *some* members; that is whether one should conduct a census or a sample. A census is a complete canvass of all population members, a sample is a selection of a smaller number of members from the population — for example, the Census of Population, 1996. Taken on the night of Sunday, 28 April 1996, 'the census figures relate to the *de facto* population, i.e. the population recorded for each area represents the total of all persons present within its boundaries on the night of Sunday, 28 April 1996, together with all persons who arrived in that area on the morning of Monday, 29 April 1996, not having been enumerated elsewhere'.[4]

Since every project has its own unique features and merits, a census or sample is thus dependent upon the particular features of the study and the compromise possible. Like many other issues in marketing research, the answer lies in balancing the different constraints of the project in hand. These constraints have a tendency to cluster around the following.

Time Requirements

Marketing problems are under severe time pressures. As a general rule, samples take less time than a census, the one exception being where there is a very small, finite, contained and accessible population. It is less time-consuming to research 1,000 people than the entire 3.6 million Irish population. However, if there are only five manufacturers of urology products in Ireland, a census is a sensible approach.

The Financial Cost

In most circumstances, a sample will physically consist of smaller numbers than a census and is therefore cheaper to pursue. However, the exception to this general rule-of-thumb is the small contained finite population, in which case a census is a practical alternative to a sample, as in the case of the urology manufacturers above.

Required Information, Related Decision

The management decision and required information has to be reviewed at this point, as more efficient use of money and time can be made by undertaking a sample. A sample can allow the researcher to control other dimensions of the project. For example, money could possibly be better spent on training interviewers and so minimising interviewer error, than talking with an additional 100 people. If properly conducted, a sample can be nearly as accurate as a census.

Pragmatic Reasons

Practical considerations often dictate the use of samples in place of a census, e.g. the destructive nature of measurement and investigation — if, as part of a quality drive, you eat all the produced Easter eggs, you would have none left to sell! Clearly, common sense calls for a sample.

A census would further be avoided if gathering information from people were a difficulty. It can happen that by talking with people, they are sensitised to the topic and so the results of the data collection process are not representative of the population's true opinion on the topic. Weiers[5] concisely expresses this when he writes 'it is desired to measure changes in the population rather than to induce changes by means of the measurement process itself'.

One development relating to the issues of census or sample is the shift from audit sampling in the retail sector to census data, based upon scanner-based tracking, giving rise to data drilling or data mining to monitor sales.

Accuracy and Confidence

The final issue to be considered in choosing between a sample or census is the needed accuracy, confidence and objectivity in the results. If little or minimum error can be tolerated in the results, the tendency is towards sampling because:

1. sampling error can be calculated and so is subject to statistical estimation, thus the accuracy of the results can be defined;
2. a census is more prone to non-sampling error, e.g. interviewer bias, analysis error;
3. sampling error can be reduced by increasing the sample size.

The accuracy and confidence required in the results is a measure of the preceding three variables. In choosing a sample or census, accuracy and confidence are the single best barometers.

A final comment on the question of a sample or census. It would appear from the above that samples are the preferred choice of most researchers and this is true in practice. Samples are generally more convenient, easier and more economical than a census.

• The Sampling Process

Once the decision has been made to undertake a sample, the researcher engages in the sampling process. It can be thought of as consisting of seven stages, as shown in Figure 10.1. These stages are essentially sequential decisions and form the discussion for the remainder of this chapter.

Figure 10.1 The sampling plan

(handwritten annotation: should have pop. defined since stage 1)

1. Defining the Target Population and Its Parameters

(handwritten: Defines who has info)

In deciding who to seek data from, the first step in sampling is about defining the population of interest. A population is defined as the total and entire group of persons, items/objects that the researcher wants to know, study and describe. A population is the totality of cases. Like problem definition, population determination has to be explicit and it can be equally difficult — there are many examples in marketing where people, objects and items do not lend themselves to easy and convenient classification. For example, consider a population that is to include all those people in Ireland who are against property taxes.

(handwritten margin note: can be a person, product, object or shop)

This aside, the objectives of the study are the sole determinants used to identify the target population. The defined population must contain all of the members of interest, otherwise it is not a population. To assist in achieving this completeness, and provide a manageable basis for defining a population, a population should have:

1. an *element*; this is the person we want to gather data from, or an entity which has the desired information. It can on occasions be the same as the unit. For example, we could be studying the smoking habits of all young teenagers to assist with government policy guidelines. Given this, the element we might wish to seek information from are 13–15 year-old-teenagers, male and female (the 13–15-year-olds are the elements of interest). In identifying the element of analysis, we often have to identify the population parameters we are also interested in. For example, we could be interested in 13–15-year-old teenagers who have smoked or are smoking (this excludes those teenagers who have not smoked). Careful planning and attention to detail are important at this point, to ensure an efficient

sampling process. A fish manufacturer wanted to find out about the perceptions and expectation of retailers with respect to new added value fish products for the Irish market. At first glance, it seemed like a good idea to talk with retail store managers. However, secondary data from Bord Iascaigh Mhara quickly highlighted that the fish counter managers had more responsibility, experience and knowledge about specific developments in the fish trade and therefore were the real element of analysis for the study.

2. *a unit* — the unit contains or houses the unit of interest. Thus, the unit is often the access point to the element of analysis. In our illustration above, to talk with and so access 13–15-year-olds, we would approach households where the majority of such people reside. Alternatively, we could approach schools, or other such places where teenagers are most likely to be found.

3. *a time* dimension — for example, during the year 2002. This provides a temporal boundary for the population. Continuing our example, we would also specify the time, e.g. year or month, 1999 or December 1998.

4. *a geographic* boundary — this defines the extent of the population. In most Irish circumstances, this is either Ireland; a province(s); a county(s); a city(s) or a town(s). Completing our example, the geographic extent could be the island of Ireland, as we wish to generalise about all teenagers.

In practice, population definition can be easier for the consumer market than for the industrial market. This is attributable in part to the fact that there are more documented secondary data sources available for the consumer market. Secondly, population or universe definition is increasing in difficulty due to the collapsing boundaries between industries and organisations — a trend being fuelled by the 'global village' syndrome. Thirdly, as the number of variables used to define the population increases, say age and income plus social class, occupation and education, the cost of population definition increases. One method of dealing with these difficulties is to conduct exploratory research to determine the population.

2. Choosing the Appropriate Sampling Frame/List

A sampling frame is a list of all of the units (and elements) of the defined population, where no member is excluded and all members are mentioned once, and once only. If observable or documented, the frame is referred to as a direct list. Secondary sources of data can be of immense help in compiling such a list. Directories such as Kompass and Thoms are regularly used to this effect. The Register of Electors is commonly used as well, as are association/professional memberships, e.g. surgeons, dentists, lawyers. These are examples of sample frames — where every member is included and written down.

On occasions, it may be possible to generate a required list, but impractical to do so. Given such a situation, the researcher can work under the assumption that they have such a list. For example, in wishing to study the general public, a researcher would need a list of every individual who resides in Ireland at a given point in time. It is theoretically possible to compile such a sample frame, but unrealistic: it would absorb too much time and money. To this end, the researcher would assume that the list is readily available, in the form of households, and continue with the sampling process. This is an example of an indirect sample frame. Commonly used sample frames in Ireland are presented in Table 10.1.

Table 10.1 Sample frame list examples in Ireland

Consumer/households	Manufacturing firms	All firms	Miscellaneous
1. Register of Electors	1. IDA	1. Chambers of Commerce	1. Bord Failte
2. Postal Districts	2. Forbairt	2. Golden Pages	2. Business & Finance Top 1,000
3. AC Nielsen	3. Kompass	3. Kompass	3. Financial Times

Sampling frames can be a difficult area for researchers in Ireland. Depending upon the population definition, it can be hard to generate or access lists easily. Industrial markets, services and small businesses are a few illustrations where generating a sample frame can be difficult. In such circumstances, creativity is called for — the researcher may need to collate a number of different and existing sources to generate their list. Other sampling frames, e.g. persons with the HIV virus, may not be available for confidentiality reasons.

A further problem associated with frames is sampling frame error. Frame error is said to have occurred when a list of the population is incomplete or inaccurate, due to missing, duplication or incorrect elements. That is, there is a discrepancy between the defined population and the actual list or sample frame of that population. The effect of sampling frame error may be to introduce a bias in the results of the research. A classic frame error illustration in most countries is the telephone directory. At first glance, the telephone directory would seem to provide a listing of all residents. But it excludes those who do not have a phone, those who are ex-directory, those who have recently moved residence, those who have a mobile phone, but no fixed phone, those with only e-mail addresses and those who are nomadic, such as the travellers and homeless. Another example is the Register of Electors — a list of the names and addresses of all people over the age of 18. It is up-dated and published every year, but suffers from missing elements, persons who have not registered, duplication, students who have moved address and are registered twice or three times, and incorrect elements, persons returned from abroad or persons who have died.[6]

310   *Marketing Research in Ireland*

In conclusion, the perfect and ideal sample list is rarely available, implying that many researchers experience frame error. Nevertheless, potential sources of such error are best recognised in advance and minimised whenever possible.

3. Choosing a Sampling Method

Once we have a satisfactory population list, our next step in the sampling process is to choose between conducting a probability (random) or non-probability sample.

Probability is a type of sampling where each unit has a known chance of being selected. Inclusion and exclusion in the sample is determined by pure chance and the likelihood of this is known. This process can be likened to a number from 1–100 being picked out of a hat. Being based upon the notion of random selection, randomness in this context has a precise meaning — every member has a known (and under some circumstances discussed further on, an equal) chance of selection. Thus, probability sampling allows for generalisations to be made about the many from the few, i.e. the sample is used to make inferences about the whole population. The results generated by the sample, broadly speaking, equal those that would have been generated by a census, if sampling had been correctly undertaken. Probability sampling also enables the calculation of the sampling error. Remember, a sample statistic estimates the true population value, so sampling error tells us how different our sample statistic is from the unknown population value. Another way to think about sampling error is to reflect on how accurate the sample results are — how closely do they mirror the real population and its parameters or values? All of these issues — error, accuracy, random selection, and generalisations — can be managed through the use of probability sampling.

So, by definition, probability sampling excludes the researcher from choosing the sample members and so eliminates selection bias on behalf of the interviewer as well as subjective selection. This, as well as the sampling error estimation, is the great advantage of probability sampling. For these reasons, probability sampling is normally, but not exclusively, used for descriptive research and for causal research. Examples of marketing applications of probability sampling include advertising and promotional studies, pricing studies, sales, market forecasts and brand preferences.[7]

In practice, two things need to be known:

1. each element in the population (hence a sampling frame); and
2. the total number in the population.

In Ireland, some of the larger Irish surveys employ probability sampling on a regular basis, such as the JNRR, as described in Chapter 4.

Non-Probability Sampling

By contrast, non-probability sampling is not based upon any probability principles or laws. The probability of selection is unknown. It is inherently subjective, and not objective, as the sample members are chosen consciously by the researcher. The representativeness of the observed sample is unknown for non-probability sampling. Drawing inferences about the entire population is not possible as the amount of sampling error cannot be determined. So, non-probability sampling relies solely on the researcher's skills and experience and not on predetermined selection rules.

The main advantages of non-probability sampling are that it:

1. is cheaper, in terms of costs and the time demanded of the investigator;
2. is sometimes easier to conduct;
3. is more convenient than the probability method of sampling;
4. can be used in the absence of a sampling frame.

Talking with the first ten people who pass by in a shopping centre is the classic example of non-probability sampling. Alternatively, a researcher may have been instructed to talk with 25 UK visitors, 35 USA and 15 Japanese tourists, to reflect the breakdown in visitors to Ireland in general, according to Bord Failte statistics. (Known as quota sampling, we discuss this later in further detail.)

In the past, non-probability sampling has been closely associated with qualitative data and exploratory research. However, recent times have seen a trend towards the use of probability sampling when conducting exploratory research. With more sophisticated computer models becoming ever available, non-probability sampling is becoming more sophisticated. Quota sampling, one form of non-probability sampling, is discussed further on in this chapter.

The choice between probability and non-probability sampling becomes a question of the advantages and disadvantages of both sampling types, as applied to the particular project. As is evident from the above discussion, probability sampling is statistically superior to non-probability sampling, as probability sampling allows for the calculation of sampling error. Remember, sampling error is defined as the measurement of difference between the actual population parameter and the observed sample estimate of it. In reality, this means that the chosen sample, for whatever reasons, doesn't necessarily mirror the population. Thus, from a marketing researcher's perspective, sampling error can be managed by either increasing the sample size, which decreases the amount of error, or using probability sampling, which calculates the amount of error present. (This statistical dimension to the sampling process is considered in more detail in the next chapter, as we turn our attention to sample size determination.) However, this theoretical advantage of probability sampling can be outweighed by practical considerations; for example, the choice of sampling type is inextricably linked to the availability of a suitable sampling frame. Thus, the choice between probability and non-probability sampling is a question of balancing the purpose of the study, with likely error, time and costs. A basic checklist to assist with the decision-making between probability and non-probability sampling is provided in Box 10.1.

Box 10.1 Probability or non-probability checklist

1. Is there a lot of existing knowledge about the problem? Yes No
2. Do you require very specific information? Yes No
3. Is the research data quantitative? Yes No
4. Is a high level of accuracy called for? Yes No
5. Do you want to generalise the results from your sample to the population? Yes No
6. Do you have an accurate sampling frame? Yes No
7. Is a defined level of confidence required about the results? Yes No
8. Do you want to be able to estimate the amount of sampling error present? Yes No
9. Is there a large budget? Yes No
10. Is serious investment being made? Yes No

More 'Yes' answers than 'No' suggest that probability is the preferred sampling mode. More 'No' answers point in the direction of non-probability sampling.

4. Choosing a Sampling Type

Once the decision has been made to pursue either probability or non-probability sampling, the researcher must then turn their attention to the selection of a specific sampling type. Under the auspice of probability sampling, one can choose from simple random sampling, systematic random sampling, stratified random sampling, cluster sampling, area sampling or multi-stage sampling. Non-probability encompasses convenience, purposive, judgment and quota sampling.

Box 10.2 Sampling methods

Probability sampling
- Simple random sampling
- Systematic random sampling
- Stratified random sampling
- Cluster and area random sampling
- Multi-stage random sampling

Non-probability sampling
- Quota sampling
- Purposive sampling
- Judgment sampling
- Convenience sampling

[handwritten note: Use if you decide you have enough experience + knowledge of topic]

Simple Random Sampling

Simple random sampling (SRS), is the best-known method of probability sampling. It underpins other probability methods and for these reasons it serves as a useful point to begin our discussion.[8]

In simple random sampling, sample members are selected randomly from a population list that contains every member. Each member has a known and an equal chance of being selected. The 'equal' chance of a sample member being selected is a unique feature of simple random sampling. SRS can be with or without replacement. With replacement SRS means that a member, when picked, is put back into the hat, so to speak, and can be picked again. Without replacement, the more common form of SRS, means that once a member is selected, it is not returned to the list, and so the sample member cannot be chosen again.

The single biggest strength of simple random sampling is its simplicity. Computer-generated random numbers make the administration of simple random sampling very easy and effortless. This is particularly true for a relatively small population. One of the biggest disadvantages of SRS is its dependency upon a complete and accurate sampling frame. Without such a listing, SRS is not possible. Another problem for SRS is its inability to control for sample variation. If the population is heterogeneous, and the sample selected is small, it could potentially be non-representative of the population — you can technically draw all those who are similar and miss some members who are different. An illustration is presented by manufacturing firms in Ireland. Suppose you generate an accurate and complete list of all firms, large, medium and small, who are manufacturing products at present. It is conceivable, though highly unlikely, that a SRS could result in 90% of the drawn sample being small firms, or 99% being large firms — to the exclusion of the other firms. This would result in an overestimation or underestimation of the sample statistics, e.g. the mean. Such a situation is likely when dealing with a small sample size. A further drawback of SRS is the possible wide geographical spread of the selected sample and therefore the increased costs of travel and data collection. This problem becomes more accentuated when researching and sampling in and across Europe.

Therefore, there are two practical requirements to be fulfilled for a researcher to evoke simple random sampling. These are:

1. an accurate, complete sample frame; and
2. a random selection procedure, e.g. computer-generated random numbers or traditional random tables.

In practice, the generalised procedure for simple random sampling is as follows:

1. Define the population, i.e. unit, element, time, geographic boundary and population parameters of interest.
2. Obtain or generate an accurate, up-to-date, valid and reliable list of defined population.

3. Number the population members or items from 1 to N.
4. Use a random selection procedure (a computer can generate a list of random numbers or alternatively pick a random starting point and select numbers from tables of random numbers).
5. Continue selecting sample members/items until sample size is reached (sample size is predetermined using the relevant formula in the next chapter).
6. Numbers selected constitute the sample members.

Suppose we want to mail our new Christmas hamper catalogue to a sample of managing directors in Ireland. We obtain a relevant and accurate listing from a commercial organisation. We can assign a number to each member and either use computer-generated random numbers or use random tables to select the sample, as illustrated in Box 10.3.

Box 10.3 Hypothetical listing of managing directors in Ireland

Numbers assigned to population members	Managing directors
1	Ruth Kelly
2	Judy Casburn
3	Niall Daveron
4	Denis Nielson
5	Robert Nielson
6	Richard Dunne
7	Kevin Long
8	Catherine O Connor
9	Michael Keady
10	James Kelly
11	Brian O'Mahony
12	Catherine Bane
13	David Clancy
14	Siobhan Taxter
15	Bernard Kenny.

Based upon the tables in Appendix 1, taking the right-hand column, the following numbers and associated directors were selected: 2, 4, 5, 7, 10 and 11.

If there are 10 items in the population, number items from 1–10 and take 2 digits at a time in the random tables.

If there are 100 items in the population, number items from 1–100 and take 3 digits at a time in the random tables.

If there are 1,000 items in the population, number items from 1–1,000 and take 4 digits at a time in the random tables.

Systematic Random Sampling

Systematic random sampling is a variation on simple random sampling.[9] Every n^{th} member of the population is chosen from the sample frame, having started from a random starting point. For example, you have a population of 400 and want a sample of 40. 400 divided by 40 = 10, so n^{th} = every tenth member on the list — hence the name systematic. 1/10 is the sampling fraction. A random starting point is chosen between 1 and 10 (from computer-generated random numbers or random tables) for the first sample member selected and from then, on every following 10th.

The main benefit of systematic random sampling is its ability to deal with a sampling list where ordering is involved, i.e. the population is arranged according to some criteria. For example, if companies are listed according to size or turnover, a systematic sample will produce a selection of elements with varying turnover or size that may be more representative of the population than a simple random sample might be. Another reason for using systematic sampling is its ease of administration. It is not necessary to number every item/member, but just to have a list of the population. Furthermore, we work on the assumption that the population being studied is homogenous — all population members are similar, so systematic sampling is useful as in the case of some commercial directories and professional/trade bodies.

As with simple random sampling, systematic sampling may not satisfactorily deal with periodic population heterogeneity. For example, a highly dispersed population living in different European countries will increase the cost of the research, because it is possible, in drawing a systematic sample, to have most of the sample from one country — which does not fully represent the actual population. Thus, variations that occur in parts of the population (and not all of the population) can result in systematic random sampling producing a less representative sample. Given this, a researcher should consider such 'periodicity' when considering systematic random sampling.

The generalised procedure for systematic sampling is:

1. Define the population, unit, element, time, geographic boundary and population parameters of interest.
2. Obtain or generate an accurate, up-to-date, valid and reliable list of defined population.
3. Calculate the sampling interval.
4. Pick a random starting point, using computer-generated random numbers or random tables between 1 and N/n.
5. Take every n^{th} member/item, until sample size is reached.

Let's say we have a population of 200 students who went parachuting during their summer holidays. Using the formulae in Chapter 11, suppose we require a sample size of 50 students from our population. According to the procedure for systematic sampling, the sampling interval is 200/50 = 4. We select a random starting point, between 1 and 4, say 2, using random tables in Appendix 1 or computer-generated random numbers. We then return to our population list and select the sample. We start with the second population member, and take every following fourth. So, our systematic sample consists of sample members 2, 6, 10, 14 and 18 and so on. We then collect the needed information from the corresponding respondent.

Stratified Random Sampling

Suppose in our previous example, we knew that our parachuting student population was broken down into 100 females and 50 males. We might want to use this information to give us more detailed knowledge about our population (we know from secondary data, that female students are more likely to take up parachuting than male students and want to investigate why). In such circumstances, we could use stratified random sampling, a form of probability sampling that allows the researcher to account for variations within the total population. Thus, the concept of segmentation, well known to marketing people, is reflected in stratified random sampling. An entire and whole population is taken and divided into mutually exclusive and collectively exhaustive smaller parts or strata. Members within an individual stratum are similar, while the strata are heterogeneous and vary with respect to the parameter of interest. Within each stratum, simple or systematic random sampling, or another form of probability sampling, is applied. Thus, stratified sampling involves sampling of sub-populations or strata as if they were a separate population. The advantage to such an approach lies in the ability of stratified random sampling to facilitate a researcher in examining the relationship between the selected strata and the parameter(s) of interest, which can result in a better estimate of the parameter(s) of interest, than either simple or systematic random sampling could produce. This superiority of stratified random sampling is related to the degree of variability across strata and within strata. The higher the similarity within strata and the greater the difference between strata, the more effective the stratified random sampling.

Numbers and Dimensions of Bases of Strata

Once the decision to use stratified sampling has been taken (i.e. there is high variation between population groups and low variation within groups) the researcher has to choose the numbers of strata relevant to the project, along with the differentiating factors, or bases for strata. A decision also has to be made regarding the use of proportionate or disproportionate stratified random sampling.

Generally speaking, it is recommended that there are no more than five or seven strata within the sample (this also assumes a relatively large population). Any more groupings within the sample and the researcher can experience administration and cost difficulties that outweigh the usefulness of stratification. Diminishing returns arise as one increases the number of strata.

The dimensions or bases for selecting the strata are dependent upon the parameters of interest and generally follow usual segmentation principles in marketing — these can be based upon demographic factors, such as age, income, social class, occupation and/or education, psychographic variables, i.e. lifestyle and personality or behavioural variables, heavy or light consumer, brand loyal or usage pattern. Such sub-population detail demands that the researcher has prior knowledge to stratify the population. This knowledge, secured from secondary sources and/or previous research, is used in advance of the sample selection. It is normally recommended to have strata in which the members are as similar as possible while being as different as possible from other members of other strata.

A further issue for the researcher to consider is the question of stratified random sampling being either proportional or disproportional. Proportional stratified sampling signifies that all group strata are proportionally represented in the sample, as in the population. So, if you have 10% of small firms in the population, then the sample contains 10% of small firms. Disproportionate stratified sampling signals that one stratum is weighted as more important than another in the population, with respect to the parameter of interest and therefore should be sampled more extensively. Thus, some strata have more or less variability than others. A commonly used rule in disproportionate sampling is the 80%/20% rule or the Pareto principle. For example, 80% of food sales are accounted for by 20% of the grocery outlets, the major multiples. So, 80% of the sample is drawn from the major multiples and the remaining 20% of the sample is taken from the other grocery sellers, such as corner shops, petrol forecourt shops and tobacco outlets.

The generalised procedure for stratified random sampling is:

1. Define the population, unit, element, time, geographic boundary and parameters of interest.
2. Obtain or generate an accurate, up-to-date, valid and reliable list of defined population.
3. Obtain reliable secondary sources of data to stratify population, or alternatively, conduct exploratory research to establish key variables.
4. Choose number and bases of strata.
5. Stratify population list into sub-population lists.
6. Using the relevant formula, determine the sample size.
7. Determine whether to use proportionate or disproportionate sampling.
8. Pick a random starting point, between 1 and N/n, using computer-generated random numbers or random tables.
9. Take every nth member/item, until sample size is reached within stratum one and proceed to stratum
10. Repeat steps 6 and 7, until sample is selected.

As is evident from the above discussion, the strength of stratified sampling lies in its ability to combat the issue of population heterogeneity, which can plague simple and systematic random sampling, especially in marketing. This lends more reality to the study. Another advantage of stratified sampling is where the 'strata' vary in size, some being very small and some being large — stratification provides a more accurate picture of the population. In effect, stratified sampling also allows the researcher to treat each stratum as a separate sample, thus allowing for detailed analysis within and across strata (as described in Chapters 13 and 14). Thus, stratified sampling decreases and controls for sampling error. It is less likely to over- or under-estimate the sample statistics, e.g. the mean. This ability to deal with population heterogeneity is very useful from a marketing perspective, as two or more groups can be compared. For example, most branded products compare the attitudes of heavy consumers to light consumers to assist with decisions about product positioning or new advertising campaigns.

From a practical perspective, good secondary data is needed to stratify the population. This may be a potential pitfall, if such information is not readily available. Linked to this potential drawback is the inherent rise in costs associated with the relative complexity of administering stratified random sampling.

The Household Budget Survey 1994–1995 conducted by the CSO[10] (as detailed in Chapter 4), makes use of stratified sampling, where 'an overall random national sample of approximately 16,000 private households (i.e. 8,000 originals and 8,000 substitutes) was initially selected so that each private household in the State had an equal chance of being selected'.

Box 10.4 Stratification of 1994-95 Household Budget Survey

Sampling stratification

Town survey areas

1. County boroughs.
2. Suburbs of county boroughs.
3. Towns and their environs with population of 5,000 or over at the 1986 Census of Population (large urban).
4. Towns and their environs with population of 1,000 to 5,000 at the 1986 Census of Population (other urban).

Country survey areas

5. Mixed urban/rural areas bordering on the suburbs of county boroughs.
6. Mixed urban/rural areas.
7. Rural areas.

Source: CSO, Household Budget Survey 1994–1995, Appendix 4.[11]

Cluster Sampling

Under this form of probability sampling, the population is sub-divided into manageable clusters or groups, as opposed to individuals, and simple random sampling is conducted to select the clusters or groups. So, cluster sampling selects groups rather than individuals and involves sampling from a sample of the population. Unlike stratified sampling, a list of the population members is not required, the idea being that groups naturally form or cluster together. As the old adage goes, 'birds of a feather, flock together', i.e. social classes tend to live in the same areas, people of like professions or interests congregate together in clubs. To use cluster sampling:

1. Define the population of interest, i.e. element, unit, time, geographic boundary and parameters of interest.
2. Classify the population according to predetermined cluster information drawn from secondary sources of data or previous research.
3. Randomly select a sample of clusters or groups for further sampling.
4. Collect data from members within the selected cluster, by conducting either a sample or census.

For cluster sampling to work, the clusters have to be mutually exclusive and collectively exhaustive. Advantage-wise, cluster sampling saves time and money, as well as providing an estimate of the sampling error. Against this, cluster sampling can suffer from too tightly defined clusters and so hinder the administration of the study.

From first appearances, cluster sampling is identical to stratified sampling, and there are obvious similarities. Both forms of sampling divide the population into sub-groupings. Both use criteria to break down the total group into smaller groups (the same criteria can be used in either forms). However, there is one fundamental difference. In stratified sampling, we have a complete population list which is then stratified according to predetermined variables. This implies that each population member (regardless of stratum) has a known chance of inclusion in the sample. The sample is selected from each sub-group. By contrast, in cluster sampling, there is no physical population listing (though the researcher works on the assumption that one could be developed, given time and cost constraints), and the clusters are chosen first; and from within each chosen cluster, sample members are selected. So, in cluster sampling, one chooses a sample of sub-groups and thus utilises probability sampling twice.

Area Sampling

Area sampling is a variation upon cluster sampling. When a population is concentrated in certain areas, it is normal to use area sampling. A simple random sample is taken of groups or areas instead of a simple random sample of individuals. In this manner, area sampling is a form of cluster sampling based upon geography. *eg county, province etc.*

Suppose you are establishing a pizza and fast-food restaurant chain in Leinster. You break the population down into mutually exclusive and collectively exhaustive groups. In this case, we might use the CSO classification of country or county borough for our area sampling.

Figure 10.2 Area sampling in operation

Area sampling is a practical method for conducting a probability sample when no sample listing is available, but it is theoretically possible to generate a list. The geographic restriction tends to decrease costs and time constraints while still enabling sample error calculations. Compared to simple random sampling, area sampling can suffer from the fact that people with similar demographic and psychographic profiles tend to live in similar areas — potentially leading to a reduced statistical efficiency for this approach.

Multistage Sampling

Multistage sampling (as opposed to single stage, such as cluster sampling described above) is where probability selection methods are pursued at a number of different stages within a sampling procedure. The effect of this is a probability sample where every member has a known chance of being included in the final sample. For example, in proceeding from province to county to urban and rural districts to particular households, we are using a four-stage sampling approach. In this manner, multistage sampling combines the advantages of cluster and area sampling for practical application, and cost and labour savings. It allows researchers to use probability sampling at a macro level, where there is no relevant sampling frame or list.

Multistage sampling is different from stratified sampling, in that multistage sampling divides the population into groups or clusters, from which a few clusters or areas are sampled. Remember, in stratified sampling, the population is also divided into groups, or strata, and all strata are sampled.

Non-Probability Sampling

There are occasions in marketing research when probability sampling is not required or feasible. For example, as is often the case with exploratory research, becoming more familiar with the population and their views is more important than having a representative sample. In such circumstances, non-probability samples, which are not statistically derived, provide no estimate of sampling error and do not enable one to generalise from the sample to the population, are valid. They are, however, very popular when there is no sample frame, and ease of use, cost and time are a concern.

Consider the situation where a small kitchen-units manufacturing firm for the Dublin market, wants to look at potential ways of expanding the business. With three employees and very limited marketing resources, the firm just wants initial ideas to consider. Surveying and probability sampling are neither required, nor possible for this company at this time. Instead they may be better served to talk with ten important customers and ask them what other furniture needs they have or have had in the recent past. Such customers might be in the office at an appropriate time, or the firm might have such discussions when fitting the kitchen. Either way, the results would not be used to generalise about other customers or the market, but would be of great value in suggesting further avenues of investigation.

As already identified, there are four types of non-probability sampling, convenience, purposive, judgment and quota sampling. Quota sampling is the most popular of all the non-probability methods, because of the ready availability of demographic data which assists with the administration of quota sampling. In recent years, hybrid sampling is occurring with increasing regularity. This is where probability and non-probability are combined to improve the overall results. For example, area sampling is first chosen and then followed by judgment sampling. The broad types of non-probability sampling are now discussed.

Convenience Sampling

Here, the units or members for sampling easily present themselves to the investigator for selection — customers walk into your shop, people in the street or shopping centre. Respondents are chosen 'because they are there', or by accident, because they are walking down the street, hence the name, convenience. Radio chat-shows are an example. This sample is the easiest to access, relatively cheap compared with probability sampling, and not time-bound. It has the advantage of facilitating large numbers of questionnaires to be completed, quickly and economically. Against these advantages, convenience sampling may be seriously non-representative. Take people walking down a street — it excludes those working, those in shops at that time, and those elsewhere, so the results generated pertain to the sample and the sample only. As with all non-probability sampling, inferences and generalisations about the population are not possible. For these reasons, convenience sampling is acceptable for exploratory research, where it may assist in developing further hypotheses. It is not generally recommended for descriptive or causal work.

Purposive Sampling

Purposive non-probability sampling is where the sample members or units are chosen specifically because they are *not* representative of the population. They are chosen according to some predetermined important factor(s) or their extreme position(s) with respect to the product, service, company or attitude they hold. The assumption here is that representativeness is explicitly rejected as the marketing problem calls for the abnormal data, instead of the normal data. A drinks manufacturer might purposively pick respondents who either hate or love the new flavoured carbonated drink to establish the range of opinion. A car manufacturer may select professionally qualified drivers because of their ability to handle difficult driving conditions, or a fast-food restaurant may choose to talk with strict lifelong vegetarians when introducing new vegetarian product alternatives. So, sample members are selected in light of important, predetermined criteria, that are not necessarily representative of the population, but relevant to the success of the project on hand, as laid down by the researcher.

Judgment Sampling

This form of non-probability sampling uses the expertise of the researcher to hand-pick the sample units, in an attempt to bring representativeness to the sampling approach. The units are judged by the researcher to be representative or typical of the population. For example, the Consumer Price Index from the CSO is based upon a judgment sample of market basket items.

Alternatively, the researcher can use 'experts' to identify the sample. If dealing with a small finite population, such as those Irish companies hand-making customised carpets, judgment sampling can be effective. It is cheap, easy and time-saving. It is dependent on the researcher having an excellent knowledge of the population. It is based on the premise that the researcher *thinks* the sample is representative of the general population, rather than actually being so.

Snowball sampling is another term often associated with judgment sampling. It is where the researcher asks the respondent to name other potential participants who are experts or conform to the population definition. For example, in examining the effect of the Internet on marketing practice in Ireland, snowball sampling was effectively used to identify Internet experts who may not have been nationally known, but possessed in-depth knowledge and/or experience of the topic. While a cost-effective method for a small population or emerging area, it can suffer from 'friends recommending friends' and so detract from the results, i.e. respondents from a similar background will tend to hold similar attitudes, opinions, views and expectations. Furthermore, it cannot be guaranteed that the judgment or snowball sample is representative of the population (as is the case with all non-probability samples).

Quota Sampling

The most popular of all the non-probability sampling methods is quota sampling. It is the one non-probability method that *attempts* to replicate the population *without* using random selection. Predetermined controls, such as age, sex, social class, are used to select sample units. These controls are proportionate to the population. If the population has 20% female members, then 20% of the observed sample is also female. The assumption is that the sample is representative from a practical dimension (if conducted correctly), but theoretically speaking, there is no calculation of sampling error. Quota sampling thus attempts to select a sample that resembles the population, but there is no mechanism to confirm or falsify this.

To illustrate, take the following hypothetical situation. You are marketing manager for an organic yogurt product, and are considering introducing a new variety and wish to test the market. You don't have a complete listing of all yogurt purchasers, so you segment the market by age and social class, using Census of Population and Household Budget Survey figures from the government publications by the CSO. It results in the matrix shown in Figure 10.2.

Figure 10.3 Hypothetical yogurt consumption, 1998

```
35% = ABC1          65% = C2DE
55% = 15–35         45% = 36+
```

You now deliberately select elements for your sample that reflect the population statistics, so that the aggregate picture from your research reflects the total population. Accordingly, since 35% of the population are ABC1, you require 35% of your sample to be ABC1; and since 45% of the population are 36+, you require your sample to have 45% of respondents 36+. On this basis, fieldworkers select respondents that conform to the pre-determined criteria for the quota sampling. Interviewing of respondents continues, until the desired number of respondents is fulfilled. In Ireland, quota variables are readily available from the CSO at a district electoral division (DED).

Controls can be one-dimensional, such as age; two-dimensional such as age and social class; or more, such as age, social class, occupation and income. Regardless of the number of controls selected, they have to be easy to use, current, available, accessible and relevant. As a result, good secondary sources are critical to quota sampling, and used extensively in the administration of quotas. An added benefit to quota sampling is that a sampling frame is not needed. Furthermore, the researcher does not have to call back to a particular respondent if they are not at home. They can proceed to another respondent who meets the quota criteria and is at home, thus saving money and time for the researcher. For example, the first election day survey in Ireland was conducted among a representative quota sample of 1,239 electors who had voted or actually intended to vote in the 1997 election. The sample extended across 200 locations covering all 41 constituencies in the Republic.[12] Quota sampling is therefore commonly used in the consumer markets, but less so in the services and industrial markets. Nevertheless, quota sampling, like all other non-probability sampling methods, may not be representative of the population, despite the researcher's efforts.

One of the biggest hurdles to employing quota sampling can be the interviewer bias that is naturally present in selecting units. This can be counteracted by employing trained, experienced interviewers and stringent field controls. Another disadvantage of quota sampling concerns those who refuse to be interviewed. Their very refusal could mean they are different in some way from those who positively respond. This inherent selection bias, in effect self-selection, results in us having no estimate of sampling error or knowing how representative the sample is of the population.

Of all of the non-probability sampling methods, quota sampling is the most extensively used method in Ireland for survey work by professional research organisations.[13] The quota pre-determined criteria are drawn from CSO Census of population data, normally at district electoral division. This offers all firms a practical, cost-effective and speedy alternative to probability sampling.

5. Sample Size Determination

Sample size is the next issue for the researcher to confront in the sampling process — this is given special attention in the next chapter.

6. Selection and Validation of Sampling

This step in sampling overlaps with fieldwork, normally considered under the data collection heading. Suffice it to say that actual selection and validation of the sample occurs during the fieldwork stage of the marketing research project. This administration of the sampling procedure should aim to maximise the collection of information and minimise the amount of error. The validation of the sample is a simple checking that the actual sample units or members are who they are meant to be, i.e. they are part of the defined population.

- ## Summary

Sampling is central to the success of a marketing research study and is one of the most powerful tools a researcher has. Sampling allows us to study some of the cases of interest, at the same time drawing useful conclusions for all.

Throughout this chapter, we have examined the basic concepts of sampling — the population, the sample, population parameters, sample estimate and sampling error, along with the sampling process itself.

The first consideration is whether to conduct a census or a sample. If a sample is chosen, the researcher proceeds with defining the population, generating a sampling frame, selecting a sampling type and form, determining a sample size and selecting the actual sample.

The researcher can choose between probability and non-probability sampling, depending on the nature of information sought, population of interest, error tolerance, time and cost constraints. The probability sampling methods include simple random sampling; systematic random sampling; stratified random sampling; cluster sampling; area sampling and multistage sampling. Non-probability embraces convenience sampling; judgment sampling; purposive sampling and quota sampling. Each form of sampling has its own advantages and disadvantages which need to be considered for the project on hand.

Key Terms

Sampling
Population
Sample estimate
Probability
Sampling process
Unit
Sampling proportion
With replacement
Simple random sampling
Stratified random sampling
Cluster random sampling
Multistage random sampling
Judgment sampling
Quota sampling
Sample size

Census
Sample
Population parameter
Non-probability
Element
Sampling error
Selection bias
Without replacement
Systematic random sampling
Strata
Area random sampling
Convenience sampling
Purposive sampling
Hybrid sampling
Validation

Questions

1. Why is sampling used so often in marketing research?
2. Distinguish between a census and a sample.
3. Identify the steps involved in the sampling process.
4. What is meant by the term 'population'?
5. What is meant by a 'sampling frame'?
6. Give an example of a perfect sample frame. Justify your choice.
7. Why is a telephone directory often not an acceptable sample frame of a particular city or area?
8. What distinguishes a probability sample from a non-probability sample?

9. How should a simple random sample be selected? Describe the procedure.
10. Which sampling method typically produces more precise estimates of a population mean — simple random sampling or stratified sampling? Why?
11. What is a convenience sample?
12. Distinguish, using examples, between the different types of non-probability sampling procedures.
13. What are the benefits of stratified sampling?
14. Simple random samples are rarely used for door-to-door interviewing. Why do you think this is true?
15. Compare and contrast stratified random sampling with quota sampling.

Problems and Assignments

1. XYZ Q-Stacker supplies computer chips to the car and consumer electronics industries. XYZ Q-Stacker sells to different-sized companies in each of these industries and to companies in all regions of the world. Historically, XYZ Q-Stacker management has noted sales differences by industry type, size, and geographic region. XYZ Q-Stacker desires to select a quota sample to predict the sales level of a new product offering.
   (a) What control characteristics should be used for this quota sample?
   (b) What would one need to know about these control characteristics for them to be useful in this study?
   (c) State how many respondents would be specified for each cell.
   (d) What inferences could be drawn about XYZ Q-Stacker's entire customer base from such a sample?
2. You are asked to make recommendations as to the type of sample to be used, the method of selecting the sample, and the sample size, in each of the following situations:
   (a) The manager of the appliance department of a local department store chain is planning a major one-day non-price promotion of food processors, supported by heavy advertising in the two local newspapers. The manager asks you to recommend a method of sampling customers coming into the department. The purpose is to assess the extent to which customers were drawn by the special advertisement, and the extent to which the advertisement influenced their intentions to buy. A pre-test of the questionnaire indicates that it will take about three minutes to administer. The manager is especially interested in learning whether there are significant differences in the response to the questionnaire among (a) males versus females, (b) gift buyers versus other buyers, and (c) age groups.
   (b) A major airline wants to run a preliminary study on the attitudes of university students towards air travel. The company's research director already has

submitted an interview plan and has estimated that, on average, each interview will require between an hour and an hour-and-a-half to administer. It is estimated that the cost of interviewing and interpreting the interview will be roughly £75 per respondent.
    (c) A sample of homeowners in the Dublin South area is desired for a major segmentation study conducted by a large financial institution. A lengthy personal interview lasting over one hour will be conducted with each respondent. A sample size of 3,000 is targeted.
3. The host of a phone-in programme on a local radio station suggests that listeners call in to record their 'votes' concerning whether or not the city council should permit free parking on parking meters in the city centre area on Saturdays. Of 230 telephone calls recorded during the three-hour programme, 84% of callers felt that parking should be free on Saturdays. What is your opinion of this sampling technique? If you were the county council or mayor, how would you respond?
4. 'The Big Shirt Company', a manufacturer of clothing for large-sized consumers, was in the process of evaluating its product and advertising strategy. Initial efforts consisted of a number of focus-group interviews. Each focus group consisted of ten to twelve large men and women of different demographic characteristics who were selected by the company's research department using on-the-street observations of physical characteristics.
    (a) What type of sampling method was used?
    (b) Critically evaluate the method used.
5. A leading film-processing company wishes to investigate the market potential for a new line of digital processing equipment. Because this is a completely new technology, it is felt that industry leaders might offer insights into the desires of customers and consumers. However, a list of industry leaders does not exist. Discuss possible methods of generating a sampling frame for the influential people in the digital processing industry.
6. A mobile telephone company wants to investigate the needs of its customers. Propose a stratification scheme for the sample and discuss the benefits of your scheme.
7. John Murphy, the owner of a local hotel, is interested in assessing customer satisfaction with his hotel. John's hotel does not accept reservations. Because all of his customers are walk-ins, John has no way of knowing how many people will stay in his hotel on any given night. All of the hotel guests must check in with the front-desk receptionist; due to the small size of the hotel, there is only one check-in desk. John has decided to distribute a survey to every tenth room that checks in:
    (a) What type of sampling is to be used?
    (b) Critically evaluate this method.
8. Name some possible sampling frames for the following:
    (a) Patrons of a wine bar.

(b) Owners of hamsters.
(c) Tennis players.
(d) Fishing rod owners.
(e) Retailers of *Home and Garden Magazine.*
(f) Emigrants to the US of less than two years.
(g) Women wearing size 10 dresses.

9. Identify the following sample designs:
   (a) The names of 20 patrons of a bingo hall are drawn out of a hat and a questionnaire is administered to them.
   (b) A radio talk-show host invites listeners to call in and vote 'Yes' or 'No' on banning nuclear weapons.
   (c) A dog-food manufacturer wants to test a new cat food. It decides to select 100 cat owners who feed their cats canned food, and 100 who feed their cats dry food.

10. A financial services company wants a survey of Internet users to see if they are interested in using the company's financial planning Internet services. Previous studies have shown that Internet usage differs greatly by age, education and gender. The total sample size will be 1,000. Using actual information about Internet usage, or supplying reasonable assumptions, indicate how stratified simple random sampling should be applied for each of the following stratification situations:
    (a) Age ranges of 18–25, 26–50, and 51–65.
    (b) Education levels of second-level, some third-level, third-level qualification and postgraduate qualification.
    (c) Gender: males versus females.

11. A 'Lotto' player is curious about the randomness of winning lottery numbers. He has kept track of the winning numbers in the past five weeks and finds that most numbers were selected 25% of the time, but the number 6 was one of the winning numbers 50% of the time. Will he be more or less likely to win if he picks a 6 in this week's lottery, or will it not make any difference in his chances? Relate your answer to simple random sampling.

12. A local retailer has asked you to select a sample of 50 'fashion leaders'. These leaders will be paid £20 each to 'evaluate' the shop's layout and merchandise selection. The shop carries men's and women's clothing. Describe the sampling process you would use.

13. For each situation below, critique the method used and suggest alternatives you consider better where appropriate:
    (a) To study attitudes toward a fast-food chain, interviewers were stationed in the car parks of the chain, and questioned all those willing to answer.
    (b) In studying the results of a screening method for credit card applications for a department store, folders of applicants were selected at a fixed interval beginning at the front for each file drawer.

(c) To develop information on the purchasers of its new video game, the manufacturer made the activation of the product warranty conditional upon the receipt of the warranty card, which also contained a short questionnaire.
14. Define the appropriate target population and the sampling frame in each of the following situations:
   (a) The manufacturer of a new cereal brand wants to conduct in-home product usage tests in Dublin.
   (b) A national chain store wants to determine the shopping behaviour of customers who have its store charge card.
   (c) An Irish TV station wants to determine households' viewing habits and programming preferences.
   (d) The regional branch of the Marketing Institute wants to test the effectiveness of its new-member drive in Waterford.

Case Study
Irish Bank*

Irish Bank operates branches in 34 cities and towns throughout the country. The bank offers a complete range of financial services, including credit cards, pension plans and corporate loans.

Irish Bank currently has 45,000 businesses using its corporate loan facilities. From the original applications, it has certain information about these companies, including names, addresses, county, telephone and fax number, turnover, size of firm and industry sector.

Irish Bank is interested in determining whether there is a relationship between the size of corporate loans and characteristics of the firm. For example, are businesses in certain parts of the country more or less likely to be heavy users of loan facilities? Is there a relationship between the firm's pattern of sales and loan usage? Are Irish Bank corporate loan clients similar to other businesses across the country? Hugh Muslin is Marketing Director for Irish Bank and is currently in the process of developing a design for the research. Using the resources in your nearest library, develop an appropriate plan to answer in full the following questions:

1. How would you define the population of interest for this study?
2. What sample frame would you use for the study? (Provide an illustrative example of internal and external secondary sources of data that you would combine for use as a sampling frame.)
3. How would you select a stratified sample from the sampling frame you have chosen?
4. How would you select a quota sample from the sampling frame you chose? How would this differ from your answer to the previous question?

5. Which, of *all* possible sampling methods, would you choose for the study, and why?

*This case was written by C. Domegan, NUI, Galway. It is intended as a basis for class discussion rather than to illustrate either effective or ineffective handling of an administrative situation.

Case Study
Aer Arann: Rising Above the Waves**

Aer Arann began flying between Galway and the Arann Islands in August 1970. Its initial launch was shaky in a literal sense, as the first flight was almost blown away by a ferocious storm sweeping across the island from the Atlantic. Nine hefty islanders were called on to fill the plane that night to prevent it from being carried off by the wind. The staying power of Aer Arann remained to see it through several reorganisations and changes of ownership. Today, the company flies from its airfield fifteen miles west of Galway to purpose-built runways on the three Arann Islands, covering the distance in just under ten minutes.

Aer Arann competes with two ferry companies transporting people from Galway to the islands throughout the year. One further ferry company operates between Co. Clare and the islands during March and September only. The market is characterised by severe seasonal shifts — almost two-thirds of the traffic occurs during June, July and August when up to 5,000 people per day travel to the islands.

An adult return fare to the islands is approximately £15 by ferry, which takes about an hour, and £35 by Aer Arann. While Aer Arann can boast the advantage of speed and comfort, the ferry companies have been improving their boats to include attractions such as dining facilities and a bar.

It is estimated that around 250,000 people travel out to the Arann Islands in a year. Island Ferries takes approximately 40% of this number, Arann Ferries hold 35%, and the seasonal operator, Doolin Ferries, takes about 20%. Aer Arann currently holds about 5%. Almost three quarters of Aer Arann's business comes from non-islanders, though this figure is skewed by the influx of tourists in the summer when their two nine-seater planes make a total of 25 flights per day. Even in the depths of winter a minimum of four flights are made each day to serve the 1,322 Arann Islanders and visitors. Travellers between the mainland and the Islands can be characterised by five main types (Box 10.5).

After a successful season, the management of Aer Arann considered expanding its service to cover some of the less frequently travelled islands of the west coast such as Clare Island off the coast of Mayo, and Tory Island off Donegal.

Box 10.5 Profile of travellers to the islands	% of total
Islanders: time factor important, journeys spread throughout the year.	11
Backpackers: very cost-conscious, may stay in budget guest house, B&B, or bring tent, may also travel either side of peak, mainly continental European.	24
Returning relatives: staying with family, seasonally skewed — Summer, Christmas and Bank Holidays.	10
Culture-seekers: least cost-conscious, looking for distinctive experiences, peak season, mainly US and European origin.	21
Day trippers: limited time, perfunctory visit as part of wider itinerary, includes some passing trade, peak season.	34

Another line of potential expansion was through a variety of package deals which combine Aer Arann transport to the islands with travel from other parts of the country, and include accommodation on the island. However, the company was still very dependent on the seasonal nature of the business and was searching for opportunities to develop.

Questions

1. What secondary and primary research would you undertake to determine the size and profile of Aer Arann's target customer?
2. What sampling process would you recommend? Why?
3. How might it respond to seasonal variations in passenger numbers?
4. Suggest ways in which further marketing research could facilitate the development of the business.

**This case was written by Alan J. Whelan and Brenda Cullen, Marketing Department, UCD, 1997. It is intended as a basis for class discussion rather than to illustrate either effective or ineffective handling of an administrative situation. The case is based on a real situation, though some information has been disguised. The authors and NUI, Galway wish to thank Aer Arran for their kind permission to use the material in this case.

Case Study
Judy Greene Pottery***

'If at first you DO succeed, try something harder!'
Ann Landers, Syndicated Columnist

Background

This is exactly what Judy Greene did. She has established herself as a master potter and is recognised as being among one of the most prominent contemporary potters in Ireland. With respect to her handmade pottery, she is not only engaged in developing designs and products, but also in managing the manufacturing and retail operations. To date, her business has been quite successful, experiencing phenomenal growth rates over the last ten years.

In addition to her core business, Judy has established two additional enterprises: Design Concourse Ireland and Greene Corner. Both enterprises are centred around unique retail concepts. Design Concourse Ireland was initially conceived as a showcase for Irish designers and craftsmen. It has now expanded its operations to a full retail outlet offering a range of handmade, Irish-designed products such as jewellery, clothing, art, modern glass, furniture, and assorted home furnishings. Greene Corner grew out of Judy's interest in conserving the natural environment. This retail enterprise offers a wide selection of goods made from recycled materials such as clothing, art, jewellery, furniture and accessories.

Strategic Considerations

Currently, Judy is contemplating what to do next, especially when all appears to be going well. She is not interested in diversifying into additional enterprises and prefers to consolidate her current ventures. Her primary area of concern is her core business of pottery. As mentioned, her handmade pottery has been extraordinarily successful and she wishes to focus on developing future strategies to ensure continued prosperity.

One strategic issue pertinent to her future progress relates to her customer base. In the past, customer demand was 'too fine'. Customers were looking for products that were 'too perfect' to be handmade. Now, customers are more educated and understand that handmade products will not be identical, nor is it desirable for them to be so. Customers now appreciate variations as part of the crafted product. However, Judy is still concerned about how to continue to communicate and make tangible the handmade aspect to customers. This is particularly important to support price increases in labour costs. She has several ideas to enhance communication of the handmade feature such as placing a potter's wheel in the store, to let people experience what it is like to work with clay. Another idea is to establish an additional retail shop in her workshop and give tours of her manufacturing operations.

Changing Customer Profile and Trends

Another strategic issue related to her customer base is her expectation that customer tastes will change. Pottery, in general, has been very fashionable for the last ten years. In fact, the china, porcelain and cut glass (i.e. crystal) markets have suffered at the expense of natural earthy designs. Now, customer trends are changing and their tastes appear to be moving slowly away from pottery back to china, porcelain and cut glass. The imminent questions are when will the trends change and in which manner? Most importantly for Judy, is how to stay ahead of the trends, to ensure her future profitability.

Judy has considered that perhaps she needs to investigate her customer base more precisely. Her current customers are mostly female, but with a good representation of male buyers, 30 years of age and older, coming from mostly middle and upper-middle incomes. Ten years ago, when Judy started, flowers and flowery designs were very 'in'. Now, she has to consider what the upcoming generations want. The younger age groups are more interested in simpler, more classical lines of design. As a result, Judy introduced her 'Connemara Collection' to appeal to the younger markets. To date, it has proved to be very attractive and popular with young customers.

In addition, Judy has introduced her limited edition, 'Millennium Line' to appeal to the more sophisticated tastes of an older market. These are pieces which are either once-off designs or which are produced in small numbers and will no longer be made after the year 2000. Furthermore, Galway being a tourist town, there are the tastes of visitors to consider, especially those from other countries. Essentially, Judy is aware that she needs to capitalise on ideas for new lines to 'stay fresh' in a highly competitive market. Yet, at the same time, she is also aware of how important it is to stay true to her own style. Balancing these two concerns is challenging while trying to satisfy customer demand.

To answer many of these questions relating to current and future customers, Judy is thinking of doing some kind of survey. Although she is confident about her craft, she is concerned about acquiring the 'right' information she needs to make better decisions, particularly for those decisions relating to her customer base. She is also quite busy and doesn't have a lot of time to waste, so she wants to ensure she has the appropriate research plan.

Judy does have at her disposal a database of her current (Irish) customers. She can also get information about customers from the major retailers who sell her product. In addition, as a member of the Galway Chamber of Commerce, she has access to a research report, *Galway Tourism 1997*, which the Chamber of Commerce produced. According to this report, there were 920,000 visitors to Galway City in 1996. These visitors stayed an average of 3.5 days in the city and spent an average of £60 per day. Typically, for every £1 spent by tourists in Galway City, about 8p was spent on souvenirs and gifts.

Despite having this information, she is considering how best to use it in developing her strategies. How would you advise her?

Data and Information Needs

1. With respect to Judy Greene's customer base, how would you define the population?
2. What sources of information could she use to develop a sample frame?
3. Do you believe she should engage in probability or non-probability sampling or perhaps both?
4. Given your answers to the above questions, what suggestions would you make to Judy Greene in designing a survey which will address her informational needs?

***This case was written by Ann Torres, National University of Ireland, Galway. It is intended as a basis for class discussion rather than to illustrate either effective or ineffective handling of an administrative situation. The case is based on a real situation, though some information has been disguised. The author wishes to thank Judy Greene for her kind permission to use the material in this case.

Chapter 11

SAMPLE SIZE DETERMINATION

> - **Chapter Overview**
> - Introduction • Non-Probability Sample Size Determination
> - The Normal Distribution Curve • The Sampling Distribution for the Mean • The Sampling Distribution for the Proportion • Confidence Intervals • Sample Size Formulae • Sample Size Determination, Finite Populations • Summary

- **Introduction**

We have seen from the last chapter that there are five key questions every researcher needs to ask about sampling.[1]

1. How has the population been defined?
2. What sampling method was used?
3. What level of accuracy was chosen?
4. How big was the sample?
5. What degree of confidence can be placed in the findings?

So far, we have answered these with the one exception of 'How big a sample to select?' This issue, sample size determination, is the focus of this chapter.

In choosing an appropriate sample size, we are deciding upon the accuracy we want our sample to have and the amount of error we can or cannot tolerate. That's to say, sample size is about how similar we want our sample to be, compared to the population from which it is drawn. At this point, it would seem as if sample size is all about statistics. While this is true of probability sampling, it is important to know that there are a number of alternative methods available to marketing researchers in determining the sample size for non-probability samples. This aside, statistical theory continues to play an important part in sample size determination.

As with the previous discussion about sampling theory, statistical sample size determination has its own terminology. At this point, it is useful for the reader to review some of the basic concepts in statistics, such as measures of central tendency and dispersion, as these and others impact upon sample size. Chapter 12 presents some of these together with worked examples. That done, we examine the normal distribution, standard deviation, mean and confidence intervals, to understand how accuracy, confidence, error and sample size are related. As one would expect, this discussion can get complex, so we confine ourselves and our discussion of statistical principles to simple random sampling. Formulae for stratified random sampling and cluster sampling[2] are beyond the scope of this book. Thus, by the end of this chapter, the reader will become knowledgeable about the:

1. characteristics and properties of a normal distribution curve;
2. standardised value Z;
3. confidence interval estimates;
4. computing of sample size formulates for large and small samples;
5. non-statistical considerations for non-probability sample size determination.

• Non-Probability Sample Size Determination

When we are using a non-probability sampling procedure, such as convenience or quota sampling, we do not need statistical formulae for non-probability sampling. Instead, we can employ less objective strategies to determine the best-suited sample size for our sample. Suppose you are conducting exploratory research to gauge if there is an opening for a complementary school of alternative medicine and healing in Ireland. Time and money are severely limited. You have already chosen non-probability sampling. How do you decide on the number of people to include in your sample? Faced with such a situation, you can choose from the following options: *[use less objective strategies to determine size:]*

1. Intuition, Convenience *[Judgement]*

You pick a particular number for no other reason other than it is what suits you, the time and budget constraints and it is a figure you are psychologically comfortable with. For example, you choose 1,000 people as a nice round, even number. This is very much the 'thumbs in the air' approach.

2. Cost Limitations, Affordability

This translates into how large a sample we can afford — what our budget constraints are at the sampling phase, but also at other stages, such as fieldwork, photocopying, etc. *[Time]*

3. Industry Standards, Comparability

This is where you try to emulate what other similar projects or industry standards have done in an effort to be comparable with them, e.g. other healing schools have been set up in France and Switzerland, and have interviewed 5% of the total adult population, so you take 5% of the Irish population as your sample size. This assumes that the previous projects had chosen suitable sample sizes. *[Time/money limited]*

Remember, in choosing a sample size for non-probability samples, statistical generalisation is not required, therefore, we can be more flexible in selecting the

The sampling Distrib of Proportion => the larger the samples taken, the more likely the sample proportions will be closer to the actual population proportion

exact number of respondents to gather information from, as each of the above approaches demonstrate. Now, we are ready to consider statistical sample size approaches used for probability samples. To this end, we begin by examining the normal distribution curve.

• The Normal Distribution Curve

Suppose that the marketing researcher collects a large set of data, say 10,000 values from a sample, relating to the daily sales figures for a retail outlet. If these sales figures were listed individually, the sheer volume of numbers would obscure any information contained in the sample figures. Hence the maxim, 'a picture is worth a thousand words'. A histogram can provide a pictorial or graphical view of how such data is distributed. Even more useful, it is possible to express the distribution (of a histogram) in a neat and compact form by a mathematical formula. Hence, in the interest of extracting information from a sample, we can go from raw data to a histogram to a mathematical formula for the distribution of the data.

One of the more useful and popular probability distributions is the normal distribution, also known as the normal curve, as shown in Figure 11.1.

Figure 11.1 The normal distribution curve

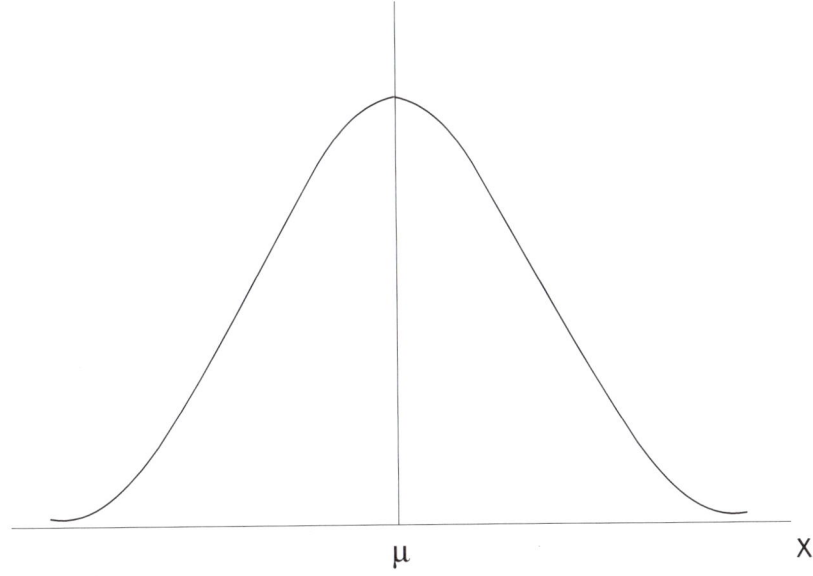

The appropriate mathematical formula for this normal curve is X~N(μ,σ). This formula tells us that:

1. X is just a symbol and represents the random variable of interest, e.g. shop sales, the height of students, the number of shoes purchased, etc. X is not a fixed quantity, it is random, i.e., shop sales are not fixed, but randomly change from day to day and hour to hour.
2. '~' reads 'distributed as'.
3. N stands for normal.
4. μ is the expected value of X, or the long-term average of X.
5. σ^2 refers to the variance of X and is a measure of the spread or dispersion of the data in a sample about its own sample mean.

The properties, among others, of this N (μ,σ^2) curve are:

1. The curve is symmetric about its mean.
2. It is a bell-shaped curve, the highest point being the mean. The curve falls away relatively slowly at first either side of the mean, μ, in other words, there is a high probability of the data values occurring just a little above or below the mean. The further one moves away from the mean, in either direction, the smaller the probability of a data value occurring.
3. Prob (a < X < b) = area under the curve between a and b. Don't get lost in the symbols. X is the random variable of interest and a and b are simply specified values of X. For example, say X represents the daily sales figures of newspapers in Ireland and we want to find the probability that the daily sales figures on any given day will exist between 140,000 and 210,000 papers. We simply write this as Prob(140,000< X <210,000) or P(140,000< X <210,000).
4. X~N(0,1) reads that the curve has a mean = 0 and standard deviation = 1.

This characteristic X~N(0,1) is often referred to as the *standard normal distribution*, where we denote the random variable X, by the special symbol, Z where Z~N(0,1). In other words, the standard normal distribution is very valuable to us, as it enables us to transform any ordinary variable X e.g. X~N(5,1) or X~N(2,12) into a standardised value, Z, using the equation:

$$Z = \frac{X - \mu}{\sigma}$$

which reads as the value to be transformed minus the mean, divided by the standard deviation[3]. Suppose that the auditing times for companies in Cork city are well described by a normal distribution with a mean of 7 hours and a standard deviation of 3 hours. What is the probability that an accountant will spend more than 10 hours auditing any particular company in Cork city? Well, using the terminology above, let X = auditing time of a Cork city company. Then, X ~N (7, 3). We require P (X > 10). Using the transformation $Z = \frac{X-\mu}{\sigma}$, we obtain

$$P(X>10) = P\left(\frac{X-\mu}{\sigma} > \frac{10-7}{3}\right) = P(Z>1) = 0.3413.$$

Therefore, there is a 34.13% probability that an accountant will spend more than 10 hours auditing any particular company in Cork city. The advantages of applying this transformation lie in probabilities of the resultant variable Z being found in Appendix 2.

Thus, Z represents the standard deviations from the mean. Using a normal distribution table such as that in Appendix 2, we can say as shown in figure 11.2 that:

68% of observations will occur between Z = -1 and Z = +1; area = .682
95% of observations will occur between Z = -2 and Z = +2; area = .955
99% of observations will occur between Z = -3 and Z = +3; area = .977
(Note, these figures have been rounded up, e.g. 95% implies Z = –1.96 to Z = +1.96).

Figure 11.2 The normal distribution curve and Z values

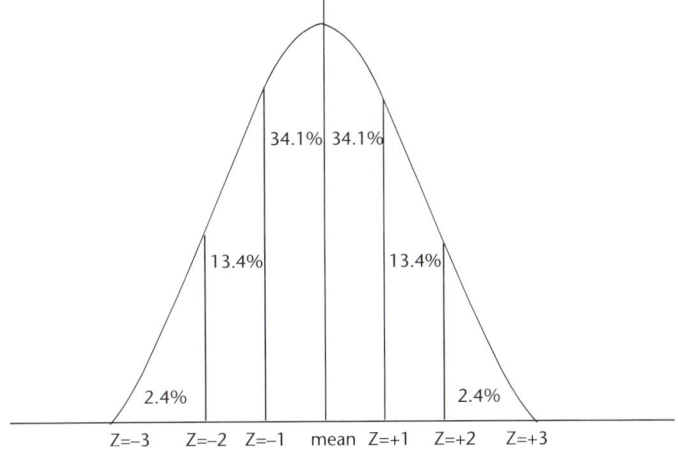

• **The Sampling Distribution for the Mean**

Suppose that a clothing company wishes to estimate the average income of female shoppers in Ireland. To this end, a simple random sample of 120 females was selected and the average X noted. Now suppose we draw another 99 samples, each with a sample size of 120, to obtain a total of 100 samples. The variable X is subject to fluctuations, so the value of X changes from sample to sample. What is interesting is that the different means from the different samples from the same population can be arranged in a frequency distribution and that this sampling distribution (of the mean) will be approximately normally distributed[3]. So, the sampling distribution of the mean for large n (n ≥ 30) is normally distributed with

$$\bar{X} \sim N \left(\mu, \frac{\sigma^2}{n}\right)$$

As the sample size increases, the more likely our sample mean is to cluster around the true population mean and so, the standard error of the mean decreases, as is intuitively expected. Furthermore, based upon the normal distribution, we can say that 95% of the sample means would be within ±1.96 standard error units of the population mean. The same logic applies to the sampling distribution for the proportion.

• **The Sampling Distribution for the Proportion**

The larger the samples taken, the more likely the sample proportions will be closer to the actual population proportion. Increasing the sample size will decrease the variability of the sampling distribution for the proportion. The sampling distribution for a proportion (P) for large samples, i.e. n ≥ 30, is also normally distributed with

$$P \sim N \left(\pi, \frac{\pi(1-\pi)}{n}\right)$$

where P = sample proportion
       π = population proportion
       n = sample size.

We can also say that –95% of the sample proportions would be within +/–1.96 standard error units of the population proportion.

Another issue for the researcher is to decide how much sampling error to tolerate; or, asked in another way, how confident does the researcher wish to be about the sample results? This introduces the concept of confidence intervals.

• **Confidence Intervals**

In attempting to estimate a population value, the confidence interval is a statistical expression of how close we believe we have come to estimating it. It is a range of values that we are confident, but not certain, reflects the population parameter. It is based on the premise that μ = X̄ ± sampling error. Consider the example where the gross earnings of a sample of 64 industrial workers in Dundalk is found to have a mean of £260 and a standard deviation of £32. The mean of £260 is a single estimate of the true average earnings of industrial workers in Dundalk. We know that if we took another sample of 64 workers, we would, more than likely, obtain a different value. To combat this shortfall, we use the confidence interval formula

$$\text{Confidence interval} = \bar{X} \pm Z \frac{\sigma}{\sqrt{n}}$$

where X̄ = sample mean
Z = Z value reflects the level of confidence we would like
σ = standard deviation of the population
n = sample size

So, in our example, there is a 95% chance that μ is contained between £252.16 and £267.84. In this manner, we often report the confidence interval for the unknown parameter in addition to the sample statistic. For 90% confidence, Z = 1.65; for 99% confidence, Z = 2.58. The 95% confidence interval is the most popular in marketing research. If we require any other confidence level, the normal distribution table (Appendix 2) is consulted to locate the Z that corresponds to the required level. For example, an 80% confidence, Z = 1.28.

Similar logic applies in calculating the confidence level for the mean μ, when samples are small, i.e. samples with less than 30 respondents. The appropriate formula is:

$$\text{Confidence interval} = \bar{X} \pm t_{(n-1)} \frac{s}{\sqrt{n}} \quad \text{where } \frac{s}{\sqrt{n}} = \text{standard error of the mean}$$

The only difference between this formula and the previous one is that instead of referring to a normal distribution table (and therefore Z values), we now reference a t-table, as in Appendix 3, with n–1 degrees of freedom.

To estimate the confidence interval for the proportion P, we use:

$$P \pm Z \sqrt{\frac{P(1-P)}{n}}$$

where P = sample proportion
Z = the Z value that equates with the level of confidence sought
n = sample size.

As an example of the construction of a confidence interval for the population proportion, assume we have drawn a random sample of 50 shoppers from a shopping centre in Athlone. 75% of the shoppers have a credit card in their possession. We want to obtain a 90% confidence interval for the true population proportion of shoppers with a credit card. Using the formula above for population proportion, P = 0.75,

Z = 1.65 and n = 50. Based on this, we could be 90% confident that the percentage of the shoppers with a credit card is between 65.9% and 85.1%.

• Sample Size Formulae

We are now in a position to use the concept of the confidence interval, the sample mean and standard deviation, along with the normal distribution curve to determine, in advance, the degree of confidence we seek. Thus, when estimating the population mean, the sample size formula is:

$$n = \frac{Z^2 \sigma^2}{E^2}$$

where n = unknown, to be determined, sample size
Z = number of standard error units reflecting the required confidence level (95% confidence ⇒ Z = 1.96)
σ = known or estimated standard deviation of the population
E = allowable error, the maximum difference we will tolerate between our sample mean and the population mean.

For example, a department store wishes to determine, within £150, the average credit card purchases for shoppers in Dublin. Based on past experience, the standard deviation of this population is estimated at £1,500. The manager in question wants to be 95% confident of the results and has asked you, the marketing assistant, what sample size is required? Using the formula above, where Z = 1.96; σ = 1500 and E = 150,

$$n = \frac{1.96^2 \; 1500^2}{150^2}$$

and the required sample size is 385.

Thus, by drawing a sample of 385 from this population, we are 95% certain that the sample mean (X) will not differ from the population mean, μ by more than £150. If the manager reduced the allowable error from £150 to £50, in this scenario, Z = 1.96; σ = 1500 and E = 50. So, the required sample size would be:

$$n = \frac{1.96^2 \; 1500^2}{50^2} = 3457.44 = 3458 \text{ rounded up.}$$

That is to say, by drawing a sample of 3558 from this population, we are 95% certain that the sample mean, X will not differ from the population mean, μ by more than £50. You'll note from these examples, that in order to achieve a more accurate estimate of μ, the sample size has increased. This result is to be expected, because in order to reduce error, we require more information from the sample, which is reflected by an increased sample size.

Turning our attention to the population proportion and sample size, the same logic applies. In this case, the formula is given by:

$$n = \frac{Z^2 (\pi)(1-\pi)}{E^2}$$

where n = required sample size
Z = Z value reflecting the associated level of confidence (for 95% confidence, Z = 1.96)
π = proportion of the population with the attribute of interest
E = allowable error or the maximum difference between the sample and population proportion that we are willing to tolerate.

For example, a financial body would like to determine, within 5 percentage points, the proportion of Irish women who have taken out a mortgage within the past month. Assuming a confidence level of 90% is satisfactory to you, the true proportion to be no more than 0.3, you wonder what sample size is required.

Employing the above formula for population proportion, where Z = 1.65; π = 0.3 and E = 0.05, n can be calculated as:

$$n = \frac{1.65^2 \, 0.3 \, (1 - 0.3)}{0.05^2} = 228.69 = \text{rounded up to 229.}$$

Thus, by drawing a sample of 229 from this population, we are 90% certain that the sample proportion (P) will not differ from the population proportion π by more than 5%.

If we do not know the value of π, which is frequently the case in marketing, the researcher still applies the above formula for population proportions. The question still remains, what value does the researcher assign to π? The only choice is where π = 0.5 implying that there is no reason to assume that the proportion of women who took out a mortgage in the past month is greater than those who did not, or vice-versa, hence let π = 0.5. Applying the sample size formula, we obtain:

$$n = \frac{1.65^2 \, 0.5 \, (1-0.5)}{0.05^2} = 272.25, \text{ rounded up to 273.}$$

This says that by drawing a sample of 273 from this population, we are 90% certain that the sample proportion (p) will not differ from the population proportion, π, by more than 5%. This tells us, that when we possess no information pertaining to the population proportion, π, we require more information from the sample (in the form of a larger sample size) to obtain the same error that is obtained when information about π is available. One final comment, rather than opt to let $\pi = 0.5$ when it is unknown, in the interests of obtaining an estimate of the true proportion, π, we can undertake exploratory research or utilise secondary sources of data to identify π.

- ## Sample Size Determination, Finite Populations

The discussion so far, of sample size determination, assumes that the sample is relatively small compared to the total population from which it is drawn. However, when the sample itself accounts for 5% or more of the population from which it is drawn, the sample size formulae derived earlier must be modified.

When estimating the mean of a finite population, the sample size formula is given by:

$$n = \frac{\sigma^2}{\frac{E^2}{Z^2} + \frac{\sigma^2}{N}}$$

where all the terms have been explained earlier, noting that N is the population size. Consider the previous example where the department store wishes to determine, within £150, the average credit card purchases for shoppers in Dublin where, based upon past experience, it is estimated that the standard deviation for this population is about £1,500. Assuming a confidence level of 95%, what sample size is required if we suppose the population consisted of 2,500 members. Employing the last formula, with N = 2500, we obtain:

$$n = \frac{1500^2}{\frac{150^2}{1.96^2} + \frac{1500^2}{2500}} = 332.99, \text{ rounded up to 333.}$$

If the population consisted of 1,000 members, then the sample size is given by:

$$n = \frac{1500^2}{\frac{150^2}{1.96^2} + \frac{1500^2}{1000}} = 277.54, \text{ rounded up to 278.}$$

From this, we note that the decrease in sample size depends on the population size.

When dealing with the sample size required when estimating the proportion of a finite population, the sample size formula is given by:

$$n = \frac{\pi(1-\pi)}{\frac{E^2}{Z^2} + \frac{\pi(1-\pi)}{N}}$$

where all the terms are as before and N = population size. Returning to our financial body who would like to determine, within 5 percentage points, the proportion of Irish women who have taken out a mortgage within the past month. If we assume that $\pi = 0.3$, the population = 2,500 members and we employ a confidence level of 90%, the required sample size is:

$$n = \frac{0.3(1-0.3)}{\frac{0.05^2}{1.65^2} + \frac{0.3(1-0.3)}{2500}} = 209.52, \text{ rounded up to } 210.$$

If the population consisted of no more than 1,000 members, then the sample size required is given by:

$$n = \frac{0.3(1-0.3)}{\frac{0.05^2}{1.65^2} + \frac{0.3(1-0.3)}{1000}} = 186.13, \text{ rounded up to } 187.$$

As was observed when determining the sample size for the mean of a finite population, decreases in sample size depend on the population size.

• **Summary**

In this chapter, we have been primarily concerned with the statistical methods used to determine sample size for probability simple random samples. Our examination began with the normal distribution curve, the distribution of the sample mean or proportion and the confidence interval giving the range of values likely to contain the population parameter. These assist in determining sample size formulae. The implementation of the formulae requires specification of the maximum desired error between the sample estimate and the population parameter and the selection of the level of confidence required. The larger the size of the sample drawn from the population, the closer the sample estimate will be to the value of the population parameter. An inverse relationship exists between sample size and the desired error, i.e. as sample size increases, error decreases and vice-versa.

Key Terms

Mean
Sample statistics
Frequency distribution
Standardised normal distribution
Parameter
Sample mean
Sampling distribution

Standard deviation
Population parameters
Normal distribution
Confidence interval
Sample statistic
Sample proportion
Standard error

Questions

1. What methods can be used to determine the sample size for non-probability samples?
2. What is the mean and how can it be calculated?
3. What is the standard deviation and how can it be calculated?
4. Describe the properties of a normal distribution curve.
5. In a normal distribution, what value of Z is necessary for the area from −Z to +Z to be 0.75, 0.80, 0.85, and 0.97?
6. What is the sampling distribution of the mean?
6. What role does accuracy and levels of confidence play in sample size determination?
7. What is the most popular level of confidence in marketing research, and why?
8. Describe the appropriate sample size formula for:
   (a) dealing with a population mean
   (b) dealing with a population proportion
   (c) dealing with a finite population mean and
   (d) dealing with a finite population proportion?
9. When is the t-table employed in sample size determination?

Problems and Assignments

1. Suppose that the average monthly food bill for residences in Cork city is £600, with a standard deviation of £200. What is the probability the resulting sample mean will be greater than £650, if a simple random sample of 100 homes is selected in the city?
2. Suppose it is known that 25% of Irish households are inadequately heated. What percentage of a simple random sample of 100 homes would have estimated the population proportion as 0.18 or more?
3. A sample of 64 items resulted in a sample mean of 160 and a standard deviation of 15.
   (a) compute the 90% confidence interval for the population mean;
   (b) compute the 95% confidence interval for the population mean;

(c) assume the same sample mean and sample standard deviation were obtained from a sample of 120 items. Provide a 90% confidence interval for the population mean;
(d) assume the same sample mean and sample standard deviation were obtained from a sample of 120 items. Provide a 95% confidence interval for the population mean;
(e) what is the effect of a larger sample size on the interval estimate of a population mean?

4. In a simple random sample of 1,225 persons, the sample average annual consumer expenditure on leisure activities is found to be £900, with a standard deviation of £420. What is the 95% confidence interval for the population mean?

5. A random sample of industrial workers finds that 64% have one or more children. The survey is claimed to have an error of no more than 5 percentage points. Assuming the 95% confidence level, what sample size was used?

6. A simple random sample of 1,200 people includes 750 individuals who have a personal pension plan. What is the 90% confidence interval for the proportion of people in this population who have a personal pension plan?

7. A researcher would like to determine, within 6 percentage points, the proportion of the Irish population who have visited the cinema within the past week. Assuming a confidence interval of 90% is satisfactory:
(a) without making any assumptions about the true value of the population proportion, what sample size is required?
(b) assume that the true proportion to be no more than 0.35, by how many individuals would it be possible to reduce the sample compared to the sample size above?

8. In Question 7, what would be the required sample size if the population of interest consisted of students at a college with an enrolment of 1,600?

9. A simple random sample of the general public found that 76% own a cat or dog. The results claim to have an error of no more than 5 percentage points. Assuming the 95% confidence level, what sample size was used?

10. A bank, in surveying 700 of its customers, has found the average savings account to have £550, with a standard deviation of £250. What is the 95% confidence interval for the population mean?

Case Study
The Examiner in association with Dairygold National Women's Survey*

A national women's survey was conducted by Rigney Dolphin Ltd, consultants, for *The Examiner* newspaper in association with Dairygold. 1,143 women were surveyed, in-home, during December (between the 9th and 19th), at 76 locations throughout the country. The margin of error in the results of the study is estimated at plus or minus 3%.

Women were interviewed about a range of attitudes and behaviours including crime, parenting, finance, working outside the home, working in the home, equality, feminism, media, home entertainment, sexuality, and eating habits. The questionnaire was developed to a stage where most questions were capable of being closed-ended. The inclusion of an 'other' category facilitated variability in response. The question format meant that data was collected in a standardised way, making computer coding and analysis easier, and minimising interviewer–interviewee interaction bias. A sample question is reproduced in Box 11.1.

Box 11.1 A sample question

Question 6 When you relax which of the following would you do?
(Tick all that are identified) (Prompt 3)

(a) Have your hair done □ (b) Have a social drink □
(c) Walk □ (d) Talk to a friend □
(e) Have a cup of tea □ (f) Aerobics □
(g) Gardening □ (h) Eat □
(i) Read □ (j) Listen to music □
(k) Sports □ (l) Other □

The Sampling Procedure
The sample was designed to represent Irish women. Multi-stage cluster sampling was deemed the most appropriate method. It was chosen as the method best able to capture the diversity of the members of the population both in terms of their opinions and geography. Multi-stage methods are often used where a heterogeneous group is being studied at the one time. The first stage of the sampling procedure involved a demographic breakdown of the research population. Women were demographically divided under the following headings:

A. Location: urban, rural-overall, rural (non-farming), farmers
B. Age: 15–24, 25–44, 45–64, 65+
C. Marital status: married, single, other
D. Parents/non parents
E. Working outside the home/working in the home

Following the demographic division of the sample, the second stage of the process was a locational split. Forty-four urban locations were selected in the towns and cities listed in Box 11.2, and a rural sample was selected from 32 locations throughout the country.

Box 11.2 Urban locations

Category 1	Category 2	Category 3	Category 4	Category 5
Dublin	Clonmel	Cavan	Gorey	Castlerea
Cork	Sligo	Portlaoise		
Limerick	Tralee			
Galway				
Waterford				

The Sample Frame

The sample frame was chosen to be representative of the population under study. Box 11.3 details the actual sample frame used in the study. As can be seen from the table a sample size of 1,143 women was used. This was a large sample size which gave the authors of the study some confidence in the generalisability of their findings. Census and labour force survey data is provided in Box 11.4 for comparison purposes.

Box 11.3 Sample Frame

N = 1,143 women

Overall	100%
Urban	61%
Rural-overall	39%
Rural (Non-farming)	22%
Farmers	17%
Age 15–24	23%
Age 25–44	40%
Age 45–64	25%
Age 65+	12%
Married	52%
Single	31%
Martial status — Other	17%
Parents	60%
Non-parents	40%
Working outside home	40%
Working in-home	60%

Box 11.4
Census and labour force survey data

Total population*	3,523,900
Males	1,759,000
Females	1,765,000

Females in age categories:

0–14	459,600
15–24	300,300
25–44	463,300
45–64	310,800
65 or over	231,000
Total	1,765,000

Female marital status:

Single	453,500
Married	667,000
Separated/widowed	56,400

> *Female work status:*
>
> | | |
> |---|---|
> | Outside home | 377,000 |
> | In-home | 640,600 |
>
> * Figures may vary with rounding. Data in table is from similar time frame as the Women's survey.
> Source: Central Statistics Office — Population and Labour Force Surveys.

Questions

1. Discuss the appropriateness of the multi-stage cluster sampling procedure for this particular study.
2. Examine the reasons why such a methodology was chosen.
3. (a) What alternative methods of sampling would be available for the study? Consider factors such as representativeness in your answer.
   (b) If you were a marketer constrained by budget, what alternative sampling methods would you have considered in this case, and what trade-offs would this have involved?
4. In terms of the sample size used in the study, is it representative and why? How confident would you be in the results?
5. Determine the factors used to arrive at the sample size in this case.

* This case was written by Dr Tom O'Toole, IT, Waterford and Dr Frank Dolphin, Rigney Dolphin Research. It is intended to be used as a basis for class discussion rather than to illustrate either effective or ineffective handling of an administrative situation. The case is based on a real situation, though certain information has been disguised. The authors would like to thank *The Examiner*, Dairygold and Rigney Dolphin Research for their kind permission to use the material in this case.

Part 4

DATA ANALYSIS AND PRESENTATION

Chapter 12

DATA PREPARATION AND PROCESSING

- **Chapter Overview**
- Introduction • Data Analysis • Editing • Coding • Tabulating the Data • Statistical Summarisation • Tables and Graphs

---

• Introduction

Most of the preceding chapters have dealt with the collection of data. This chapter is concerned with what we do after it has been collected, i.e. taking the raw data we have collected and converting it into a form that facilitates analysis and reporting. The end objective of most research is to provide information. There is a difference between raw data and information. Often a research survey will result in several hundred usable questionnaires of up to ten pages each. This represents a sizeable stack of paper. Data analysis helps transform this raw data into the 'list of needed information' which was established at the beginning of the marketing research process. That is to say, the raw data collected in the field must be transformed into information that will answer the marketing manager's questions.

• Chapter Objectives

Having read Chapter 12 you will be able to:

1. Discuss what is meant by data analysis.
2. Describe the editing process.
3. Understand the coding process.
4. Explain simple and cross tabulation.
5. Discuss measures of central tendency and measures of dispersion.
6. Outline the main graphical methods of summarisation and presentation.

• Data Analyis

Data analysis can be defined as 'a set of methods and techniques that can be used to obtain information and insights from the data'.[1] Data analysis, while unique to each study, requires the research to perform the following tasks:

1. Editing.
2. Coding.
3. Tabulation.
4. Summarisation.

- **Editing**

After receiving all questionnaires from the field, a preliminary check is made before they are subjected to editing. This preliminary examination helps weed out unusable questionnaires. These may, perhaps, have missing pages, have sizeable portions or sections unanswered, been completed by a demographically incorrect respondent or by a respondent that clearly did not take seriously (questionnaire dotted with 'funny' comments) or understand the task at hand, or the questionnaire was received after the pre established cut-off date. Whatever the problem, this initial screening identifies returned questionnaires that are clearly unusable and unsuitable to more rigorous editing.

Editing is the process of reviewing questionnaires with the objective of increasing accuracy and precision. It requires checking for completeness, consistency and legibility of data and making the data ready for coding. Questionnaires are normally edited at least twice before being submitted for data entry. Fieldworkers and field supervisors are frequently responsible for conducting initial field editing on the same day as the interview. Less editing is required for CAPI and CATI interviews since checks can be done during the interview.[2] After editing at field level, the questionnaires or interview forms are later subsequently edited in-house by the analyst. It is important that editing be done consistently. If possible, all (or sections) of the questionnaires should be edited by the same person. It is unwise to erase original data. Edited data should be inserted in a different coloured pen. Likewise another colour should be used for coding. The editing function is time-consuming and tedious. It involves checking for a number of problems including:

1. *Ambiguity*. A response might be legible or it might be unclear, e.g. which of two boxes in a multiple choice question is ticked. Illegibility is more likely to occur when open-ended questions are used and when no interviewer is present.
2. *Inconsistent*. Many surveys use filter questions that direct the sequence of questions according to the respondents' answers. The editor must determine if the answers a respondent gave to one question are consistent with those for other, related questions. For example, a respondent who claims to have a college education may have later checked a box indicating that he has just completed Leaving Certificate.
3. *Incomplete*. Respondents often fail to answer a single question, or a section of the questionnaire, either deliberately or inadvertently. When an individual question is

unanswered, on an otherwise completed questionnaire, it is referred to as *item non-response*. If a questionnaire has too many missing answers it may not be suitable for further data analysis.

4. *Inaccurate.* Unfortunately, most errors are not evident, but factual errors may be recognised.
5. *Interviewer error*, e.g. interviewers may not be giving respondents the correct instructions.
6. *Non-adherence to sampling instructions.* An inappropriate respondent may be included in the sample. For example, if the sampling is supposed to include homeowners, interviews with renters would not be acceptable.
7. *Responses too consistent.* If, for example in a questionnaire containing a large number of multiple-choice questions the respondent has checked the first response category in each, it raises a doubt as to how seriously the respondent took his role as respondent.

When editing identifies one or more of these problems, there are several courses of action open to editors.[3]

1. Where practical, the questionnaire may be returned to the interviewer for his interpretation or for re-interview of the respondent.
2. The editor can attempt to interpret or infer what is recorded.
3. Throw out the particular questionnaire as non-usable.
4. Eliminate only the problem questions and retain the balance of questions.
5. Code illegible or missing answers into a category as 'Don't know' or 'No opinion'.

• Coding

The primary purposes of editing and coding are to eliminate errors in the raw data and to process the data into categories so that tabulation can occur.[4] Editing eliminates errors or points of confusion in the raw data. Coding assigns the data into pertinent categories, to speed up tabulation. Careful editing makes the coding job easier. The design of the questionnaire should anticipate the editing and coding work since the physical arrangement of the form must allow editing and coding space. Where possible, codes are assigned to the alternative answers, and included in the questionnaire format. This is referred to as pre-coding. Pre-coding is appropriate with dichotomous and multiple-choice questions, which have only limited selection of predetermined responses. When responses are of the open-ended type, it will be necessary to assign responses to categories that have been selected after the data have been collected. More about this later.

Coding Process

Coding is an important step in preparing survey documents for data entry. Coding means assigning a code, usually a number, to represent each specific response to each specific question.

There are two different methods of coding questionnaires depending on the type of software being used to analyse the data. One method of inputting is to use ASCII data which breaks down the data set into individual columns. The code will include the column position and the data field, e.g. if gender is a question, 1 could represent male and 2 female. Therefore the question for gender would be assigned one column since both responses are not possible in that they are in fact mutually exclusive. This column is termed a 'field', which means a single item of data. All the combined fields, for instance containing the demographic characteristics of the respondent, are then referred to as a record. Therefore when the data is printed in a numerical format the columns represent the fields and the rows represent the records. Each record typically contains 80 columns and a number of records may be used for each respondent depending on the size of the questionnaire.

Table 12.1

	Fields Column 1–4	Column 5–6	Column 7	Column 8–9
Record 1	1247	27	1	12
Record 2	1248	32	2	14
Record 3	1249	45	2	11
Record 4	1250	58	1	09

In the above example, column 1–4 represents the individual questionnaire, column 5–6 represents the age of the respondent, column 7 represents the gender and column 8–9 represents the employment status of the respondent. Therefore record one refers to questionniare number 1247 who is a male aged 27 with a job coded as 12. This example assumes that the oldest person to be interviewed will be aged 99 years. Therefore should a respondent be aged 100 years or more either the age will be entered incorrectly as 99 years or the entire coding system will have to be changed. This is because 100 would obviously take up three columns whereas the system has only allocated two columns for the age of the respondent.

This method of encoding is of benefit when the data input is being done independently of the analysis and the person inputting does not know which software package is being used.

The more usual method nowadays is to use statistical packages, e.g. SPSS, MINITAB or SAS which use a spreadsheet or similar to assign a variable to each column and a row to every response.

Table 12.2

Respondent No.	Q.1	Q.2	Q.3a	Q.3b	Q.3c
1234	1	2	5	0	4

Using this format requires the researcher to take care in designing the questionnaire, particularly in relation to mutually exclusive and non-mutually exclusive responses. For example if asking the respondent for their gender, as in a previous example, the answer will be male or female which as before will be assigned a single column for the variable 'gender'. But if the question asks the respondent to tick 'all which apply' then a column will need to be assigned to each possible response as above Q. 3a, Q. 3b etc. It is immaterial whether the columns are headed with the question number or the subject of the question once the person inputting the data is totally aware of the protocol being used. Once again the questionniare will contain the relevant codes for the responses beside each question and the responses are input as before, except in a spreadsheet format.

If a questionnaire contains only or mainly structured questions it may be pre-coded which means that the codes are assigned before the survey work is conducted and the codes printed on the questionnaire. If the questionnaire is unstructured and contains many open questions the codes may be assigned after the field work is completed or by the interviewer from a codebook.

Categories

In a structured questionnaire containing many multiple-choice or dichotomous questions the categories are established at the questionnaire design stage. It is important that all possible categories be included, so a response such as 'Other' may be required.

Box 12.1

Please indicate *how many* of the following types of accounts or products you have in *your own name*. Please leave blank any boxes which do not apply to you. (For instance, if you have two current accounts with Bank of Ireland you should write '2' in the appropriate column)

	How many with B/I	How many with other financial institutions
Current account	☐	☐
Bank savings account	☐	☐
Other savings or investment account	☐	☐
Credit card	☐	☐
Life assurance	☐	☐
Mortgage	☐	☐
Other loans	☐	☐
Laser card	☐	☐
Other (please specify)	_____	

It is just as important to assign a category for non-responses or missing data. The norm is to assign the number 9 or a multiple of 9 to missing data to overcome blanks in the questionnaire. This is because many software packages will read blanks as zero which may be the value assigned to another response. Obviously the number 9 could not represent a legitimate response in this case.

Box 12.2

Bank of Ireland	Strongly agree	Agree	Neither agree nor disagree	Disagree	Strongly disagree	
Strives to meet customer needs	5	4	3	2	1	12
Is honest in its advertising	5	4	3	2	1	15
Treats customers fairly	5	4	3	2	1	251
Gives value for money	5	4	3	2	1	16

Precoded Questionnaires

Many questionnaires, particularly if being completed over the telephone or independently by the respondent, will be pre-coded. In this type of questionnaire the record number, column number and response value are all printed on the questionnaire. Each questionnaire is assigned the same number of columns containing details of the questionnaire such as week number, sampling point number as well as the responses to each question.

In this example from a Bank of Ireland customer survey each response is numbered 1–5 representing the customer's attitude towards Bank of Ireland. At the right-hand side of the question the field number is shown. Therefore the computer operator knows that the response to the first statement is to go in column number 12.

Postcoded Questionnaires

Coding is usually required for open-ended questions, where respondents write in their answers long-hand as opposed to choosing from existing answer categories listed on the questionnaire. Coding allows these qualitative answers to be further processed on a quantitative basis. The researcher will choose a number of questionnaires, e.g. 100. From these responses a categorisation of the responses to the open questions is designed and then applied to the entire survey. Again it is important that the categories be mutually exclusive and exhaustive. This means that each response should fit into one, and only one category. It also means that every response must fit into a category even if it means adding an 'Other' or 'None of the above' category.

The coding process usually begins with a 'comment summary' (a list of paraphrased verbatim responses from a portion of completed surveys). From the comment summary, numeric codes are built for the most frequently occurring response categories. The advantage of postcoding is that the full range of responses is known in advance of data inputting. This allows for the elimination, or reduction, of the 'Other' category, resulting in more accurate findings.

Box 12.3

Please use the space below for any comments you would like to make about Bank of Ireland, the service we provide and your dealings with us.

_____

_____

_____

Postcoding is difficult to use as there is a danger of inconsistency between coders unless very specific instructions are issued beforehand. In practice more than one coder may be used, each independently coding the completed questionnaires in an attempt to reduce the number of errors. Coding may be carried out before the completion of the questionnaire if the survey is based on work carried out previously. In this case a code book is developed whereby the interviewer will transcribe the verbatim answer of the respondent and then assign a code from the codebook to the response either on a separate codesheet or onto the actual questionnaire.

Development of a 'Code Book'

A code book provides explicit instructions as to coding and recording each variable. It may be used in the field to assist the interviewer or by the researcher to code the variables after the completion of the fieldwork. For example if a respondent is asked a question such as 'What brand of beer did you last buy?' the interviewer will have a list of possible responses in a code book. This allows the interviewer to input a number rather than recording the response. On the other hand the interviewer could simply write down the brand name and the coder would enter the relevant code prior to data entry.

It is important to emphasise that the person with responsibility for developing the code book should have input into the questionnaire design and meetings about the design involving the client. This helps to overcome problems which may not be apparent until the analysis stage and could prove to cause an expensive error. For example a question may ask 'How many times in the past week did you read the *Irish Times*?' The code book could state '0–2 per week means an irregular reader' while '3–6 times equates with a regular reader'. However, the actual data might prove more beneficial than coded data in this case as the use of the code book serves only to limit the analysis to the prescribed categories. Alternatively if the variable 'Other' proves to be a significant variable after data entry it could indicate that at the precoding stage an insufficient number of choices were given to the interviewee.

• Tabulating the Data

Having assigned responses to categories, it is then necessary to count how many responses are in each category. This is called tabulation. Tabulation consists of three activities: sorting, counting and summarising. There are two types of tabulation — simple tabulation and cross tabulation. Tabulation can be done manually or by computer. When the tabulation is done by hand it is referred to as 'tallying'. Otherwise, particularly for large amounts of data, a complete statistical package may be used (more about these later). Before tabulation can begin, the researcher should initially prepare a plan outlining which items of data are to be tabulated separately or in combination with other items. The type and number of tabulations should be determined early in the research process with research objectives and list of needed information stated.

Simple Tabulation

Simple tabulation (also called marginal or one-way tabulation) involves counting a single variable, i.e. on a question-by-question, or item-by-item basis. Tabulation for each variable is independent of the tabulation for the other variables. This leads to a frequency distribution (frequency table) of how many responses were in each of the categories. The relative occurrence, or frequency, of different values of the variable is expressed in percentages. The percentage is often easier to interpret than the actual numbers. A brief discussion on percentages will follow later.

Table 12.3 Example of frequency table for a simple tabulation

Type of PC	Number respondent	%
Dell	85	28
Gateway	92	31
Compaq	90	30
Other	33	11
Total	300	100

Cross Tabulation

Cross tabulation (also known as bivariate cross tabulation) is an extension of simple tabulation. While a frequency distribution describes one variable at a time, cross tabulation describes two or more variables simultaneously. The premise is to look at the responses to one question in relation to responses to one or more other questions. A bivariate tabulation typically results in a table consisting of two or more rows, and two or more columns. Thus, the frequency distribution of one variable is subdivided according to the values or categories of the other variables. Cross tabulation tables are also called contingency tables. A series of cross tabulations may provide greater insights into a complex phenomenon than a single multivariate analysis.[5]

Table 12.4 Example of 2 x 2 matrix

Usage rate	Usage rate of store loyalty card			
	Males		Females	
	No.	%	No.	%
Regularly	50	17	80	27
Occasionally	100	33	120	40
Never	150	50	100	33
Total	300	100	300	100

Cross tabulation is one of the most popular ways of summarising marketing research data. Stopping with simple tabulation may not yield the full value of the research. While cross tabulation could be done manually, it is more common practice to do the analysis using a computer. A number of spreadsheet programs (Lotus 1-2-3, Excel, Quattro Pro) and nearly all statistical packages (e.g. SPSS, MINITAB, and SAS) can generate cross tabulations. Most cross tabulations are of the two-way variety. Yet little difficulty is presented when there are more than two variables being measured. What is required is to present the variables in a two-at-a-time fashion. If there are n-variables, there would be $[n(n-1)]/2$ different presentations. For example, for four different variables, there would be $[4(4-1)]/2$, or six two-way presentations required.

Perhaps the main issue in bivariate and multivariate tabulation is deciding which combination of questions should be tabulated. Surveys may contain dozens of questions. How many of these should be cross tabulated? It is easy to become swamped by the sheer volume of computer printouts if a careful tabulation plan is not developed. The number of cross tabs should be determined early when research objectives are stated. It is often tempting to add variables and develop different relationships among the variables because they might be of interest. However, any awareness of time, cost and spurious relationships should constrain the researcher from such an analysis. Through a preliminary investigation and a continuous contact with the situation, the researcher should be able to develop an intuitive feeling for what the key variables are. Common sense and experiences will go a long way in determining what relationships need to be analysed. To facilitate the comparison of data, one should show percentages rather than frequencies, for it will indicate more clearly the relative size of two or more values. The total number of respondents or observations may be used as a base for computing the percentage. The simplicity of calculating percentages has led to its wide applicability as a statistical tool in marketing research.

Box 12.4 Statistical packages on personal computers

PC-based statistical packages serve a useful purpose for the analysis of small-scale experiments or for teaching. The range of statistical software available on personal computers is quite limited and expensive to purchase. Some packages lack the ability to read external files, e.g. Excel or other spreadsheets, requiring users to type in data. The available facilities and the size of the dataset, while restricted in some cases, are more than adequate for the needs of students and most researchers. The following is a brief description of three of the more commonly used statistical packages. The URL for each of the companies is given to allow students to browse the sites and occasionally access working samples of new products.

MINITAB

MINITAB is a general-purpose data analysis system for organising, analysing, and reporting statistical data. It provides a wide range of basic and advanced functionality while maintaining a high ease of use. MINITAB 10 excels at exploratory data analysis and includes full font, editing, and printing support. The program's import and export commands let you handle Excel, Lotus 1-2-3, Access, Filemaker, FoxPro and other database files.

MINITAB is designed especially for students and research workers with no previous experience of computers. MINITAB 10, which runs on Macs and Windows PCs, is easy to use thanks to a good interface with pull-down menus and dialogue boxes. As such it is generally recommended as an entry-level package for new users. It will meet the requirements of most users but some may need to use one of the more powerful packages.

MINITAB is primarily an interactive package, i.e. commands are submitted one by one from the terminal, and results or errors are displayed on the screen. As you run your Minitab sessions, an editable session window makes it easy to go back and re-try an analysis with different options. This enables the user to carry out further analysis or correct errors.

MINITAB contains a wide range of statistical facilities including descriptive statistics, data manipulation, T tests, analysis of variance, frequency tables, multiple regression, non-parametric statistics, matrix manipulation (including inversion and the calculation of eigenvalues and vectors) and exploratory data analysis.

URL: http://www.minitab.com

SPSS

SPSS stands for Statistical Package for Social Scientists but is used by researchers from many other disciplines. SPSS is an integrated system for statistical data analysis. There is an SPSS Manager that helps you build commands and review output. The Manager includes a menu-based command generator, context-sensitive help, an on-line glossary, and extensive editing capabilities.

Its very powerful data manipulation facilities make it useful for analysing large quantities of data (both numeric and non-numeric, with limited facilities for free text). It has all the facilities available in MINITAB, except for matrix manipulation and exploratory data analysis, but also includes life tables, survival analysis, multivariate analysis and more advanced analysis of variance. SPSS is best suited for analysing medium to large data files or carrying out more advanced analysis than MINITAB can provide. If your requirements meet these criteria then we recommend you to start with SPSS although it is slightly more complex to master than MINITAB.

URL: http://www.spss.com

SAS (Statistical Analysis System)

SAS software provides statistical and graphical tools for analysing market research data. The SAS System also includes a point-and-click interface that provides easy access to commonly used techniques in market research analysis, including conjoint analysis, correspondence analysis, and discrete choice analysis.

SAS/STAT software provides extensive statistical capabilities. Ready-to-use procedures handle a wide range of statistical analyses, including analysis of variance, regression, categorical data analysis, multivariate analysis, survival analysis, psychometric analysis, cluster analysis, and nonparametric analysis.

SAS/STAT software is fully integrated with the rest of the SAS System, so you can easily access data from any source, perform data management, carry out statistical analyses, and then present your findings in a variety of reports and graphs — all within a single software environment.

URL: http://www.sas.com

- **Statistical Summarisation**

There are two major kinds of summarising statistics.[6] The first provides measures of the midpoint of the distribution and is known as measures of central tendency. The second gives an indication of the amount of variation in the data comprising the distribution and is known as measures of dispersion.

Measures of Central Tendency

The three most common ways to describe the centrality of a set of data are the arithmetic mean, median and mode.

Mean

The arithmetic mean is properly computed from interval or ratio scale data. it is the most commonly used measure of centrality of a set of data and in non-statistical applications is frequently referred to as the 'average'. It is calculated by summing all the observations in a batch of data and then dividing the total by the number of items involved.

Thus, for a sample containing a batch of n observations $x_1, x_2 \ldots x_n$, the arithmetic mean (denoted by the symbol $\overline{X}$ — called 'X — bar') can be written

$$\overline{X} = \frac{(x_1, x_2 + \ldots + x_n)}{n}$$

For example, suppose that we have five scores: $x_1 = 10$, $x_2 = 12$, $x_3 = 15$, $x_4 = 18$, and $x_5 = 20$. Then the mean $(\overline{X})$ would be:

$$\overline{X} = \frac{10 + 12 + 15 + 18 + 20}{5}$$

$$= \frac{75}{5} = 15$$

Instead of writing the equation for the mean as above, we can shorten it to

$$\overline{X} = \frac{\sum_{i=1}^{n} x_i}{n}$$

or simply:

$$\overline{X} = \frac{\sum x_i}{n}$$

where $\overline{X}$ = sample arithmetic mean
 n = sample size
 x_i = ith observation of the random variable X
 $\sum_{i=1}^{n} x_i$ = summation of all x values in the sample.

An important characteristic of the mean is that we can calculate it without having to first arrange the data into a frequency distribution or to rank order the scores. Occasionally, however, arithmetic means must be calculated from absolute frequency distributions. In practice, the formula that we have already for the (arithmetic) means need extending, because real-life figures occur in groups, not individually. Suppose that we group the figures of our simple example (see Table 12.3). The xf column merely saves us the trouble of adding each x value separately. We would never add 12 equal heights of 5ft 10 inches separately, for example; instead we multiply to get the total contribution of 12 times 70 in. (i.e. 840 in.) from that height category. With grouped data the midpoint of each category is multiplied by the number of observations in that category, the resultant values are summed, and this total is divided by the total number of observations. This process is represented in the following formula:

$$\overline{X} = \frac{\sum_{i=1}^{h} f_i x_i}{n}$$

where:
f_i = frequency of the ith class
x_i = midpoint of that class
h = number of classes
n = total number of observations

Table 12.5 Calculation of weighted arithmetic mean

x_i	f_i	$x_i f_i$
3	2	6
4	1	4
5	1	5
6	1	6
7	3	21
8	1	8
9	0	0
10	1	10
	10	60

$$\bar{X} = \frac{\Sigma x_i f_i}{\Sigma n} = \frac{60}{10} = 6$$

Averaging Means

Often we are given the means of two or more samples and we wish to find the mean of all the measures combined into one group. This is done by computing the weighted mean. Suppose that a test is given to three groups with the following results:

$\bar{X}_1 = 60 \quad n_1 = 10$
$\bar{X}_2 = 50 \quad n_2 = 60$
$\bar{X}_3 = 40 \quad n_3 = 30$

where $\bar{X}_i$ and n_i stand for the mean and the number of individuals in groups 1, etc. We wish to find the mean of the three groups combined, $\bar{X}_t$.

Previously we learned that the mean is equal to the sum of the measures divided by the number of cases:

$$\bar{X} = \frac{\Sigma x_i}{n}$$

If we have the mean ($\bar{x}$) and the number of cases (n), we can obtain the sum of the measures by solving the equation:

$$\Sigma x = n \bar{x}$$

This is exactly the procedure followed in obtaining the mean for the total group. We get the sum of the observations for each group and add these, then divide this obtained sum by the total number of cases as follows:

$\bar{X}$	n	$n\bar{x}$
60	10	600
50	60	3000
40	30	1200
	N = 100	$\Sigma n\bar{x}$ = 4800

$$\bar{X}_t = \frac{4800}{100} = 48$$

It should be noted that this mean cannot be obtained by averaging the three sample means. In this case the average of the three means would be 50. Only when the number in each sample is identical can the means of the samples be averaged directly to obtain the mean of the total group.

The widespread use of the mean to describe the 'middle' of a set of data is not accidental. Aside from the fact that it is a simple, familiar measure, the mean has the following desirable properties:
1. It can be calculated for any set of numerical data, so it always exists.
2. A set of numerical data has one and only one mean, so it is always unique.
3. It lends itself to further statistical treatment (for instance, the mean of several sets of data can be combined into the overall mean of all the data).

Probably the key weaknesses of the mean as a description of the centre of a set of data is its susceptibility to extreme values.

Median

If the data is of an interval nature we may use the mean as a measure of central tendency. The median is the middle observation in data that have been arranged in ascending or descending numerical sequence. For example, the following data represents the number of times each of nine customers used ATM machines last month. (Note, the data has been arranged in numerical order).

2, 4, 5, 5, 7, 8, 10, 10, 13

When an array has an odd number of observations, the median is $(N + 1)/2$ observations from either end. Thus the median number of banking machine transactions for these nine customers is the fifth observation from either the top or bottom of the sequence (i.e. $(9 + 1)/2 = 5$). Therefore the median is 7. If the array has an even number of observations, the median is any point between the two middle values. Generally the median is taken to be the mean of the middle two values.

Say, on ten days, a bank has 18, 13, 15, 12, 8, 3, 7, 14, 16, and 3 foreign currency transactions. Arranging these figures according to size, we get:

3, 3, 7, 8, 12, 13, 14, 15, 16, 18.

The median is 12.5, the mean of 12 and 13.

The mean of the numbers in this example is 10.9 and it should not come as a surprise that it differs from the median, which is 12.5. Each of these averages describes the middle of the data in its own way. Like the mean, the median always exists and is unique for any set of data. It can also be used to define the middle of a number of objects, properties, or quantities which are not really quantitative in nature.

The median is most useful as a measure of central tendency, or central location, in situations where the data contains some extreme observations. Unlike the mean, the median is not easily affected by extreme values. If in the previous ATM use example, the highest banking machine use rate for nine customers was 50 rather than 13, the median would still be 7. On the less desirable side, ordering large sets of data manually can be a very tedious job.

Mode

The mode can be computed for all types of data (nominal, ordinal, interval, and ratio). This is not true for the mean and median. The mode is the observation that occurs most frequently in a data set. In the following set of data the mode is 7. 10

4, 18, 11, 7, 10, 5, 33, 9, 12.
3, 11, 10, 6, 26, 37, 15, 7, 18, 10, 21.

The two main advantages of the mode are that it requires no calculations, only counting, and that it can be determined for qualitative as well as quantitative data.

A set of data may have two or more values that tie for most frequently occurring. When this happens the distribution is bimodal or mulitmodal. Also a data set may have no mode if no one value occurs more frequently than another, e.g. there is no mode of the ages 18, 22, 28, 30, 25, 26. A weakness of the mode is that the most frequently recorded measurement may not really be very typical of the entire set of results obtained.

Measures of Dispersion

In the previous section, we saw that the mean, median and mode describe the central location of a distribution. However, the centrality of a set of data is only one characteristic of interest to decision-makers. It is also useful to determine the amount of dispersion (or spread) that exists among a set of measurements. Frequently used measures of how 'spread out' the data are include: the range, variance and standard deviation. The smaller these three values are, the more compact are the data.

The Range

The range is the difference between the largest and smallest observations in a batch of data. It is the simplest measure of spread.

$$\text{Range} = X \text{ largest} - X \text{ smallest}$$

Using the following data (e.g. daily rates from a sample of eight Killarney hotels):

$$£60, £52, £48, £58, £73, £69, £75, £64$$

the range is £75 — £48 = £27

Although the range is the easiest measure of dispersion to calculate, it also conveys the least information. Since the range is determined by only the two extreme values, it provides no indication about the spread of the other values. It is unwise to use the range as a measure of dispersion when either one of its components are extreme observations. Of all the measures of variability, range is the most unstable. By this we mean that from sample to sample, the range varies more than any of the other measures. An illustration will show why this is so. Suppose that we have a distribution of scores, the lowest of which is 30 and the highest is 103. The next score below 103 happens to be 90. By the use of our formula, the range is found to be 74; but 13 of the points making up this range are the result of the high score of 103. The chances are good that the next sample will not contain this high deviate score, and hence the range will be much smaller. The range, like the mode, is a very unstable statistic, since it may vary considerably from sample to sample.

The Variance and Standard Deviation

The two most frequently used measures of spread are the variance and the standard deviation. Unlike the range, the variance and standard deviation consider all the data in their computation.

The variance and standard deviation provide numerical measures of how the data tend to vary around the mean. If the data are highly clustered around the mean, both the variance and standard deviation will be relatively small. If, however, the data are widely scattered around the mean, the variance and standard deviation will be relatively large.

Computing the Variance and Standard Deviation

The first step in computing the variance is to find the algebraic difference between each x_i value and the mean. As the sum of these differences for any set of raw data is zero, we must square each of the differences. The sum of the differences squared is then calculated. The final step in computing the variance of the population is to divide the sum of the squared differences by the population size, n. (When calculating the standard deviation for a sample, it is necessary for technical reasons to divide by n-1 instead of n).

i.e. $$\sigma_x^2 = \frac{\sum_{i=1}^{n} (x_i - \mu_x)^2}{n}$$

The notation for the population variance is σ_x^2

If we take the square root of the variance, we compute the standard deviation.

$$\sigma_x = \sqrt{\frac{\sum_{i=1}^{n} (x_i - \mu_x)^2}{n}}$$

For practical purposes the most common measure of dispersion is probably the standard deviation. The steps to follow when calculating the standard deviation can be summarised as follows:

1. Find the arithmetic mean of the distribution.
2. Find the deviations of the value of all items from the arithmetic mean (AM).
3. Square each deviation.
4. Add the squared deviations.
5. Divide the total of squared deviations by the number of items (the result is the variance).
6. Find the square root of the variance. The result is the standard deviation.

A short example will make this explanation a little clearer.

Value of item		Deviations from AM	Square of deviations
5		-2	4
8		+1	1
12	AM = 35/5 = 7	+5	25
3		-4	16
7		0	0
35		0	46

Variance = $\frac{46}{5}$ = 9.2

Standard deviation = $\sqrt{9.2} = 3.03$

In this example, ungrouped data have been used in a very short calculation. For grouped data (e.g. class intervals) the calculation of the standard deviation is a little more complex. For a more in-depth discussion on the calculation of standard deviation for grouped data, students should refer to a statistics textbook.

Finally, then, we can make the following generalisations regarding our measures of dispersion:

1. The more 'spread out' or dispersed the data, the larger our measures will be.
2. The more 'concentrated' or homogenous the data, the smaller our measures will be.
3. If the observations are all the same (i.e. no variation in the data), our measures will be zero.

A Word on Percentages

A percentage is just another summary measure, like the average or standard deviation. It simplifies and reduces data to a representative figure which is easier to grasp. In marketing research applications, a percentage is the proportion who answered a question in a certain way, multiplied by 100. The percentages are a popular way of summarising data and reporting research findings. Much statistical analysis depends on percentages. Whenever we want to compare different sizes or different shares or different rates of change, we call on percentages. Index numbers (e.g. cost of living, retail prices, wage rates, production, imports and exports), mark-ups, and discounts are all variants of the percentage. Where would we all be in ordinary conversation without the percentage? After all, it is easy to calculate and universally understood.

Unfortunately misproper use of percentages can lead to distortion, misinterpretation and even deception.[7] Therefore when one examines a percentage, two basic questions should be asked: in what direction should the percentage be computed; and how do you interpret the percentage of difference? When the objective of the research is to identify a relationship between the two questions (or variables) one of the questions is commonly chosen as a base for determining percentages. Conventionally, the rule to apply in determining which direction to use to compute percentages is to calculate percentages in the direction of the causal factor. The researcher needs to identify which variable is the independent variable and which is the dependent variable. The percentages should then be computed in the direction of the independent variable across the dependent variable.

Consider, for example, the question of the relationship, if any, between the number of cars that a family owns and family income. In this case, income is logically considered to be the cause, or independent variable, and multiple car ownership to be the effect, or dependent variable. The independent variable should be used as the base for computing the percentages.

The following are some caveats when using percentages:

- Distinguish between percent and percentage point, e.g. an increase from 40–65% is an increase of 25 percentage points or 61.5%.
- Averaging of percentages is not possible, unless each percentage is based on the same number of items. A solution is to use a weighted average. This weights each percentage by its relative sample size.
- Percentages based on a very small number of items are misleading.
- Using percentages that are too large can be confusing to the reader, e.g. 'A 750% increase was observed'. It would be simple to say a 'seven and a half times increase'.
- A percentage decrease can never exceed 100%. However, it is not uncommon to come across statements such as 'a 250% decrease'. This is not true and results from an incorrect figure being chosen as the base for analysis.

• Summarising Data Using Tables and Graphs

Eventually the researcher must develop some conclusions from the data analysis and present the results. Data can be presented in tabular or graphic form.[8] Tables allow numerical presentation of data. Graphics present data in terms of visually interpreted sizes. Because tables and graphs are used to summarise and present data, this section is also relevant to Chapter 15 which describes the research report and the presentation of research findings.

The proper use of visuals within the marketing research report enhances the presentation of numerical data. It is often said that 'a picture is worth a thousand words'. Regardless of which type of visual is used, it should be uncluttered and self-explanatory. Visuals should be referred to by number and, needless to say, the key points of all visuals should be explained in the text preceding it. Each visual should be located on the same page or next page (unless it is placed in the appendix) to the text paragraph which refers to that same visual. Visuals should be referred to by number, e.g. 'as shown in Fig. 2.1'. Placing the visual within easy reach of the text which deals with it, makes it easier on the readers. When reading a report nobody wishes to have to sift through pages to find the relevant table or pie chart.

All the main spreadsheet programs such as Excel, Lotus 1-2-3, and Quattro Pro have graphics capabilities. There are also several specialised programs available to the researcher to create high quality graphics. The main software programs for this purpose are Power Point and Harvard Graphics. Several data analysis packages such as SPSS, SAS and MINITAB are also capable of generating tables and graphics. With current computer graphics, virtually all charts can now be made three-dimensional. It should, however, be recognised that graphical presentation is not a substitute for statistical analysis.

Tables

Tables are extremely useful for summarising and presenting numerical data. Tables allow the reader to compare numerical data. They enable the researcher to present important information without getting bogged down in detail.

As a rule, the main section of the report should only contain relatively short summary tables. More detailed and comprehensive tables are best placed in the appendix.

Guidelines for Using Tables in Reports

Each table in the report should include the following:

1. A table number for reference purposes.
2. A title that illustrates the content of the table.
3. A sub-head containing the captions for the rows of the table.
4. A bannerhead which contains the captions for the columns.
5. A footnote, if required, to explain particular items in the table.
6. A source note to acknowledge a secondary information source.

Graphs and Charts

The most common graphical methods are as follows.

Line Graph

Line graphs are often used to show movements in a variable over time. Data values for each time period are joined to show trends in data at equal intervals. The dependent variable is generally shown on the vertical axis with the independent variable allocated to the horizontal axis. The x-axis is frequently used to depict time and if so we have what is known as a time series. A multiple line graph shows the relationship of more than one dependent variable to the independent variable.

Bar Chart

Bar charts are most suitable for categorical and discrete data, and are similar to a line chart. Discrete data are grouped into classes corresponding to a rectangle. The height of the bars represents the frequency of occurrence with the base of the column representing the class interval. Bar charts can be drawn horizontally or vertically, and can be plain, clustered, stacked, or multiple row. In the case of more complex bar charts, each bar should be clearly identified with a different colour or pattern.

Histograms are similar to bar charts except that no gaps are left between the bars and, unlike bar charts, histograms can be used for depicting either discrete or continuous data. The continuous nature of the data is emphasised by the absence of gaps between bars. In addition, the area of each column represents the frequency (rather than its height as is the case with bar charts). Therefore, if a class interval is twice as wide as the others in a histogram, the height of the column must be taken as half of the frequency for this larger class interval. Bar charts can be used to show trends between discrete time periods, and histograms used for continuous time periods.

Pie Chart

The pie chart is one of the simplest and perhaps most effective ways to show proportional relationships. Each segment of the pie represents its share of the total value. It can be difficult to interpret pie charts with more than eight to ten segments. A pie chart always shows only one data series and is useful when you want to emphasise a significant element. It is also possible to 'explode' or separate an important segment of the pie from the main part. In order to make smaller segments easier to see, a solution is to group them together as one collective 'other' category in the pie chart. You can then break down that category into a smaller pie or bar chart next to the main chart.

A problem with pie charts is that they do not allow you to show the passage of time nor do they allow you to compare more than one group of data within a single chart. This can only be done by using multiple pie charts.

Other types of charts used for summarisation and presentation purposes include:[9]

- An *XY (scatter) chart* either shows the relationships among the numeric values in several data series or plots two groups of numbers as one series of XY co-ordinates.
- An *area chart* emphasises the magnitude of change over time. By displaying the sum of the plotted values, an area chart also shows the relationship of parts to a whole.
- Like a pie chart, a *doughnut chart* shows the relationship of parts to a whole, but it can contain more than one data series. Each ring of the doughnut chart represents a data series.
- In a *radar chart*, each category has its own value axis radiating from the centre point. Lines connect all the values in the same series. A radar chart compares the aggregate values of a number of data series.
- A *surface chart* is useful when you want to find optimum combinations between two sets of data. As in a topographic map, colours and patterns indicate areas that are in the same range of values.
- A *bubble chart* is a type of xy (scatter) chart. The size of the data marker indicates the value of a third variable.
- The *high-low-close chart* is often used to illustrate stock prices. This chart can also be used for scientific data; for example, to indicate temperature changes.
- *Pictogram*. A visual representation of categorical data in which pictures are used to summarise data, each picture being scaled in size or repeated a number of times to indicate relative magnitudes.

Guidelines for Using Charts in Reports

The guidelines for using charts are similar to those for tables, with some small exceptions. At a minimum charts should have:

1. A figure number, which is separate from that of any tables contained in the report.
2. A title which describes the content of the chart. However, unlike tables, where the number and title are placed above the table, the chart number and title are usually placed below the chart.
3. Explanatory legends to highlight the components of the chart.
4. Footnotes (less common with charts than tables) and a source note if necessary.

• Summary

Data analysis helps transform raw data into the 'list of needed information' which was established at the beginning of the marketing research process. Data analysis, while unique to each study, requires the research to perform the following tasks: editing, coding, tabulation and summarisation.

Editing is the process of reviewing questionnaires with the objective of increasing accuracy and precision. It requires checking for completeness, consistency and legibility of data and making the data ready for coding. After editing at field level, the questionnaires or interview forms are later subsequently edited in-house by the analyst. It is important that editing be done consistently.

Coding assigns the data into pertinent categories, so as to speed up tabulation. Careful editing makes the coding job easier. There are two different methods of coding questionnaires depending on the type of software being used to analyse the data. One method of inputting is to use ASCII data which breaks down the data set into individual columns. This method of encoding is of benefit when the data input is being done independent of the analysis and the person inputting does not know which software package is being used.

The more usual method nowadays is to use statistical packages, e.g. SPSS, MINITAB or SAS which use a spreadsheet or similar to assign a variable to each column and a row to every response. If a questionnaire contains only or mainly structured questions it may be pre-coded which means that the codes are assigned before the survey work is conducted and the codes printed on the questionnaire. If the questionnaire is unstructured and contains many open questions the codes may be assigned after the field work is completed or by the interviewer from a codebook.

Having assigned responses to categories, it is then necessary to count how many responses are in each category. This is called tabulation. Tabulation consists of three activities: sorting, counting and summarising. There are two types of tabulation: simple tabulation and cross tabulation. Tabulation can be done manually or by computer. Simple tabulation (also called marginal or one-way tabulation) involves counting a single variable, i.e. on a question-by-question, or item-by-item basis. Cross tabulation describes two or more variables simultaneously.

There are two major kinds of summarising statistics. The first provides measures of the midpoint of the distribution and is known as 'measures of central tendency'. The second gives an indication of the amount of variation in the data comprising the distribution and is known as measures of dispersion. The three most common ways to describe the centrality of a set of data are the arithmetic mean, median and mode. Frequently-used measures of how 'spread out' the data are include: the range, variance and standard deviation. The smaller these three values are, the more compact are the data.

Data can be presented in tabular or graphic form. Tables allow numerical presentation of data. Graphics present data in terms of visually interpreted sizes

Questions

1. Describe the process of data preparation.
2. What is meant by editing a questionnaire?
3. Why is it necessary to edit survey questionnaires prior to analysing the data collected? What are some of the difficulties that can be uncovered and resolved at this stage of data collection and analysis?
4. Distinguish between the preliminary data analysis steps of editing, coding and tabulation.
5. What should an editor do with incomplete answers? Obviously wrong answers? Answers that reflect a lack of interest?
6. How do you identify data collection instruments that are unacceptable for data processing?
7. Differentiate between precoding and postcoding.
8. How does one go about developing a code book?
9. How should multiple responses be handled?
10. What are some potential problems that might arise when coding open-ended questions?
11. What is the difference between one-way tabulation and cross tabulation? Provide examples to illustrate this difference.
12. Give a brief description of two of the more commonly used PC-based statistical analysis packages.
13. Differentiate between measures of central tendency and measures of dispersion.
14. What generalisations can be made regarding measures of dispersion?
15. Detail some caveats associated with using percentages.
16. How does the use of visuals enhance the presentation of data?

Problems and Assignments

1. Shown below is part of a questionnaire used to determine consumer preferences for shoes. Set up a coding scheme for the following three questions.

    Q.6 Please rate the following factors you would consider when shopping for a new camera:

		Not so important				Very important
a.	DX film speed setting	1	2	3	4	5
b.	Auto film advance	1	2	3	4	5
c.	Autofocus	1	2	3	4	5
d.	Autoloading	1	2	3	4	5

    Q.7 Where do you get most of your photo processing done? Please check only one option

    a. ____ Chemist
    b. ____ Corner shop
    c. ____ Camera stores
    d. ____ Department store
    e. ____ Supermarkets
    f. ____ Mail order
    g. ____ Other

    Q.8 If you were to buy a new camera, which of the following outlets would you visit? Please check as many as apply.

    a. ____ Pharmacy
    b. ____ Camera shop
    c. ____ Department store
    d. ____ Supermarket
    e. ____ Other

2. You are president of a company that analyses and tabulates incoming data from mail surveys. One survey is causing you some trouble because a few of the questions deal with whether the respondent uses drugs on occasion. What could you do to ensure that a high percentage of respondents answer these sensitive questions truthfully? If you end up having received many surveys with these questions left unanswered, what might you recommend to your client company?

3. (a) Establish response categories and codes for the following question that was asked to a sample of business executives. 'In your opinion, which types of companies have not been affected by the present economic climate?'
   (b) Code the following responses using your categories and codes:
   (1) *Sunday Independent* (4) Hoover (7) Faberge
   (2) Gillette (5) Colgate Palmolive (8) *The Star*
   (3) Jury's Inn (6) Holiday Inns (9) Singer
4. You have been assigned the task of preparing a coding manual for a study of personal computer users in 15 countries: Ireland, Canada, Mexico, Brazil, Japan, China, the UK, France, Italy, Germany, Spain, Austria, Hungary, Australia, and New Zealand. Outline your approach.
5. Using data from a business magazine report create the following types of graphs:
   (a) Line chart (b) Bar chart (C) Pie chart
6. (a) Find the standard deviation of the numbers (a) 3, 6, 2, 1, 7, 5; (b) 3.2, 4.6, 2.8, 5.2, 4.4; (c) 0, 0, 0, 0, 0, 1, 1, 1.
   (b) By adding 5 to each of the numbers in the set 3, 6, 2, 1, 7, 5 we obtain the set 8, 11, 7, 6, 12, 10. Show that the two sets have the same standard deviations but different means.
7. In a survey of 100 people 15 respondents answer 'don't know' to a question that has 'yes' and 'no' as alternatives. The researcher uses 85 as a base for calculating the percentage of respondents who answer 'yes' or 'no'. Is this correct?
8. Suppose you were preparing two-way tables of percentages for the following pairs of variables. How would you run the percentages?
   (a) Age and consumption of alcohol.
   (b) Family income and eating out frequency.
   (c) Marital status and purchase of fashion clothing.
   (d) Crime rate and unemployment rate.
9. A researcher investigated attitudes toward her company and noticed that one individual answered all image questions at one end of a bipolar scale. Should she decline to use this questionnaire in the data analysis?
10. A researcher asks, 'What do you remember about advertising for Gillette Sensor Excell razors?' How should the code book for this question be structured?

Chapter 13

FUNDAMENTAL DATA ANALYSIS

> - **Chapter Overview**
> - Introduction • Tests of Significance • Steps in Hypothesis Testing
> - Tests Concerning Means • P-Values • Tests Concerning a Proportion
> - The Chi-Square Test For Goodness Fit • Other Significance Tests
> - Analysis of Variance • The Significance of Relationships and Associations, Simple Linear Regression and Correlation • The Spearman Rank-Correlation Coefficient • Summary

- **Introduction**

As we have seen from the previous chapter, measures of central tendency, the mode, median and mean, together with measures of dispersion, the range, variance and standard deviation make much sense of quantitative data. When used in conjunction with simple and cross tabulation, such data reduction and summarisation techniques assist the researcher in identifying, describing and displaying data.

While useful, there are many occasions in marketing when patterns emerge from the data, and describing such patterns is not enough. As well as observing patterns, we need to question their very existence. Perhaps the results occurred as a result of sampling error. Perhaps there is a pattern in the data, but it may not be significant. Or perhaps there is a pattern in the data, but it cannot be seen due to its complexity. In all of these circumstances, the researcher can perform statistical tests to measure the significance of differences between numbers, and to measure the relationships, associations and strength between variables. This takes the researcher into the domain of univariate and bivariate data analysis. Univariate analysis is data analysis concerned with one variable, while bivariate analysis focuses on two variables. When three or more variables are being simultaneously investigated, it is classified as multivariate analysis (this area is dealt with in Chapter 14).

While the terminology and mathematical formulae of data analysis can be overwhelming upon first reading, computer packages can readily perform the necessary calculations. Thus, the onus upon the researcher is to be knowledgeable of and understand the premise and purpose of the various analysis methods,[1] together with the appropriate circumstances in which to apply the techniques. Against this background, by the end of this chapter, the reader will be able to:

1. Understand univariate and bivariate data analysis;
2. Discuss the steps for significance testing;
3. Conduct a hypothesis test for a population mean;
4. Conduct a hypothesis test for a population proportion;
5. Detail the chi-squared test;
6. Describe the basis of analysis of variance;
7. Explain the concepts of regression and correlation.

- **Tests of Significance**

Hypothesis testing is one approach to making inferences about the population. Hypothesis testing is a statistical procedure that uses sample data to determine whether or not a statement about the value of a population parameter should be rejected. We can construct hypothesis tests for situations involving one population mean and one population proportion², two sample means and two sample proportions for example.

Hypothesis testing involves two hypotheses. Recall from Chapter 3 that a hypothesis is a tentative statement about the expected outcome. Given this, we can now introduce the notion of a *null hypothesis* and *alternative hypothesis*, for the purposes of statistically testing the differences we observe in numbers, generated by quantitative data methods such as surveys, observation or experiments.

A *null hypothesis* is a hypothesis that states that our results do not show any significant difference between the population and our sample(s) statistics, e.g. sample mean, sample proportion. The null hypothesis is symbolised by H_0. If it is proven to be true (by means of a statistical test), our findings show the differences in the observed numbers is due to chance and therefore not significant.

An *alternative hypothesis* is a hypothesis that says our sample findings reflect a real difference between population groups. It is represented by H_1. If H_1 is accepted, on foot of the appropriate statistical test, then H_0 is rejected and the results are significant and worthy of the researcher's attention, as they did not occur by chance.

Essentially, a researcher proceeds on the assumption that any differences between a sample and population measures are due to chance, unless proven otherwise, in which case the null hypothesis is rejected, the alternative hypothesis is accepted and the results are therefore significant. In this manner, it is the null hypothesis, and not the alternative hypothesis, that is subjected to hypothesis testing.

Hypothesis testing can be either non-directional or directional. The term 'non-directional' implies that the null hypothesis can be rejected if a sample finding is either very low or very high, i.e. there are two rejection regions. For this reason, non-directional testing is sometimes referred to as 'two-tail significance testing'. One-tail, or directional testing, is where there is one rejection region. It includes a > or < sign, while a two-tailed test includes a ≠ sign.

• Steps in Hypothesis Testing

Suppose that you are in the process of buying a chain of restaurants from an existing owner who assures you that the average amount spent by patrons in such restaurants is at least £22. However, you may feel/believe/claim that this figure is too high. How do you test this? To test for significance in differences in numbers, we can follow a three-step procedure outlined below. (This basic procedure can then be adapted to different circumstances and different problems, as explained later on in the chapter.)

Step 1 — Formulate the Null and Alternative Hypothesis

[margin note: one or the other will either be true or not but not both]

In hypothesis testing we begin by making some assumption about a population parameter, e.g. in this example we make the assumption that μ (the true average amount spent by patrons in restaurants) ≥ £22. Thus we write

$$H_0: \mu \geq 22$$

We now define an alternative hypothesis which is the direct opposite of that stated in the null hypothesis, i.e. we define an alternative hypothesis which is a contradiction of the null hypothesis. Thus we write

$$H_1: < 22$$

The general approach adopted in hypothesis testing is to take a random sample from the population of interest. If this sample information is not inconsistent with the statement in the null hypothesis then such a statement cannot be rejected. However if the sample information is inconsistent with the null hypothesis, then it (H_0) can be rejected.

The null and alternative hypothesis are contradicting statements. Either the null or alternative hypothesis is true, but not both. The ideal hypothesis-testing procedure is one in which we reject H_0 when it is false and reject H_1 when it is false.

Step 2 — Determine the Observed Value of the Test Statistic

[margin note: what is the actual statistic we wish to test e.g. the mean (might ask for proportion — this set before testing)]

Here, we concern ourselves with the actual value of the statistic we wish to test. It could be either a sample mean or a sample proportion. In hypothesis tests pertaining to a population, we use,

$$Z = \frac{\bar{X} - \mu}{\frac{\sigma}{\sqrt{n}}}$$

where $\bar{X}$ = sample mean
μ = population mean
σ = standard deviation
n = sample size

In our restaurant example, we conduct a survey of 64 patrons and find the average amount of money spent to be £20, with a variation of £5.50. Under such circumstances, the actual value of our observed test statistic becomes

$$Z = \frac{20-22}{\frac{5.5}{\sqrt{64}}} = -2.91$$

Step 3 — Choose the Appropriate Rejection Rule

At what level do we reject the null hypothesis? eg above or below 10%. General Rules 15%

Now, we find the critical value, from appropriate statistical tables, of the test statistic. The critical region is that set of values of the test statistic for which we reject Ho. Thus the critical value defines the acceptance and rejection regions for Ho.

To determine the relevant critical value, we need to select a level of significance. The significance level is the probability of making a mistake; of rejecting a true null hypothesis. This is chosen by the researcher with 0.05 being the most popular level of significance in marketing practice. A 0.05 level of significance equates with $Z = +/-1.96$, as shown in figure 13.1 below; a 0.10 level of significance implies $Z = +/-1.65$, while 0.01 level of significance results in $Z = +/-2.58$.

This 3 stage process will be used for significance testing; tests concerning a mean; critical tests; tests concerning a proportion etc.

Figure 13.1 Hypothesis testing and Z values

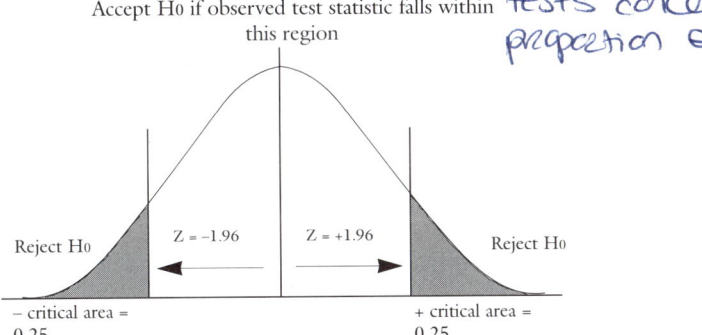

Note: Critical areas, – and +, when added equal the desired level of significance, 0.05.

Returning to our restaurant example, we select a 0.05 level of significant. This implies a critical value, $Z = +/-1.96$. Since our observed test statistic, $Z = -2.91$ is less than the critical value of Z, we reject Ho.

This procedure of hypothesis testing, a statistical method for measuring the probability of an observed difference between sample results being a real difference and not due to chance, can be applied to various different scenarios, such as the population mean, the population proportion, two sample means, large or small samples.[3] These different cases for hypothesis testing are now outlined.

- ## Tests Concerning a Mean

Given a random sample $X_1, X_2, X_3, \ldots X_n$ from a population with unknown mean μ and variance σ^2, how do we test the null hypothesis

$$H_0: \mu = \mu_0$$

against various alternative hypotheses? To answer this question, we follow the hypothesis-testing procedure outlined above, and adapt it to cater for the appropriate sample size.

Large Sample Case

If σ is not known then it is sufficient to replace σ by

$$S = \sqrt{\frac{\sum_{i=1}^{n}(X_i - \bar{X})^2}{n-1}}$$

Then the test statistics and critical region are given by test statistics:

$$Z = \frac{\bar{X} - \mu_0}{\frac{\sigma}{\sqrt{n}}}$$

Critical regions (at a specified level of significance α) are given in Table 13.1.

Table 13.1 Critical regions

H_1	Critical region
$\mu > \mu_0$	$Z > Z_\alpha$
$\mu < \mu_0$	$Z < -Z_\alpha$
$\mu \neq \mu_0$	$Z > Z_{\frac{\alpha}{2}}$ or $Z < -Z_{\frac{\alpha}{2}}$

where $Z \sim N(0,1)$.

We can also see that the form of the critical region, i.e. greater than, less than or use of both directional operators is determined by H₁. Tests in which the alternative hypothesis is of the form $H_1: \mu > \mu_0$ and $H_1: \mu < \mu_0$, i.e. tests in which a directional operator (<, >) is used, are known as one-tailed tests and a test of the form $H_1: \mu \neq \mu_0$ as a two-tailed test.

Consider the following three hypothesis tests:

(a) $H_0: \mu \geq 22$ (b) $H_0: \mu \leq 22$ (c) $H_0: \mu = 22$
(a) $H_1: \mu < 22$ (b) $H_1: \mu > 22$ (c) $H_1: \mu \neq 22$

The corresponding critical regions are given by, respectively,

(a) $Z < -Z_\alpha$ (b) $Z > Z_\alpha$ (c) $Z > Z$ or $Z < -Z$

or, adopting a pictorial representation, these corresponding critical regions are given by, respectively,

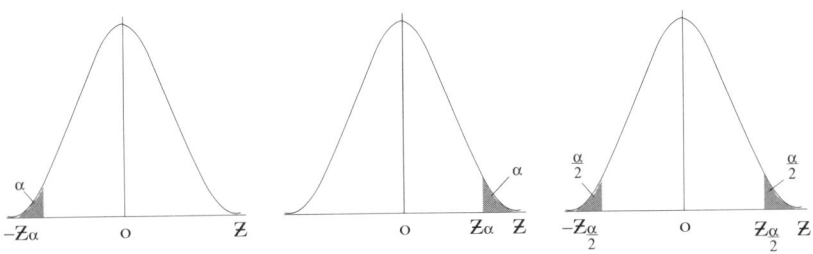

Recalling that Z_α is the value such that Prob $(Z > Z_\alpha) = \alpha$, e.g. Prob $(Z > 1.65) = 0.05$ Table 13.2 reports Z_α and $Z_{\frac{\alpha}{2}}$ for some of the more commonly used levels of significance.

Table 13.2 Levels of significance

α	Z_α (application to one-tail test)	$Z_{\frac{\alpha}{2}}$ (application to two-tail test)
0.01	2.33	2.58
0.05	1.65	1.96
0.1	1.28	1.65
0.2	0.84	1.28

For example, a retail credit association wants to test the hypothesis that for all shops in Tralee, Co. Kerry the average charge account is £110.20. To be specific, it wants to test this hypothesis against the alternative hypothesis that the average is not

£110.20. Assuming a significance level of 0.1, what can they conclude if 110 accounts, selected at random, have a mean of £112 and a standard deviation of £8.5? There are three steps involved in the solution:

Step 1 — Specify the Null and Alternative Hypothesis

Let μ = true average of charge account. Thus we may write the null and alternative hypothesis as:

$$H_0: \mu = 110.20$$
$$H_1: \mu \neq 110.20$$

Step 2 — Determine the Value of the Test Statistic, Noting that S = 8.5 and σ = 110

$$\text{Test statistic} = Z = \frac{\bar{X} - \mu_0}{\frac{\sigma}{\sqrt{n}}} = \frac{112 - 110.20}{\frac{8.5}{\sqrt{110}}} = 2.11$$

Step 3 — Choose the Appropriate Rejection Rule

From examination of Table 13.1 we employ the rule *reject H_0 if $Z > Z_{\frac{\alpha}{2}}$ or $Z < -Z_{\frac{\alpha}{2}}$* where, referring to Table 13.2 (application to two-tail test). Finally, since the value of the test statistic, 2.11, is greater than the critical value 1.65, we reject H_0.

Small Sample Case (n <30)

Under this scenario, the test statistics and critical region are given by

$$\text{Test statistic} \quad t = \frac{\bar{X} - \mu_0}{\frac{S}{\sqrt{n}}}$$

where $\bar{X}$ = sample mean
μ_0 = population mean under H_0
$\frac{S}{\sqrt{n}}$ = estimated standard error of the mean

Critical regions (at a specified level of significance α)

Table 13.3 Critical regions

H₁	Critical region
$\mu > \mu_0$	$t > t_\alpha$
$\mu < \mu_0$	$t < -t_\alpha$
$\mu \neq \mu_0$	$t > t_{\frac{\alpha}{2}}$ or $t < -t_{\frac{\alpha}{2}}$

where t is described by t distribution with n–1 degrees of freedom. In each case the critical region is chosen so that Prob (test statistic is in the critical region/H₀ is true) = α.

For example, the manufacturer of a toy claims that it takes no longer than 13 seconds to assemble it. A suspicious parent believes that the true figure is greater and gave the toy to eleven children to put together. He obtained the following random sample of assembly times: 15.1, 12.7, 12.01, 13.5, 15.01, 16.9, 11.6, 13.4, 15.4, 17.9, and 14.4 seconds. Assuming a level of significance equal to 0.01, what can the suspicious parent conclude from this data? Following the hypothesis-testing procedure where:

Step 1 — Specify the Null and Alternative Hypothesis

Let μ = true average assembly time of toy, so we write the null and alternative hypothesis as:

$$H_0: \mu \leq 13$$
$$H_1: \mu > 13$$

Step 2 — Determine the Value of the Test Statistic

Noting the calculated values of s and X from the observed assemble times 15.1, 12.7 . . . 14.4 are given by s = 1.97 and X = 14.36.

$$\text{Test statistic} = t = \frac{\bar{X} - \mu_0}{\frac{s}{\sqrt{n}}} = \frac{14.36 - 13}{\frac{1.97}{\sqrt{11}}} = 2.29$$

This test statistic is appropriate as the sample size n < 30, as given above.

Step 3 — Choose the Appropriate Rejection Rule

From examination of Table 13.3, we use the rule reject H₀ if t (n–1) >T$_\alpha$ (n–1) where, referring to Appendix 3, t₀.₀₁ (11–1) = 2.764. Finally, since the value of our test statistic, 2.29, is not greater than the critical value, 2.764, we do not reject H₀, rather we accept it.

• P-Values

This provides an alternative approach in deciding whether or not to reject H₀. The p-value reports the probability of obtaining a sample result that is at least as unlikely as that observed when the null hypothesis is true. It is often called the observed level of significance. The p-value can be used in making a decision in a hypothesis test by noting that the value of the test statistic is in the critical region. Thus the decision in a hypothesis test will always be the same whether the p-value or test statistic approach is adopted. A small p-value indicates a sample result that is inconsistent given the assumption that H₀ is true. Small p-values lead to rejection of H₀ whereas large p-values indicate that the null hypothesis cannot be rejected. The decision rules based on these p-values are given in Table 13.4.

Table 13.4 P-Value decision rules

H_1	Reject H₀ if
$\mu > \mu_o$	p-value $< \alpha$
$\mu < \mu_o$	p-value $> \alpha$
$\mu \neq \mu_o$	p-value $< \frac{\alpha}{2}$

We can apply the p-value method to the earlier example of a retail credit association wishing to test:

$$H_0: \mu = 110.20$$
$$H_1: \mu \neq 110.20$$

where the level of significance = 0.1. In our earlier solution, we rejected H₀ as the observed value of the test statistic (2.11) was greater than the critical value (1.65). The p-value for this test is given by:

$$\text{Prob}(Z > 2.11) = 0.0174.$$

The appropriate rejection rule is given by the third row of Table 13.4 and thus we reject H₀ if P-value $< \frac{\alpha}{2}$ i.e. in this case we reject H₀ as $0.0174 < \frac{0.1}{2} = 0.05$.

• Tests Concerning a Proportion

In many areas of research the random variable of interest is the sample proportion. Frequently the researcher may wish to compare the sample proportion with a value that has hypothesised for the population. The procedure for conducting such tests is the same as that adopted for tests concerning a mean, considered earlier. We consider the case of large samples only, i.e. $n \geq 30$. The test statistic and critical region are given by:

Test statistic:

$$Z = \frac{P - \pi_o}{\sqrt{\frac{\pi_o(1-\pi_o)}{n}}}$$

where P is the sample proportion and
π_o is the hypothesised proportion, i.e. the value of π under H₀.

Critical regions: (at a specified level of significance α)

Table 13.5

H₁	Critical region
$\pi > \pi_o$	$Z > Z_\alpha$
$\pi < \pi_o$	$Z < -Z_\alpha$
$\pi \neq \pi_o$	$Z > Z_{\frac{\alpha}{2}}$ or $Z < -Z_{\frac{\alpha}{2}}$

where $Z \sim N(0,1)$. In each case the critical region is chosen so that Prob (test statistic is in the critical region/H₀ is true) = α.

To illustrate, a telesales company has observed that they have a 14% success rate in obtaining a personal meeting with customers contacted by telephone. A particular employee, Renee Scarry, has telephoned 290 individuals so far this year and has been able to meet 29 of them. In a non-directional test, at the 0.05 level of significance, is Renee's performance significantly different from the company's past performance?

Step 1 — Specify the Null and Alternative Hypothesis

Let π = company success rate in obtaining a meeting with clients. Thus we may write the null and alternative hypothesis as:

$$H_0: \pi = 0.14$$
$$H_1: \pi \neq 0.14$$

Note, we are assuming that Renee's performance is the same as the company's and we are looking for evidence to contradict this assumption.

Step 2 — Determine the Value of the Test Statistic

$$\text{Test statistic} = Z = \frac{P - \pi_o}{\sqrt{\frac{\pi_o(1-\pi_o)}{n}}}$$

where P = the sample proportion = 0.29
       π_o = the value π of under H₀ = 0.14
       n = sample size = 290.

Thus the observed value of the test statistic is 7.36.

Step 3 — Choose the Appropriate Rejection Rule

From examination of Table 13.5, we use the rule reject H₀ if $Z > Z_{\frac{\alpha}{2}}$ or $Z < -Z_{\frac{\alpha}{2}}$ where, $Z_{\frac{0.05}{2}} = 1.96$ and $-Z_{\frac{0.05}{2}} = -1.96$. Finally, since the value of the test statistic, 7.36, is greater than the critical value, 1.96, we reject H₀. Thus Renee's performance is significantly better than the company's performance.

Another example: an entrepreneur has developed, so he claims, a new ingredient which if added to stout will substantially improve its taste. The entrepreneur approaches a drinks company hoping to sell his new ingredient. The company, being somewhat sceptical, asked 90 people to test this new stout and a conventional stout. Of the 90, 50 reported an improvement in taste over the conventional stout. At the 0.05 level of significance, should the entrepreneur's assertion be accepted by the company?

Step 1 — Specify the Null and Alternative Hypothesis

Let π = the true proportion of people who think that the new ingredient improves taste. We would expect 50% of those trying both formulations of stout to choose the new formulation by chance alone if the ingredient fails to improve taste. Thus we obtain H₀, i.e.

$$H_0: \pi = 0.5$$

The entrepreneur claims that the new ingredient improves taste and thus we obtain H₁, i.e.:

$$H_1: \pi > 0.5$$

Step 2 — Determine the Value of the Test Statistic

$$\text{Test statistic: } Z = \frac{P - \pi_0}{\sqrt{\frac{\pi_0(1-\pi_0)}{n}}}$$

where P = the sample proportion = 0.556
       π = the value of π under H₀ = 0.5
       n = sample size, 90

Thus the observed value of the test statistic is 1.06.

Step 3 — Choose the Appropriate Rejection Rule

From examination of Table 13.5, we employ the rule reject H₀ if $Z > Z$ where, referring to Table 13.2, $Z_{0.05} = 1.65$. Finally, since the value of the test statistic,

1.06, is not greater than the critical value, 1.65, we do not reject H₀. Thus the company would be ill-advised to add this new ingredient to its existing stout.

• The Chi-Square Test for Goodness Fit

Often in marketing, we deal with frequency distribution data, i.e. data in the form of rows and columns. We use the chi-square test to test such data for significance, regardless of sample size. In fact, the chi-square test is one of the more popular statistical techniques used in marketing research.[4]

In chi-square testing the fundamental approach is to compare an observed table of sample data with an expected table of sample data, this expected table of frequencies being derived under the assumption that the null hypothesis is true. If the two tables differ too greatly from one another then this provides us with evidence to reject H₀. The steps involved in conducting the chi-squared test are the same as those involved in the earlier significance tests pertaining to the population parameters μ and π. The test statistic and critical values of the chi-square test are defined as follows:

$$\chi^2 = \frac{\Sigma (O_c - E_c)^2}{E_c}$$

where Σ = 'sum over all cells in the table'
O_c = observed frequency for each cell (the sub-script stands for 'cell')
E_c = expected frequency for each cell. The formula for E_c is given by E_c = np_c where n = sample size and p_c is the calculated probability, under H₀ for each cell. Note that for this test to be valid, E_c must be at least 5. If this does not hold, adjacent categories should be amalgamated to ensure that this condition is satisfied.

We reject H₀ if $\chi^2 > \chi^2_\alpha$ (k–1) where k = the number of categories and k–1 are the associated degrees of freedom. The critical value χ^2_α (k–1) is obtained from a χ^2 table, as in Appendix 4.

Traditionally, a magazine's new subscribers have had the following as their highest level of education: 15% less than secondary, 35% secondary school, 43% degree and 7% postgraduate degree. A recent sample of 200 new subscribers has, respectively, the following numbers of people from these four groups: 32, 86, 70, and 12. At the 0.10 level of significance, do the findings suggest that a change has occurred in the educational attainment of new subscribers? Applying the chi-square test:

Step 1 — Specify the Null and Alternative Hypothesis

H₀: A magazine's new subscribers have the following as their highest of education: 15% less than secondary, 35% secondary, 43% degree and 7% postgraduate degree.
H₁: The proportions specified in H are incorrect.

Step 2 — Determine the Value of the Test Statistic

Test statistic:

$$= \chi^2 = \frac{\Sigma (O_c - E_c)^2}{E_c}$$

The value of the test statistic = 7.074. Note that all the expected frequencies are greater than 5.

Step 3 — Choose the Appropriate Rejection Rule

Reject H₀ if $\chi^2 > \chi^2_\alpha (k-1)$. Referring to Appendix 4, $\chi^2_{0.10} (4-1) = 6.25$. Finally, since the value of the test statistic, 7.074, is greater than the critical value, 6.25, we reject H₀. In this manner, in chi-square testing, a table of observed data is compared with one that assumes a certain hypothesis to be true.

• Other Significance Tests

Some other tests to measure significance,[5] under specific circumstances, include:

1. the Mann-Whitney test; when data is from the ordinal scale, this test is used to compare two groups;
2. the Wilcoxom test; when data is non-metric, ordinal in nature and there are two matching samples, this test is employed;
3. the Kruskal-Wallis test; utilised when the data is non-metric and the researcher is drawing upon three or more independent samples.

• Analysis of Variance

Analysis of variance is used to specifically evaluate the results of experiments, i.e. to determine the influence of the independent variable on a dependent variable(s). It is based upon the premise that the total variance can be attributed to specific factors by means of mathematics formulae. Thus, this is a technique for simultaneously testing the equality of the means of several populations. This approach is known as the analysis of variance, or simply ANOVA. The method is best explained through the medium of an example.

A fast-food chain, Characters, expect mean gross sales of £800,000 per year per franchise. A random sample of outlets in Donegal, Cork and Dublin, over a period of four years, gave the following results in units of £100,000:

Franchise s / Observations

Donegal	8.7	7.4	8.0	7.5
Cork	8.7	9.2	9.1	8.3
Dublin	7.8	7.6	6.9	5.7

Assuming these to be independent random samples from normal populations with the same variance, is there evidence at the 5% level of significance of a difference in means gross sales among the three cities?

Fundamental Data Analysis

Let μ_1 = mean gross earnings for population 1 (Donegal franchise)
μ_2 = mean gross earnings for population 2 (Cork franchise)
μ_3 = mean gross earnings for population 3 (Dublin franchise).

The null and alternative hypothesis are stated as:

$H_0: \mu_1 = \mu_2 = \mu_3.$
$H_1:$ Not all population means are equal.

In this example, the number of populations is three but more generally we let k denote the number of populations. If the means of the three populations are statistically equal then we expect the three means to be close together. The closer the sample means the more evidence that the population means are equal. Conversely the greater the distance between means the greater the evidence that the population means are not equal. We may state these observations thus: if the variability between means is small it supports H_0 but if this variability is large it supports H_1. If the null hypothesis, $H_0: \mu_1 = \mu_2 = \mu_3$, is true (but not otherwise) then it can be shown that the variability among sample means can be used to estimate σ^2. In Table 13.6 we show some summary statistics for the three populations in question.

Table 13.6 Statistics for franchise outlets

Investigate further

Observations	Donegal	Cork	Dublin
1	8.7	8.7	7.8
2	7.4	9.2	7.6
3	8.0	9.1	6.9
4	7.5	8.3	5.7
Sample mean	7.9 *near to average*	8.83 *Above Average*	7 *Below Average*
Sample standard deviation	0.59	0.41	0.95

If the null hypothesis is true then we may regard $\bar{X}_1 = 7.9$, $\bar{X}_2 = 8.83$ and $\bar{X}_3 = 7.0$ as 3 observations drawn from the same distribution.

Here, $\bar{X} \sim N(\mu, \frac{\sigma^2}{n})$. We require an estimate of the mean μ and variance σ^2. Intuitively an estimate of μ can be obtained from $\bar{X}_1$, $\bar{X}_2$, and $\bar{X}_3$, i.e., the mean of the sampling distribution of $\bar{X}$ is obtained by averaging the sample means $\bar{X}_1$, $\bar{X}_2$ and $\bar{X}_3$. Hence the overall sample mean is given by *near to target 8.00000*

$$\frac{7.9 + 8.83 + 7}{3} = 7.91$$

We compute the variance by calculating the sum of the squared deviations of the sample means from this overall mean, thus

$$s_{\bar{x}}^2 = \frac{(7.9-7.91) + (8.83-7.91)^2 + (7-7.91)^2}{3-1} = (0.915)^2 = 0.837$$

But since $\sigma_{\bar{x}}^2 = \frac{\sigma^2}{n}$ solving for σ^2 gives

$$\sigma^2 = n\,\sigma_{\bar{x}}^2 = 4\,(0.837) = 3.35$$

The result $n\,\sigma_{\bar{x}}^2 = 3.35$ is referred to as the between samples estimate of σ^2 and is based on the assumption that the null hypothesis is true. A second estimate of σ^2 is now obtained. This estimate is based on the fact that when a simple random sample is drawn from each of the k populations, each of the sample variances pertaining to these populations provides an estimate of σ^2. These k estimators are pooled into a single estimator known as the within-samples estimate of σ^2. The within-samples estimate of σ^2 is not affected by the equality/inequality of population means because each of the k sample variances are calculated within each sample only, i.e. not between each sample. When the sample sizes are equal, the within-samples estimate of σ^2 can be computed by obtaining the mean of the individual sample variances, e.g. for the example in hand we obtain the within-sample estimate of σ^2 by:

$$\sigma^2 = \frac{0.59 + 0.41 + 0.95}{3} = 0.65$$

Thus, irrespective of whether the null hypothesis is true or not, a second estimate of σ^2 (the within-sample estimate of σ^2) is given by $\sigma^2 = 0.65$. Let us now compare the between-samples estimate of σ^2 and the within-samples of σ^2. The ratio of these two estimates is given by:

$$\frac{3.35}{0.65} = 5.15$$

As stated earlier the between-samples estimate of σ^2 is only appropriate if the null hypothesis is true. If the null hypothesis if false the between-samples estimates will be too large, i.e. it will overestimate. This remark provides us with the basis to conduct a hypothesis test — if the null hypothesis is true then the ratio

$$\frac{\text{between-sample variance}}{\text{within-sample variance}}$$

will be close to 1 but if the null hypothesis is false than the between-samples estimate will be larger than the within-sample estimate and thus the ratio above will be large.

The only question remaining is to define large, i.e. how large a value of the ratio is required to indicate that the null hypothesis is false. If we let

MSB denote between-samples variance and
MSW denote between-samples variance

then the quantity MSB/MSW is the test statistic used in testing hypothesis pertaining to the equality of k means. It is known to follow an F distribution (refer to Appendix 5) with k–1 and N–k degrees of freedom, where N is the total sample size drawn from the k populations. We reject H0 if

$$F = \frac{MSB}{MSW}$$

is large, i.e. if F is greater than the critical value F_α (k – 1, N – k), where Prob $(F > F_\alpha) = \alpha$.

In our example the value of the test statistic F = 5.85. From examination of the F-Tables in Appendix 5 we obtain $F_{.05}(2,9) = 4.26$. Since the test statistic F = 5.85, is greater than the critical value $F_{.05}(2,9) = 4.26$, we reject $H_0: \mu_1 = \mu_2 = \mu_3$.

This concludes our discussion of significance testing. We now turn our attention to the significance of relationships between variables. The aim of these data analysis techniques is to examine the relationship, if any, between variables and assess the degree of association between variables. The former is called 'regression' and the latter is known as the correlation coefficient. The term 'correlation' reflects that variables are in some way related. While there is a huge array of such bivariate measures of association, we confine our discussion here to the more popular techniques.

• The Significance of Relationships and Associations, Simple Linear Regression and Correlation

From the above discussion, simple regression and correlation are concerned with the significance of relationship between pairs of observations, e.g. price and quantity, height and weight etc. These quantities measure the extent of and the nature of the relationship between two interval or ratio-scale variables.[6]

With simple linear regression we fit a straight line that provides the 'best fit' between the dependent variable, Y, and the independent variable, X, while correlation is used to measure the strength of this relationship between the two variables. A frequent implementation of simple linear regression is to provide a prediction of the value of Y given a value of X. Typical applications of both of these techniques in marketing research include describing the relationships between such dependent variables as sales, and independent variables such as price, advertising expenditure, quality of product, and other quantities under the control of the marketing manager.

For example, an environmental consulting firm is considering hiring its own statistician rather than continuing to use the services of a statistical consulting service. The firm wants to know how much to pay that statistician based on years of experience. A check on salaries provides the following information.

Annual salary (thousands of £)	24	20	32	34	35	47
Experience (years)	2	1	3	4	5	7

How can such data be of use to the researcher?

Let Y denote salary and X denote experience. More generally Y is known as the dependent variable and X as the independent variable. This allows for a scatter plot, as presented in Figure 13.1.

Figure 13.1 Scatter plot

From a visual examination of the scatter plot, we observe that a straight line relationship seems to exist between Y = salary and X = experience. We would like to fit a straight line through this set of data. Although many straight lines could be drawn we concentrate on a particular line know as the 'least squares regression line'. The formula for this line is given by $Y = \alpha + \beta X$

where $\alpha = \bar{y} - \beta \bar{x}$

and $\beta = \dfrac{n \Sigma xy - \Sigma x \Sigma y}{n \Sigma x^2 - (\Sigma x)^2}$

Note n = Number of data points
Σx = Sum of all the X values
Σx² = Sum of the squared values of X
Σy = Sum of all the Y values
Σxy = Sum of the products of X times Y
X = Mean of the X values
Y = Mean of the Y values
α = Slope of the least squares equation
β = The constant term in the least squares equations i.e. where the line intersects the Y axis,

In calculating a and b it is helpful to lay out the calculation as follows:

X	Y	XY	X²
2	24	48	4
1	20	20	1
3	32	96	9
4	34	136	16
5	36	180	25
7	47	329	49

Then

$$\beta = \frac{n \Sigma xy - \Sigma x \Sigma y}{n \Sigma x^2 - (\Sigma x)^2} = \frac{6(809) - 22(193)}{6(104) - (22)^2} = \frac{608}{140} = 4.34$$

and

$$\alpha = \overline{Y} - \beta X = 32.17 - 4.34\,(3.67) = 16.23$$

Finally the least squares equation is given by Y = 16.23 + 4.34X. Using the equation to predict the salary as a statistician after six years of experience i.e. find Y, when X = 6. Substituting for X = 6 we obtain Y = 16.23 + 4.34 (6) = 42.27.

The Pearson's product moment correlation coefficient, commonly known as the sample correlation coefficient, denoted by r, is given by

$$r = \frac{n\,(\Sigma x y) - (\Sigma x)\,(\Sigma y)}{\sqrt{(n(\Sigma x^2) - (\Sigma x)^2)\,(n(\Sigma Y^2) - (\Sigma Y)^2)}}$$

and is a numerical measure of the linear association between two variables that takes values between -1 and +1. Values near +1 indicate a strong positive linear relationship, values near -1 indicate a strong negative linear relationship, and values near zero indicate lack of a linear relationship. Figure 13.2 gives the values of the correlation coefficient for several scatter plots.

Figure 13.2 Correlation coefficients

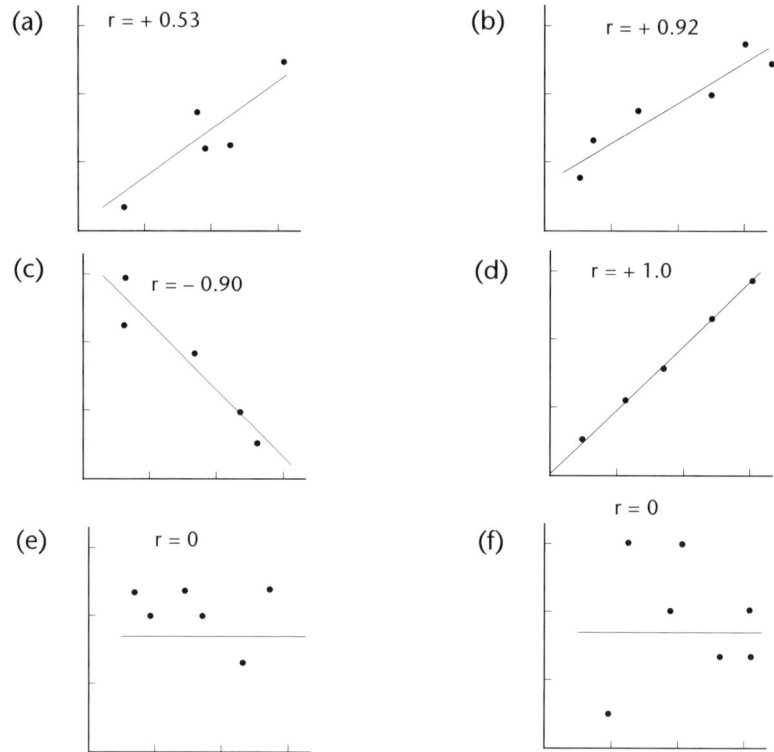

Thus returning to our example, r = 0.986.

The sample correlation coefficient is almost equal to unity, so we say that a near perfect linear relationship exists between salary and experience.

The coefficient of determination is a measure of the goodness of fit of the estimated regression equation. It can be interpreted as the proportion of the variation in dependent variable Y that is explained by the estimated regression equation. This coefficient, denoted R^2, is given by

$R^2 = r^2$ i.e. the square of the sample correlation coefficient.

Thus $R^2 = (0.986)^2 = 0.972$, or 97.2% of the variation in Y is explained by the estimated regression equation.

The correlation coefficient is a measure of the linear association between two variables for which interval or ratio data are available. We now discuss a measure of the association between two variables when only *ordinal data* are available, i.e. the Spearman Rank-Correlation Coefficient.

• The Spearman Rank-Correlation Coefficient

The Spearman Rank-correlation Coefficient is defined as

$$R_s = 1 - \frac{6 \sum_{i=1}^{n} d_i^2}{n(n^2 - 1)}$$

where n = the number of items or individuals being ranked
        x_i = the rank of item i with respect to one variable
        y_i = the rank of item i with respect to a second variable and
        d_i = $x_i - y_i$.

For example, the student union at the Institute of Technology, Sligo, surveyed both recent and current students to obtain information on the quality of lecturing at the Institute. An analysis of the responses provided the lecturing-ability rankings reported in Table 13.7 for ten lecturers.

Table 13.7 Responses concerning lecturer ability

Lecturer	Current students	Recent students (Graduates)
1	4	6
2	6	8
3	8	5
4	3	1
5	2	2
6	1	3
7	5	7
8	10	9
9	7	4
10	9	10

The computations for the required coefficient are given in Table 13.8.

Table 13.8 Spearman Rank-correlation Coefficient

Lecturer	x_i = Ranking by current student	y_i = ranking by recent student	$d_i = x_i - y_i$	d_i^2
1	4	6	−2	4
2	6	8	−2	4
3	8	5	3	9
4	3	1	2	4

Table 13.8 continued

Lecturer	x_i = Ranking by current student	y_i = ranking by recent student	$d_i = x_i - y_i$	d_i^2
5	2	2	0	0
6	1	3	−2	4
7	5	7	−2	4
8	10	9	1	1
9	7	4	3	9
10	9	10	−1	1

From this, $R_s = \dfrac{1 - 6(40)}{10(100-1)} = 0.24$

The Spearman Rank-correlation Coefficient ranges from −1.0 to +1.0 and its interpretation is similar to that of the sample correlation coefficient in that positive values near 1.0 indicate a strong association between the rankings, i.e. as one rank increases, the other rank increases. Rank correlations near −1.0 indicate a strong negative association between the rankings, i.e. as one rank increases the other rank decreases. The value obtained in our example, $R_s = 0.24$, indicates a weak correlation between current and recent students. Lecturers ranked high by current students do not tend to rank high by recent students.

• **Summary**

Once data has been reduced and summarised, the researcher is then in a position to further analyse the data. One such analysis is to test the data for significance of differences of numbers, i.e. hypothesis testing.

Hypothesis testing is a statistical procedure that uses samples data to determine whether or not a statement about the value of a population parameter should be rejected. The hypothesis must be composed of two competing statements, a null hypothesis H0 and an alternative hypothesis H1. Hypothesis testing can be applied to a sample mean or proportion for either a large or small sample. If the data is in a frequency distribution form, the chi-square goodness of fit test is used. If dealing with experimental data, the analysis of variance is employed. Finally, regression and correlation measure relationships, that is, the extent of and degree of association between variables.

Key Terms

Null hypothesis
Critical region
Test statistic

Alternative hypothesis
Critical value
Level of significance

One-tailed test
Analysis of variance
Chi-square test
ANOVA table
Dependent variable
Correlation

P-value
Spearman Rank-correlation coefficient
Dependent variable
Correlation coefficient
Independent variable
Simple linear regression

Questions

1. What is univariate and bivariate analysis?
2. Discuss the role and function of significance testing in marketing.
3. Discuss a hypothesis for (a) a population mean for large samples, and (b) a population proportion for small samples.
4. Detail the steps for undertaking hypothesis testing.
5. What is meant by the significance level of a test?
6. Explain why the chi-square test is popular in marketing.
7. What is analysis of variance?
8. Detail two techniques for measuring and testing the significance of relationships between two variables.
9. Define the Spearman Rank-correlation Coefficient.

Problems and Assignments

1. The owner of a food manufacturing plant claims that 45% of Irish consumers purchase his product at least once a week. In a sample of 200 consumers, 80 purchased his product within the last week. For this situation:
   (a) Formulate the appropriate null and alternative hypothesis.
   (b) At the 0.10 level of significance, conduct a non-directional test of the null hypothesis.
2. The manager of a restaurant contends that patrons spend an average of 50 minutes in his establishment. In observing a sample of 80 customers, a market analyst finds their average stay to be 45 minutes, with a standard deviation of 15 minutes. In a non-direction test at the 0.10 level of significance, evaluate the manager's claim.
3. Using the data of question (2), repeat the test at the 0.01 level of significance.
4. In an experiment concerning the process of learning, the average time required by nine adults to comprehend a mathematical procedure was five minutes with a standard deviation of 1.3 minutes. At a level of 0.05, does this support the claim that the average time required by a group of adults to comprehend such a mathematical procedure is not more than four minutes?
5. Consider the following hypothesis test, where p is the population proportion: a sample of 220 provided a sample proportion P = 0.58

(a) Compute the value of the test statistic, when H₀ : π ≤ 0.6 and H₁: π > 0.6.
(b) What is your conclusion?

6. Telecom Eireann find that, at national level, 45% of phone bills are paid on time, 35% are paid two weeks in arrears and the remainder are paid a month in arrears. From a survey of 400 customers in the south of Ireland, the corresponding percentages were 65%; 30% and 5%.
   (a) At the 0.05 level, is the payment period of the south consumers significantly different from the rest of the country?
   (b) At the 0.025 level, is there a significant difference?

7. A sample of 200 individuals was randomly selected from all candidates who recently took the examination of a certain professional body in Ireland. The examination results (pass/fail) and existing education qualifications of individuals in the sample were examined and were as follows

	Pass	Fail
Postgraduate	68	22
Graduate	17	9
Leaving Certificate	20	32
No qualifications	12	20

   Analysis of these data produced a chi-square (X_2 = 25.704) with d.f. = 3,0 = .000019
   (a) State the null hypothesis tested and indicate whether it would be accepted or rejected.
   (b) Interpret the statistical information cited.
   (c) Suggest at least one other statistical measure/index which might be used to further analyse these data.

   (Adapted from a Marketing Institute of Ireland Examination Question, 1996)

8. The attached table is extracted from the SPSS printout.
   Cross tabulation of willingness to purchase from catalogue (V3) with whether respondent has purchased from it before (V4)

Count Row percent Column percent Total percent	Never ordered	Ordered before but not within past year	Ordered within past year	Row rotal
Unwilling	20 40.0 46.5 16.1	20 40.0 51.3 16.1	10 20.0 23.8 8.1	50 40.3
Somewhat willing	7 20.0 16.3 5.6	11 31.4 28.2 8.9	17 48.6 40.5 13.7	35 28.2

Very willing	16	8	15	39
	41.0	20.5	38.5	31.5
	37.2	20.5	35.7	
	12.9	6.5	12.1	
Column Total	43	39	42	124
	34.7	31.5	33.9	100.0

Raw chi square = 10.997 with 4 degrees of freedom
Significance = .027
Contingency coefficient = .285

(a) Interpret the table.
(b) Show clearly in your analysis which are the null and alternative hypotheses and illustrate the role of hypothesis testing in marketing research.
(c) Explain some of the dangers and pitfalls in the use of cross tabulations and their associated statistics.
(Adapted from a Marketing Institute of Ireland Examination question, 1993)

9. A group of 30 customers is randomly selected from those shopping in a large supermarket. They are asked, as they leave the store, to indicate on a ten-point equal interval scale, their assessment of value for money obtained in the store. A score of 1 indicate very poor value and a score of 10 represents excellent/unbeatable value. They are also asked to state to the nearest point how much they have just spent in the store. In the situation outlined:
   (a) State a suitable null hypothesis which the researchers are likely to wish to test.
   (b) Identify an appropriate statistical test which would be used to test the null hypothesis and explain your choice.
   (c) How would you decide whether or not to accept the null hypothesis?
   (d) Can you suggest an alternative method of analysing these data?
   (Adapted from a Marketing Institute of Ireland Examination question, 1997)

10. An analysis of the sales performance and scores on a psychological test of 'salespersonship' of twelve sales executives produced the following data:

Table 13.9

Person	Number of units sold	Test score out of 100
A	59	75
B	37	45
C	45	16
D	32	72
E	16	34
F	11	16
G	23	40
H	16	32

Table 13.9 *contd*

Person	Number of units sold	Test score out of 100
I	43	25
J	21	32
K	25	45
L	17	35

Analysis of these data produced the following results:

	Mean	Standard deviation	Est. standard error
Units sold	28.75	14.60	4.21
Test score	38.91	18.71	5.40

The value of t is −1.9512. The corresponding probability value with eleven degrees of freedom for a two-tailed test is .074.

(a) State the null hypothesis tested and indicate, giving reasons, whether or not you would accept it.
(b) Interpret carefully the statistical results cited.
(c) Can you think of another way of analysing these data?

(Adapted from a Marketing Institute of Ireland Examination question, 1997)

11. A sample of 100 adults is randomly chosen from the population of an Irish city. An examination of the employment status and educational qualifications of individuals in the sample reveals the following pattern:

Education	Employed	Unemployed
No qualifications	10	12
Leaving Certificate	20	15
Higher education	30	13
	60	40

A chi-square (X^2) statistic and associated information is calculated and is as follows:

X^2 = 3.768   d.f. = 2   p = .152

A second random sample of 200 adults is drawn and it reveals a strikingly similar pattern.

Education	Employed	Unemployed
No qualifications	20	24
Leaving Certificate	40	30
Higher Education	60	26
	120	80

X^2 = 7.535   d.f. = 2   p = .0231

(Adapted from a Marketing Institute of Ireland Examination Question, 1992)

Chapter 14

MULTIVARIATE DATA ANALYSIS

> - **Chapter Overview**
> - Introduction • What is 'Multivariate' Analysis? • Types of Multivariate Techniques • Multiple Regression Analysis • Multiple Regression Illustrated • Discriminant Analysis • Discriminant Analysis Considerations, Classification of Groups • Discriminant Analysis Illustrated • Factor Analysis • Factor Analysis, Basic Principles • Factor Analysis Illustrated • Cluster Analysis • Cluster Analysis Illustrated • Multidimensional Scaling (MDS) • MDS Considerations, Direct versus Derived • MDS Illustrated • Multivariate Techniques, Concluding Comments • Summary

• Introduction

In this last chapter concentrating on data analysis, we turn our attention to 'multivariate' analysis and away from univariate analysis (dealing with one variable, e.g. mean) and bivariate analysis (association between two variables, e.g. age and the right to vote). Our discussion here of multivariate techniques is rudimentary. The researcher is not obliged to have the degree of knowledge and understanding that a statistician would have of multivariate methods. However, as marketing researchers, we need to know what these techniques are, when to employ them, and their limitations, to enable effective and efficient management decision-making.

With this in mind, by the end of this chapter the reader will be able to:

1. explain the term 'multivariate' analysis;
2. distinguish between univariate, bivariate and multivariate techniques;
3. describe five commonly used multivariate techniques, namely:
   - multiple regression analysis;
   - discriminant analysis;
   - factor analysis;
   - cluster analysis;
   - multidimensional scaling.
4. identify the appropriate marketing circumstance for their application, and specify their limitations.

• What is 'Multivariate' Analysis?

Multivariate analysis is data analysis dealing with several variables simultaneously — a distinguishing feature which differentiates multivariate techniques from other data analysis methods, i.e. univariate and bivariate analysis, as outlined above. More formally, multivariate techniques can be defined as 'all statistical methods that simultaneously analyse multiple measurements on each individual or object under investigation'.[1] Thus, multivariate techniques differ from univariate and bivariate, in that they *simultaneously* analyse multiple combinations of variables that are inter-related and thus cannot be separately interpreted.

In defining the term 'multivariate', the use of preprogrammed computer packages, for example, SPSS, Minitab and SAS, is inescapable, as such computer applications are intrinsic to the processing and analysis of complex, large sets of data, utilising multivariate techniques. Recent technological advancements and the widespread availability of PC statistical packages are encouraging a significant growth in the use of multivariate applications — a trend which will no doubt continue to seriously impact upon marketing research.[2] Linked to this, is the development of new multivariate methods.[3,4]

Multivariate techniques have the ability to deal with complex situations — reflected in the need to analyse several variables at any one point in time. This dimension to multivariate techniques is very valuable in marketing because it facilitates a more realistic analysis of markets, consumers, products and suppliers facing most firms (compared to univariate or bivariate techniques).[5] This said, any researcher planning to employ such techniques has to appreciate the assumptions, data collection requirements and limitations of such approaches. Be warned — failure to do so often results in a multivariate technique being applied in incorrect circumstances and thus giving rise to a potentially disastrous management decision. The old adage applies here — 'no information is better than wrong information'.

Therefore, multivariate techniques are appropriate for data analysis when:

1. the collected data pertains to multiple variables;
2. there are a large number of observations or respondents;
3. there may be interaction and/or interdependency between the variables;
4. there is a serious need by management to capture the realistic, complex and competitive marketplace, as is often the case in new product development, market segmentation studies, product positioning and media selection.

• Types of Multivariate Techniques

Multivariate techniques fall into two broad camps:

1. dependent techniques;
2. independent techniques.

The terminology here is reminiscent of that in experimentation. Dependent multivariate methods refer to the fact that the dependent variable is affected by the independent variable. For example, brand awareness is influenced by advertising, hence, brand awareness is the dependent variable and the advertising could be considered the independent variable. In this chapter, we confine ourselves to multivariate techniques that are based upon one dependent variable. There are multivariate dependent techniques that deal with two or more dependent variables, but these are beyond the scope of this chapter.[6,7] If there is no identified dependent variable, the researcher is then dealing with a host of variables (several or more) that are independent or interdependent upon each other. For example, age, social class, occasion, education, attitudes, lifestyle and personality all interact to influence the type and brand of coffee one drinks.

This classification of multivariate methods into either dependent or independent is used by researchers to choose the relevant and appropriate technique, given a particular situation, as shown in Figures 14.1 (a) and (b).

Figure 14.1 (a) Choosing the appropriate multivariate technique

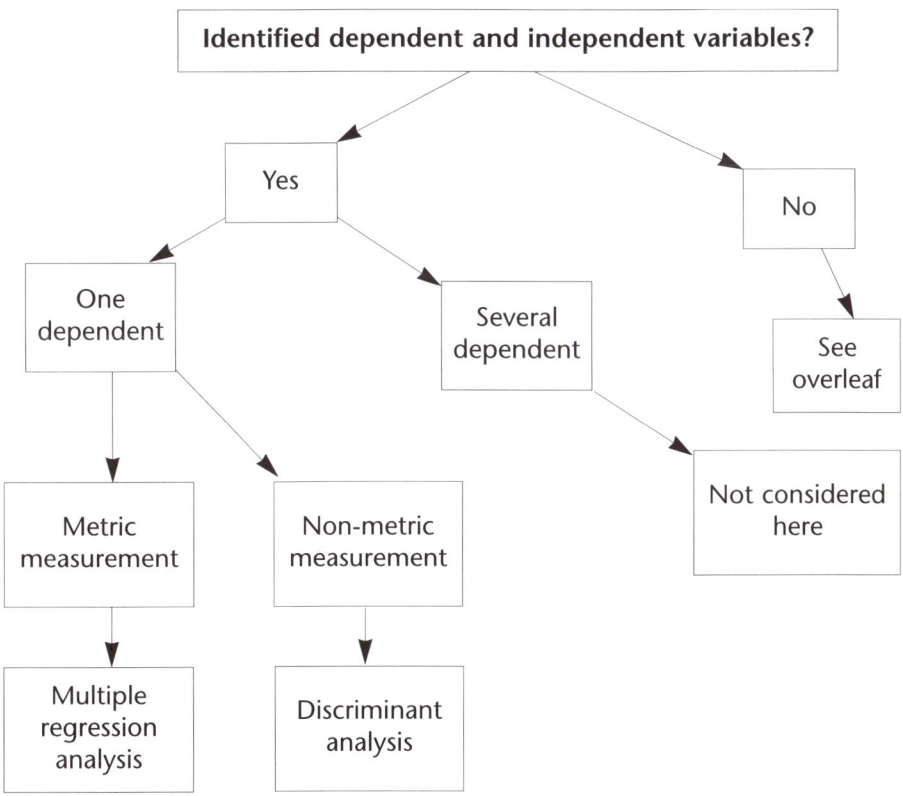

Figure 14.1 (b) Choosing the appropriate multivariate technique

```
                  Identified dependent and independent variables?
                         /                            \
                       Yes                            No
                        |                           /    \
                        v                          v      v
                See previous                  Metric      Non-metric
                  diagram                  measurement   measurement
                                             /    \           |
                                            v      v          v
                                      Summarise/  Summarise
                                       reduce    groups /
                                      variables  individuals
                                          |          |          |
                                          v          v          v
                                       Factor     Cluster      MDS
                                      analysis   analysis
```

From the above figures, another dimension is brought to bear in deciding what technique to employ or how to classify multivariate methods — the issue of metric or non-metric data. Metric data is data based upon an interval or ratio scale of measurement and thus quantitative, while non-metric data is generated by either a nominal or ordinal scale and is qualitative in nature. It is also worth noting at this point, that the metric/non-metric debate has to be factored into the design of a questionnaire or any other data collection instrument, to allow for the use of multivariate techniques at the data analysis stage, if so desired. As multivariate methods grow in popularity, the data collection process will increasingly reflect this.[8]

We now consider the more commonly used multivariate techniques in marketing, with the following questions in mind:

1. What does the technique do?
2. How does the technique work?
3. How is it used in reality?

Multiple Regression Analysis

Multiple regression analysis is the study of how a dependent variable Y is related to two or more independent variables. Since many regression problems involve more than one independent variable, multiple regression is a valuable technique. Based upon an extension of regression analysis as presented in Chapter 13, the output and interpretation of multiple regression is similar.

Multiple Regression Illustrated

Table 14.1 shows the monthly sales at a tourist attraction over a twelve-month period, together with the admission price and the mean number of hours sunshine in each month. The number of visitors to the attraction per month is also given. Using a statistical package such as SPSS or Minitab, and the data provided in Table 14.1, consider the following questions:

1. How can we estimate the influence of the price, number of visitors and hours of sunshine on sales?
2. How can we use the results to predict sales when 28,000 visitors pay an admission of £5 during a month with a mean ten hours of sunshine?

Table 14.1 Regression printout

Month	Sales (£,000)	Price	Visitors (£,000)	Sunshine (Mean daily hours)
Jan	33	3	10	3.0
Feb	42	3	11	3.5
Mar	45	3	14	4.5
Apr	68	3	16	5.5
May	75	3	17	6.5
Jun	180	5	25	10.5
Jul	195	5	30	11.0
Aug	210	5	35	11.0
Sep	78	3	18	6.0
Oct	42	3	12	3.5
Nov	32	3	10	2.5
Dec	26	3	8	2.0

The concepts of a regression equation and a regression model introduced in Chapter 13 can be applied here, i.e. the regression equation is:

$$E(Y) = \alpha + X_1 + X_2 + X_3.$$

In the context of the present example if we let:

Y = Sales
α = slope of the least squares equation
X_1 = Price
X_2 = Visitors and
X_3 = (mean daily hours of) sunshine

then the regression equation is given by:

$$E(Y) = \alpha + \text{Price} + \text{Visitors} + \text{Sunshine}.$$

When the given data is submitted to a statistical computer package for analysis, the estimated multiple regression equation is given by:

$$E(Y) = -99.0 + 29.4 \,(\text{Price}) + 2.70 \,(\text{Visitors}) + 6.11 \,(\text{Sunshine}).$$

This tells us that, since the data relates to a tourist attraction, it is believed that peak season prices would be higher than off-peak prices due to price promotion being carried out to stimulate visitor interest. This belief is validated by the data, i.e. sales increase as prices increase (the coefficient of Price in the regression equation is positive). We further observe that there is a positive relationship between sales and the number of visitors and a positive relationship between sales and the mean daily hours of sunshine. Next, the units of measurement are used in interpreting the size of the coefficients:

- A one-unit increase in price will increase sales by 29.4 units or £29,400.
- A one-unit increase in visitor numbers means an extra 1,000 visitors and a sales increase of 2.70 units or £2,700.
- An extra hour of sunshine will account for 6.11 extra units of sales or £6,110.

To date, we have interpreted the regression coefficients. We now wish to test for a significant regression relation, i.e. in the multiple regression model, so we wish to test

H_0: $X_1 = X_2 = X_3 = 0$
H_1: One or more of the parameters is not equal to zero.

If H_0 is rejected, we have sufficient statistical evidence to conclude that one or more of the parameters is not equal to zero and that the overall relationship between Sales and the set of independent variables Price, Visitors and Sunshine is significant. Alternatively, if H_0 cannot be rejected, we do not possess sufficient evidence to conclude that a significant relationship is present.

F-test

To conduct the required hypothesis test we perform an F-test, i.e. adopt either one of the following decision rules.

1. Reject H_0 if $F > F_\alpha (p, n - p - 1)$

where

F is the value of the test statistic and
$F(p, n - p - 1)$ is the critical value, which is obtained from an F distribution with p (number of independent variables) and $n - p - 1$ degrees of freedom (see Appendix 5).

2. Reject H_0 if the p-value associated with the test statistic is less than the level of significance α.

The calculation of this test statistic F is beyond the scope of this book; however in practice such calculations are performed by statistical packages and thus the emphasis here will be placed on interpreting and utilising such output. In our example, the output is given in Table 14.2.

Table 14.2 Regression computer printout

The regression equation is
Sales =.−99.0 + 29.4 Price + 2.70 Visitors + 6.11 Sunshine

Predictor	Coef	Stdev	t-ratio	P
Constant	-98.995	7.022	−14.10	0.000
Price	29.353	3.243	9.05	0.000
Visitors	2.7019	0.5979	4.52	0.000
Sunshine	6.108	1.609	3.80	0.005

s = 3.930   R-sq = 99.8%   R-sq(adj) = 99.7%

Analysis of variance

Source	DF	SS	MS	F	P
Regression	3	51353	17118	1108.5	0.000
Error	8	124	15		
Total	11	51477			

Source	DF	SEQ SS
Price	1	47961
Visitors	1	3170
Sunshine	1	223

Unusual observations

Obs.	Price	Sales	Fit	Stdev. Fit	Residual	St. Resid
3	3.00	45.00	54.38	1.36	−9.38	−2.54R

In the analysis of variance part of the output, we obtain the value of the test statistic, i.e. F = 1108.50. With a level of significance a = 0.05 and referring to the F-tables in Appendix 5, the critical value is given by:

$$F\alpha\ (p, n - p - 1) = F0.05\ (3.12 - 3 - 1) = F0.05\ (3,8) = 4.07.$$

Since the test statistic is greater than the critical value (i.e. since 1108.50 is greater than 4.07) we reject H_0: $X_1 = X_2 = X_3 = 0$ and conclude that one or more of the parameters is not equal to zero and that the overall relationship between Sales and the set of independent variables Price, Visitors and Sunshine is significant. The p-value = 0.000 in the last column of the analysis of variance table also indicates that we can reject H_0 as the p-value is less than α.

In our discussion of simple linear regression we used the coefficient of determination to measure the goodness of fit for the estimated regression equation. The term 'multiple coefficient of determination' is applied when we are measuring the goodness of fit for the estimated multiple regression equation and again is denoted by R^2.

In this example, R^2 = 99.8%. Therefore 99.8% of the variability in Sales is explained by the estimated multiple regression equation with Price, Visitors and Sunshine as the independent variables.

• Discriminant Analysis

Discriminant analysis discriminates between respondents who fall into one group or category from those who fall into another group or category,[9] for example, jeep owners versus car owners. That is, discriminant analysis determines the characteristics of one group that differentiate it from the characteristics of another group. So, discriminant analysis classifies objects/subjects into groups and identifies those variables that best determine group membership. Thus, the objective in using discriminant analysis is to classify people/objects into one of two or more groups, based on the measurements of various independent variables, and predict which particular group or class an individual or entity belongs to.

On a technical level, discriminant analysis is a statistical technique which distinguishes one dependent variable with respect to a set of independent variables. The dependent variable is of the nominal/ordinal scale of measurement and represents a group measurement. So, for discriminant analysis it is important that the number and measurement level of the dependent variable is known in advance.

Discriminant analysis is utilised when:

1. there is an identified dependent variable;
2. there is only one dependent variable (other multivariate techniques can be used if there are two or more dependent variables;
3. the dependent variable is measured using non-metric scales;
4. there is a large set of observations or responses, i.e. large data set.

- **Discriminant Analysis Considerations — Classification of Groups**

An important feature of discriminant analysis is the identification of those variables that best determine group membership. Here we examine members of known groups to identify those variables which best determine group membership. For example, if we are in the business of direct mail sales we may wish to determine those variables that best discriminate between past interviewees who have purchased goods by direct mail, and past interviewees who have not purchased goods by direct mail. Such variables may include age, sex, marital status and proximity to shopping centres.

For the purpose of conveying the concepts in discriminant analysis we will suppose that for buyers and non-buyers of three types of car we have information pertaining to two independent variables — the age of each buyer/non-buyer and the number of children for each buyer/non-buyer. Scatter diagrams for each type of car are shown in Figure 14.2.

Figure 14.2 (a, b and c) Scatter diagram for discriminant analysis

(c)

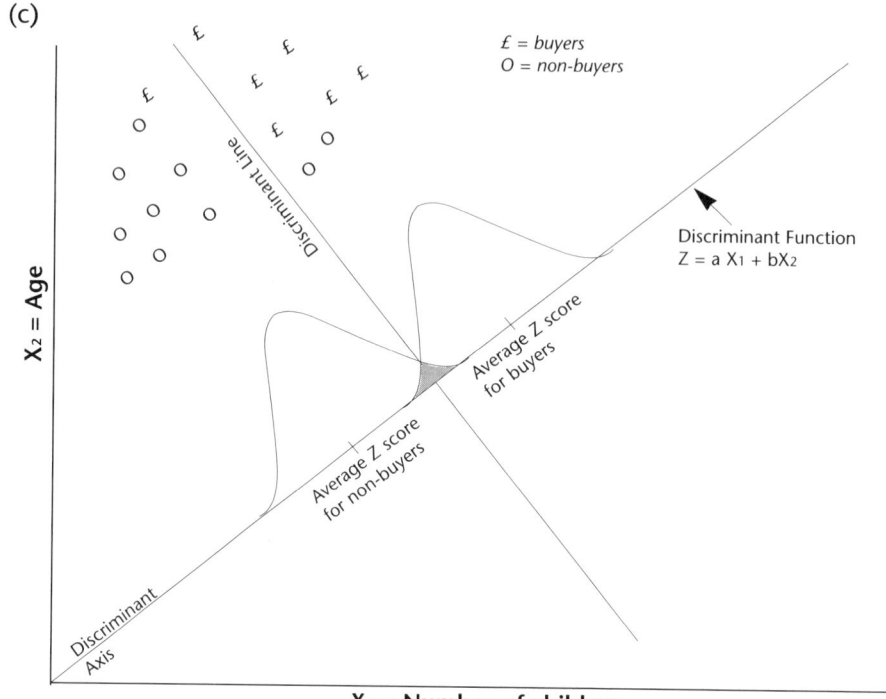

X_1 = Number of children

Car type 1:

Referring to part (a) in Figure 14.2 the ability of X_2 (age) to discriminate between buyers and non-buyers is very weak, particularly in comparison to variable X_1 (number of children) where the two groups are very distinct from each other along this dimension or variable. Thus the dimension X_1 is the only one that really separates the two groups.

Car type 2:

Referring to part (b) in Figure 14.2 the ability of X_2 to discriminate between buyers and non-buyers is very strong. This is in contrast to the discriminatory power of X_1. Thus the two groups are separated from each other only in the vertical direction.

Car type 3:

Referring to part (c) in Figure 14.2 the groups are not separated by a single dimension as with car type 1 and 2 but with respect to both dimensions, indicating that both variables differentiate between the members of the two groups.

The discriminant axis is the line along which the groups are most separated. Discriminant analysis tries to find this straight line which discriminates one group from another, when imposed upon a scatter diagram, such as the one above.

Multivariate Data Analysis 415

Statistically, it is the direction along which the ratio

$$\frac{\text{Variation between groups}}{\text{Variation within groups}}$$

is maximised. Maximisation of this ratio is intuitively appealing as we wish to distinguish between groups in such a manner that the variation within each group (or spread of data within each group) is small compared to the variation between each group (or spread of data within each group). If this ratio is large, then individuals in each group will be very close, or alike, to one another in contrast to the distance, or dissimilarity, of individuals between groups. The term 'centroid' can be taken to refer to the multidimensional mean.

• **Discriminant Analysis Illustrated**

To gain some insight into this technique of discriminant analysis, consider an example of a used-car salesman, Bernard Kenny. Bernard, in an attempt to identify genuine car buyers, has collected considerable survey data for three variables:

X_1: The customer's approximate age.
X_2: The number of minutes the customer spends examining the car in the forecourt before discussing a price with Bernard.
X_3: Whether or not the customer bought a car.

Figure 14.3 Scatter diagram pertaining to X_1 and X_2.

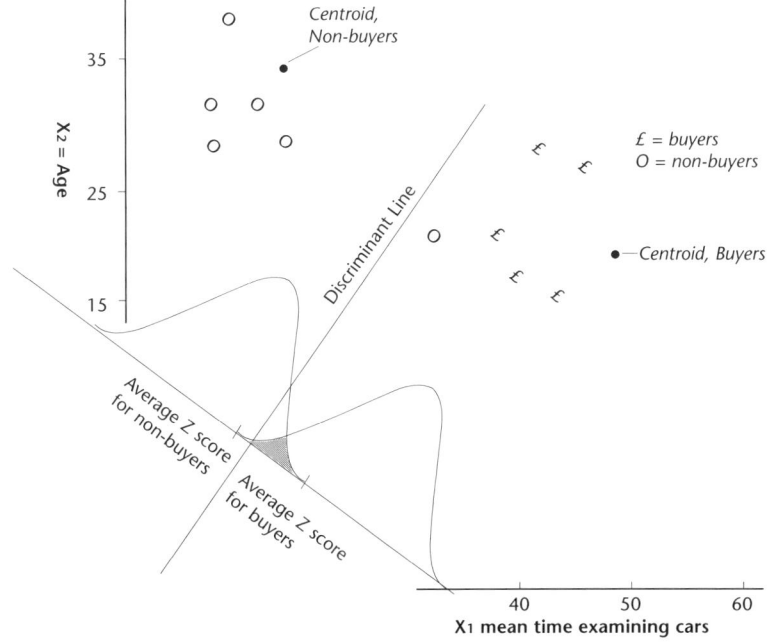

From observation alone, we note that both dimensions/variables X_1 and X_2 help to classify individuals into one of two groups. Buyers tend to be younger and spend greater time examining a car than non-buyers. The examination of centroids for both groups shows that the averages for buyers and non-buyers differ on both dimensions, i.e.

Table 14.3
Centroids for discriminant analysis

	Non-buyers	Buyers
X_1: Mean time spent examining cars	22.1	40.0
X_2: Mean age	37.0	27.3

In Table 14.3 the two groups have been classified by means of discriminant analysis. (The calculation of those entities pertaining to discriminant analysis has not been included here but in practice these calculations are performed by appropriate software, as previously noted.) The discriminant axis is neither horizontal or vertical but diagonal, indicating that both variables help to differentiate between individuals of the two groups. The discriminant line, i.e. our cut-off point for determining group membership, is located halfway between the centroids and is perpendicular to the discriminant axis.

With this information, Bernard can now classify future customers into one of two groups: potential buyers and potential non-buyers, and reflect this in his marketing strategy.

- **Factor Analysis**

Factor analysis is concerned with the identification of 'a few number of variables that are responsible for the correlation of a large number of variables',[10] i.e., factor analysis attempts to identify underlying common dimensions that explain the relationships in a complex set of large data. For this reason, it is sometimes referred to as a data reduction method. Essentially, the aim of this technique is to condense the larger data into a reduced data set or factors.[11]

A researcher frequently ends up with a large number of variables from a set of respondents drawn from a given population. However, it is frequently the case that many of these variables may be highly correlated and thus much of the information contained in one variable is contained in another variable. For example, if you own a very expensive house then you probably own a very expensive car and vice-versa. Thus, information on the respondent's house price is somewhat redundant, if information pertaining to car type is available. In this vein, we employ factor analysis to reduce the number of variables without an undue loss of information.

Factor analysis is of further use, in that we can also identify the dimensionality of the data. If we had 100 variables measuring only five different basic characteristics of our sample, then obviously the employment of 100 variables represents gross inefficiencies. (The money could possibly have been better spend on managing response or non-response error, for example.)

Therefore, factor analysis is used by a researcher when:

1. the researcher cannot distinguish between the dependent variable(s) and the independent variable(s);
2. the variables are metric-based;
3. a large number of variables are to be reduced or summarised into a smaller set, as in new product development, product positioning, measuring opinion leaders and opinion-seekers,[12] assessing advertising readership or establishing product/service quality factors.

Factor Analysis, Basic Principles

Factor analysis typically starts with a matrix of correlations between the variables of interest, as shown in Table 14.4. We note that variables X_1 and X_2 are highly correlated. This suggests 'variable redundancy'.

Table 14.4 Correlation between variables

	X_1	X_2	X_3
X_1	1	0.91	0.20
X_2	0.91	1	0.15
X_3	0.20	0.15	1

Factor analysis attempts to generate three important measures:

1. the proportion of responses (statements) variability explained by the factors, commonly labelled 'communalities';
2. a standardised score, 'eigenvalues', which is the actual response measured in terms of the number of standard deviations from the mean;
3. the correlation between each statement score and the various original variables, called 'factor loadings'. An illustration serves to explain these terms and factor analysis further.

Factor Analysis Illustrated

A survey is conducted to examine those attributes which influence consumers in their choice of car. The researcher measured a sample of customers by means of the nine statements shown in Table 14.5 below.

Table 14.5 Customer responses

Statements	I	II	III	Communalities
I like sport cars	0.75	0.20	0.03	0.60
I insist that my car has good acceleration	0.68	0.30	0.09	0.56
I watch a lot of Grand Prix racing	0.81	−0.16	0.15	0.70
I like cars with improved heating	0.21	0.73	0.21	0.62
I like cars with leather seats	0.33	0.69	0.04	0.59
I prefer a quiet car	0.25	0.56	−0.04	0.38
I insist on a robust car	0.29	0.33	0.68	0.66
I prefer a car with a ten-year warranty	0.31	0.11	0.71	0.61
I insist on a car which rarely requires servicing	−0.18	0.08	0.62	0.42
Eigenvalues	2.11	1.61	1.43	
Percent of variance explained	23.4%	17.8%	15.8%	
Cumulative percent of variance explained	23.4%	41.2%	57.0%	

The question to be addressed here is whether these statements are measuring nine different aspects of the sample or are the nine measurements representative of a smaller number of more basic consumer characteristics? The data was processed by means of a factor analysis software program (such as those in SPSS, SAS or Minitab) and some of the output is shown in Table 14.5. The computer printout demonstrates that there are only three distinct aspects being measured by the nine statements, or at least three factors account for an acceptable proportion of the variation in the sample. These three factors are as follows:

Factor 1

Each of the first three statements in Table 14.5 has a high loading or correlation with the first factor and thus these three statements are identifying a single underlying attribute of consumer demand which may be termed 'I prefer fast cars'.

Factor 2

The next three statements in the table have a high loading on the second factor. These statements are measuring 'I prefer comfortable cars'.

Factor 3

The last three statements are measuring the underling factor 'I prefer reliable cars'.

Thus the nine statements may essentially be reduced to only three. The factor loading in the table, on each of the nine statements, is high on a single factor only.

Table 14.5 also contains additional information in the form of communalities and eigenvalues. The communality is the proportion of each statement's variability that is explained by the three factors. The three factors are better at explaining the variability in some statements than in others. For example the factors explain 70% of the variability in the statement 'I watch a lot of Grand Prix racing' but only 38% of the variability in the statement 'I prefer a quiet car'. In seven of the nine statements, the three factors explain at least 56% of the variability in these statements. The eigenvalue is the sum of the squared factor loadings for each factor.

• Cluster Analysis

This is a technique which groups or clusters objects or individuals so that objects/individuals within each group are more similar to each other than they are to objects/individuals of different groups.[13] Cluster analysis procedures search through large amounts of data and 'identify respondents who have given identical or similar answers to a certain combination of questions', these respondents then form a cluster.[14] Cluster analysis is utilised in marketing research when:

1. the dependent variable(s) and independent variable(s) cannot be differentiated;
2. the data is metric data;
3. a large group of people or objects is to be summarised, as is the case with market segmentation studies or facilitating the selection of test markets for experimentation purposes.

Cluster analysis measures 'similarity' between respondents. This similarity is normally measured in terms of distance between respondents. One commonly used distance measure is the 'euclidean' distance.[15]

Cluster Analysis Illustrated

Suppose we are considering the clustering of customers based on attitudes towards shopping. Suppose five attitudinal variables are employed upon which consumers are asked to express their degree of agreement using a six-point scale (1 = disagree, 2 = agree). The variables are given by:

Var. 1: I shop for bargains
Var. 2: I only buy designer brands
Var. 3: I only shop during the sales
Var. 4: I insist on a guarantee with products
Var. 5: I shop mostly at discount shops

A computer application (SPSS, SAS or Minitab etc.) on analysing the responses would include a table of centroids for the desired number of clusters. Suppose that we specify that the desired number of clusters is two and that these centroids produced by the computer are given by Table 14.6 (each entry corresponds to the mean value of each variable for all objects/respondents in that cluster).

Table 14.6 Cluster analysis and centroids

	Var. 1	Var. 2	Var. 3	Var. 4	Var. 5
Cluster number 1	5.1	2.8	4.8	2.9	5.0
Cluster number 2	3.0	4.9	1.0	5.1	1.9

All objects/respondents have being grouped into either cluster 1 or cluster 2. We see that objects/respondents in cluster 1 have a high value on variables 1, 3 and 5 but low values on variables 2 and 4. Such objects/respondents could be termed 'shoppers concerned with price'. Alternatively, objects/respondents in cluster 2 have a high value on variables 2 and 4 but low values on variables 1, 3 and 5 and could be termed 'shoppers concerned with quality'.

• Multidimensional Scaling

Multidimensional scaling (MDS) is a class of procedures for describing and representing consumer attitudes, especially perceptions and preferences. In this manner, MDS attempts to identify important consumer attributes, and measure their relative importance. It results in a visual map, such representations often being called 'spatial maps'. The axes of the map are assumed to denote the underlying variables/dimensions respondents use to form perceptions and preferences. MDS is employed in a large number of applications and has been used in marketing for segmentation studies, product life-cycle examinations, vendor evaluations and media selection.

MDS Considerations, Direct versus Derived

One issue for the researcher to consider in employing MDS is whether to utilise direct or indirect MDS. In gathering perception data, the direct MDS approach asks respondents to judge how similar or dissimilar various brands or objects are using their own criteria. Respondents are frequently required to rate all possible pairs of objects in terms of similarity on a Likert scale. Direct approaches have the advantage that the researcher does not have to identify a set of pertinent attributes. Respondents form their judgments using their own criteria.

In derived MDS approaches to collecting perception data, the respondents are required to rate these objects on a set of specified attributes/criteria. The advantage of the derived approach is that it is easy to identify clusters of respondents based on the attribute ratings. Also the labelling dimensions, which result from implementation of MDS, may be considerably simplified when the derived approach is adopted.

Once the collected perceptual data has been input into a computer program, three further issues are investigated. First, how many dimensions underlie consumer perceptions; and second, what is the configuration of those perceptions, i.e. which products are perceived to be most alike and which are most dissimilar? These two questions produce a goodness-of-fit or lack-of-fit, referred to as a stress index. Third, the actual attributes are identified, and can be compared to the ideal point, a point that describes the consumer's first preference (regardless of whether it is real or imagined).

Multidimensional Scaling Illustrated

Suppose respondents are asked to rate, using their own criteria, five brands of soap using the following five-point Likert scale.

Table 14.7 Respondent's comparison of soap brands

	Very dissimilar			Very similar	
	1	2	3	4	5
Soap 1 versus Soap 2.					
Soap 1 versus Soap 3.					
Soap 1 versus Soap 4.					
Soap 1 versus Soap 5.					
Soap 2 versus Soap 3.					
Soap 2 versus Soap 4.					
Soap 2 versus Soap 5.					
Soap 3 versus Soap 4.					
Soap 3 versus Soap 5.					
Soap 4 versus Soap 5.					

The data from one respondent might be as follows:

Table 14.8 Similarity ratings of soap brands

	Soap 1	Soap 2	Soap 3	Soap 4	Soap 5
Soap 1	—				
Soap 2	5	—			
Soap 3	1	2	—		
Soap 4	2	3	4	—	
Soap 5	1	2	2	2	—

On supplying this similarity matrix as the basis for an MDS procedure a typical output is given in Figure 14.4.

Figure 14.4 Typical output in MDS

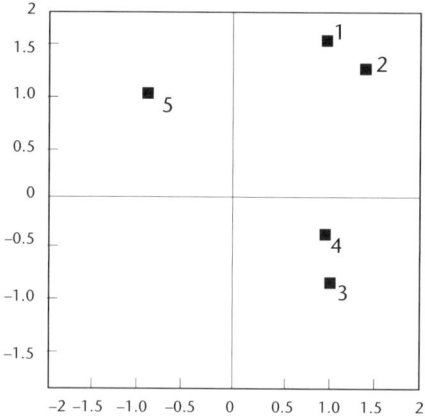

From examination of the map we find that soaps 1 and 2 are clustered together, soaps 3 and 4 are clustered together and soap 5 is not clustered with any other soap. Suppose the respondents are shown this map and asked to label the dimensions — the horizontal and vertical axes, as they provided similarity measures based on their own dimensions/criteria. In doing so, they could label soaps 1 and 2 as 'dirt removing and pleasant smelling'; soaps 3 and 4 as 'dirt removing and failing to leave a pleasant smell' and soap 5 as 'poor dirt remover and pleasant smelling'.

• Multivariate Techniques, Concluding Comments

Before concluding our discussion on multivariate techniques, a number of points are worthy of our attention again. The use of multivariate approaches is significantly increasing; one force fuelling this trend is the ready availability of relevant, user-friendly

PC software. Coupled with this, new multivariate techniques, such as LISREL,[16, 17] are emerging and will continue too, as a result of the commercial imperative to survive and sustain competitiveness in the marketplace and marketspace. Against this background, multivariate techniques are to be treated with caution, and an eye kept on the ten commands of multivariate analysis:[18]

1. Do not be technique-oriented.
2. Consider multivariate models as information for management.
3. Do not substitute multivariate methods for researcher skill and imagination.
4. Develop non-technical communication skills.
5. Avoid the temptation to over-analyse.
6. Beware of generalisations.
7. Beware of the peculiarities of the method.
8. Start at the beginning.
9. Don't use the technique in isolation, ignoring other descriptive methods.
10. Keep an eye on the cost-benefit factors.

• **Summary**

This chapter focused upon some of the more popular multivariate data analysis techniques in marketing research, namely, multiple regression analysis, discriminant analysis, factor analysis, cluster analysis and multidimensional scaling. These methods are applicable only to a certain type of variable, dependent or independent and to a certain type of data, metric or non-metric. They make extensive use of computer procedures, reflect the complex and dynamic nature of many marketing situations and are growing in popularity. When used with caution by a researcher, they can provide invaluable insights and information to assist the manager or management team with their decision-making.

Key Terms

Univariate analysis
Multivariate analysis
Discriminant axis
Dependent variable
Metric data
Factor analysis
Cluster analysis
Multidimensional scaling

Bivariate analysis
Discriminant analysis
Communality
Independent variable
Non-metric data
Centroid
Eigenvalue
Factor loading

Questions

1. What are multivariate techniques?
2. Provide real or hypothetical examples where multivariate analysis might be beneficial to a marketing researcher.
3. How does multiple regression analysis differ from regression analysis as described in Chapter 13?
4. What are the objectives of discriminant analysis?
5. What is factor analysis and why is it useful in the analysis of marketing research data?
6. In factor analysis, what is the difference between a factor and a factor loading? What is meant by the eigenvalue associated with each factor?
7. What is cluster analysis?
8. Describe how factor and cluster analysis differ.
9. What is meant be the term 'Multidimensional scaling'?
10. Why is the use of multivariate methods increasing?
11. Differentiate between direct and derived approaches to MDS.

Problems and Assignments

1. A marketing company wishes to conduct a cluster analysis study of the fast-food industry in Ireland. What variables associated with this industry should be measured?
2. Suppose that a marketing department has collected data on the leisure equipment expenditure of 500 consumers. Members of the sample have also completed surveys measuring 30 psychological variables and 20 different demographic variables. Discuss how each of the following could contribute to analysis of such data:
   (a) Discriminant analysis.
   (b) Cluster analysis.
   (c) Factor analysis.
3. Use the Internet to go to the SPSS home page at http://www.spss.com and examine the package with respect to multivariate techniques.
4. Illustrating your answer with examples, distinguish between discriminant analysis and multiple regression analysis in respect of:
   (a) the usual or most common purpose of the technique; and
   (b) the type of variables involved.
   (*Adapted from a Marketing Institute of Ireland Examination Paper, 1996*)
5. Describe three different problems in marketing which you feel might be suited to analysis by multi-dimensional scaling. Show how you would use multi-dimensional scaling in each case. (*Adapted from a Marketing Institute of Ireland Examination Paper, 1993*)

6. An oil company has developed a multiple regression model to predict the sales of 50 of its filming stations. The variables used are:
   Y = average monthly sales in gallons;
   X_1 = square foot area of station property;
   X_2 = average daily traffic flow;
   X_3 = number of competing filling stations.
   The empirical results are shown in Table 14.9.

   Table 14.9

Variable	Variable mean	Variable range	Regression coefficient	t-value
Y_1	10,000			
X_1	10,000	3,000–20,000	b1 = 4.0	1.3
X_2	6,000	2,500–12,500	b2 = 4.0	1.0
X_3	12	0 – 25	b3 = -1000	
r2 = .45			bo = 10,000	

   (a) What is the regression equation?
   (b) Which variable seems to be the most significant predictor?
   (c) Provide a prediction of sales given the following inputs:

   X_1 = 5,000
   X_2 = 2,000
   X_3 = 2

   (d) Comment on the usefulness of your prediction.
   (*Adapted from a Marketing Institute of Ireland Examination Paper, 1993*)

7. (a) Define cluster analysis and indicate some common uses of the procedure in marketing research.
   (b) Comment briefly on the options/considerations when conducting a cluster analysis in relation to the following:
      (i) Selection of a distance/similarity measure.
      (ii) Selection of a clustering procedure.
      (iii) Decisions on the number of clusters.
   (*Adapted from a Marketing Institute of Ireland Examination Paper, 1997*)

8. Illustrating your answer with examples distinguish between discriminant analysis and multiple regression analysis in respect of:
   (a) the usual or most common purpose of the technique; and
   (b) the type of variables involved.

9. Choosing multidimensional scaling and illustrating your answer with a suitable example discuss the method briefly under the following headings:
    (a) The basic (or most usual) purpose of the technique.
    (b) How the input data are generally obtained.
    (c) An analytical/mathematical rationale for the procedure (it is not essential to include particular mathematical models or expressions in your answers).
    (d) The type of output from the analytical method.

    (Adapted from a Marketing Institute of Ireland Examination Paper, 1996)

Chapter 15

COMMUNICATION OF RESEARCH FINDINGS, REPORT WRITING AND PRESENTATION

- **Chapter Overview**
- Introduction • Written Research Report Guidelines • The Contents of the Marketing Research Report • The Oral Report • Summary

- **Introduction**

The final step in the research process is the preparation and presentation of the research report. After spending days, weeks or even months working on a project, the researcher may view the preparation of the report as just a mere formality. This is far from the truth. In marketing we frequently hear of product failure that can be attributed to poor packaging. This final phase could very well be the most important part of the research process. No matter how appropriate the research design, how proper the statistical analysis, how representative the sample, how carefully worded the questionnaire, how well the fieldwork is managed etc., everything will be for nought if the report is confusing, poorly written and communicated ineffectively to the appropriate decision-makers. Often the research report is the only part of the research project that others will ever see. The quality of the report (written and oral presentation) is often used as a major indicator of the quality of the research itself. In fact, management's decision to undertake research in the future (or to use that research firm again!) will be greatly influenced by the perceived usefulness of the report and the presentation. The perceived quality of the research report by managers is also a primary determinant of whether the managers will use the research findings.[1] In this chapter we will discuss two vital ingredients of this communications process, the written research report and the oral presentation.

The objectives of this chapter are thus:

1. to discuss the importance of the research report;
2. to outline and explain the contents of the written research report;
3. to detail the requirements for an oral presentation.

• Written Research Report Guidelines

The market research report has three primary roles: to communicate findings, to serve as a reference document, and to provide credibility for the work carried out. No two people will prepare a written report in exactly the same way. Situational differences in the personality, background and responsibility of the researcher and the manager to whom the report is addressed should conspire to give each report a unique flavour. There are, however, a series of guidelines which should be followed.

Consider the Audience

The researcher should use only words familiar to the readers and define all technical terms. The technical sophistication of the reader(s) determines their capacity for understanding methodological decisions such as sampling plan, measurement device, experimental design, analysis technique etc. The readers of your reports are busy people, and very few of them can balance a research report, a cup of coffee and a dictionary at the one time.[2] In fact, most managers are extremely busy and are probably much less interested in the technical and logical aspects of a research problem than the researcher is. Depending on your audience, your research report may be either *technical* or *popular* in orientation. While both approaches describe the research study, its methodology, findings, conclusions and recommendations, they can differ considerably in terms of detail, writing style, use of technical terms and length of report.

The technical report is generally intended for other researchers, or for research managers. For example, the majority of articles which appear in the *Journal of Marketing Research* tend to use a format and language style that is typical of the technical report. The popular report, on the other hand, is intended for a more general audience. The writing style and complexity will tend to resemble what we find in the business section of the *Irish Times* or in a magazine such as *Business and Finance*. The report writer's difficulties in tailoring the report are often compounded by the existence of several audiences. A possible solution is to place the more technical aspects of the report in a separate section such as the appendix and to use a more balanced writing style in the main body of the report suitable for both levels of reader. Over-use of technical terms not common to the reader is likely to result in misunderstanding, suspicion and even hostility.

Address the Information Needs

A good report is designed to communicate information to decision-makers by answering the questions derived from the statement of objectives. This requires the research report-writer to be familiar with and to adhere to the study objectives. The report should reflect the interest of the reader rather than that of the researcher. The report should be built around the decision and how the resultant information is relevant to the decision. Unfortunately, researchers are often more interested in the research problem and the methodology used to solve it.

Be Complete, Concise, Accurate and Clear

No report was ever written that contained everything known on the given subject. If too much is included there is a danger that the important points will be lost in the detail. Yet completeness is required. A report is complete when it addresses all of the questions raised in the original assignment. And although the report must be complete it must also be concise. 'Concise writing makes maximum use of every word . . . no word in a concise discussion can be removed without impairing or destroying the function of the whole composition . . . To be concise is to express a thought completely and clearly in the fewest words possible'.[3] If something does not pertain directly to the subject, it should be omitted. One way of ensuring that the report is concise is to read the draft aloud. 'The eye can grow accustomed to the appearance of a sentence, but it is much more difficult for the tongue, lips and jaw to deal with what the eye might readily accept.'[4]

Lengthy discussions of commonly known methods should also be avoided. The writer of the research report must avoid restating the obvious or quoting numbers which the reader can easily see in a table. The challenge is to make the report complete and brief. For example, when discussing the survey method used, it is not necessary to devote page upon page to justifying your decision to use that particular method. Researchers must use their judgment in deciding what can be omitted.

Even with accurate input from the previous steps in the research process, the research report may generate inaccuracies because of carelessness in handling the data, illogical reasoning or inept phrasing.[5] Examples of inaccuracies in report writing include:

- Mathematical errors such as subtraction and addition.
- Confusion between percentages and percentage points.
- Grammatical errors in punctuation, spelling, tense, subject and verb agreement, etc.

If the report contains errors, the reader is likely to ask 'How can I be confident that they know what they are doing?' Word processing software will not identify all errors. For important documents, two proof readers should be used.

Clarity in report-writing is also important. Clear and logical thinking and precise expression produce clarity. The writer should make an outline of the major points. These points should be ordered logically and supporting details should be placed in their proper position. Tell the reader what you are going to do, do it and then tell them what you have done. Choose your words carefully. Don't expect to get it right first time. Few people write well enough to produce a polished draft the first time. The writer should plan at least one major rewrite.

The report should be visually attractive, interesting and easy to read. Sprinkle the report with short quotes from the respondents. This can vitalise a perhaps otherwise dull report. Because the report represents the research firm (and the writer) it should convey positive professional impressions. It should have clear headings which correspond directly with the table of contents. The report should flow logically from topic to topic (corresponding to the research objectives, or questionnaire sequence).

The researcher should:

- write in the present tense and use the active voice;
- avoid jargon, slang and clichés;
- avoid 'I, we' etc. Write in the third person?
- write naturally and simply — the way you talk;
- avoid using too many difficult words or technical complex language. Words should be chosen that provide variety and change of pace to the report;
- choose to use short words over long words that mean the same thing;
- avoid long-windedness and unnecessary complexity in sentence structure. Always prefer the simple to the complex;
- vary the length and structure of sentences;
- within a sentence keep the subject and verb together. This makes it easier for the reader to understand the message;
- use brisk, business-like English;
- the report should have a uniform style and format. Headings and subheadings with sufficient white space is important. Page after page of type is not a good idea. The typography should be varied. It is better to 'break up' the text of the report with headings, subheadings, bullets, indentations and the like. Visual aids such as tables, graphs and charts should also be built into the report.

Be Objective

Objectivity is a virtue which must at all times be maintained. Researchers should never overlook their scientific role, even though from time to time they will probably encounter situations whereby the research findings will not be easily accepted by the client. The results may not concur with the readers' judgment, accumulated industry experience or past decisions taken. The research should resist slanting the findings to conform to the expectations of management. Instead the research findings should be presented in an objective manner and their validity defended if challenged by the client.

Contents of the Marketing Research Report

> **Box 15.1**
>
> *Title Page*
> 1. Title
> 2. Client
> 3. Research company
> 4. Date of submission
>
> *Letter of transmittal*
>
> *Executive Summary*
> 1. Concise statement of objectives
> 2. Concise statements of methodology
> 3. Concise statement of major finding(s)
> 4. Concise statement of conclusions and recommendations
> 5. Other pertinent information as required (e.g. special limitations or techniques)
>
> *Table of Contents*
> 1. Section titles and sub-headings with page numbers
> 2. List of tables
> 3. List of figures
> 4. List of exhibits
> 5. List of appendices
>
> *Introduction*
> Background to the research undertaken
> Problem definition and objectives
>
> *Research methodology (design)*
> a. Type of research design
> b. Information needs
> c. Data collection from secondary sources
> d. Data collection from primary sources
> e. Scaling techniques
> f. Questionnaire development and pre-testing
> g. Sampling techniques
> h. Field work
>
> *Data Analysis*
> Data Analysis methodologies and techniques

> *Results/Findings*
>
> *Limitations*
>
> *Conclusions and recommendations*
>
> *Appendices*
> 1. Questionnaire and forms
> 2. Statistical output
> 3. Other appendices as necessary e.g. geographical map, bibliography, tables not included in findings section, instructions to field workers.

Report Format

There is no single, acceptable organisation for a report. The format chosen depends on the audience and the topic of the report. However, a general format is suggested in Box 15.1. This can be easily altered as required. It should not be thought of as a rigid outline that must always be followed. The format given here is for the most formal type of report. For less formal reports some parts may be shorter or omitted. The general rule is to include all parts needed for effective communication in the particular circumstances and no more.

The Parts of the Report

Each of the report format items is discussed briefly in the following paragraphs.

Title Page

The title page should state a title that conveys the essence of the report, by whom the report was prepared, the name of the recipient organisation and the date of release or presentation.[6] Addresses and telephone numbers of the research firm and recipient may also be included. The title should be brief and informative but 'catchy' if possible. Some research reports are confidential and for limited distribution; in such cases a list of people to whom the report should be circulated may be named on the title page.

Letter of Transmittal

The letter of transmittal is included in relatively formal to very formal reports. It is the 'Here it is' dimension of the report. It should be brief, to the point and should include:

1. the authorisation for the report;
2. a carbon-copy (cc) notation;
3. broad comment(s) on the report findings;
4. a reference to implementation or future related research.

Executive Summary

It is reasonable to assume that some key individuals within the recipient organisation may not have time to read the report in its entirety. The executive summary is a condensed, accurate, one- to two-page statement of what is important in the report. The summary should be written only after the rest of the report has been completed. It represents the essence of the report, and should not be viewed as a miniature of the main report. A good test of a summary is self-sufficiency. Can it stand on its own? It will rarely be broken down through the use of headings and sub-headings. If you can't hold your breath while reading it, most likely it is probably too long. As a variation, the summary may be detached from the main report and circulated by itself.

The executive summary should:

1. State the objectives of the research report.
2. Outline the nature of the decision problem.
3. Identify the methodology and key findings.
4. State conclusions.
5. State recommendations (this is optional).

Table of Contents

The table of contents lists, in order of appearance, the divisions and subdivisions of the report with page references. The purpose of a table of contents is to help readers find the particular sections of the report that are of most interest to them. All items, except title page and table of contents, are listed with page numbers in the table of contents. As a rule, front matter pages are numbered with lower-case Roman numerals (e.g. i, ii, etc). The main body uses Arabic numerals. If the report includes numerous tables, graphs and charts, they should be listed in a separate page immediately following the table of contents. This is referred to as a list of illustrations. It may comprise two separate pages, one for tables, the other for figures. Tables are words or numbers that are arranged in rows or columns. Figures are graphs, charts, pictures, maps etc. Within each, the table or figure, the individual table or figure should be referenced by number, title description and corresponding page number(s).

Introduction

This section begins the main body of the report and bridges the gap between the table of contents and the data analysis/results sections. The introduction begins with the background information as to why the report was undertaken. In some cases a description of the company or product involved may also be required. Reference and short review should be made to any previous related research work carried out on the decision problem. It must explain the nature of the decision problem and state explicitly the objectives of the study. Frequently this is presented as primary and secondary research objectives.

Research Methodology

The section on research methodology contained in the introduction should specify these details, e.g. 'how' the research was conducted, i.e. how the information was collected to achieve the research objectives. Enough detail must be included to document the nature of the methodology used, yet it should not be the major section of the report. Technical details should be included in the appendix. Readers must be told whether the research design was exploratory, descriptive or causal. Are the results based on secondary or primary data or both? If a primary data collection method was used was it based on observational or survey research? If a survey, was the questionnaire administered in person or by telephone or post? An account must be given of the sampling plan. How was the population defined? What sampling frame was used? Was probability or non-probability sampling used, and which technique? How large was the sample size? How were fieldwork issues dealt with? These are all questions which must be answered by the research methodology section. It is also best to provide a brief argument as to why you chose a particular approach, e.g. postal versus telephone, probability versus non-probability, etc. However, you do not need to defend every aspect of your methodology. As mentioned earlier, readers requiring a more detailed methodology discussion should be referred to the appendix.

Data Analysis

Relatively little can be said about the analysis and interpretation methods. The results tend to show what has been done in this regard. However, it can be useful to include a brief discussion on analysis before presenting the results. You may wish to make reference to the data analysis techniques employed, including computer statistical packages, if any are used. Again, it is probably better not to get too technical at this point. A more detailed discussion of methods of analysis including raw data and calculations can be presented in the appendix.

Results/Findings

The 'results' section is the 'meat' of the report. It may comprise several chapters. It makes up the bulk of the report and is organised around the research objectives and information reeds. A combination of continuous narrative text with liberal use of relevant tables, charts, graphs etc. tends to work best. Personal computers and graphics software packages provide a quick and low-cost means of preparing graphics of all types, both simple and sophisticated 3D. The findings must be presented in a clear, logical, organised and attractive way. It is not merely an assortment of tables, graphs and text. The findings section should not read as a series of response frequencies to questionnaire items. Greater creativity is required than that if the report is to retain the interest of the reader. Comprehensive or detailed tables and charts should be confined to the appendix. The researcher should avoid the temptation to present everything that has been learnt regardless of its bearing on the research objectives. This can be overcome by continual reference to the study objectives and by placing less pertinent findings in the appendix.

Limitations

Almost every research project has limitations. Many of these are time, budget or organisational based. Many of the research errors described in Chapter 2 are potential project limitations or caveats. The limitations section should indicate the nature of any potential weaknesses without unduly degrading the readers' credibility in the overall quality of the work. Rather than belabouring the minor weaknesses of the study, the limitations section should instead provide a realistic basis for assessing the validity of the study results. The ethical researcher does not overstate the weaknesses but instead assumes a balanced perspective. In fact an open, frank admission of the study limitations can actually increase, rather than diminish the readers' confidence in the quality of the work undertaken.

Conclusions and Recommendations

Conclusions and recommendations are not the same. A conclusion is an opinion based on the results, while recommendations are suggestions for action. Ideally, the reader should be able to read the objectives, turn to the conclusions section and find specific conclusions relative to each objective. There are two schools of thought as to whether recommendations should be included in the report or not. One says that, because the researcher is probably not familiar with the bigger picture of the client firm, he should not include recommendations in the research report. That is seen as the job of the client's management team. Managers may prefer to determine the appropriate courses of action for themselves. Alternatively, those people from the other school feel that the researcher is in the best position to suggest a course of action. If recommendations are included in the research report they should be practical and actionable and based on the study results. The recommendations may or may not be followed by the management team.

Appendix

The appendix should be reserved for material that is too technical or too cumbersome to place in the main body of the report. This includes materials of interest only to some readers or subsidiary materials not directly related to the objectives. The appendix will typically contain a copy of the questionnaire or observational form used, interviewer instructions, details of the sampling plan, detailed statistical tables, geographical maps, bibliography etc. Each appendix item should be titled, referenced, explained and listed in the table of contents. The writer should not put material in the appendix if its omission from the body of the report would create gaps in the presentation.

Evaluating Research Reports

The following is a number of guidelines for evaluating research reports.[7]

Origin — what is behind the research. The report should contain a clear statement of why the research was conducted, who sponsored it, and who conducted it. Key questions:

- Does the report identify the organisations (divisions, departments) that requested the research?
- Does it contain a statement of purpose that clearly states what the research was to accomplish?
- Are the organisations that defined and conducted the research identified?

Design — the concept and the plan. The research approach, the sample, and the analysis should be described clearly and they should be appropriate for the purpose of the study. Key questions:

- Is there a complete non-technical description of the research design?
- Is the design consistent with the purpose for which the research was conducted?
- Does any aspect of the design, including the measuring instrument(s), induce any bias (particularly bias in favour of the sponsor)?
- Does the design control for patterns of sequence or timing or other external factors which might prejudice the results?
- Are the respondents capable of answering the questions raised?
- Is there a precise statement of the populations the research is to represent?
- Does the sampling frame fairly represent the population?
- Does the report describe how the data are analysed?
- Are copies of the questionnaire, field and sampling instructions, and other materials available in the appendix or on file?

Execution — collecting and handling the information. Data should be carefully collected by competent people using forms and methods appropriate for the task. Key questions:

- Does the report describe the data collection procedures including 'quality control' procedures?
- Does the report specify the proportion of the selected sample from which information was collected?
- Where those who collected the data treated in a manner that would minimise any bias they might introduce?

Stability — sample size and reliability. The sample size should be reported and it should be large enough to yield stable results. Key questions:

- Is the sample large enough to provide stable findings?
- Are sampling error limits shown (if applicable)?
- Is the calculation of sampling error, or the lack of such a calculation, explained?
- Does the treatment of sampling error make clear that it does not include non-sampling error?
- For the major findings, are the reported error tolerances based on direct analysis of the variability of the collected data?

Applicability — generalising the findings. The research report should clearly indicate the boundaries which limit the findings. Key questions:

- Does the report specify when the data were collected?
- Does the report state clearly whether its results apply beyond the direct source of the data?
- Is it clear which groups, if any, are under-represented in the data?
- If the research has limited applications, is there a statement describing who or what it represents and the times and conditions under which it applied?

Meaning — interpretations and conclusions. All assumptions and judgments involved in reaching any findings, conclusions or recommendations should be clearly specified. Key questions:

- Are the measurements described in simple and direct language?
- Does the use of the measurements make sense?
- Are the actual findings clearly differentiated from any interpretation of the findings?
- Has rigorous objectivity and candid reporting been used in interpreting research findings as evidence of caution or as predictive of future behaviour?

Candour — open reporting and disclosure. The research report should be an honest, complete description of the research process and outcome. Key questions:

- Is there a full and forthright disclosure of how the research was done?
- Have all the potentially relevant findings been presented?

The Oral Report

In addition to one or more written reports, you may also have to give an oral report of your research. While not unlike public speaking, presentation of the research report has a number of distinguishing characteristics:

- Generally a smaller group of people is involved.
- Statistics, graphics and key points make up the bulk of the presentation.

As a researcher you may be required to deliver an oral presentation at one or more stages of the research project, namely:

- The research proposal stage.
- Progress to date reports.
- Presentation of final report and research results.

Barriers to Communication

It is the listener or reader who will determine the extent to which the message is understood. What we hear, see or understand is shaped very largely by our own experience and background. In reality many barriers to good communications exist. The main ones are as follows.[8]

1. *Language:* Some individuals may have vocabulary deficiencies due to age, education or environment. Words can also have different meanings to different people. For example look at the possible communication difficulties that arise between Americans, English and Irish who all speak the English language. Jargon used by specialists can also cause difficulties.
2. *Perception:* Our personal feelings will often affect the way we interpret communications. Its is often difficult to separate what we hear from our feelings about the person who says it. Sterotyping would be a prime example.
3. *Listening:* Communication involves receiving as well as issuing information. Some individuals are good talkers but poor listeners, hearing only what they want to hear and disregarding any critical comments. Communication overload can also occur.
4. *Authority:* An individual's position in an organisation may be relevant. Communications from senior managers will be considered important and significant. On the other hand research has shown that people with low status within an organisation find difficulty communicating with those who have a higher status.
5. *Distortion of message:* Lines of communication may be too long, resulting in a dilution of the information. Personality clashes may also contribute.
6. *Non-verbal communication:* Body language can be a help but sometimes it can prove a barrier if misinterpreted. This can often arise in contacts with individuals from different cultures.
7. *Emotions:* Emotions can colour our ability to convey or receive the true message.
8. *Time:* The individual may not have been accorded sufficient time to deal with a particular communication.

A good oral presentation is as much an art as a science. Some people have a natural flair for presenting, but for the less fortunate, spoken communication is a skill that can be acquired like any other and, given time and proper tutoring, excelled at.[9]

A couple of years ago a survey was conducted in the UK which considered mans' greatest fears — anything that put the fear of God into respondents. The results surprised the researchers. From the survey it appears that man's greatest fear is not fire, not drowning, not great heights but publicly speaking to a group of people. Yes, it appears that the one thing guaranteed to turn an otherwise rational, logical and organised individual into a quivering mass is — talking to people. Crazy isn't it?[10]

The key success factor in any presentation: apply the KISS principle — Keep it short and simple. Overall, tell them what you are going to tell them, tell them, and tell them what you have told them. In other words:

- Have an opening to grab their attention.
- Have a short introduction.
- Have a body (middle section) that is logically structured.
- Have a strong close.
- *Finish before you are expected to.*

Some Tips for Effective Presentations

You and Your Audience

- Where are the audience members from — internal or external?
- What knowledge and experience do they have?
- Why are they attending (is attendance voluntary or compulsory)?
- What do they think of me?
- What do they think of my subject matter?
- What is the prevailing mood of the audience likely to be?
- What do they expect from me?
- What is the audience's age range and educational background?

Language

- Given that your audience has not spent as much time researching the subject area, it is reasonable to assume they will probably not be as familiar as you are with your basic ideas or concepts.
- Keep the wording of your presentation formal but also conversational. Use familiar words and have examples to explain.
- Try to avoid unnecessary abstract terms or overly theoretical examples. Keep the explanation simple and use short, precise sentences.
- Avoid slang, catchphrases and 'in jokes' which might alienate your audience.
- Avoid using jargon or inappropriate technical language.

- Be careful not to over-use certain words or phrases, for example 'like'.
- The above applies when answering questions, too.

Visual Aids
- The more commonly used visual aids include: whiteboard, flip-chart, overhead projector, slide projector, video, samples and hand-outs.
- Stick to one, or at most two kinds of visual aids, and use them only when you need them.
- By distributing samples or handouts before or during your presentation, you may end up competing with them for your audience's attention.
- It may be better not to have a prepared flipchart or OHP visible before you need it, as your audience will be looking at it rather than you.
- If you are going to write on a flipchart or board there are three points to remember:
  — Don't talk while you write with your back to the audience. Turn and write in silence. This may also be used as a pause in the presentation.
  — Don't scribble; write slowly and legibly. Do use colours.
  — Do not mask the visual aid with your own body.
- Visual aids are not a substitute for an oral presentation. If a visual aid does not add to the content of your presentation, do not use it.
- Make sure you check that you have everything you need beforehand. Is all of the equipment working?

Body Language and Eye Contact
- Start with a smile.
- You are on show, and every move you make conveys a message to your listeners.
- Stand with both feet flat on the ground and slightly apart. This will give an impression of confidence. You will also feel steadier.
- Be prepared to make eye contact with your audience. Don't avoid eye contact as this undermines what you are saying.
- Don't talk to the one person who looks at you most — that person is probably already interested; it's the others you need to convince.
- Watch for signs of boredom — people looking at their watches, tapping feet, sighing. Use your voice, eye contact, or even a question to get them interested again.
- Identify and eliminate distracting mannerisms such as fiddling with your watch, or other accessories. Remove all coins from your pocket. Do you know what to do with your hands?

Voice
- Use your voice to add interest and emphasis to your speech. Work on your voice for volume, speed, tone and variety.

- Practise by reading a passage from a book out loud. Use a tape-recorder if you wish. Do you sound interesting?
- Nervousness on the day of the presentation can make you speed up. A good trick is to take several deep breaths before you start, or hold your breath occasionally or try speaking in an unnatural voice.

Using Notes

- Write your headings and main points on index cards. Write any visual aid prompts on these too. You can put them on the desk or table in front of you and turn them over when you have finished with each one.
- Don't read your whole presentation out. If you do, you reduce eye contact and do not properly involve the audience. You will probably sound monotonous and look impersonal and uninteresting. You also reduce audibility as your voice is directed to the ground.
- Repeat important bits.

Above all, try to RELAX and be yourself. Remember: practice makes perfect. If you fail to prepare, prepare to fail.

Questions

1. Why is the research report important?
2. Differentiate between the technical report and the popular report as applied to marketing research findings.
3. Why is it important to focus on the audience when writing a research report?
4. What is meant by the research criteria of completeness, accuracy, clarity, and conciseness?
5. How do the objectives of the study relate to the writing of the report?
6. Discuss the importance of objectivity in writing a marketing research report.
7. Why is it critical to avoid spelling and grammar errors in research reports?
8. Discuss the difference between conclusions and recommendations in research reports.
9. Describe the following parts of the report: title page, table of contents, executive summary, research design, data analysis, conclusions and recommendations. What should go in each part?
10. In what circumstances is it appropriate to use the various forms of tables and charts which might be included in the body of the research report?
11. Why is the limitations and caveats section included in the report?
12. By what criteria would you evaluate an oral presentation? Develop an evaluation form.
13. What visual aids are available for oral presentations?

Problems and Assignments

1. Re-phrase each of the following titles so that the communication will be on a more professional level.
   (a) 'A study of what students at UCD like and don't like about their contact lenses.'
   (b) 'A study to see if residents of Malahide own different kinds of cars than the people who live in Leixlip.'
   (c) 'Age, income, education level, and some other demographic measurements describing households owning a Whirlpool washer and dryer.'
2. Select any paragraph from this chapter, then use a thesaurus to help you rewrite it at the most complex level possible. Might there ever be any benefit from employing such language?
3. The Director your local Chamber of Commerce asked the marketing research class of UCG to prepare a research report on members' attitudes toward the service offerings of the Chamber. Evaluate the completeness of the executive summary portion of their report, which follows:

   > To provide a foundation for a comprehensive marketing plan, the Chamber of Commerce (CC) undertook a membership survey in November 1996. Eighty-four usable surveys were returned from a stratified proportionate sampling plan of 172 CC members.
   >
   > Results showed that members were familiar with all of the services except National Safety Council materials and employers' manuals. Newsletters were found to be the most often used as well as the most important service offered by the Chamber. Government regulation and mandated employee benefits were thought to be the most threatening issues facing business, according to eleven statements about Chamber of Commerce services.

4. Observe three specific oral presentations outside of class. Consider the following:
   (a) Were there any distracting mannerisms?
   (b) What did the presenters do with their hands?
   (c) How was the audience involved, if at all?
   (d) Evaluate the visual aids used. Would you recommend the use of other visual aids?
   (e) Did you become confused or bored? Was there anything the presenter could have done differently to counteract that tendency?
5. You are giving a presentation of a marketing report related to which new advertising campaign your food product employer should run for its new low-fat snack cookies. There has been a great deal of debate among the marketing managers as to whether the product should take a 'health' position or a 'taste' position. Your research has results related to this positioning issue, as well as the test results for the copy test of ads for each position. Discuss how you would handle the following events at the presentation.

(a) One manager keeps interrupting you to ask questions about issues that will be presented later in your report.
(b) A professional health positioning manager argues that your whole research has far too small a sample (n = 300), has a sample that was collected improperly (you used a syndicated ad testing service mall intercept), and that the statistical test (the z test) is suspect due to the lack of an underlying normal distribution in the population. These and other similar technical arguments arose when your early results seemed to question health positioning.
(c) A professional taste manager draws a conclusion about what the strategy and execution should be — a conclusion that uses your results improperly.
(d) One manager states, 'I don't care what the copy testing results are. That ad will lack true impact in the marketplace. I've been in this business too long to accept that test result.'
(e) The general manager asks what decision you would make based upon the marketing research.

6. There are a number of graphic presentation forms. Which would you suggest using to show each of the following? Why?
   (a) A comparison of changes in average annual *per capita* income for the United States and the Soviet Union from 1988 to 1998.
   (b) The percentage composition of average family expenditure patterns, by the major types of expenditure, for families whose heads are under 30 years compared with families whose heads are 50 years or older.
   (c) A comparison of the change between 31 December 1995, and 31 December 1996, of the share price of six major technology firms.

7. Outline a set of visual aids that you might use in an oral briefing on:
   (a) How to write a research report.
   (b) The outlook for the economy over the next two years.
   (c) The major analytical article in the latest *Business and Finance*.

8. Go to the library and try to find some research reports. How do they meet the standards set forth in this chapter?

9. Using the business section of newspapers or business magazines find examples of good/bad table and graphic presentation. How might they be improved?

APPENDIX 1
Random Digits

37751	04998	66038	63480	98442	22245	83538	62351	74514	90497
50915	64152	82981	15796	27102	71635	34470	13608	26360	76285
99142	35021	01032	57907	80545	54112	15150	36856	03247	40392
70720	10033	25191	62358	03784	74377	88150	25567	87457	49512
18460	64947	32958	08752	96366	89092	23597	74308	00881	88976
65763	41133	60950	35372	06782	81451	78764	52645	19841	50083
83769	52570	60133	25211	87384	90182	84990	26400	39128	97043
58900	78420	98579	33665	10718	39342	46346	14401	13503	46525
54746	71115	78219	64314	11227	41702	54517	87676	14078	45317
56819	27340	07200	52663	57864	85159	15460	97564	29637	27742
34990	62122	38223	28526	37006	22774	46026	15981	87291	56946
02269	22795	87593	81830	95383	67823	20196	54850	46779	64519
43042	53600	45738	00261	31100	67239	02004	70698	53597	62617
92565	12211	06868	87786	59576	61382	33972	13161	47208	96604
67424	32620	60841	86848	85000	04835	48576	33884	10101	84129
04015	77148	09535	10743	97871	55919	45274	38304	93125	91847
85226	19763	46105	25289	26714	73253	85922	21785	42624	92741
03360	07457	75131	41209	50451	23472	07438	08375	29312	62264
72460	99682	27970	25632	34096	17656	12736	27476	21938	67305
66960	55780	71778	52629	51692	71442	36130	70425	39874	62035
14824	95631	00697	65462	24815	13930	02938	54619	28909	53950
34001	05618	41900	23303	19928	60755	61404	56947	91441	19299
77718	83830	29781	72917	10840	74182	08293	62588	99625	22088
60930	05091	35726	07414	49211	69586	20226	08274	28167	65279
94180	62151	08112	26646	07617	42954	22521	09395	43561	45692
81073	85543	47650	93830	07377	87995	35084	39386	93141	88309
18467	39689	60801	46828	38670	88243	89042	78452	08032	72566
60643	59399	79740	17295	50094	66436	92677	68345	24025	36489
73372	61697	85728	90779	13235	83114	70728	32093	74306	08325
18395	18482	83245	54942	51905	09534	70839	91073	42193	81199
07261	28720	71244	05064	84873	68020	39037	68981	00670	86291
61679	81529	83725	33269	45958	74265	87460	60525	42539	25605
11815	48679	00556	96871	39835	83055	84949	11681	51687	55896
99007	35050	86440	44280	20320	97527	28138	01088	49037	85430
06446	65608	79291	16624	06135	30622	56133	33998	32308	29434

Source: *Exploring Marketing Research*, sixth edition, by William G. Zikmund. The Dryden Press. Copyright © 1997.

APPENDIX 2
Area Under the Normal Curve

z	.00	.01	.02	.03	.04	.05	.06	.07	.08	.09
0.0	.0000	.0040	.0080	.0120	.0160	.0199	.0239	.0279	.0319	.0359
0.1	.0398	.0438	.0478	.0517	.0557	.0596	.0636	.0675	.0714	.0753
0.2	.0793	.0832	.0871	.0910	.0948	.0987	.1026	.1064	.1103	.1141
0.3	.1179	.1217	.1255	.1293	.1331	.1368	.1406	.1443	.1480	.1517
0.4	.1554	.1591	.1628	.1664	.1700	.1736	.1772	.1808	.1844	.1879
0.5	.1915	.1950	.1985	.2019	.2054	.2088	.2123	.2157	.2190	.2224
0.6	.2257	.2291	.2324	.2357	.2389	.2422	.2454	.2486	.2518	.2549
0.7	.2580	.2612	.2642	.2673	.2704	.2734	.2764	.2794	.2823	.2852
0.8	.2881	.2910	.2939	.2967	.2995	.3023	.3051	.3078	.3106	.3133
0.9	.3159	.3186	.3212	.3238	.3264	.3289	.3315	.3340	.3365	.3389
1.0	.3413	.3438	.3461	.3485	.3508	.3531	.3554	.3577	.3599	.3621
1.1	.3643	.3665	.3686	.3708	.3729	.3749	.3770	.3790	.3810	.3830
1.2	.3849	.3869	.3888	.3907	.3925	.3944	.3962	.3980	.3997	.4015
1.3	.4032	.4049	.4066	.4082	.4099	.4115	.4131	.4147	.4162	.4177
1.4	.4192	.4207	.4222	.4236	.4251	.4265	.4279	.4292	.4306	.4319
1.5	.4332	.4345	.4357	.4370	.4382	.4394	.4406	.4418	.4429	.4441
1.6	.4452	.4463	.4474	.4484	.4495	.4505	.4515	.4525	.4535	.4545
1.7	.4554	.4564	.4573	.4582	.4591	.4599	.4608	.4616	.4625	.4633
1.8	.4641	.4649	.4656	.4664	.4671	.4678	.4686	.4693	.4699	.4706
1.9	.4713	.4719	.4726	.4732	.4738	.4744	.4750	.4756	.4761	.4767
2.0	.4772	.4778	.4783	.4788	.4793	.4798	.4803	.4808	.4812	.4817
2.1	.4821	.4826	.4830	.4834	.4838	.4842	.4846	.4850	.4854	.4857
2.2	.4861	.4864	.4868	.4871	.4875	.4878	.4881	.4884	.4887	.4890
2.3	.4893	.4896	.4898	.4901	.4904	.4906	.4909	.4911	.4913	.4916
2.4	.4918	.4920	.4922	.4925	.4927	.4929	.4931	.4932	.4934	.4936
2.5	.4938	.4940	.4941	.4943	.4945	.4946	.4948	.4949	.4951	.4952
2.6	.4953	.4955	.4956	.4957	.4959	.4960	.4961	.4962	.4963	.4964
2.7	.4965	.4966	.4967	.4968	.4969	.4970	.4971	.4972	.4973	.4974
2.8	.4974	.4975	.4976	.4977	.4977	.4978	.4979	.4979	.4980	.4981
2.9	.4981	.4982	.4982	.4983	.4984	.4984	.4985	.4985	.4986	.4986
3.0	.49865	.4987	.4987	.4988	.4988	.4989	.4989	.4989	.4990	.4990
4.0	.49997									

Source: *Exploring Marketing Research*, sixth edition, by William G. Zikmund. The Dryden Press. Copyright © 1997.

APPENDIX 3
Distribution of *t* for Given Probability Levels

d.f.	Level of Significance for One-Tailed Test					
	.10	.05	.025	.01	.005	.0005
	Level of Significance for Two-Tailed Test					
	.20	.10	.05	.02	.01	.001
1	3.078	6.314	12.706	31.821	63.657	636.619
2	1.886	2.920	4.303	6.965	9.925	31.598
3	1.638	2.353	3.182	4.541	5.841	12.941
4	1.533	2.132	2.776	3.747	4.604	8.610
5	1.476	2.015	2.571	3.365	4.032	6.859
6	1.440	1.943	2.447	3.143	3.707	5.959
7	1.415	1.895	2.365	2.998	3.499	5.405
8	1.397	1.860	2.306	2.896	3.355	5.041
9	1.383	1.833	2.262	2.821	3.250	4.781
10	1.372	1.812	2.228	2.764	3.169	4.587
11	1.363	1.796	2.201	2.718	3.106	4.437
12	1.356	1.782	2.179	2.681	3.055	4.318
13	1.350	1.771	2.160	2.650	3.012	4.221
14	1.345	1.761	2.145	2.624	2.977	4.140
15	1.341	1.753	2.131	2.602	2.947	4.073
16	1.337	1.746	2.120	2.583	2.921	4.015
17	1.333	1.740	2.110	2.567	2.898	3.965
18	1.330	1.734	2.101	2.552	2.878	3.992
19	1.328	1.729	2.093	2.539	2.861	3.883
20	1.325	1.725	2.086	2.528	2.845	3.850
21	1.323	1.721	2.080	2.518	2.831	3.819
22	1.321	1.717	2.074	2.508	2.819	3.792
23	1.319	1.714	2.069	2.500	2.807	3.767
24	1.318	1.711	2.064	2.492	2.797	3.745
25	1.316	1.708	2.060	2.485	2.787	3.725
26	1.315	1.706	2.056	2.479	2.779	3.707
27	1.314	1.703	2.052	2.473	2.771	3.690
28	1.313	1.701	2.048	2.467	2.763	3.674
29	1.311	1.699	2.045	2.462	2.756	3.659
30	1.310	1.697	2.042	2.457	2.750	3.646
40	1.303	1.684	2.021	2.423	2.704	3.551
60	1.296	1.671	2.000	2.390	2.660	3.460
120	1.289	1.658	1.980	2.358	2.617	3.373
∞	1.282	1.645	1.960	2.326	2.576	3.291

Source: *Exploring Marketing Research*, sixth edition, by William G. Zikmund. The Dryden Press. Copyright © 1997.

APPENDIX 4
Chi-Square Distribution

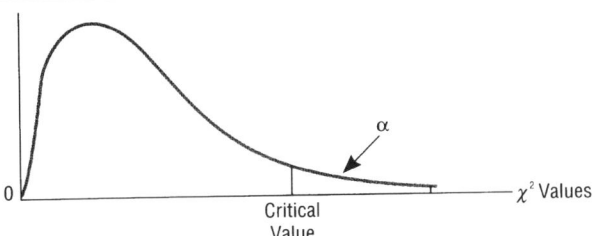

Degrees of Freedom (d.f.)	Area in Shaded Right Tail (α)		
	.10	.05	.01
1	2.706	3.841	6.635
2	4.605	5.991	9.210
3	6.251	7.815	11.345
4	7.779	9.488	13.277
5	9.236	11.070	15.086
6	10.645	12.592	16.812
7	12.017	14.067	18.475
8	13.362	15.507	20.090
9	14.684	16.919	21.666
10	15.987	18.307	23.209
11	17.275	19.675	24.725
12	18.549	21.026	26.217
13	19.812	22.362	27.688
14	21.064	23.685	29.141
15	22.307	24.996	30.578
16	23.542	26.296	32.000
17	24.769	27.587	33.409
18	25.989	28.869	34.805
19	27.204	30.144	36.191
20	28.412	31.410	37.566
21	29.615	32.671	38.932
22	30.813	33.924	40.289
23	32.007	35.172	41.638
24	33.196	36.415	42.980
25	34.382	37.652	44.314
26	35.563	38.885	45.642
27	36.741	40.113	46.963
28	37.916	41.337	48.278
29	39.087	42.557	49.588
30	40.256	43.773	50.892

Example of how to use this table: In a chi-square distribution with 6 degrees of freedom (d.f.), the area to the right of a critical value of 12.592—i.e., the α area—is .05.

Source: *Exploring Marketing Research*, sixth edition, by William G. Zikmund. The Dryden Press. Copyright © 1997.

APPENDIX 5
Critical Values of $F_{v_1 v_2}$ for $\alpha = .05$

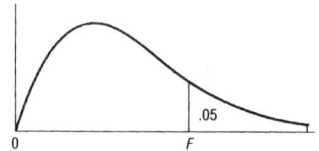

v_1 = Degrees of Freedom for Numerator

v_2	1	2	3	4	5	6	7	8	9	10	12	15	20	24	30	40	60	120	∞
1	161	200	216	225	230	234	237	239	241	242	244	246	248	249	250	251	252	253	254
2	18.5	19.0	19.2	19.2	19.3	19.3	19.4	19.4	19.4	19.4	19.4	19.4	19.5	19.5	19.5	19.5	19.5	19.5	19.5
3	10.1	9.55	9.28	9.12	9.01	8.94	8.89	8.85	8.81	8.79	8.74	8.70	8.66	8.64	8.62	8.59	8.57	8.55	8.53
4	7.71	6.94	6.59	6.39	6.26	6.16	6.09	6.04	6.00	5.96	5.91	5.86	5.80	5.77	5.75	5.72	5.69	5.66	5.63
5	6.61	5.79	5.41	5.19	5.05	4.95	4.88	4.82	4.77	4.74	4.68	4.62	4.56	4.53	4.50	4.46	4.43	4.40	4.37
6	5.99	5.14	4.76	4.53	4.39	4.28	4.21	4.15	4.10	4.06	4.00	3.94	3.87	3.84	3.81	3.77	3.74	3.70	3.67
7	5.59	4.74	4.35	4.12	3.97	3.87	3.79	3.73	3.68	3.64	3.57	3.51	3.44	3.41	3.38	3.34	3.30	3.27	3.23
8	5.32	4.46	4.07	3.84	3.69	3.58	3.50	3.44	3.39	3.35	3.28	3.22	3.15	3.12	3.08	3.04	3.01	2.97	2.93
9	5.12	4.26	3.86	3.63	3.48	3.37	3.29	3.23	3.18	3.14	3.07	3.01	2.94	2.90	2.86	2.83	2.79	2.75	2.71
10	4.96	4.10	3.71	3.48	3.33	3.22	3.14	3.07	3.02	2.98	2.91	2.85	2.77	2.74	2.70	2.66	2.62	2.58	2.54
11	4.84	3.98	3.59	3.36	3.20	3.09	3.01	2.95	2.90	2.85	2.79	2.72	2.65	2.61	2.57	2.53	2.49	2.45	2.40
12	4.75	3.89	3.49	3.26	3.11	3.00	2.91	2.85	2.80	2.75	2.69	2.62	2.54	2.51	2.47	2.43	2.38	2.34	2.30
13	4.67	3.81	3.41	3.18	3.03	2.92	2.83	2.77	2.71	2.67	2.60	2.53	2.46	2.42	2.38	2.34	2.30	2.25	2.21
14	4.60	3.74	3.34	3.11	2.96	2.85	2.76	2.70	2.65	2.60	2.53	2.46	2.39	2.35	2.31	2.27	2.22	2.18	2.13
15	4.54	3.68	3.29	3.06	2.90	2.79	2.71	2.64	2.59	2.54	2.48	2.40	2.33	2.29	2.25	2.20	2.16	2.11	2.07
16	4.49	3.63	3.24	3.01	2.85	2.74	2.66	2.59	2.54	2.49	2.42	2.35	2.28	2.24	2.19	2.15	2.11	2.06	2.01
17	4.45	3.59	3.20	2.96	2.81	2.70	2.61	2.55	2.49	2.45	2.38	2.31	2.23	2.19	2.15	2.10	2.06	2.01	1.96
18	4.41	3.55	3.16	2.93	2.77	2.66	2.58	2.51	2.46	2.41	2.34	2.27	2.19	2.15	2.11	2.06	2.02	1.97	1.92
19	4.38	3.52	3.13	2.90	2.74	2.63	2.54	2.48	2.42	2.38	2.31	2.23	2.16	2.11	2.07	2.03	1.98	1.93	1.88
20	4.35	3.49	3.10	2.87	2.71	2.60	2.51	2.45	2.39	2.35	2.28	2.20	2.12	2.08	2.04	1.99	1.95	1.90	1.84
21	4.32	3.47	3.07	2.84	2.68	2.57	2.49	2.42	2.37	2.32	2.25	2.18	2.10	2.05	2.01	1.96	1.92	1.87	1.81
22	4.30	3.44	3.05	2.82	2.66	2.55	2.46	2.40	2.34	2.30	2.23	2.15	2.07	2.03	1.98	1.94	1.89	1.84	1.78
23	4.28	3.42	3.03	2.80	2.64	2.53	2.44	2.37	2.32	2.27	2.20	2.13	2.05	2.01	1.96	1.91	1.86	1.81	1.76
24	4.26	3.40	3.01	2.78	2.62	2.51	2.42	2.36	2.30	2.25	2.18	2.11	2.03	1.98	1.94	1.89	1.84	1.79	1.73
25	4.24	3.39	2.99	2.76	2.60	2.49	2.40	2.34	2.28	2.24	2.16	2.09	2.01	1.96	1.92	1.87	1.82	1.77	1.71
30	4.17	3.32	2.92	2.69	2.53	2.42	2.33	2.27	2.21	2.16	2.09	2.01	1.93	1.89	1.84	1.79	1.74	1.68	1.62
40	4.08	3.23	2.84	2.61	2.45	2.34	2.25	2.18	2.12	2.08	2.00	1.92	1.84	1.79	1.74	1.69	1.64	1.58	1.51
60	4.00	3.15	2.76	2.53	2.37	2.25	2.17	2.10	2.04	1.99	1.92	1.84	1.75	1.70	1.65	1.59	1.53	1.47	1.39
120	3.92	3.07	2.68	2.45	2.29	2.18	2.09	2.02	1.96	1.91	1.83	1.75	1.66	1.61	1.55	1.50	1.43	1.35	1.25
∞	3.84	3.00	2.60	2.37	2.21	2.10	2.01	1.94	1.88	1.83	1.75	1.67	1.57	1.52	1.46	1.39	1.32	1.22	1.00

v_2 = Degrees of Freedom for Denominator

Source: *Exploring Marketing Research*, sixth edition, by William G. Zikmund. The Dryden Press. Copyright © 1997.

REFERENCES

Chapter 1

1. Ward, J. and Domegan, C., 'A Closer Look at Our Top 1,000 SME's', Presentation at the Irish Marketing Teachers Conference, UCD, 1997.
2. Quinn, Feargal, *Crowning the Customer, How to Become Customer-Driven*, Dublin: O'Brien Press, 1990, 57.
3. Barabba, V. and Zaltman, G., *Hearing the Voice of the Market, Competitive Advantage through Creative Use of Market Information*, Harvard Business School Press, 1991.
4. Interview with John Casey, Chief Executive, The Marketing Institute of Ireland, 1996.
5. The Market Research Society (UK), *Definition of Market Research*, www.marketresearch.org.uk, 1998.
6. American Marketing Association, *Definition of Marketing Research*, Chicago, 1988.
7. Boyd, H., Westfall, R. and Stasch, S., *Marketing Research, Text and Cases*, 5th edition, Illinois: Irwin, 1981, 29–35.
8. Baker, Michael, *Research for Marketing*, London, UK: Macmillan, 1995.
9. Irish Trade Advertisement, *MII Newsletter*, March 1998.
10. 'Duty free promises huge liqueur sales', *Sunday Tribune*, 1st December 1996.
11. McCraith, Joe, 'Critical Incident Research', *MII Newsletter*, March/April, Vol. 9 No. 2, 1996, 6–7.
12. 'Cheesestrings Tackle UK Market After Successful Granada Test', *IMJ*, October 1996, 8.
13. 'Goodfella's Market Slice', *Sunday Business Post*, 23rd December 1994.
14. 'HB to Launch New Corporate Identity', *Irish Media Journal*, November 1997.
15. Harrison, B., 'In Cod's Name, What's Happened to Capt. Birdseye?', *Irish Times*, June 1998.
16. Bank of Ireland Customer Satisfaction Survey, 1997.
17. 'Goodfella's Pizza', *MII Newsletter*, 1997; and Marketing Institute of Ireland, *Yearly Diary*, 1996, 74.
18. Interview with Roger Jupp, *LMR*, 1996.
19. Brophy, M., *IMJ*, April 1997, 50.
20. *MII Newsletter*, March/April 1996, Vol. 9 No. 2, 16–17.
21. Laitin, J. and Klaperman, B., 'The Brave New World of Marketing Research, Market Research Forum', *Medical Marketing and Media*, July 1997.
22. der Vegt, Van, 'We are Drowning in Data but We Lack Information', *Marketing and Research Today*, May, Vol. 27 No. 2, 1998, 73–100; *Irish Media Journal*, April 1997, 50.
23. Rodger Jupp, Managing Director, Lansdowne Market Research, 1999.

24. ESOMAR Press Release, September 1997, Amsterdam and ESOMAR 1995, 'ESOMAR Market Research Industry Turnover Trend Report, 1990–1994', Amsterdam, The Netherlands, and the Association of Irish Marketing Research Organisations, 1995, Press Release, Dublin.
25. *Ibid.*
26. Co-operation North Study, 'Marketing Practice, The Republic of Ireland and Northern Ireland', undertaken jointly by the College of Marketing and Design, Dublin, and the University of Ulster, Jordanstown, 1991.
27. Brannick, Theresa, 'Information Quandary', *Marketing Institute Newsletter*, March/April 1995, 10–11.
28. *Ibid.*

Chapter 2

1. 'Does Colour Make a Difference?', *IMJ*, April 1996, 18.
2. Marketing Institute of Ireland, 1996, *Yearly Diary*, 74.
3. 'Omega 3 Research Beneficial', *CEX*, 20th January 1996.
4. Syedain, H., 'Cadbury: Sweet Dreams', *Management Today*, September 1989, 4.
5. *Irish Independent*, 30th May 1996.
6. 'Gilbey's Targets Wine Buyers', *Sunday Business Post*, 1st September 1996.
7. Curtis, J., 'Giving Birth to the Male Pill (Branding Contraceptives)', *Marketing*, 25th September 1997, 30–2.
8. *IMJ*, February 1997, 6.
9. Gray, R., 'Keeping up With the Kids (Researching Children's Tastes)', *Marketing*, 24th April 1997, 26–8.
10. Quinn, F., *Crowning the Customer*, Dublin: O'Brien Press, 1990.
11. Harper, T., 'Quantitative Research', in *Perspectives on Marketing Management in Ireland*, edited by Mary Lambkin and Tony Meenaghan, Dublin: Oak Tree Press, 1994, 369–80.
12. Domegan, C., 'An Evaluation of AnCO's Distance Learning Package for Marketing Managers', MBS dissertation, UCD, 1984.
13. Thornton, A., 'The Use of Conjoint Analysis in the Cheese Industry in Ireland', unpublished MBS thesis, UCD, 1984.
14. Frost, F., 'Electronic Surveys — New Methods of Primary Data Collection', in the 27th EMAC Conference, 'Marketing, Theory and Practice', track 5, *Marketing Research*, 1998, 213–32.
15. Pring, D., 'All Wired Up and Ready to Go, Marketing Research in Cyberspace', in ESOMAR/JMA/ARF Conference on 'Triad 2000; Marketing and Research Towards the Millennium', New York, June 1995, 283–302.
16. Brodie, R. J., Coviello, N. E., Brookes, R. W., and Little, V., 'Towards a Paradigm Shift in Marketing? An Examination of Current Marketing Practices', *Journal of Marketing Management*, Vol. 13 No. 5, 1997, 383–406.
17. Donnellan, E., 'Changing Perspectives on Research Methodology in Marketing', *Irish Marketing Review*, Vol. 8, 1995, 81–90.
18. O'Leary, P., 'Qualitative Research, Where it's at, Where it's Going', *Irish Marketing Review*, Vol. 6, 1993, 23–8.
19. Frost, F., 1998, *op. cit.*

20. Pring, D., 1995, *op. cit.*
21. ESOMAR, 'Guideline on Conducting Marketing and Opinion Research Using the Internet', Press Release, 1998, at www.esomar.nl.
22. Cody, P., 'Marketing Information', *Irish Times*, March 1996, 10.
23. 'Guinness Test Market Range of Premium Beers', *IMJ*, November 1997.
24. Adapted from discussions with Jackie Williamson, Market Analyst, Digital, Reading, UK, April 1994.
25. Donnellan, E., 1995, *op. cit.*
26. Adapted from discussions with Clodagh Forde, Marketing Analysts, Marketing and Planning Systems Consultants, Boston, USA, February 1996.
27. Pring, D., 1995, *op. cit.*
28. *Ibid.*
29. Qsr Nudist, Qualitative Data Analysis Software, Scolari Sage Publications, London, UK, 1996.
30. Adapted from discussions with Ray Collis, Managing Director, Envision Marketing, Galway, 1998.
31. Adapted from material from Rodger Jupp, Managing Director, Lansdowne Market Research, Dublin, 1998.
32. Sparks, J. R. and Hunt, S. D., 'Marketing Researcher Ethical Sensitivity: Conceptualisation, Measurement and Exploratory Investigation', *Journal of Marketing*, Vol. 62 No. 2, 1998, 92–110.
33. Irish Marketing Surveys, 'Thank You' leaflet 20, 21 Upper Pembroke Street, Dublin, 1997.
34. The Market Research Society, 'Code of Conduct', 1998, at www.marketresearch.org.uk.
35. O'Leary, P., 1993, *op. cit.*
36. Adapted from material from Rodger Jupp, *op. cit.*
37. 'Marketing Research, Business Studies', *Business and Finance*, 14th November 1991.

Chapter 3

1. Gibson, L. D., 'Defining Marketing Problems', *Marketing Research*, Vol. 10 No. 1, 1998, 5–13.
2. Adapted from discussions with Martin MacBride, Managing Director, Envision Marketing, Belfast.
3. Assael, H., *Consumer Behaviour and Marketing Action*, 4th Edition, Boston, USA: PWS-Kent, 1992.
4. 'How to Develop and Use Marketing Information and Planning Systems', Van Mayros, Seminar in MKIS, MII, Dublin, December 1991.
5. Murrary, J., and O'Driscoll, A., *Managing Marketing*, Dublin: Gill & Macmillan, 1993, 131–45.
6. 'Aer Arran, Flying High', DMP Programme, NUI, Galway, Unpublished study, 1995.
7. Piercy, Nigel, *Market-led Strategic Change*, London: Butterworth Heinemann, 1992.
8. Barrett, Ciara, 'Marketing Information Systems — An Investigation into the Uses and Management of Marketing Information by Irish Award-winning Companies', unpublished MBS thesis, NUI, Galway, 1997.

9. O'Connor, J., and Galvin, E., 'Marketing and Information Technology — the Strategy, Application and Implementation of IT in Marketing', London: Pitman, 1997.
10. Baker, Michael Thomas, 1991, 'Research for Marketing', UK: Macmillan.
11. Dickens, J., 'The Fresh Cream Cakes Market: the use of qualitative research as part of a consumer research programme', 4–43, in *Applied Marketing and Social Research*, edited by U. Bradley, England: Van Norstrand Reinhold Company Ltd, 1982.
12. Barnes, J., 'Strategic Marketing Information', MII Seminar, Autumn 1994.
13. Harper, Tom, 'Quantitative Research', in *Perspectives on Marketing Management in Ireland*, edited by Mary Lambkin and Tony Meenaghan, Dublin: Oak Tree Press, 1994, 369–80.
14. Briks, D., 'Market Research', 238–67; and Meidan, A., and Moutinho, L., 'Quantative Methods in Marketing Research', 268–302, in *The Marketing Book*, 3rd Edition, Michael Baker, Butterworth-Heinemann, 1995.

Chapter 4

1. Williams, Jane, 'Marketing Research', talk given at MII West of Ireland Regional function, Ardilaun Hotel, Galway, October 1995.
2. Bond, C., 'Complementary Forces: Databases and Marketing Research', *Marketing*, January 1997, 29.
3. Nielson, Monica, *Tourism Marketing In Ireland*, Handout, GMIT, Dublin Road, Galway, 1998.
4. Adapted from 'Marketing Sources of information', written by Jim Ward for the 1984 AnCO Distance Learning package, *Marketing Management*.
5. Adapted from material supplied by Chris Hession, Irish Shellfish Association, 1996.
6. Central Statistics Office, *Guide to CSO Publications and Information Services*, April, Dublin and the CSO web site, http://www.cso.ie, 1999.
7. www.enterprise-ireland.com.
8. Enterprise Ireland, '53.21N 6.18W' report, Summer 1998.
9. Enterprise Ireland, *A New Approach*, 1998.
10. Bord Failte, Advisory and Research Publications, 1997/1998.
11. Bord Failte, 'Report and Accounts', 1996.
12. Bord Failte, 'The Failte Business, Tourism's Role in Economic Growth', 1997.
13. www.idaireland.com.
14. Udaras na Gaeltachta at www.udaras.ie.
15. Shannon Development, Shannon Development Annual Report, 1997.
16. Shannon Development, 'Innovative Action — Regional Growth', 1997.
17. Shannon Development at http://www.commerce.ie/shannon-dev/.
18. Nielson, Monica, 'Tourism Marketing In Ireland', Handout, GMIT, Dublin Road, Galway, 1998.
19. Shannon Development 1997, Shannon Development Annual Report.
20. Kompass, http://www.kompass.ie.
21. Pring, David, 'All Wired Up and Ready to Go? Marketing Research in Cyberspace', in ESOMAR/JMA/ARF, Conference on 'Triad 2000: Marketing and Research towards the Millennium', New York, USA, 11th–14th June 1995, 283–302.

22. *Online/CD-ROM Business Sourcebook*, edited by Pam Foster, 1999, Headland Business Information, London.
23. *World Directory of Business Information Web Sites*, 1998, Euromonitor.
24. *The On-line Manual, A Practical Guide to Business Databases*, 6th edition, edited by Louise Amor, 1997, Rowe Ltd.
25. Pring, David, *op. cit.*
26. AC Nielsen at http://acnielsen.com/ie/ieoffc.htm.
27. Lansdowne Market Research, Joint National Readership Research, 1996/97.
28. AC Nielsen, *op. cit.*
29. IPA Diary, 1998, 19–159.
30. Wilson & Hartnell, 'The Irish Market Facts and Figures', Leeson Park, Dublin 6.
31. McConnell's 'Media Facts', Charlemont Place, Dublin 2.
32. Shannon Development, 'Innovative Action — Regional Growth', 1997.

Chapter 5

1. From glossary of *Principles of Marketing*, Brassington and Pettitt, Pittman Publishing, 1997.
2. 'Prospecting for That Research Gold', *Marketing*, 23rd May 1996.
3. *Irish Independent*, 30th May 1996.
4. *MII News*, March/April, Vol. 8 No. 3, 1995, 3.
5. *Sunday Tribune*, 21st April 1996.
6. Penny, Richard, 'Using the Right Method', *Sunday Tribune*, 21st April 1991, 31.
7. O'Leary, Phelim, 'Qualitative Research: Where it's at, Where it's Going', *Irish Marketing Review*, Vol. 6, 1993.
8. Gulledge, Larry, 'Satisfaction Measures', *Marketing News*, Vol. 30 No. 22, 21st October 1996.
9. Darling, Eleanor, 'Banking Leaves Nothing to Chance', *BusinessPlus*, April 1998.
10. McLoughlin, Damien and Feely, Finola, 'Successful Brand Name Selection: Finches Soft Drinks', *Irish Marketing Review*, 31st August 1996.
11. 'The Name Game', *Marketing*, 22nd August 1996.
12. Lyons, Madeline, Goodfella's launch £350,00 ad blitz, SBP, 1995.
13. *Irish Times*, 18th September 1996.
14. *MII News*, January/February 1996, Vol. 9 No. 1, 7.
15. 'The Big Pint', SBP, 13th April 1997.
16. Greenbaum, Thomas, 'Using Focus Groups Effectively in Packaging Research', *Marketing News*, Vol. 29 No. 12, 5th June 1995.
17. Bristol and Fern, 'Exploring the Atmosphere Created by Focus Group Interviews', *Journal of Marketing Research Society*, Vol. 38 No. 2, April 1996.
18. Moran, William T., 'The Science of Qualitative Research', *Journal of Advertising Research*, 26, June–July 1986, RC-16.
19. Calder, Bobby, 'Focus Groups and the Nature of Qualitative Marketing Research', *Journal of Marketing Research*, 14, August 1977, 353–64.
20. Krueger, Richard, *Focus Groups, A Practical Guide*, Sage publications, 1988.
21. Calder, Bobby, *op. cit.*

22. Nelson, James E. and Frontczak, Nancy, 'How Acquaintanceship and Analyst Can Influence Focus Group Results', *Journal of Advertising*, 17, 1988, 41–8.
23. 'Marketing', *The Wall Street Journal*, 13th January 1992, B1.
24. Sykes, W., 'Validity and Reliability in Qualitative Market Research: a Review of the Literature', *Journal of the Market Research Society*, 32, 3 1990, 289–328.
25. Fern, Edward F., 'The Use of Focus Groups for Idea Generation: The Effects of Group Size, Acquaintanceship, and Moderator on Responds Quantity and Quality', *Journal of Marketing Research*, 19, February 1982, 1–13.
26. McQuarrie, Edward F., 'New Books in Review', *Journal of Marketing Research*, February 1989, 121–4.
27. Greenbaum, Thomas, 'Focus Groups by Video', *Marketing News*, Vol. 130 No. 16, 29th July 1996.
28. Greenbaum, Thomas L., 'Focus Groups Research Is Not A Commodity Business', *Marketing News*, Vol. 27 No. 5l, 1st March 1993, 4.
29. Grinchaunas, Richard and Siciliano, Tony, 'Focus Groups Produce Verbatims, Not Facts', *Marketing News*, Vol. 27 No. 1, 4th January 1993, FG-19.
30. See John M. Hess, 'Group Interviewing', in R. L. King (ed.), *New Science of Planning*, Chicago: American Marketing Association, 1968, 4.
31. Darling, Eleanor, *op. cit.*
32. Sokolow, H., 'In-Depth Interviews Increasing in Importance', *Marketing News*, 13th September 1985, 26.
33. Knox, M. Z., 'In-Depth Interviews Can Reveal What's In a Name', *Marketing News*, 3, January 1986, 4.
34. Hazel, Kahan, 'One-on-Ones Should Sparkle Like The Gems They Are', *Marketing News*, 3rd September 1990, 8–9.
35. *MII News*, January/February 1995, Vol. 8 No. 1, 1.
36. Proctor, Tony, *Essentials of Marketing Research*, Pitman Publishing, 1997, 165.
37. Greenbaum, Thomas L., 'Focus Groups vs One-on-Ones: The Controversy Continues', *Marketing News*, 2nd September 1991, 16.
38. Penny, Richard, *op. cit.*
39. Mitchell, Vincent Wayne, 'Getting the Most from In-Depth Interviews', *Business Marketing Digest*, Vol. 18 No. 1, First quarter, 1993, 63–70.
40. Greenbaum, Thomas L., *op. cit.*
41 Hollander, Sharon L., 'Projective Techniques Uncover Real Consumer Attitudes', *Marketing News*, 4th January 1988, 34.
42. Kassarjian, H. H., 'Projective Methods', in R. Ferber (ed.), *Handbook of Marketing Research*, New York: McGraw-Hill, 1974, 3.85–3.100.
43. Lindzey, G., 'On the Classification of Projective Techniques', *Psychological Bulletin*, 1959, 158–68.
44. McLoughlin, Damien and Feely, Finola, *op. cit.*
45. O'Leary, Phelim, *op. cit.*
46. O'Leary, Phelim, *op. cit.*
47. Haire, Mason, 'Projective Techniques in Marketing Research', *Journal of Marketing*, April 1950, 649/652.
48. O'Leary, Phelim, *op. cit.*

Chapter 6

1. Oppenheim, A. N., *Questionnaire Design and Attitude Measurement*, NY: Basic Books, 1996.
2. Seymour, Harry, 'Conducting and Using Customer Surveys', *Marketing News*, 23rd September 1996, Vol. 30 No. 20, 8.
3. Sudman, Seymour, *Reducing the Cost of Surveys*, Chicago: Aldine, 1967.
4. Proctor, Tony, *Essentials of Marketing Research*, Pitman Publishing, 1997, 99.
5. DuPont, Thomas D., 'Do Frequent Mall Shoppers Distort Mall-Intercept Results?', *Journal of Advertising Research*, Vol. 27 No. 4, August/September 1987, 45–51.
6. Tyebjee, Tyzoon T., 'Telephone Survey Methods: The State of the Art', *Journal of Marketing Research*, Summer 1979, 69; Howard Gershowitz, 'Entering the 1990s: The State of Data Collection — Telephone Data Collection', *Applied Marketing Research*, Vol. 30 No. 2, Second Quarter 1990, 16–19.
7. Gates, Roger and Brobst, Bob, 'RAN-DIAL: A Program for Generating Random Telephone Numbers in Interviewer Usable Form', *Journal of Marketing Research*, 14, May 1977, 240–2.
8. Czaja, Ronald, Blair, Johnny and Sebestik, Jutta P., 'Respondent Selection in a Telephone Survey: A Comparison of Three Techniques', *Journal of Marketing Research*, 19th August 1982, 381–5; and O'Rourke, Diane, and Blair, Johnny, 'Improving Random Respondent Selection in Telephone Interviews', *Journal of Marketing Research*, 20, November 1983, 428–32.
9. *Your Opinion Counts*, 14. See also Jolene M. Struebbe, Jerome B. Kernan, and Thomas J. Georgan, 'The Refusal Problem in Telephone Surveys', *Journal of Advertising Research*, June–July 1986, 29–37.
10. Reported by Survey Sampling Inc., March 1993.
11. Becker, Emil, 'Automated Interviewing has Advantages', *Marketing News*, January, 2, Vol. 29 No. 1.
12. Berdie, Douglas, 'Reassessing the Value of High Response Rates to Mail Surveys', *Marketing Research*, September 1989, 52–63; Jean Charles Chebat and Ayala Cohen, 'Response Speed in Mail Surveys: Beware of Shortcuts', *Marketing Research*, Spring 1993, 20–5; and Robert J. Sutton and Linda L. Zeits, 'Multiple Prior Notifications, Personalization, and Reminder Surveys', *Marketing Research*, December 1992, 14–21.
13. Kanuk, Leslie and Berenson, Conrad, 'Mail Surveys and Response Rates: A Literature Review', *Journal of Marketing Research*, November 1975, 440–53; Lee Harvey, 'Factors Affecting Response Rates to Mailed Questionnaires: A Comprehensive Literature Review', *Journal of the Market Research Society (U.K.)*, July 1987, 341–53.
14. Parker, Charles D. and McCrohan, Kevin F., 'Increasing Mail Survey Response Rates: A Discussion of Methods and Induced Bias', in John Summey, R. Viswanathan, Ronald Taylor, and Karen Glynn (eds), *Marketing Theories and Concepts For Era of Change*, Atlanta: Southern Marketing Association, 1983, 254–6.
15. Darling, Eleanor, 'Banking Leaves Nothing to Chance', *BusinessPlus*, April 1998.
16. 'Data — What Companies Know About You', *Business and Finance*, 15th September 1994.
17. 'Mail Lists Key to New Markets', *Sunday Business Post*, 1995.
18. Darling, Eleanor, *op. cit.*

19. See, for example, Stephen W. McDaniel and Perry Werille, 'Do Topic Differences Affect Survey Non-Response?', *Journal of the Marketing Research Society*, Vol. 29 No. 1, January 1987, 55–66.
20. Brennan, Mike, Hoek, Janet and Aistridge, Craig, 'The Effect of Monetary Incentives on the Response Rate and Cost Effectiveness of a Mail Survey', *Journal of Market Research Society*, Vol. 33 No. 3, 229–41.
21. Darling, Eleanor, *op. cit.*
22. Kanuk and Berenson, 'Mail Surveys', 450. Reprinted from the *Journal of Marketing Research*, American Marketing Association.
23. Addis, Robin, 'Understanding Your Customers and Finding New Ones', *Business and Finance*, October 1990, 14–18.
24. *MII News*, March/April 1996, Vol. 9 No. 2, 14.
25. Zikmund, William, G., *Exploring Marketing Research*, 6th Edition, Dryden Press, 1997, 206.
26. Aaker and Day, *Marketing Research*, 4th Edition, Wiley Publications, 139.
27. Harper, Tom, 'Quantitative Research', in *Perspectives on Marketing Management in Ireland*, edited by Mary Lambkin and Tony Meenaghan, Dublin: Oak Tree Press, 1994, 369–80.
28. Harper, Tom, *op. cit.*
29. Lansdowne Market Research Promotional Material.
30. 'Market Research in Ireland', *Business and Finance*, 16th September 1993.
31. Chisnall, Peter, *Marketing Research*, 5th Edition, McGraw-Hill, 229.
32. Harper, Tom, *op. cit.*
33. Mason, Jennifer, *Qualitative Researching*, Sage Publications, 1996.
34. 'The Magic of Mystery Shopping', *Marketing*, 17th October 1996, 41–3.
35. 'Does Colour Make a Difference', *IMJ*, April 1996, 18–20
36. 'Retailing Revolt', *Business and Finance*, 28th July 1994.
37. Bowles, T. and Charbitt, C., 'Can Scanner Data Achieve their Potential in Europe?', *Marketing and Research Today*, May 1997, (25/2), 121–5.

Chapter 7

1. Campbell, D., and Stanley, J., 'Experimental and Quasi-Experimental Designs for Research', Chicago: Rand McNally, 1966.
2. Hunt, Shelby, D., *Marketing Theory, The Philosophy Of Marketing Science*, Irwin, 1983, 120–5.
3. Rothlisberger, F., and William, J., *Management and the Worker, An Account of a Research Program Conducted by the Western Electric Company, Hawthorne Works, Chicago*, Harvard University Press, 1939.
4. Fox, M., and Phua, K., 'Using Medicaid Claims Data to Evaluate a Large Physician Fee Increase', *Health Services Research*, Vol. 29 No. 3, 1994, 315–29.
5. Thornton, Sarah, 'Sales Promotion and Experimental Designs', unpublished MBS thesis, NUI, Galway, 1997.
6. Domegan, Christine, 'An Evaluation Study of ANCO's Open Learning Marketing Management Programme', UCD, 1984, 28.
7. Rothlisberger, F., and William, J., *op. cit.*

8. Churchill, G.A., 'Marketing Research Methodological Foundations', 6th Edition, London: Dryden Press, 216.
9. Weiner, J., 'Consumer Electronics Marketer Uses Conjoint Approach to Configure its New Product and Set the Right Price', *Marketing Research*, Vol. 6 No. 3, 1996, 7–11.
10. Adapted from Tull, S., and Hawkins, D., *Marketing Research, Measurement and Method*, 5th Edition, Macmillan, 207.
11. 'Guinness Test Market Range of Premium Beers', *IMJ*, November 1997.
12. 'Mars Celebrate', *IMJ*, November 1997.
13. 'World Stella Test Marketed', *Factfinder*, 31st August 1997.
14. Yarbrough, J., 'Fill 'er up', *Sales and Marketing Management*, Vol. 148 No. 9, 1996, 126.
15. 'Beamish Red Ahead of Expectations in UK', *Factfinder*, 31st March 1997.
16. Bases Worldwide, 'Simulated Test Marketing' at http://www.bases.com/stm.htm, 1998.
17. Cohen, S., and Gadd, M., 'Virtual Reality Shopping Simulation for the Modern Marketer', in the 48th ESOMAR Marketing Research Congress, ' Making the Decision', The Hague, 17th–20th September 1995, 269–83.
18. Burke, Raymond R., *Virtual Shopping Breakthrough in Marketing Research*, HBR March/April, 1996, 120–31
19. Clancy, K. J., and Shulman, R. S., 'Test for Success', *Sales and Marketing Management*, 1995, 111–14.
20. Kleinschmidt, E. J., and Cooper, R. G., 'The Impact of an International Orientation on Product Innovation', *European Journal of Marketing*, Vol. 22 No. 10, 1988, 56.
21. Phillips, A., 'Developing a Rounder Tea', *Marketing and Research Today*, Vol. 19 No. 1, 1991, 3–14.
22. Bases Worldwide, *op. cit.*
23. 27th EMAC Conference, Marketing Research and Practice, Track 5, Marketing Research, Sweden, Vol. 5, May 1998.

Chapter 8

1. Seymour, Harry, 'Conducting and Using Customer Surveys', *Marketing News*, 23rd September 1996, Vol. 30 No. 20, 8.
2. Malhotra, Naresh K., *Marketing Research, An Applied Orientation*, 1993, Prentice Hall, 318–19.
3. Haller, Terry, *Danger: Marketing Researcher at Work*, Westport, Conn: Quorum Books, 1983, 149.
4. Jones, S., 'Listening to Complexity', *Journal of the Market Research Society*, January 1981, 26–39; and McDonald, C., 'Coding Open-Ended Answers with the Help of a Computer', *Journal of the Market Research Society*, January 1982, 9–27.
5. Krosnick, Jon A., and Alwin, Duane F., 'An Evaluation of a Cognitive Theory of Response-Order Effects in Survey Measurement', *Public Opinion Quarterly*, Summer 1987, 201–19; and Payne, S. L., *The Art of Asking Questions*, Princeton, NJ: Princeton University Press, 1951, 141.
6. Morgan, Fred W., 'Judicial Standards for Survey Research: An Update and Guidelines', *Journal of Marketing*, 54, January 1990, 59–70; and Peterson, R. A., and Kerin, R. A., 'The Quality of Self-Report Data: Review and Synthesis', in Ben Enis and Kenneth Roering (eds), *Annual Review of Marketing 1981*, Chicago: American Marketing Association, 1981, 5–20.

7. Omura, G. S., 'Correlates of Item Nonresponse', *Journal of the Market Research Society*, October 1983, 321–30; and Presser, S., 'Is Inaccuracy on Factual Survey Items Item-Specific or Respondent-Specific?', *Public Opinion Quarterly*, Spring 1984, 344–55.
8. Payne, S. L., *The Art of Asking Questions*, Princeton NJ: Princeton University Press, 1951, 41.
9. Boyd, Harper W., Jr., Westfall, Ralph and Stasch, Stanley F., *Marketing Research: Text and Cases*, 7th Edition, Homewood, IL.: Richard D. Irwin, 1989, 277.
10. Smith, Tom W., 'That Which We Call Welfare by Any Other Name Would Smell Sweeter. An Analysis of the Impact of Question Wording on Response Patterns', *Public Opinion Quarterly*, Spring 1987, 75–83.
11. Payne, *op. cit.*
12. Boyd, Harper W., Jr., Westfall, Ralph and Stasch, Stanley F., *op. cit.*
13. See, for example, George F. Bishop, 'Experiments with the Middle Response Alternative in Survey Questions', *Public Opinion Quarterly*, Vol. 51, Summer 1985, 220–32; or Clinton B. Schertizer and Jerome B. Kernan, 'More on the Robustness of Response Scales', *Journal of the Marketing Research Society*, Vol. 27, October 1985, 262–82.
14. Mayer, Charles S., and Piper, Cindy, 'A Note on the Importance of Layout in Self-Administered Questionnaires', *Journal of Marketing Research*, 19, August 1982, 390–1.
15. 'Mailing List Brokers Sell More than Names to Their Many Clients', *The Wall Street Journal*, 19th February 1974, 1, 18; and Bob Davis, 'Baby-Goods Firms See Direct Mail as the Perfect Pitch for New Moms', *The Wall Street Journal*, 29th January 1986, 31.
16. Leeuw, E. and Hox, J., 'The Effect of Computer Assisted Interviewing', *JMRS*, Vol. 37 No. 4, 1995.
17. Normally pretests are done individually, but a focus group could be used. See Steven A. Long, 'Pretesting Questionnaires Minimizes Measurement Error', *Marketing News*, Vol. 25 No. 11, 27th May 1991.
18. Hunt, Shelby D., Sparkman, Richard D. Jr., and Wilcox, James B., 'The Pretest in Survey Research: Issues and Preliminary Findings', *Journal of Marketing Research*, 19, May 1982, 265–75.
19. Kiecker p. Nelson 'Do interviewers follow telephone survey instructions', *JMRS*, April 1996, Vol. 38 No. 2, 161– 76(16).

Chapter 9

1. Gordon Allport, 'Attitudes' in C. A. Murchinson (ed.), *A Handbook of Social Psychology*, Worchester, MA.: Clark University Press, 1935, 798–844.
2. Neelankavil, J. P., O'Brien, J. V. and Rashjain, R., 'Techniques to Obtain Market-related Information from Very Young Children', *Journal of Advertising Research*, June/July 1985, 41–7. See also M. C. Macklin, 'Do Children Understand TV Ads?', *Journal of Advertising Research*, February/March 1983, 63–70.
3. McDaniel, Carl Jr., Gates, Roger, *Contemporary Marketing Research*, 3rd Edition, West Publishing Company, 1996, 355.
4. See Churchill, Gilbert A. Jr., 'A Paradigm for Developing Better Measures of Marketing Constructs', *Journal of Marketing Research*, 16, February 1979, 64–73, for a procedure that can be used to construct scales having construct validity. See J. Paul Peter, 'Construct Validity: A Review of Basic Issues and Marketing Practices', *Journal of Marketing Research*, 18, May 1981, 133–45

5. Perreault, William D. Jr., and Leigh, Laurence E., 'Reliability of Nominal Data Based on Qualitative Judgments', *Journal of Marketing Research*, 25, May 1989, 135–48; Peter J. Paul, 'Reliability: A Review of Psychometric Basics and Recent Marketing Practices', *Journal of Marketing Research*, 16, February 1979, 6–17.
6. Grigg, A. O., 'Some Problems Concerning the Use of Rating Scales for Visual Assessment', *Journal of the Market Research Society*, January 1980, 29–43; and L. W. Friedman and H. H. Friedman, 'Comparison of Itemised vs Graphic Rating Scales', *Journal of the Market Research Society*, July 1986, 285–90. For a different view see S. I. Lampert, 'The Attitude Pollimeter: A New Attitude Scaling Device', *Journal of Marketing Research*, November 1979, 578–82.
7. Cose, Eli P. II, 'The Optimal Number of Response Alternatives for a Scale: A Review,' *Journal of Marketing Research*, November 1980, 407–22.
8. Friedman, H. H. and Leefer, J. R., 'Label Versus Position in Rating Scales', *Journal of the Academy of Marketing Science*, Spring 1981, 88–92.
9. Dickson, John and Albaum, Gerald, 'A Method for Developing Tailor-Made Semantic Differentials for Specific Marketing Content Areas', *Journal of Marketing Research*, 14, February 1977, 87–91.
10. Malhotra, Naresh K., 'A Scale to Measure Self-Concepts, Person Concepts and Product Concepts', *Journal of Marketing Research*, 18, November 1981, 456–64.
11. Friedman, H. H. and Leefer, J. R. 'Label Versus Position in Rating Scales', *Journal of the Academy of Marketing Science*, Spring 1981, 88–92. R. I. Haley and P. B. Case, 'Testing Thirteen Attitude Scales for Agreement and Brand Discrimination', *Journal of Marketing*, Fall 1979, 20–32.
12. Likert, Rensis, 'A technique for measuring of attitudes', *Archives of Psychology*, 140.
13. Riecken, G. and Samli, A. C., 'Measuring Children's Attitudes Toward Television Commercials: Extension and Replication', *Journal of Consumer Research*, June 1981, 57–61.
14. See Jacob Jacoby and Michael S. Matell, 'Three Point Likert Scales Are Good Enough', *Journal of Marketing Research*, November 1971, 495–506; Roger Best, Del I. Hawkins, and Gerald Albaum, 'The Effort of Varying Response Intervals on the Stability of Factor Solutions of Rating Scale Data', in *Advances in Consumer Research*, Vol. VII, Jerry Olson (ed.), San Francisco: ACR, 1979, 539–54.
15. Roberts, Mary Lou and Wortzel, Lawrence H., 'New Lifestyle Determinants of Women's Food Shopping Behaviour', *Journal of Marketing*, Summer 1979, 28–39.
16. Osgood, Charles E., Sici, George J., and Tannenbaum, Percy H., *The Measurement of Meaning*, University of Illinois Press, Urbana, 1957.
17. Malhotra, Naresh K., 'A Scale to Measure Self-Concepts, Person Concepts and Product Concepts', *Journal of Marketing Research*, 18, November 1981, 456–64.
18. Andrews, F. M., 'Construct Validity and Error Components of Survey Measures', *Public Opinion Quarterly*, Summer 1984, 432.
19. Anderson, R. C. and Scott, E. A., 'Supermarkets: Are they really alike?', *Journal of Retailing*, Autumn 1970.
20. Another way to avoid the halo effect is to have subjects rate each stimulus on the same attribute and then move to the next attribute. See Bob T. W. Wu and Susan Petroshius, 'The Halo Effect in Store Image Management', *Journal of the Academy of Marketing Science*, Vol. 15 No. 1, 1987, 44–51.

21. Garg, Rajendar K., 'The Influence of Positive and Negative Wording and Issue Involvement on Responses to Likert Scales in Marketing Research', *Journal of the Marketing Research Society*, Vol. 37 No. 3, July 1996, 234–46.
22. Menezes, Dennis and Elbert, Nobert F., 'Alternative Semantic Scaling Formats for Measuring Store Image: An Evaluation', *Journal of Marketing Research*, February 1979, 80–7.
23. Hawkins, Del I., Albaum, Gerald, and Best, Roger, 'Stapel Scale or Semantic Differential in Marketing Research?', *Journal of Marketing Research*, August 1974, 318–22.

Chapter 10

1. Rodger, Leslie, *Statistics for Marketing*, McGraw Hill Marketing Series, 1984.
2. Churchill, Gilbert A., *Marketing Research Methodological Foundations*, 6th Edition, The Dryden Press, 574–651.
3. Williams, Jane, 'The Sampling Process', 61–96, in *Business Research Methods, Strategies, Techniques and Sources*, T. Brannick and W. Roche (eds), Dublin: Oak Tree Press, 1997.
4. CSO, Census of Population, 1996, Preliminary Report, Commentary, 5.
5. Weiers, Ronald, *Marketing Research*, 2nd Edition, Prentice-Hall International.
6. Williams, Jane, *op. cit.*
7. Rodger, Leslie, *op. cit.*
8. Hague, P. and Harris, P., *Sampling and Statistics*, the Marketing Research Series, Kogan Page, 1993.
9. Maisel, R. and Persell C., *How Sampling Works*, New York: Pine Forge, 1996.
10. CSO, *Household Budget Survey, 1994–1995, Volume 1, Detailed Results for all Households*, Appendix 4, 215–24.
11. CSO, Census of Population, 1996, Preliminary Report, Table B, 'Population of each province, County and County Borough and actual and percentage change, 1991–1996', 7.
12. *The Irish Times and MRBI Ltd*, 'Fianna Fail expected to lead next government', 7th June 1997 and 'FF and PD's close to gaining majority, new poll reveals', 31st May 1997.
13. Harper, Tom, 'Quantitative Research' in *Perspectives on Marketing Management in Ireland*, Mary Lambkin and Tony Meenaghan (eds), Dublin: Oak Tree Press, 1994, 369–80.

Chapter 11

1. Rodger, Leslie, *Statistics for Marketing*, McGraw Hill, 1984.
2. Kish, Leslie, *Survey Sampling*, New York: John Wiley & Sons, Inc., 1965.
3. Zikmund, William, *Exploring Marketing Research*, 6th Edition, Dryden Press, 1997.

Chapter 12

1. Aaker, David and Day, George, *Marketing Research*, 4th Edition, John Wiley & Sons, Inc., 1990, 431.
2. Keller, Wouter J., 'Trends in Survey Data Processing', *Journal of Market Research Society*, Vol. 35 No. 3, July 1993.
3. Aaker, David and Day, George, *op. cit.* See also, D. W. Stewart, 'Filling the Gap; A Review of the Missing Data Problem', *An Assessment of Marketing Thought and Practice*, American Marketing Association, 1982, 395–9, and Malhotra, Naresh K., 'Analysing Marketing

Research Data with incomplete information on the Dependent Variable', *Journal of Marketing Research*, 24, February 1987, 74–84.
4. For a further discussion of coding see also, Philip S. Sidel, 'Coding', in Robert Ferber (ed.), *Handbook of Marketing Research*, New York: McGraw Hill, 1974, pp. 2-178–2-199.
5. Malhotra, Naresh, K., *Marketing Research, An Applied Orientation*, Prentice-Hall, 1993, 487.
6. For a detailed discussion on fundamental statistics, see Richard I. Levin, *Statistics for Management*, Englewood Cliffs, New Jersey: Prentice-Hall, 1987, or any business statistics textbook.
7. For an excellent discussion on this, see Keane, John G., 'Questionable Statistics', *American Demographics*, Vol. 7 issue 6, June 1985, 18–21.
8. For an excellent discussion on creating graphics presentations see Gus Venditto, 'Twelve Tips for Better Presentations', *PC Magazine*, 28th January 1992, 253–60
9. This discussion of charts is taken from the Excel Spreadsheet Software package.

Chapter 13

1. Bowles, B. and Blyth, B., 'How Do You Like Your Data; Raw, Al dente or Stewed?', *Journal of the Market Research Society*, Vol. 19 No. 1, 1997, 165–74.
2. Davis, E. J., 'Statistical Tests', Appendix 3, 351–64, in *The Marketing Research Process*, 4th Edition, by M. Crimp and L. T. Wright, Prentice-Hall, 1995.
3. Groebner, D. and Shannon, P., *Business Statistics, A Decision-Making Approach*, 3rd Edition, Merrill, 1989.
4. Downie, N. M. and Heath, R. W., *Basic Statistical Methods*, Harper & Row International, 1974.
5. Janpi, G. K., *100 Statistical Tests*, Sage Publications, 1993.
6. Berenson, M. and Levine, D., *Basic Business Statistics, Concepts and Applications*, Prentice-Hall, 1996.

Chapter 14

1. Hair, J., Anderson, R., Tatham, R., and Black, W., *Multivariate Data Analysis*, 5th Edition, Prentice-Hall International, 1998.
2. Hooley, Graham and Hussey, Michael, *Quantative Methods in Marketing*, London: Dryden Press, 1995.
3. Sharma, Subhash, 'Applied Multivariate Techniques', USA: John Wiley, 1996.
4. Fornell, C. and Zinkhan, G, 1987, 'Classification Schemes for a new generation of multivariate Analysis', American Marketing Association Winter Education Conference, 295–9.
5. Diamantopoulos, A. and Schilegelmilch, B., *Taking the Fear out of Data Analysis*, London: The Dryden Press, 1997.
6. Hair, J., Anderson, R., Tatham, R. and Black, W., *op. cit.*
7. Sharma, Subhash, *op. cit.*
8. Hair, J., Anderson, R., Tatham, R. and Black, W., *op. cit.*
9. Boyd, H., Westfall, R. and Stasch, S., *Marketing Research, Text and Cases*, 5th Edition, USA: Richard Irwin, Inc., 1981.

10. Sharma, Subhash, *op. cit.*
11. Johnson, D., Forward, 'Some Observations on, and Developments in, the Analysis of Multivatiate Survey Data', *Journal of Market Research Society*, Vol. 38 No. 4, 1996, 447.
12. Flynn, L., Goldsmith, R. and Eastmann, J., 'Opinion Leaders and Opinion Seekers, Two New Measurement Scales', *Journal of Academy of Marketing Science*, Vol. 24 No. 2, 1996, 137–47.
13. Inglis, J. and Johnson, D., 'Some observations on, and developments in, the analysis of multivariate survey data', *Journal of Market Research Society*, Vol. 12 No. 2, 1970, 449–71.
14. Boyd, H., Westfall, R. and Stasch, S., *op. cit.*
15. Churchill, G., *Marketing Research, Methodological Foundations*, 5th Edition, Chicago: Dryden Press, 921.
16. Diamantopoulous, A., 'Modelling with LISTREL: A Guide for the Uninitiated', in Hooley, Graham and Hussey, Michael, *Quantitative Methods in Marketing*, London: Dryden Press, 1995, 105–36.
17. Mountinho, I., Goode M. and Davis, F., *Quantitative Analysis in Marketing Management*, England: John Wiley, 1998.
18. Hooley, Graham and Hussey, Michael, *op. cit.*

Chapter 15

1. Deshpande, Rohit and Zaltman, Gerald, 'A Comparison of Factors Affecting Researcher and Manager Perceptions of Market Research Use', *Journal of Marketing Research*, 21, February 1984, 37.
2. Britt, S. H. 'The Writing of Readable Research Reports', *Journal of Marketing Research*, May 1971, 265.
3. Gallagher, William J., *Report Writing for Management*, Massachusetts: Addison-Wesley Publishing Company, Inc., 1969, 87.
4. *Ibid.*, 84.
5. See Gallagher, *Report Writing*, 80–3, for a number of examples that display some of the inaccuracies that may arise. The examples are particularly interesting because they have been extracted from actual company reports.
6. Resta, Paul, E., *The Research Report*, NY: An American Book Company, 1972, 5.
7. Tull and Hawkins, *Marketing Research*, 4th Edition, New York: Macmillan, 1987.
8. Lawlor, Kevin, 'Communicate or Die', *Business and Finance*, 12th October 1995.
9. Hayes, Stephen, 'Making Effective Presentations', *Marketing, Running Your Business*, June/July 1996.
10. *Ibid.*

INDEX

ABI Inform, CD-Rom, 104
AC Nielsen, research data, 112–13
Aer Arann, case study, 330–31
airline industry, case study, 330–31
alginate industry, case study, 79–80
Anbar Abstracts, CD-Rom, 104
Annual Services Inquiry, 88
ANOVA. *see* variance analysis
association techniques, 144–5
associative variation, 198
attitudes
  components, 265–7
  effect on behaviour, 267
  rating techniques, 281–7
    fractionation-rating scales, 286–7
    graphic scales, 281–2
    itemised scales, 282–4
    paired-comparison scales, 285–6
    rank-order scales, 284–5
  scaling techniques, 287–95
    multidimensional scaling (MDS), 420–22
    semantic differential, 291–4
    Stapel scale, 294–5

banking, case study, 329–30
Bord Failte
  as data source, 94–7
  case study, 64–6
Bord na Mona, case study, 152–4
BOTIS, on-line information, 104
branding, case study, 38–40
Bridge House Restaurant, case study, 299–301
Broccoli Quick, case study, 227–30
business environment information, 117–18
Business Information Centre, 117
Business of Advertising Agencies (CSO), 89

case studies
  airline, 330–31
  banking, 329–30
  charity organisations, 38, 40–42
  concrete products, 123–6
  electronics, 37
  footwear, 38–40
  Irish women survey, 348–51
  knitwear, 61
  newspapers, 120–23
  pharmaceuticals, 155–6
  pottery, 332–4
  restaurant, 299–301
  skin care products, 62
  solid fuel industry, 15, 152–4
  sports centre, 263–4
  television station, 191–3
  tennis clubs, 49
  tourism, 64–6
causality, 198–9
  evidence required for use, 198
census, 304
  vs. sample, 305–6
Census of Industrial Production, 90
Census of Population, 83–5
  marketing research uses, 84–5
Census of Services, 88
Central Statistics Office
  access to data, 90–91
  ad hoc analyses, 91
  Annual Services Inquiry, 88
  Business of Advertising Agencies, 89
  Census of Industrial Production, 90
  Census of Population, 83–5
  Census of Services, 88
  Consumer Price Index, 85–6
  Economic Series, 83
  Household Budget Survey, 85
  Industrial Production Index, 90
  Labour Force Survey, 88

Central Statistics Office *contd*
  library, 91
  market size data, 86–8
  Monthly Trade Statistics, 89–90
  Retail Sales Index, 89
  Statistical Abstract, 82
  Statistical Bulletin, 83
centroid, 415
Chamber of Commerce, 102–3
charity organisations, case studies, 38, 40–42
charts. *see* graphs
Checkout magazine, 115
chi-square tests, 391–2
cluster analysis, 419–20
codes of conduct, 33
coding data, 356–61
  code books, 361
  postcoded questionnaires, 360–61
  precoded questionnaires, 360
  tabulating data, 361–5
communalities, 417
completion techniques, 145–6
computer-assisted personal interviewing (CAPI), 174
computer-assisted telephone interviewing (CATI), 164–6
  advantages of, 165
concomitant variation, 198
concrete products, case study, 123–6
confidence intervals, 340–42
Connolly Produce, case study, 227–30
construction techniques, 146
Consumer Price Index, 85–6
consumer research, 5
control groups, 196
convenience foods, case study, 62–4
  correlation, of statistics, 395–8
correlation coefficients, 398–400
cross-sectional data, 56, 159
customer information, as data source, 75–6

data
  causal, 55, 56–8
  cross-sectional, 56
  descriptive, 56
  exploratory, 55, 58
  interval, 273
  longitudinal, 56
  metric, 408
  nominal, 271
  ordinal, 272, 398
  primary, 71
  qualitative, 55, 57–8
  quantitative, 56, 57–8
  ratio, 274
  secondary, 71–3
data analysis, 25–6, 380–400
  bivariate, 25, 362–3
  coding received data, 356–61
  data reduction, 25
  editing received data, 355–6
  evaluation criteria, 72–3
  multivariate, 25, 362–3, 406–23
    cluster analysis, 419–20
    dependent, 406–8
    discriminant analysis, 412–16
    factor analysis, 416–19
    independent, 406–8
    multidimensional scaling (MDS), 420–22
    multiple regression analysis, 409–12
  preparation for, 355–77
  regression and correlation, 395–8
  significance tests, 381–92
  unit of analysis, 48
  univariate, 25
  variance analysis, 392–5
  see also statistics
data collection methods, 21–3
  experimentation, 23, 195–222
  focus groups, 129–39
  future trends, 31–2
  in-depth interviews, 139–43
  Internet, 175–7
  measurement, 23
  observation, 23
  panels, 22–3
  primary data, 22, 23
  projective techniques, 143–50
  questionnaires, 23, 232–56
  secondary data, 21, 23, 71–118

surveys, 22, 157–81
data presentation, 373–6
  graphs and charts, 374–6
  tables, 374
  see also report writing
data sources
  directories, 99–102
  EU and European, 109–12
  government, 81–91
  'grey material', 115–18
  state-sponsored bodies, 92–9
  syndicated, 112–14
  trade associations, 102–4
  web sites, 107–9, 113
DATA-STAR database, 104
Department of Agriculture, Food and Forestry, 91
descriptive data, 56
  see also quantitative data
descriptive research
  observation methods, 181–8
  panels, 22–3, 179
  surveys, 157–81
desk research, 71
  conducting, 73–4
  evaluation, 71-3
Dialog database, 105
directories
  Dun and Bradstreet's Marketing Guide to Ireland, 101
  European Industrial and Trade Associations, 102
  Kelly's Business Directory, 102
  Kompass Ireland, 99–101
  Thoms Commercial Directory, 101
  Thoms Register of American Manufacturers, 101
discriminant analysis, 412–16
  centroid, 415
  group classifications, 413–15
distribution research, 5
DPLNET, 116
Dubarry shoes, case study, 38–40
Dun and Bradstreet's Marketing Guide to Ireland, 101

eigenvalues, 417
Electronic Engineering Systems, case study, 37
electronic point of sale (EPOS) data, 186
electronics industry, case study, 37
e-mail questionnaires, 176
Enterprise Ireland, 92–4
  Market Information Centre, 92, 94
errors, in research, 29–30
  history errors, 200
  instrumentation error, 201
  maturation, 200
  non-sampling, 30, 233, 306
  non-response error, 159
  reactive error, 202–3
  response error, 159
  sampling error, 159, 304
  selection bias, 202
  statistical regression, 201–2
  systematic, 29–30
  testing effect, 200–201
estimate, definition, 304
ethics, 33–4
Eurobarometer surveys, 111
Euromonitor business information, 112
European Information Centres (EICs), 109–10
Eurostat, 109
  information, 110–11
experimental research, 195–222
  case study, 227–30
  design, 205–18
    pre-experimental, 205–6
    quasi-experimental, 210–11
    statistical, 211–16
    true experimental, 206–9
  design selection, 216–18
  field vs. laboratory, 203
  simulated test marketing, 220–22
  terminology, 195–7
  test marketing, 218–22
  validity, 199–222
expert surveys, 47
expressive techniques, 147–8
external data, 75

external data *contd*
  government sources, 81–91
  source classification, 80–81
  sources, 79–81
  sources, case study, 79–80

factor analysis, 416–19
  communalities, 417
  eigenvalues, 417
  factor loadings, 417
factorial research design, 215–16
field research, 71
field workers, 256–60
  management of, 258–60
  selection, 257
  training, 257–8
fieldwork, 25
Findex directory, 105
focus groups, 22, 129–39
  advantages and disadvantages, 138–9
  analysis, 137–8
  case studies, 152–6
  discussion guide, 134–7
  managing, 131–8
  moderator selection, 133–4
  objectives of, 129–30
  recording sessions, 133
  recruiting, 132
  types, 130–31
Foinse newspaper, case study, 120–23
food industry, case study, 62–4
footwear industry, case study, 38–40
FT Profile, on-line information, 105

Goodfella's Pizza, case study, 62–4
government data sources, 81–91
  state-sponsored bodies, 92–9
graphs
  bar charts, 374–5
  line graphs, 374
  pie charts, 375
  scatter diagrams, 413–15
  use guidelines, 376
Green Isle Foods, case study, 62–4

Hawthorne Effect, 202–3
hierarchy of effects model, 267
history errors, 200
Household Budget Survey, 85
hypothesis development, 45, 49
hypothesis testing, 381–92
  alternative hypothesis, 381
    formulation, 382
  directional/non-directional, 381
  null hypothesis, 381
    formulation, 382, 388
  p-values, 388
  rejection rule, 383
  test statistic value, 382–3

Industrial Development Agency (IDA)
  data source, 97–8
Industrial Production Index (CSO), 90
instrumentation error, 201
internal data, 75–9, 81
  from company records, 76–9
  from customer information, 75–6
Internet
  market research using, 175–7
  marketing information on, 107–9
interviews
  in-depth, 22, 139–43
    advantages and disadvantages, 141
    applications, 139–41
    sample questions, 141–3
  personal, 160–61
    advantages, 160
    limitations, 161
    procedure, 160
    shopping centre intercepts, 161
  postal, 167–73
    advantages, 168
    limitations, 168–9
    non-response error, 172
    non-response reduction, 169–72
    procedure, 167–8
  telephone, 162–4
    advantages, 163
    computer-assisted, 164–6
    limitations, 163–4

procedure, 162–3
IPA Administration Yearbook, 115
Ireland, marketing research in, 9–12
Irish bank, case study, 329–30
Irish Consumer Market yearbook, 115–16
Irish Market Facts & Figures, 116
Irish Marketing profile, 116
Irish Stock Market Annual, 105

jargon, definitions, 101
jigsaw puzzle market, 40–42
Joint National Readership Research (JNRR), 113–14
Judy Greene Pottery, case study, 332–4

Kelly's Business Directory, 102
knitwear industry, case study, 61
Kompass Ireland, 99–101

Labour Force Survey, 88
Lansdowne Market Research, 113–14
Latin Square research design, 214
leisure industry, case studies, 49, 263–4
Likert's scale, 288–91
   constructing, 289–91
   for multidimensional scaling, 422
logos, marketing function, 6, 65–6
longitudinal data, 56
loyalty cards, 187

McCarthys database, 105
MacMillan Dictionary of Marketing & Advertising, 101
MAID market research, 105
Major Companies of Europe directory, 105
MAPS directory, 115
Market Information Centre (Enterprise Ireland), 92, 94
market researchers. *see* field workers
market size, estimating, 86–8
marketing information system
   model framework, 52
   problem definition and, 52–4
Marketing Institute of Ireland, 103
marketing research
   decision-driven, 4, 15

defined, 2–5, 12
errors, 29–30
ethics, 33–4
future trends, 30–33
in Ireland, 9–12
information-orientated, 4–5
methodology-led, 3–4
objectivity, 28–9
purpose, 6–9, 16
reliability, 4, 29
report writing, 428–41
successful, 28, 29
types, 5–6
validity, 4, 29, 199–204
marketing research process, 17–28
   case studies, 37–42
   managing, 26–30
   research proposals, 19–20
   secondary data, role of, 72
   stage 1, problem definition, 18–20, 34, 44–54
   stage 2, research design, 20–21, 34
   stage 3, data collection, 21–3, 34
   stage 4, sampling, 24–5, 34
   stage 5, fieldwork, 25, 34
   stage 6, data analysis, 25–6, 34
   stage 7, presenting results, 26, 35
Marketing Society of Ireland, 103
maturation errors, 200
measurement, 267–75
   of attitudes, 280–95
   case study, 299–301
   concepts and, 268–70
   four primary levels of, 275
   scales of, 270–75
Media Facts, 116
metric data, 408
MINITAB software, 364
Monthly Trade Statistics (CSO), 89–90
   marketing research uses, 90
'mortality', in research samples, 201
multidimensional scaling (MDS), 420–22
multiple regression analysis, 409–12
   F-test, 411
   regression equations, 396–400, 410

multivariate data analysis, 25, 362–3, 406–23
  cluster analysis, 419–20
  dependent, 406–8
  discriminant analysis, 412–16
  factor analysis, 416–19
  independent, 406–8
  multidimensional scaling (MDS), 420–22
  multiple regression analysis, 409–12
mystery shopping, 181–2

newspapers, case study, 120–23
non-spurious association, 199
normal distribution curve, 337–9

O'Leary, Phelim, 128, 150
objectivity, of data, 72–3
observation research, 181–8
  advantages and disadvantages, 187–8
  mechanical aids, 184–6
  mystery shopping, 181–2
  techniques, 182–6
OECD, marketing information, 111
omnibus surveys, 180–81
oral reports. *see* report writing
ordinal data, 398

panel research, 179–80
parameter, 304
pharmaceuticals, case study, 155–6
picture response tests, 146
pizza products, case study, 62–4
population, 303
  defining for sample, 307–8
  element, 307–8
  unit, 308
pottery, case study, 332–4
presentation of research. *see* report writing
pricing research, 6
primary data, 71
  advantages of, 72
  collection methods, 232
probability sampling, 310–12
  area sampling, 319–20
  cluster sampling, 318–19

multistage sampling, 320
simple random, 313–14
systematic random sampling, 315–16
problem definition, 18–20, 34, 44–54
  analytical/theoretical model, 48
  case studies, 49–51, 61–6
  errors, 51–2
  expert survey, 47
  literature search, 47
  marketing information system and, 52–4
  problem audit, 48
  research tasks, 44–9
  role of management in, 45–9
  situational analysis, 47
product/services research, 5–6
professional associations, 30, 33
Profile abstracts, 106
projective techniques, 22, 143–50
  advantages and disadvantages, 148
  association techniques, 144–5
  completion techniques, 145–6
  construction techniques, 146
  expressive techniques, 147–8
  new developments, 148–9
  non-verbal, 149
promotion research, 6
psychodrawing, 148
public opinion surveys
  Eurobarometer, 111

qualitative data, 55, 57–8
qualitative research, 127–8
quantitative data, 56, 57–8
questionnaire design, 232–56
  case study, 263–4
  development guidelines, 233–4
  layout, 253–5
  pre-coding, 255
  preliminary considerations, 234–5
  pre-testing, 255–6
  question content, 235–40
  question sequence, 252–3
  question types
    dichotomous, 244–5
    multiple-choice, 242–4

open-ended, 241–2
question wording, 245–52
response format, 240–45
unwilling respondents, 238–40

randomisation, 197, 202
  randomised research designs, 212–13
reactive error, 202–3
regression, of statistics, 395–8
  F-test, 411
  multiple regression analysis, 409–12
  regression equations, 396–400, 410
reliability assessment, of research, 278–80
  equivalent forms reliability, 280
  split-half reliability, 279–80
  test-retest reliability, 279
report writing, 428–41
  contents and format, 431–5
  evaluating reports, 436–7
  graphs, 374–6
  guidelines, 428–30
  oral reports, 437–41
  tables, 374
research design, 20–21
  case studies, 61–6
  casual, 21, 56–8
  choosing, 57–8
  defined, 54
  descriptive, 20–21, 56, 57–8
  experimental, 205–18
  exploratory, 20, 22, 55, 57–8
research findings. *see* report writing
research proposals, 19–20
restaurant, case study, 299–301
retail research
  EPOS data, 186
  interactive kiosks, 175
  loyalty cards, 187
  shopping centre intercepts, 161
  virtual reality shopping, 177–8
Retail Sales Index (CSO), 89
  marketing research uses, 89
role-playing, 147

sample, definition, 304
sample size, 24–5, 324
  case study, 348–51
  confidence intervals, 340–42
  for finite populations, 344
  for non-probability sampling, 336–7
  formulae, 342–4
  mean distribution, 339–40
  normal distribution curve, 337–9
  proportion distribution, 340
sampling, 24–5, 302–25
  case studies, 329–34
  error, 304
  frame error, 309
  frames, 308–10
  method selection, 310, 312
  non-probability, 24, 310–12
    convenience sampling, 321
    judgment sampling, 322
    purposive sampling, 322
    quota sampling, 323–4
  probability, 24
    area sampling, 319–20
    cluster sampling, 318–19
    multistage sampling, 320
    simple random sampling (SRS), 313–14
    stratified random sampling, 316–18
    systematic random sampling, 315–16
  size determination, 335–45
  stages in process, 306–7
  strata, 316–17
  target population, 307–8
  terminology, 303–4
  type selection, 312
  validation of, 324
SAS software, 365
scales of measurement, 270–75
  case study, 299–301
  interval, 273–4
  nominal, 271
  ordinal, 272
  ratio, 274
  summary table, 275
scatter diagrams, 413–15

470   Index

secondary data
    advantages of, 71–3
    case studies, 120–26
    evaluation criteria, 72–3
    external, 75, 79–81
    gathering, 73–4
    government sources, 81–91
    internal, 75–9, 81
    source classification, 74–5
    sources, 71–118
selection bias, 202
semantic differential scaling, 291–4
Shannon Development, data source, 98–9
shopping centre intercepts, 161
significance tests, 381–92
    chi-square tests, 391–2
    concerning a mean, 384–7
    concerning a proportion, 388–91
    hypothesis testing, 381–92
    'two-tail', 381
simulated test marketing (STM), 220–22
situational analysis, 47
skin care products, case study, 62
Smith and Nephew, case study, 155–6
solid fuel industry
    case studies, 15, 152–4
SPCA, case study, 38
Spearhead, on-line information, 106
Spearman Rank-correlation coefficient,
    399–400
sports centres, case study, 263–4
SPSS software, 364
state-sponsored bodies, data sources, 92–9
    Bord Failte, 94–7
    Enterprise Ireland, 92–4
    Industrial Development Agency (IDA),
        97–8
    Shannon Development, 98–9
    Údarás na Gaeltachta, 98
statistics
    analysis software for PCs, 363–5
    central tendency measures
        mean, 365–8
        median, 368–9
        mode, 369

dispersion measures, 369–73
    range, 370
    variance and standard deviation,
        370–72
percentages, 372–3
regression and correlation, 201–2, 395–8
summarisation, 365–73
variance analysis, 392–5
surveys, 157–81
    case studies, 191–3, 348–51
    combining techniques, 173–81
    cross-sectional, 159
    error sources, 159
    expert surveys, 47
    methods comparison, 178
    omnibus surveys, 180–81
    panels, 179–80
    public opinion, 111
    questionnaire design, 232–56
syndicated data sources, 112–14
    marketing research uses, 114

tables, in reports, 374
tabulating data, 361–5
    cross tabulation, 362–3
TED, on-line information, 106
Teilifís na Gaeilge, case study, 191–3
temporal sequence, 198
tennis club, case study, 49
test marketing, 218–22
    case study, 230–31
    controlled, 219
    simulated (STM), 220–22
    standard, 219
test units, in research, 196–7
testing effects, of research, 200–201
The Economist, forecasts and reports, 112
thematic apperception test (TAT), 146
third-person techniques, 147–8
Thoms Commercial Directory, 101
Thoms Register of American
    Manufacturers, 101
Thornton Readymix, case study, 123–6
Thurstone's scale, 287–8
time travel, 148

Times Index, newspaper compilations, 106
tourism
    case study, 64–6
    information sources, 94–7
trade associations, 102–4
Tradstat, on-line information, 106
Trócaire, case study, 40–42

Údarás na Gaeltachta, data source, 98
unit of analysis, 48

validity, of research, 4, 29, 199–204
    concurrent validity, 277
    construct validity, 277–8
    content validity, 276–7
    convergent validity, 278
    discriminant validity, 278
    external validity, 202–3
    internal validity, 199–202

predictive validity, 277
reliability and, 276
threat summary, 204
variables
    behavioural, 268
    dependent, 196, 392
    extraneous, 196
    independent, 195, 392
    interval or ratio-scale, 395
    state-of-being, 268
    state-of-mind, 268
variance analysis, 392–5
virtual reality shopping, 177–8
voluntary organisations, case studies, 38, 40–42

web-sites, as data sources, 107–9, 113
Who Owns Whom, 106
written reports. *see* report writing